"Drawing on newly declassified documents from the U.S., Cuba, and Russia, as well as interviews with former officials in all three countries, Blight and Brenner show how the missile crisis was caused, in large part, by a lack of empathy between Washington, Havana, and Moscow. I have known for some time that we in the Kennedy administration misunderstood the Cubans and Russians. But in *Sad and Luminous Days,* we learn the many ways the Cubans and Russians misunderstood each other, and how those misunderstandings made the crisis as dangerous as it was. The book is a superb addition to recent history and is full of important lessons for relations between Great Powers and small countries, beginning with the lesson: 'empathize with your adversary, or you may regret it!'"
—**Robert S. McNamara**, secretary of defense to Presidents Kennedy and Johnson

"This splendid book shows starkly the deep differences between Cuba and the Soviet Union during the half-dozen years that followed the 1962 missile crisis. Those differences arose from the way the Soviets negotiated with the United States in 1962, without prior consultation with the Cubans. The authors eloquently build their case with many fascinating interviews with Soviet and Cuban decision makers and a spectacular, hitherto secret 1968 speech wherein Fidel Castro explained to the Cuban Communist Party's Central Committee why the Soviets were untrustworthy. This thoughtful and learned book is also a great read."
—**Jorge I. Domínguez**, Director of the Weatherhead Center for International Affairs at Harvard University

"This challenging account of the missile crisis and its aftermath casts fascinating light on Fidel Castro and his Cuba. After *Sad and Luminous Days*, no one will be able to write the same way about Castro's relationship with the Kremlin."
—**Arthur Schlesinger Jr.**, Pulitzer prize–winning historian and former White House aide to John F. Kennedy

"Every so often a work of history comes along that turns conventional wisdom on its head and brings to light previously mysterious, indeed hidden, nuggets of truth, opening a new dimension to what we long held as the only conceivable plot line. Blight and Brenner's eloquent, beautifully written book brings to life in poignant, vivid, and solidly documented prose what until now has been a footnote in the standard accounts of the Cuban missile crisis: the Cuban perspective. *Sad and Luminous Days* demonstrates why the two authors are pioneers in writing Cold War history with newly declassified documents and sets the standard for the rest of us."
—**Julia Sweig**, author of *Inside the Cuban Revolution: Fidel Castro and the Urban Underground*

"Sad and Luminous Days is an absolutely fundamental contribution to our knowledge of the Cuban missile crisis, Soviet-Cuban relations, and the difficulties facing Great Powers and small countries in their dealings with each other. Its principal lesson—the necessity (and the difficulty) of achieving realistic empathy with one's adversary—is especially salient at a moment when the remaining superpower, the United States, has declared a "war on terrorism" involving potential confrontations between the U.S. and many other smaller countries. All U.S. decision makers should read this book and learn its lessons before they attempt to carry out their 'war on terrorism.'"
—**Sergei N. Khrushchev**, author of *Khrushchev on Khrushchev: An Inside Account of the Man and His Era, by his Son, Sergei Khrushchev*

"Using interviews with senior officials and recently declassified documents from Cuba, the United States, and the former Soviet Union, Blight and Brenner brilliantly show how a super-empowered Castro manipulated the Great Powers while posing as their innocent victim. This is a well-researched and beautifully written account of the triangular relationship that brought the world to the brink of nuclear catastrophe."
—**Robert A. Pastor**, author of *Exiting the Whirlpool: U.S. Foreign Policy toward Latin America*

"Empathy is believed by many to be a soft-hearted approach in a world that requires us to be hard-headed. This wonderful book amply demonstrates, however, that this view of empathy is false and derives from a fundamental misunderstanding of what empathy actually entails. The events of September 11, 2001, demonstrate how profoundly tragic may be the result of our failure to reach a deep and comprehensive understanding of how the world looks through the eyes of our adversaries. Blight and Brenner brilliantly explore how the failure of the U.S., Cuba and the Soviet Union to achieve such understanding brought us to the very threshold of nuclear annihilation in October 1962 and, in so doing, provide an utterly essential guide to negotiating the treacherous waters of the 21st century."
—**Paul L. Wachtel**, The City College of the City University of New York

SAD AND LUMINOUS DAYS

Cuba's Struggle with the Superpowers after the Missile Crisis

James G. Blight and Philip Brenner

ROWMAN & LITTLEFIELD PUBLISHERS, INC.
Lanham • Boulder • New York • Oxford

ROWMAN & LITTLEFIELD PUBLISHERS, INC.

Published in the United States of America
by Rowman & Littlefield Publishers, Inc.
A Member of the Rowman & Littlefield Publishing Group
4720 Boston Way, Lanham, Maryland 20706
www.rowmanlittlefield.com

PO Box 317
Oxford
OX2 9RU, UK

British Library Cataloguing in Publication Information Available

Library of Congress Cataloging-in-Publication Data

Blight, James G.
   Sad and luminous days : Cuba's struggle with the superpowers after the
Missile Crisis / James G. Blight and Philip Brenner.
      p. cm.
Includes bibliographical references and index.
   ISBN 0-7425-2288-1 (cloth : alk. paper)
   1. Cuba—Foreign relations—Soviet Union. 2. Soviet Union—Foreign
relations—Cuba. 3. Cuba—Foreign relations—United States. 4. United
States—Foreign relations—Cuba. 5. Cuba—History—1959– 6. Cuban
Missile Crisis, 1962. I. Brenner, Philip. II. Title.
   F1776.3.S65 B65 2002
   327.7291047—dc21

                                                                2002008626

Printed in the United States of America

∞™ The paper used in this publication meets the minimum requirements of American
National Standard for Information Sciences—Permanence of Paper
for Printed Library Materials, ANSI/NISO Z39.48-1992.

To jML, as always, whose own courageous struggle has inspired so many to resolve: *seremos como la janet!*

To Isaac, whose probing curiosity encourages us to wonder why things are the way they are; to Liliana, whose profound idealism encourages us to wonder why things are not the way they should be; and to Betsy, whose good sense encourages us to know when to ask the right question.

Fidel:

I have lived magnificent days, and I felt at your side the pride of belonging to our people in the sad and luminous days of the Caribbean crisis. Seldom has a statesman been more brilliant than you in those days. I am also proud of having followed you, without hesitation, identified with your way of thinking and of seeing and appraising dangers and principles.

Ever onward to victory! Our country or death!

I embrace you with revolutionary fervor.

—Che [Guevara], "Farewell Letter to Fidel," March 1965

Fidel:

He vivido días magníficos y sentí a tu lado el orgullo de pertenecer a nuestro pueblo en los días luminosos y tristes de la crisis del Caribe. Pocas veces brilló más alto un estadista que en esos días. Me enorgullezco también de haberte seguido sin vacilaciones, identificado con tu manera de pensar y de ver y apreciar los peligros y los principios.

Hasta la victoria siempre. ¡Patria o Muerte!

Te abraza con todo fervor revolucionario.

—Che [Guevara], "Carta de despedida a Fidel Castro," marzo 1965

CONTENTS

ACKNOWLEDGMENTS

It has been ten years since we first conceived this project. With the passage of each year, we acquired additional debts to people who made this book possible. At several junctures during these past ten years, our own lives intersected, especially during visits to Cuba. During other phases of the research and writing, we worked separately for periods on various parts of the book. The final product was made possible by all the people who aided us in the joint and individual phases. It is likely that in the following expressions of gratitude, we have omitted some who should have been included. If so, we apologize. In any case, the book in its final form represents a fully collaborative endeavor. The manuscript has been passed back and forth between us so many times that, with only a few exceptions, it is no longer clear to either of us who is responsible for the particular phrasing on which we eventually settled. Obviously, none of the friends and colleagues listed below are responsible for any errors contained in the book. That responsibility is ours and ours alone.

Let us start with our publishing house. The people with whom we have worked at Rowman & Littlefield have been patient, responsive, and extraordinarily efficient. Special thanks go to Jonathan Sisk, our publisher, and Mary Carpenter, our editor. Jon is an acknowledged visionary of the publishing world; the proof lay in the explosive growth that Rowman & Littlefield has experienced since he took command a decade or so ago. He understood the significance of our proposal immediately and has been wonderfully supportive throughout the process. (In return, we have tried to be sympathetic regarding his addiction to the hapless Boston Red

Sox—his only real weakness of which we are aware.) Mary has been an author's wish-come-true, and without her many editorial skills, good judgment, and endless capacity to handle multiple demands launched simultaneously from Providence, Rhode Island, and Washington, D.C., this book might have been available only for the fiftieth anniversary of the missile crisis, rather than the fortieth. Mary's assistant, Laura Roberts, has also come through in the clutch for us and for our book.

This book has emerged from a series of five international conferences on the Cuban missile crisis. The central institutional players in those historic meetings on the U.S. side have been Brown University's Thomas J. Watson Jr. Institute for International Studies and George Washington University's National Security Archive. The Watson Institute has been the scholarly headquarters of the Cuban missile crisis project since 1990. Its support for the project has been unstinting, creative, and complete. We wish to extend our thanks especially to the former director Mark Garrison, and to the present director, Thomas J. Biersteker. Though neither had a previous interest in Cuba, each has embraced the missile crisis project enthusiastically and provided a home base for its far-flung operations over the years. In addition, we wish to thank the following people (in alphabetical order) from Brown who have provided assistance: Aaron Belkin, Andrew Blackadar, Norman Boucher, Sheila Fournier, Elizabeth Garrison, Susan Graseck, P. Terrence Hopmann, Jean Lawlor, janet Lang, David Lewis, Brenda Menard, Mark Nickel, Frank Rothman, Thomas Skidmore, and Nancy Soukup. Bless them all for helping to make Brown University the missile crisis project's New England home.

The National Security Archive has, from the beginning of the decade-long process of creating this book, been the Washington, D.C., home of the missile crisis project. It is the institution that identifies, acquires, organizes, and makes available the declassified documents that are so important in the process called "critical oral history." When we say "thanks to our docu-nerds" at the Archive, we know they will take it as among the highest of compliments. Many people at the Archive also have given us personal support, insights, and encouragement. Special gratitude is due to Archive director Thomas Blanton. Although Tom is personally involved with the dozens of declassification projects underway at the Archive at any one time, he has given very special attention to the missile crisis project, and we are very grateful for it. Also important have been Peter Kornbluh, director of the Cuba Documentation Project, Malcolm Byrne, research director of the Archive, and Svetlana Savranskaya, director of Russian Programs at the Archive. Sveta provided essential assistance during interviews in Moscow, and in translating and transcribing them upon her return to the United States. In addition, we wish to thank the Archive's Will Ferrogiaro, and Vladislav Zubok (now at Temple University). Scott Armstrong, the founder of the Archive, was the inspiration behind the initial attempt to obtain Castro's January 1968 speech. His spirited defense of our rights under the First Amendment lives on at the Archive, the institution he created.

We are also indebted to many others for assistance in obtaining information and interviews, for enhancing our knowledge about Cuban and Soviet history, and for conceptual insights and intellectual support. These include Carlos Alzugaray, Pablo Armando Fernandez, Soraya Castro, Carlos Ciaño, Carlos Cossio, Elizabeth Cohn, Jorge I. Domínguez, Rafael Hernández, James Hershberg, Donna Rich Kaplowitz, Saul Landau, Sergo Mikoyan, Yoshiko Nakano, Wayne Smith, David A. Welch, Vladimir Zaemsky, and Oscar Zanetti. We have been blessed with the assistance of several superb research assistants whose skills and hard work we appreciate very much: Ryan Bock, Colin Bucher, Kristen Comeaux, Michael Compton, Johnny Holloway, Amy Luinstra, Geoffrey Plague, Katie Powers, Enrique Pumar, and Sohini Sarkar.

Several Cuban government officials (or former officials) also played essential roles. The efforts of Jose Antonio Arbesú, head of the Americas Department of the Cuban Communist Party Central Committee, were crucial. Tómas Diez Acosta, a senior scholar at Cuba's Institute of History, was especially helpful in obtaining documents. In addition, we are grateful to Julio Carranza, Fabian Escalante Font, Jorge Hernandez, the late Manuel Piñeiro, Jorge Pollo, Jorge Risquet, Fernando Remirez, Dagoberto Rodríguez, Luis Suarez, Pedro Alvarez Tabío, and Josefina Vidal.

A project like this one, spread out over time and space, cannot happen without financial support. We gratefully acknowledge assistance to Philip Brenner from the American Council on Learned Societies/Social Science Research Council, for an Advanced Research Grant that provided support during a sabbatical leave; Brown University's Watson Institute for International Relations for research support; American University's School of International Service, for research travel funds and research assistants. We also gratefully acknowledge the financial assistance given via several U.S. foundations to Brown University's Watson Institute. These include the Arca Foundation, the John D. and Catherine T. MacArthur Foundation, the Winston Foundation for World Peace, the General Service Foundation, the Ford Foundation, and the Rockefeller Family Associates. This consortium of foundations underwrote the January 1992 Havana conference, at which we first became aware of some of the contents of the January 1968 secret speech of President Fidel Castro. We should say a word here about how the concept of empathy came to occupy such a central place in this book. The literature of international relations and national security studies is virtually devoid of even a mention of empathy. Its importance has been emphasized over the years in conversations and correspondence with Watson Institute Director Thomas J. Biersteker, and with John Tirman, director of the Program on Global Security and Cooperation at the Social Science Research Council. We are grateful to both for pushing us in this new and, we believe, fruitful direction. Their influence on us, and on this book, is perhaps greater than they imagine.

Last, but far from least, our families have been the ongoing source of inspiration, for which a mere "thank you" in this acknowledgment section seems especially inadequate. janet Lang is the *deus ex machina* of this book. She helped organize the conferences; she participated fully in several critical interviews in Cuba; and in many other ways facilitated JGB's role in the research and writing of this book. Betsy Vieth has done far more than her fair share of maintaining a household and nurturing a family while work on the book has proceeded. She has encouraged PB to pursue his dreams even when it meant placing hers on hold. Liliana and Isaac have been patient with a less than attentive dad and, most importantly, have reminded him with their own bountiful spirits and creativity that together we are trying to build a more peaceful world for their generation, and those that follow.

James G. Blight and Philip Brenner
May 2002

PROLOGUE: THE DISCOVERY AND MEANING OF FIDEL CASTRO'S SECRET SPEECH

The Cuban missile crisis of October 1962 was the most dangerous moment in modern history, arguably in all of recorded history. President John F. Kennedy estimated that the chances of nuclear war during the crisis were as high as one in three, perhaps even one in two. Asked in 1993 how close the world had come to a nuclear catastrophe during the missile crisis, Cuban President Fidel Castro held up his forefinger and thumb until they almost touched and replied to an American reporter, "this close!" Recent research has proven his assessment absolutely correct. In the end the world did not only escape nuclear oblivion; the United States and Soviet Union avoided war of any kind. The escape seemed, and seems, miraculous, a cause for sober celebration and gratitude. And so it has been in the United States and the Soviet Union (now the Russian Federation). As recently as 2001 the American movie *Thirteen Days* reinforced the point of view that celebrates our good fortune, both in surviving the crisis and in having such good leadership when we were at the brink of disaster.

History, it has been said, is written by the big winners. In October 1962, the United States and the Soviet Union were the "winners." They made a deal at the last minute, withdrew from the crisis, and then started on a course toward improving their relations. But, usually forgotten, there was also a big "loser" in October 1962. Cuba had accepted the Soviet missiles at great risk—making itself a strategic target on the front line of the Cold War against the United States—only to become even more vulnerable at the end of the crisis. Cuban leaders saw the Soviets acquiesce to virtually every U.S. demand without seriously acknowledging Cuba's perception of the threat it faced. The Soviets agreed to withdraw the ballistic missiles (and their one megaton warheads), tactical nuclear missiles, cruise missiles, almost all the Soviet military forces on the island, and even World War II vintage bombers, all of which Cuba had hoped it could use to deter or repel an American attack. Cubans took no stock in the U.S. pledge not to invade the island, which they believed was a thoroughly hollow promise. They fully expected that they would once again need to defend themselves against the United States, especially because U.S. aggression would be encouraged by the Soviet Union's seeming lack of will to defend its Caribbean partner. And so over the next five years Cuba approached its putative ally, the Soviet Union, with bitterness and distrust.

What was this *Cuban* Cuban missile crisis like? What was it about? Until recently, detailed information about the Cuban reality in the missile crisis has been largely unavailable or virtually ignored outside Cuba. The few public comments by Cuban leaders over the years generally have been discounted as cryptic and meaningless by American scholars specializing in the missile crisis. No statement has been accorded this denigration more strongly than that of Ernesto "Che" Guevara, in his famous March 1965 "Farewell Letter" to Fidel Castro, written as he was leaving Cuba to spark revolutions in Africa and South America.

Guevara wrote, "I have lived magnificent days, and I felt at your side the pride of belonging to our people in the luminous and sad days of the Caribbean [missile] crisis."[1] The key words here are "sad" and "luminous." These are not the words that come to the minds of most people who experienced the crisis or who have learned about it. More typical are "reprieved" (from the terrible calamity we almost suffered) and "harrowing" (because of the stress during the crisis). What, one might plausibly ask, could possibly be "sad" about the resolution of the missile crisis? And what was radiant or "luminous" about going to the brink of Armageddon? Why would one of Cuba's most revered leaders express a view that is at such odds with the received wisdom in the United States and much of the rest of the world? Our purpose in *Sad and Luminous Days* is to unravel the meaning in Guevara's judgment about the peaceful resolution of a nuclear confrontation that so many others have regarded as preternaturally fortunate and sobering. It is an effort that began in 1986.

CRITICAL ORAL HISTORY

In 1986 James Blight had started to assemble a team of scholars and former U.S. policymakers to reassess the 1962 Cuban missile crisis using a method of inquiry that has since come to be called "critical oral history." This method involves the creative interaction between those who knew firsthand the burden of responsibility in an event and analysts who know secondhand (on the basis of archival documents, oral histories, and interviews) what the documentary record shows. Declassified documents are essential to this process, because they stimulate the memories of former officials and they provide a reality check on mistaken impressions and unsubstantiated beliefs the policymakers may have had even at the time of an event. On the other hand, scholars often are unable to interpret the significance of particular documents because they do not know the context in which they were written, how officials interpreted them, or what use they made of the documents. The process, then, of placing policymakers, scholars, and documents together can overcome some of the shortcomings of both traditional oral history and traditional archival research.

At the same time, the National Security Archive, under the guidance of its founding director, Scott Armstrong, had begun to use the Freedom of Information Act to secure the release of classified U.S. government documents about the crisis. The National Security Archive is a private, nonprofit research organization in Washington, D.C., whose mission is to expand public access to government information.[2] Armstrong sought to supplement what was then known or believed about U.S. decisionmaking during the missile crisis, in order to develop the most accurate account of an episode on which so many policymakers had relied for lessons about crisis decisionmaking. He also hoped to use the new documents to encourage the Cuban government to open its archives on the crisis.

Armstrong and Philip Brenner had received rumors from some sources in Cuba about the existence of a long "report," supposedly written by Castro himself, about Cuba's role in and perspective on the missile crisis. In July 1987 they traveled to Havana with Donna Rich Kaplowitz, then a researcher at the Archive, under the impression that they would be given this document. They waited in vain for nearly a week before leaving empty-handed. Even so, we at least had confirmation now from some Cuban officials that a remarkable and potentially significant Cuban document about the missile crisis did exist. We ultimately discovered it was Castro's secret 1968 speech on the missile crisis, the longest and most detailed account of the crisis the Cuban leader had ever offered. This speech also may be the best reflection of his perceptions at the time of the 1962 crisis, because the events were still so fresh in his mind when he delivered his remarks. But in mid-1987 we merely hoped this document would fill a glaring blank space that had prevented us from seeing the whole picture of the missile crisis.

A few months earlier, in March 1987, the critical oral history process got underway at a conference center in the Florida Keys. Several scholars and former ExComm members (President Kennedy's so-called Executive Committee of the National Security Council, the group of his key advisers during the crisis) convened both to examine what we knew then about the missile crisis and to review National

Security Council and Defense Department documents that had been obtained by the National Security Archive.[3] For the sake of historical accuracy, it was important to understand the ExComm members' evaluations of how the scholars had interpreted the newly released documents. Blight and David Welch then used the knowledge gained from the March meeting to conduct in-depth interviews with several Kennedy administration officials about the missile crisis. Both of them were based at Harvard University's Center for Science and International Affairs. That summer, Kurt Campbell returned to the center from an extended visit to the USSR. A specialist about the Soviet Union, Campbell was impressed by but skeptical about Soviet General Secretary Mikhail Gorbachev's announced policy of *glasnost*, or "openness," and he suggested a small "test" or challenge. Would Gorbachev permit hidden parts of Soviet history to be revealed by people who had access to Soviet information about the missile crisis or who had been privy to the inner Kremlin circle at that time? Would such knowledgeable Soviets be allowed to engage in a serious joint study of the missile crisis? The twenty-fifth anniversary of the crisis was approaching quickly. A conference at which Soviets could offer a wholly new perspective on this historic confrontation seemed so worthwhile that it became a high priority to probe the reality of *glasnost*. Soviet specialist Bruce Allyn followed up, and ultimately three participants from Moscow came to an October conference in Cambridge.[4]

Their candor and the new information they provided was breathtaking.[5] Still, the three argued, they could offer only the tip of the iceberg. The iceberg itself was waiting, and available they said, in the Soviet Union. So in January 1989 the venue shifted to Moscow. There, for the first time, the highest level Soviet political leaders—including former Foreign Minister Andrei Gromyko, former ambassador to the United States Anatoly Dobrynin, and senior Soviet military personnel—took part in uncovering their own history. The Soviets also invited former Cuban officials to participate in this chapter of the evolving critical oral history of the missile crisis.[6]

In conversations with some members of the Cuban delegation to the Moscow conference, we learned that the group had relied on a long and detailed report, probably written by Castro himself, to prepare for the meeting. We were also told, interestingly, that they were not permitted to bring this briefing document with them to Moscow. They had to return it, more or less as if it were checked out from a lending library. At the conclusion of the Moscow conference, the Cuban delegation invited the other two parties to a "concluding conference" in Havana, to complete the series.

This proved to be easier said than done. In July 1989 the Hungarians opened their borders, which led in six astonishing months to the collapse of international socialism, and consequently to a severe economic crisis in Cuba. By mid-1990,

Castro had announced that Cuba would begin "a special period in time of peace." For the indefinite future, Cubans would need to endure the sorts of shortages and hardships associated with a war.[7] As this economic crisis unfolded, the United States invaded Panama in December 1989 to oust Panamanian strongman Manuel Noriega.[8] Two months later Nicaraguans voted to oust the Sandinistas from power. Cuba had given considerable support to Nicaragua and the United States had waged a low intensity war against the Sandinistas for ten years. A gleeful Bush administration taunted Cuba that it would be the next to fall, and in March 1990 it inaugurated "TV Marti," an operation that broadcasts propaganda television programs to Cuba, which are intended to foment internal pressure against the regime. Meanwhile the United States was pressuring the Soviet Union to cut off military aid to Cuba.[9] With this heightened tension between Cuba and the United States, a project involving former U.S. policymakers (who once had tried to overthrow the Cuban government) and current Cuban officials (several of whom also were prominent in 1962) became even more sensitive and challenging than it would otherwise have been.

At the same time, the strains in Cuba's relations with the crumbling Soviet Union grew into fissures as Gorbachev sought to end the Cold War with the United States and to redirect funds from expensive overseas programs to the Soviet economy.[10] In 1991, without consulting Cuba in advance, Gorbachev announced the withdrawal of all Soviet military forces from the island. Pointedly, he did so after meeting with and in the presence of U.S. Secretary of State James Baker.[11] Virtually overnight Cuba felt itself isolated and deserted by its supposed ally. The Soviet Union was more willing to placate the other superpower—Cuba's avowed enemy—than to give Cuba even the mere courtesy of prior notification. It was a situation that bitterly reminded every Cuban over forty of the way in which the 1962 missile crisis was resolved, when Soviet leader Nikita Khrushchev publicly declared on October 28—prior to informing Castro—that the Soviets were withdrawing the missiles.

As Cuba suddenly began to face a world without a socialist community, the critical oral history of the missile crisis became a two-level exercise. The "text," so to speak, remained the history, the testimonies of veterans interacting with scholars on the basis of declassified documents. But the "subtext" became so thickly political, so analogically pertinent to the present moment, that the preparatory discussions in Havana bristled with intense emotions that seemed to emerge from the very crisis we were trying to dissect. Once again Cuba felt severely threatened by the United States and abandoned by the Soviets. Might these circumstances engender Castro to unveil the document we had long sought, this "rosetta stone" that could reveal Cuba's role in the missile crisis, even if it contained harsh comments (as was rumored) about Soviet unreliability, duplicity, and disloyalty?

CLOSING IN ON THE SPEECH

Havana, January 1992: Cuban participants in this latest conference on the missile crisis told us that, as in 1989, they had prepared for the meeting by reading the same document that the Cuban delegation had used in Moscow. Over meals and during corridor conversations in Havana, some details regarding this sought-after chronicle began to emerge. We learned that it was part of an oral report Castro had presented in January 1968 to the first plenary meeting of the Cuban Communist Party's Central Committee (the Cuban Communist Party was established in October 1965). It had taken the Cuban leader about twelve hours to deliver the whole speech. A substantial portion of it was devoted to instructing his audience—approximately 100 members of the Central Committee of the Party—about Soviet behavior before, during, and after the missile crisis.

The U.S. delegation had arrived in Havana with considerable press attention because of a fascinating set of documents that had just become public. Fortuitously, the day before the group left for the conference, the State Department finally had responded to appeals from the National Security Archive to release secret correspondence between Kennedy and Khrushchev during the immediate aftermath of the missile crisis. These were presented to Cuban officials at the airport, and Castro reportedly read the letters carefully through the night. The next day he was present at the conference, and he remained as a full participant throughout.[12]

When it came time for Castro's main presentation—a chronological narrative of Cuba's role in the crisis—he began to refer to the text of the 1968 speech. He even read directly from it, especially those sections containing original documents, such as the agreement between Cuba and the Soviet Union authorizing the deployment of the strategic missiles and some of the text of a thirty-page-long letter from Khrushchev to him in January 1963. The very existence of that letter was not generally known to American scholars then. Castro remarked at one point that "I'm declassifying here." Then, warming to his subject, he inquired facetiously and hilariously, "Does 'declassification' [of documents] have anything to do with to the class struggle?"[13]

Prompted by the Cuban leader's sudden enthusiasm for historical openness,[14] we approached the Cuban government in May 1992 with a request to declassify the 1968 secret speech. Two months later the long portion of the speech that focused on the missile crisis was delivered to us in Washington—in its original Spanish version and with an official English translation by the Cuban Council of State. We then verified the translation independently as a faithful and nuanced English rendering. At last we had in our hands a document offering us the closest possible vicarious, retrospective view of the fateful events as they unfolded in Havana from the summer of 1962, when the Soviets first proposed the missile deployment to the

Cubans, through the late spring of 1963, when Castro returned from his first trip to the Soviet Union.

THE MISSILE CRISIS, AND MORE

We read Castro's speech with eager anticipation. To our surprise, it seemed to be as much about Cuban–Soviet relations in 1968 as it was about the missile crisis. Castro's review of the crisis clearly was meant to provide the Cuban Communist Party's Central Committee members with a pointed moral: Cuba could not trust the Soviet Union. Some of the central questions it raised for us were: What had happened between October 1962 and January 1968 to provoke this distrust? Why would Castro want his comrades to take away that lesson about the Soviets precisely at that moment? And why would Castro deliver a *secret* speech to the leadership rather than taking the issues directly to the Cuban people in a major address, as was (and remains) his custom?

In the United States the general impression about Cuba's relationship with the Soviet Union is that Cuba had been a pawn of its more powerful benefactor. Scholars familiar with recent Cuban history, especially Cuban–Soviet history since 1961, had discounted this characterization. But U.S. officials often asserted or assumed that for thirty years—from 1961 until the Soviet Union's collapse—the relationship was consistently steadfast and symbiotic: the Soviets extracted obedience from the Cubans in exchange for oil and military hardware; the Cubans gratefully received Soviet oil and security sufficient to allow them to engage in what came to be called their "export of revolution." Castro's speech provides strong evidence to the contrary.

In fact, by January 1968 the relationship may have been near a breaking point. Tension between the two countries had increased steadily during the prior three years over Cuba's support for insurgencies in the Third World, especially in Latin America, the traditional U.S. sphere of influence. In the process Cuba not only undermined the Soviet Union's self-proclaimed leadership of the Third World. Cuba's Western Hemispheric provocations endangered the Soviet goal of peaceful coexistence with the United States and emerging policy of "détente." The Soviets believed they had papered over their differences with Cuba at a December 1964 meeting of Latin American communist parties, which resolved that armed struggle was *one* valid means of achieving socialism *and* that each communist party should assess the particular means appropriate for its country. Cuba, moreover, agreed to deal only with the established communist parties in Latin America.[15]

The January 1966 Tricontinental Conference, a major international meeting of revolutionaries in Havana, upset the fragile peace. While the Soviet Union fully endorsed the meeting, because it hoped the conference would undermine China's influence with revolutionary movements (and which it apparently did), it was taken aback by the conference's barely veiled criticism of allegedly weak Soviet support for North Vietnam. During the meeting Castro also read a letter addressed to the group from his former comrade-in-arms, Che Guevara, an outspoken advocate of armed struggle who had left Cuba in 1965. Guevara declared that through "liberation struggles" in Latin America, "the Cuban Revolution will today have a task of much greater relevance: creating a Second or a Third Vietnam."[16] Then, in his closing speech, Castro repeated the call for armed struggle as he sharply criticized Latin American communist parties:

> if there is less of resolutions and possibilities and dilemmas and it is understood once and for all that sooner or later all or almost all people will have to take up arms to liberate themselves, then the hour of liberation for this continent will be advanced.[17]

Over the following months, the Cuban leader reinforced these views through speeches critical of the Soviet models of socialism and of world revolution, and he supported Guevara's November 1966 expedition to Bolivia, which the Bolivian Communist Party opposed.[18] When Soviet Premier Alexsei Kosygin came to Cuba in July 1967, Castro gave him an icy reception and decried Soviet aspirations for détente with the United States. The Cuban leader also rejected renewed Soviet pressure to end Cuba's support for guerrilla movements in Latin America. The next month, at the first meeting of the Organization for Latin American Solidarity (OLAS)—which had been created by the Tricontinental Conference—Cuba arranged for nearly all of the delegations to be dominated by noncommunist revolutionary organizations. Two months later Che Guevara was killed in Bolivia. Castro suspected Bolivian Communists had sabotaged Guevara's operation.[19] He also may have assessed that the Bolivian Communist Party, one of Moscow's most obedient adherents, would not have dared to act without first consulting their Soviet masters. Cuba then chose to absent itself from a preparatory meeting of world communist parties in Budapest organized by the Soviet Union.[20] As the new year opened, Castro honored Guevara and emphasized Cuba's dispute with the Soviet Union by declaring 1968 to be the "Year of the Heroic Guerrilla."

The Soviet Union did not take this challenge lightly, and it cut back on oil deliveries to Cuba. At the time, political scientist Jorge Domínguez explains, "the USSR [Union of Soviet Socialist Republics] supplied 99.3 percent of all Cuban petroleum imports," and in prior years had matched increased Cuban needs with more oil. "In 1967, however, Cuban oil consumption increased 8 percent while Soviet oil supplies increased only 2 percent." The shortfall had its greatest impact toward the end of the year. As it had done in previous years, Cuba then requested an advance against the next year's allotment, but "the Soviets granted only 64.2 percent of the requested fuel oil."[21] Castro announced the reduction solemnly on January 2, 1968, and warned the Cuban people that "sacrifice will be necessary."[22]

A PARADOX EMERGES

Cuba's intense standoff with its Soviet patron provided the context for the first plenary meeting of the Central Committee, which opened on January 23, 1968. The main agenda item for this auspicious convocation was the removal of Aníbal Escalante and a group of his supporters—dubbed the *microfaction*—who had been critical of Cuba's deviation from Soviet orthodoxy.[23] Escalante had been a leader of the Popular Socialist Party (PSP), which was Cuba's communist party before 1959. In 1961 he became the organizational secretary of the newly established Integrated Revolutionary Organizations (ORI), a party created to mesh Castro's July 26th Movement, the Revolutionary Directorate, and the PSP into one unit. Escalante used his position to place old communists in key ORI posts, providing himself with a base from which it appeared he might challenge Castro's leadership. But Escalante's ambitions were cut short in March 1962 when Castro exiled him to Czechoslovakia and denounced the "sectarianism" that Escalante had introduced into the ORI.[24]

Escalante returned in 1964, unrepentant but more cautious. When the Cuban Communist Party was established in 1965, he became a member but sought no leadership role. Now, in 1968, Escalante was the focal point of the Central Committee meeting. His crime? He had once again conspired to undermine Castro's leadership. But this time the alleged conspiracy involved Soviet, East German, and Czech officials too. The microfaction that Escalante led purportedly had distributed "false and slanderous information" to these "foreigners" in order to encourage their countries to reduce aid to Cuba. The microfaction members were nothing less than traitors, Carlos Rafael Rodriguez charged. They had "reached the point of treason, of wanting our country's situation to deteriorate so that the Soviet Union might intervene politically in a 'friendly' way . . . to have their leader, Aníbal, called in to govern."[25] The crime, then, was not merely ideological deviation. Had the microfaction succeeded, the Central Committee agreed, Cuba would have ceded its rightful control over foreign and domestic affairs to the Soviets. The group's machinations would have enabled the Soviets to violate the very independence and sovereignty for which the Cuban revolutionaries had fought.[26]

The significance of Castro's "lesson" to the Central Committee now seemed even more poignant. Of course Cuba could not trust the Soviets. Not only did they

want Cuba to abandon its revolutionary principles and its commitment to internationalism; they were prepared to support a coup to rob Cuba of its independence.
Castro's invective in the secret speech became more understandable. It was no
longer possible, he appeared to be saying, for Cuba and the Soviet Union to maintain fraternal relations. The relationship was at the point of rupture. In an interview
with us twenty-five years later, one Cuban official recalled that a sense of impending crisis—not unlike the missile crisis—permeated the atmosphere. The meeting
was the low point, he said, "after so many instances when our relations with the
Russians hung by a slender thread."[27]

Granma reported that "On the third and last day of the [Central Committee]
meeting the First Secretary of our Party and Prime Minister of the Revolutionary
Government, Major Fidel Castro, began his remarkable report at 12:20 P.M., which,
brief recesses intervening, he concluded after midnight."[28] Nothing else about his
secret speech was published. But now that we had a large portion of the speech in
hand, it seemed possible to expose a story about which most Americans had little
knowledge. The speech, we believed, gave us a glimpse into a *danse macabre*, a
dance of death in which Cuba and the Soviet Union relentlessly entangled each
other as they careened with deadly abandon toward the abyss.

Yet a mere seven months after privately lambasting the Soviet Union in front of
the Cuban leadership, Castro pleasantly surprised the Soviets with a statement that
did not censure their August 1968 invasion of Czechoslovakia.[29] "We acknowledge," he declared, "the bitter necessity that called for the sending of those forces
into Czechoslovakia; we do not condemn the socialist countries that made that decision." This was not an easy speech for Castro to make, and he waited three days
after the invasion before announcing Cuba's reaction. The key problem for him was
this: Would the Soviet intervention in Eastern Europe establish the basis for a U.S.
invasion of Cuba? As a lawyer, Castro instinctively worried about precedents. The
Soviet Union had viewed the "Prague Spring" in Czechoslovakia as a threat to its
continued domination of countries that both the East and West blocs regarded as
within the Soviet "sphere of influence." Similarly the United States perceived Cuba
as a threat in the traditional U.S. sphere. Castro acknowledged that the Soviet invasion repudiated international law. He flatly asserted that

> what cannot be denied here is that the sovereignty of the Czechoslovak State was vio-
> lated. . . . From a legal point of view, this cannot be justified. This is very clear. . . . Not
> the slightest trace of legality exists. Frankly, none whatever.

How then could Cuba—which constantly feared a U.S. attack—justify a powerful neighbor's disregard for a small country's sovereignty? And why would Castro,
in light of his intense distrust of the Soviets and Cuba's near rupture with the So-

viet Union, now take this risk for the sake of the invader? The Soviet action was justified, he argued, because "Czechoslovakia was moving toward a counterrevolutionary situation, toward capitalism and into the arms of imperialism." The socialist camp, Castro reasoned, thus had an obligation to prevent "the breaking away of a socialist country, to its falling into the arms of imperialism."

This certainly seemed like a dramatic turnabout. What had happened in seven months, we wondered, to move Castro from condemning the Soviet Union as a feckless ally to endorsing the Soviet violation of Czech sovereignty, and in so doing, possibly handing the United States an implicit justification for invading Cuba? Perhaps we had misinterpreted the January speech. Was it in fact a gauntlet thrown at the feet of the Soviets, signaling the start of a last reckless challenge that had the potential to break the relationship? Or was it the beginning of an unorthodox approach to reestablishing better relations with the Soviets—on terms that would try to preserve essential aspects of Cuban sovereignty? Was it an overture that only became apparent with the August 1968 speech? The answers to these questions were not evident from the text of the speech alone. Thus, our success in obtaining Castro's secret missile crisis report did not end our quest. We were now confronted by the paradox of two apparently incompatible speeches delivered seven months apart. How was it possible to reconcile the anti-Soviet bitterness of January 1968 with the conditional approval of ostensibly "illegal" Soviet behavior in August 1968? Clearly, we needed to look more deeply into Cuban–Soviet relations during this critical period. Of particular interest was the role played in this drama by the Cuban memory of the missile crisis.

Castro invoked the missile crisis in the August speech as he warned the United States that a Cuban response to an American invasion would be the antithesis of the docile Czech reaction to Soviet tanks. "What has protected this Revolution," he asserted,

> what has made it possible, has been the blood shed by the sons of this people, the blood shed fighting against the Batista's thugs and armies, the blood shed fighting against the mercenaries [at the Bay of Pigs], the determination that exists here to die to the last man in defense of the Revolution that was demonstrated in the October Crisis.

Once again, the missile crisis. It is the vehicle that carries the lessons in Castro's January 1968 speech; he relies on it in August to underscore Cuban dignity and bravery. The missile crisis had become for Cubans what psychologists call a "primal event," one in which the pattern, fear, and outcome of a very traumatic experience becomes so layered over time that it is difficult for outsiders even to detect the influence of the precipitating event. So it was with the missile crisis and subsequent

Cuban–Soviet relations from 1962 through 1968. The Cuban interpretation of the missile crisis lay at the core of the way Cubans assessed every new incident with one of the superpowers in this period, even though each event was connected to the crisis in ways that differed subtly from the others. Over time, officials remembered a particular event as unique, offering its own lesson about an appropriate course of action to take. The October 1962 crisis thus became embedded with multiple meanings for Cubans, as the initial trauma was recalled in association with later incidents. This psychological process challenges any effort to identify a simple or singular explanation for the unfolding Cuban–Soviet relationship, though we now feel confident in asserting that Cuban leaders were influenced more by the way they experienced the October Crisis than by the lessons they derived from later confrontations.

So, our exploration of the paradox had to begin with the missile crisis. To understand this drama, this mystery, about Cuban–Soviet relations we had to go to the origin of the troubles. Guevara captured the Cuban perspective eloquently in recalling those days as sad and luminous. They were sad for Cubans because the island was left so vulnerable by the U.S.–Soviet resolution of the crisis, and because the Soviet Union had betrayed its faithful ally. They were luminous, because of the exhilaration in preparing to fight arm-in-arm, to the death, for one's beliefs, dignity, and salvation. Ultimately, we discovered, the enduring legacy of the October 1962 crisis has relevance today, as the United States continues to relate to Cuba as a U.S. enemy, and as the United States confronts two, three, many Cubas throughout the world.

* * *

The centerpiece of the book—Castro's secret 1968 speech about the missile crisis—is framed on one side by the first chapter, where we examine the crisis itself to help readers recall the events of 1962 and to focus on Cuba's perspective. On the other side of the speech, in the third chapter, we analyze why Soviet behavior and attitudes during and immediately after the missile crisis made Cuba so angry. We then provide in this chapter a description of the growing tension between Cuba and the Soviet Union from 1962 to mid-1967. The fourth chapter focuses on the denouement between the two countries, beginning in August 1967 and ending one year later, in August 1968, with Castro's speech about the Soviet invasion of Czechoslovakia. We examine how Cuba developed its strategy during this time for trying to maintain independence while moving back into the Soviet orbit. In the epilogue, we bring the drama up to the present by drawing parallels between Cuba's circumstances in the 1960s and its relationship with the United States today. Our analysis of U.S.–Cuban relations is rooted in an approach we call *realistic empathy*, which interprets a conflict by putting oneself in the shoes of each side. From the Cuban perspective, what is central to the struggle with the United States is the asymmetry between the two countries. Cuba is a small country, and the United States is the most powerful country that has ever existed. This approach makes clear why it is necessary for the United States to take the first steps in ending the hostility between the two countries. It also suggests that perhaps the most important lesson the missile crisis offers us today, in the current search for security and a stable world order, is that great powers need to imbue foreign policy with *empathy* both for smaller and weaker allies, and especially for smaller and weaker adversaries.

And now we must begin with the October Crisis, something that must be understood by the comrades.

—Fidel Castro, January 25, 1968

[O]ne of the most important lessons of this event is that we must look at ourselves from the point of view of others. And I want to state quite frankly that with hindsight, if I had been a Cuban leader, I think I might have expected a U.S. invasion.

—Robert S. McNamara, 1989[1]

THE OCTOBER CRISIS

"Deep disappointment, bitterness and pain."

Fidel Castro's secret speech to the Cuban Communist Party's Central Committee was intended to provide lessons to the committee members about the Soviet Union, and to help them understand his point of view about the history and future of Cuban–Soviet relations. But first, it was an account of the Cuban missile crisis, which Cubans call the *October Crisis*. So in analyzing the speech, it is useful to follow his admonition by starting with the missile crisis itself.

We will focus on Cuba's perspective of the crisis, which we emphasize was different from that of the United States or the Soviet Union at the time. Each country brought its own interests, goals, and fears into the crisis, and the distinctive personalities of the officials and the operation of key organizations in the three countries influenced the perspective of each. Segmenting the crisis into the views of each country enables us to understand why the crisis developed as it did and how its resolution affected subsequent relations between both Cuba and the Soviet Union, and Cuba and the United States.

THE U.S. PERSPECTIVE: THIRTEEN DAYS

The view Graham Allison articulated in 1971 summarizes nearly all early approaches to the crisis: "For thirteen days in October 1962, the United States and the Soviet Union stood 'eyeball to eyeball,' each with the power of mutual annihilation in hand. The United States was firm but forebearing. The Soviet Union looked hard, blinked twice, and then withdrew without humiliation."[2] In essence, the Cuban missile crisis was a confrontation between the two superpowers that lasted from October 16, when President John Kennedy's advisers informed him that the Soviet Union was installing ballistic missiles in Cuba, until October 28, when Premier Nikita Khrushchev announced that the Soviet Union would withdraw the missiles in exchange for a U.S. pledge not to invade Cuba.

The Gravest Issues Arise

It was a crisis unlike any the world had seen before or has seen since, when human civilization came closer to the brink of destruction than at any other time. Not only did we all escape catastrophe, but the United States achieved its objective of removing Soviet missiles ninety miles from Florida while suffering the loss of only one life.[3] From this perspective it is understandable why it became important to investigate narrowly how such a remarkable success was achieved. Scholars sought to identify the achievement's recipe so that it might be reproduced in ensuing crises. The thirteen days framed their analyses as they focused on the decisionmaking process.[4]

To be sure, it has been well understood that there were intimations of the brewing crisis before October 16, 1962. In midsummer, the Central Intelligence Agency warned the president that the Soviet Union was transporting large quantities of military supplies to Cuba. These were judged to be exclusively defensive equipment, such as surface-to-air missiles (SAMs), and the estimate was that no offensive weapons were included in the buildup.[5] However, several Republican senators—especially Kenneth Keating (NY), Homer Capehart (IN), and Minority Leader Everett Dirksen (IL)—repeatedly charged in speeches that the Soviets were placing ballistic missiles in Cuba. In order to deflate the impact of these charges, Kennedy issued a statement on September 4 acknowledging the buildup, but pointedly denying any evidence of "ground-to-ground" (ballistic) missiles. He then warned, "Were it otherwise the gravest issues would arise."[6] Congress followed up with a joint resolution in October sanctioning the use of force against Cuba.[7]

In 1987 Kennedy's National Security Adviser McGeorge Bundy explained the significance for the ensuing crisis of the president's statement and the congressional declaration. He observed that

> we had already staked out a public position on the issue: if the Soviet Union does anything to threaten the safety of the United States or Latin America, we cannot tolerate it. We said it in September twice. Congress had passed a resolution to that effect. . . . These were the things that were of primary concern to us.[8]

Theodore Sorensen, Kennedy's special counsel, added that the president "recognized the right of the Soviets to send defensive arms to Cuba. . . . When the line was drawn at no offensive weapons, I believe President Kennedy drew that line there confident that the Soviet Union had no intention of going beyond it."[9] In effect, the option of doing nothing seemed not to be politically viable when missiles were discovered, because Kennedy would have had to back down on his firm stance, and he would have had to answer to Congress. At one point he handed his brother Robert a note saying that if he did nothing he had to expect that impeachment would follow.[10]

Shortly after Bundy brought the news to Kennedy on October 16, the president convened a group of advisers that came to be known as the Executive Committee of the National Security Council, or ExComm.[11] Throughout the crisis this group deliberated about courses of action the United States should take, first as an initial step in dealing with the missiles and, after October 22, in response to events as they unfolded. On the 22nd President Kennedy announced to the nation—and the world—that the United States had discovered ballistic missiles in Cuba, and that it was placing a blockade around the island to prevent any further military equipment from arriving there. Kennedy then demanded that the Soviet Union withdraw the missiles.

There is little question that the president and the ExComm members had an advantage rarely available to presidents today. Their deliberations and the crisis itself were kept completely secret from the glare of publicity, so that they felt no immediate pressure from politicians who might want to take advantage of the crisis for their own political gain or from pundits who might arouse public opinion. The group focused on Soviet motivations and on consequences of various courses of action for removing the missiles.

A consensus quickly emerged that this was a Soviet challenge to the United States. In part, this was engendered by their surprise. Khrushchev had conveyed a message through several different channels that the Soviet Union was not installing offensive missiles in Cuba. He assured Kennedy the Soviets would do nothing provocative before the November congressional elections.[12] The secrecy of the move—in contrast to the public way in which the United States installed missiles in Turkey—helped to convince the group's members that this was a threat to the United States.

The Soviet Challenge

The ExComm discounted the likelihood that the Soviet Union sought to defend Cuba from a possible U.S. invasion. There would have been less provocative ways to do that, they reasoned. No, in their view Cuba was essentially irrelevant to this issue. This was the height of the Cold War, and tension between the two superpowers might have erupted in any number of locales. There was nothing special about Cuba other than its proximity to the United States.

The Soviet challenge appeared to have three dimensions. First there was the matter of U.S. credibility. As presidential adviser Arthur Schlesinger recalls:

> In a general sense, the decision obviously represented the supreme Soviet probe of American intentions. No doubt a "total victory" faction in Moscow had long been denouncing the government's "no-win" policy and arguing that the Soviet Union could safely use the utmost nuclear pressure against the United States because the Americans were too rich or soft or liberal to fight. . . . Every country in the world, watching so audacious an action ninety miles from the United States, would wonder whether it could ever thereafter trust Washington's resolution and protection.[13]

In the early 1960s, the idea that international credibility—the belief by your opponents that you are willing to use force, especially nuclear weapons—provided stability in an environment of nuclear weapons had become a central tenet for national security managers.[14] Because the use of nuclear weapons would be so horrific, a country could not easily demonstrate its willingness to use them. Yet if an adversary believed the United States were unwilling to use everything at its disposal, then it might not be deterred from acting against U.S. interests, even to the point of launching a nuclear attack on the United States. However, credibility is an intangible factor in international relations because it is so subjective. There are few ways to measure when a country has attained a sufficient amount and so it can become a Holy Grail, the pursuit of which seems to legitimate any excess. Still, fear of losing it seems to have guided the ExComm members.[15]

A second, related dimension was Kennedy's personal credibility. He emerged from a 1961 summit with Khrushchev in Vienna believing that the Soviet leader judged him to be "young and inexperienced," that having backed away at the April 1961 Bay of Pigs invasion, Kennedy "had no guts."[16] In his memoirs, Khrushchev later remembered his opinion of Kennedy at Vienna quite differently: "He impressed me as a better statesman than [President Dwight D.] Eisenhower."[17] Still, it was Kennedy's perception that governed his judgment, and he feared that if the Soviet leader viewed him as weak, that would encourage Khrushchev to give into his adventurist impulses, which is in part how the placement of missiles was interpreted. Worse, it might have encouraged the Soviets to advance on many fronts, in Europe, Africa, the Middle East, and Asia. So, drawing a line and taking a firm stand seemed to be an imperative response given the ExComm's perception that Kennedy lacked credibility.

The front of greatest immediate concern was West Berlin. Surrounded by East Germany, it was West German territory, and its link to the West had been threatened since the 1948 Soviet blockade of the city that led to the legendary Berlin Airlift. In 1961 Khrushchev threatened to sign a separate peace treaty with East Germany—thereby giving control over the West Berlin–West German corridor to a country with which the United States did not have diplomatic relations—instead of working through a treaty among the four World War II allies. When the Soviets built a wall between East and West Berlin in August 1961, this was seen as further provocation, though it served to dampen the pressure on Khrushchev to do something about the flow of migrants from East to West, and thus it actually eased tension. Still, given Khrushchev's repeated attention to the enclave city, there was suspicion among ExComm members that the Soviets were using the missiles in Cuba as a bargaining chip to secure what they wanted in Berlin.

Finally, there was the matter of the strategic nuclear balance. In October 1962 the Soviet Union had only twenty Intercontinental Ballistic Missiles (ICBMs) that could be launched against the United States. Neither its bombers nor submarine-launched ballistic missiles offered the serious capability of delivering nuclear bombs on U.S. territory. In any case it had fewer than 300 nuclear warheads. In contrast, the United States had 5,000 nuclear bombs that could be launched from more than 300 missiles capable of hitting the Soviet Union and 1,450 bombers that could penetrate Soviet territory.[18] "We saw the principal Soviet objective as redressing a strategic inferiority," Raymond Garthoff explains. As the Soviets tried to catch up with the United States, the "missiles in Cuba could . . . provide an interim substitute, ersatz ICBMs, so to speak."[19] During the first day of ExComm meetings, National Security Adviser McGeorge Bundy succinctly summarized this view by asserting, "I'm sure his [Khrushchev's] generals have been telling him for a year and a half that he was missing a golden opportunity to add to his strategic capability."[20]

It appears there was general agreement among the ExComm members that U.S. nuclear superiority prompted the Soviets to place missiles in Cuba. But there was considerable disagreement as to whether the missiles there actually would have affected the balance. Former Secretary of Defense Robert S. McNamara asserted in 1987, for example, that "the assumption that the strategic nuclear balance (or 'imbalance') mattered in any way was wrong." He argued that adding 40 warheads in Cuba to the Soviet's 300 would alter very little. "Can anyone seriously tell me," he asked rhetorically, "that their having 340 would have made any difference?"[21] In contrast, former Secretary of the Treasury C. Douglas Dillon—who also was an Ex-Comm member—contended that "what we should really be paying attention to is the number each could *deliver* [emphasis his] on the other. Before the Soviets put missiles in Cuba, it was doubtful whether they could deliver any warheads from Soviet territory at all. So . . . my impression at the time was that . . . they [the missiles in Cuba] significantly increased Soviet capability."[22]

In short, it was the Soviet perception of the imbalance that was most important to the ExComm. As with credibility, strategic balance is largely a subjective determination, and each adversary tends to worry about how the other is perceiving the superpower relationship. U.S. objectives and concerns during the crisis focused on the maintenance of power and the exercise of power in a way that was not destabilizing. Thus, the outcome of the crisis was seen as a great success, as Schlesinger explained, because Kennedy demonstrated "the ripening of an American leadership unsurpassed in the responsible management of power."[23]

The Success of Coercive Diplomacy

Alexander George argues, further, that this was a textbook case in which "the strategy of coercive diplomacy" worked, because "Kennedy limited his objective and the means he employed on its behalf."[24] Several members of the ExComm had advocated using the crisis as an opportunity to overthrow the Cuban government. Plans had been prepared for a U.S. invasion, and by October 20 U.S. forces were ready for a full-scale attack.[25] Yet the president focused the issue on the singular goal of removing the missiles, to address his primary concern about the superpower relationship rather than to aim at multiple goals involving U.S.–Cuban relations too.[26]

U.S. concerns about a Soviet military presence in Cuba began to develop well before October 16. As the White House watched the Soviets send large amounts of equipment to the island in August and September, it feared that the superpower adversary was building a major military base there. On August 23 the president ordered the Defense Department to examine ways of removing the Soviet military presence in Cuba, and in September he approved Air Force plans for aerial attacks against Cuba. The commander-in-chief of Atlantic forces then ordered on October 1—more than two weeks before the ballistic missiles were discovered—that U.S. forces be readied to implement the plan of air attacks. Two days later he ordered that they be reconfigured for a blockade of Cuba, to be in place by October 20.[27]

During the thirteen days, U.S. strategic forces went to the highest state of alert short of actual war—DefCon 2—where bombers flew at the "fail safe" point and the conditions of readiness placed everyone at a hair trigger. But the termination of the thirteen-day period did not end this status. The Soviet presence in Cuba remained a worry until November 20, after the Soviets—and finally the Cubans—agreed to remove IL-28 bombers from the island and all but 3,000 Soviet troops. Though the bombers were obsolete, U.S. officials viewed them as offensive weapons because they could be outfitted to carry a nuclear bomb. In a series of tense exchanges with Khrushchev from November 4 to November 15, Kennedy insisted that the Soviets remove the bombers.[28] Khrushchev acknowledged Kennedy's concern about the IL-28s on November 11, and he offered his "gentleman's word" to remove them, "although not now but later." This echoed the promise the president's brother made to Soviet Ambassador Anatoly Dobrynin on October 27, to remove U.S. missiles from Turkey within six months. Robert Kennedy had insisted, though, that the promise be kept secret lest it offend Turkey and undermine U.S. credibility. Despite the seemingly parallel circumstances that Khrushchev faced with Cuba, President Kennedy demanded the Soviets publicly announce their withdrawal of the IL-28s. For the United States, the Cuban missile crisis ended on November 20, when it was clear Soviet offensive weapons would leave Cuba, and U.S. power had been firmly reestablished.

THE SOVIET PERSPECTIVE: THIRTEEN MONTHS

The Soviets speak of the Cuban missile crisis as the *Caribbean Crisis*. While Cuba figured into their calculations about the emplacement of missiles, the actual confrontation for them occurred in the Caribbean—on the high seas as well as in Cuba. Like U.S. officials, the Soviets viewed it principally as a clash between the two superpowers, but they set the starting date much earlier than August 1962, because they perceived it emerging from events in 1961.

Rattling U.S. Sabers

During the 1960 presidential campaign, then Senator John F. Kennedy charged that the Eisenhower administration had permitted a dangerous gap to materialize between U.S. and Soviet missile forces. The missile gap became the symbol of an allegedly lackadaisical Republican government that Kennedy promised to replace with a vigorous administration. Whether he knew otherwise at the time is still uncertain, but within weeks of taking office Secretary of Defense McNamara accidentally revealed that "if there was a gap, it was in our favor."[29] Though the press reported the revelation, the prevailing perception remained that the Soviets were ahead of the United States in strategic weaponry. This was fueled in part by their success at space exploration, which required large rockets that could propel cosmonauts into orbit.

Inside the Soviet Union, those responsible for Soviet Strategic Rocket Forces were well aware of the reality. For several years Khrushchev had been attempting to balance domestic pressures for more consumer goods and internal Soviet economic development with military demands for increased spending on arms, especially missiles. The Soviet leader had repeatedly resisted the calls for greater defense spending. Now the military was becoming increasingly alarmed about a U.S. threat. They pointed to the Kennedy administration's quick moves to increase the Defense Department budget, especially for strategic forces; to references made by U.S. officials in 1961 about the desirability of the "first use" of nuclear weapons; and to tests of nuclear weapons early in 1961.[30] Their concern mounted further on October 21, 1961, when Deputy Secretary of Defense Roswell Gilpatric forcefully announced that the missile gap was indeed in the U.S. favor, and that despite this lead the United States would continue to build up its forces at a rapid pace.[31]

Gilpatric's speech had several intended audiences. First, it was a warning to the Soviets that the Kennedy administration was prepared to challenge any provocative Soviet moves and there should be no misconceptions that the United States had the military might to back up this warning. Second, it contained a message meant for U.S. allies, to assure them that despite recent Soviet pronouncements of strength, the United States provided a strong bulwark on which they could rely. Third, it was a broadside aimed at domestic critics, who continued to charge—in the wake of the Bay of Pigs and the 1961 construction of the Berlin Wall—that the Kennedy administration was not sufficiently tough.[32] Two days later, in response to Gilpatric's speech, the Soviet Union detonated a thirty-megaton hydrogen bomb—the largest any country had ever exploded. Defense Minister Rodion Malinovsky charged that Gilpatric's announcement indicated "the imperialists are planning . . . a surprise nuclear attack on the USSR and the socialist countries."[33] The Soviets could not trust that the Kennedy administration was rattling its sabers merely to placate hawks in the U.S. Senate.

The Soviet fear of a U.S. first strike—an aggressive attack aimed at Soviet strategic forces—had some reasonable foundation. In 1987 McNamara recalled that even though he was certain the president would never launch such an attack,

> People in the Pentagon were even talking about a first-strike. In March 1961, I went out to look at the SIOP [Single Integrated Operational Plan] and found that there were four regular options, plus a fifth called I(a) which was a first-strike plan. [Air Force Chief of Staff General Curtis] LeMay talked openly about a first strike against the Soviet Union.[34]

Gilpatric's speech unwittingly may have fueled this fear and led Soviet military officials to seek a way of closing the gap.

The Defense of Cuba

At about the same time, Soviet officials assessed that the United States had decided to overthrow the Cuban government. Indeed, on November 30, 1961, Kennedy signed a National Security Action Memorandum that authorized a multifaceted plan—the CIA called it Operation Mongoose—to achieve this goal.[35] This last aspect of the plan was evident as early as January 1962, when the United States pressured Latin American countries to suspend Cuba's membership in the Organization of American States (OAS). Soviet leaders viewed the suspension ominously, as a certain prelude to a U.S. attack.[36] Shortly after the suspension, Aleksei I. Adzhubei, the editor of *Izvestia* and Khrushchev's son-in-law, reported to Castro and the Soviet leadership that he had the strong impression from an interview with

Kennedy that the United States was planning an invasion. Fursenko and Naftali explain that Adzhubei said that Kennedy viewed Cuba's threat to the United States as analogous to the Soviet perception of the threat Hungary posed in 1956, when the Soviet Union invaded Hungary.[37]

In his memoirs, Khrushchev cites the defense of Cuba as the primary reason for installing the missiles in Cuba, though he adds that "our missiles would have equalized what the West likes to call 'the balance of power.'"[38] More recent testimony from former Soviet officials confirms the finding that at least one major Soviet objective in placing missiles in Cuba was to secure it against a possible U.S. invasion.[39] This goal probably was related to the Soviet ambition of claiming the right to guide the socialist world in the face of Chinese challenges. Indeed the Soviets viewed newly independent countries in the Third World as a battleground in a conflict against both the United States and China for global leadership. According to Kiva Maidanik, the Soviets were obsessed about China's challenge in the Third World, which he called "the fear of fears." Maidanik spent three decades in several Soviet institutes working on Latin America in various capacities analyzing Cuba. The loss of Cuba, he said, would have been perhaps the final nail in the coffin of the Soviet Union's claim as the "natural" leader for developing countries.[40] Cuba was one of the founding members of the recently created Non-Aligned Movement (NAM), an organization of Third World nations, and was the only country in the NAM from Latin America. Khrushchev noted in his memoirs that "We had an obligation to do everything in our power to protect Cuba's existence as a Socialist country and as a working example to the other countries of Latin America."[41]

Given this apparent Soviet desire to defend Cuba, it is notable that once the United States announced it had discovered the missiles, the Soviet Union related far more to its superpower adversary than to Cuba. There was little coordination or consultation with Cuba.[42] Khrushchev's first reaction to Kennedy's October 22 speech was to denounce it as a "serious threat to peace." The Soviet Union, he said, could not "recognize right of United States [sic] to establish control over armaments essential to Republic of Cuba for strengthening of its defensive capacity."[43] Yet without notifying the Cubans, Soviet officials decided on October 25 to remove the missiles. The only issue for them was the deal they could strike in return, which led to the famous complication of Khrushchev's two letters on October 26 and 27.[44]

The first letter was an emotional appeal to Kennedy, in which Khrushchev wrote about the horrors of war which "ends when it has rolled through cities and villages, everywhere sowing death and destruction. . . . We and you ought not now to pull on the ends of the rope in which you have tied the knot of war, because the more the two of us pull, the tighter that knot will be tied. And a moment may come when . . . even he who ties it will not have the strength to untie it." The Soviet leader then suggested a bargain by which the United States would pledge not to invade Cuba and the Soviet Union would remove the missiles ("the armaments which you call offensive"). The second letter arrived less than twenty-four hours after the first. It was less personal and was released to the public, which made bargaining more difficult. This letter toughened the requirements for a peaceful settlement by adding that U.S. missiles would need to be removed from Turkey in addition to the U.S. noninvasion pledge.

In 1991 Georgy Kornienko, who was deputy Soviet ambassador to the United States in 1962 and later deputy foreign minister, explained that after the second letter had been drafted on October 25, the Presidium received "alarming information" that the U.S. would be invading Cuba very soon. A Soviet intelligence agent in Washington, he said, had received information from an informant who had overheard a conversation between two U.S. journalists on the evening of October 24. One of them said he was headed to Florida the next day (October 25) "to accompany the troops" and report on the invasion of Cuba, which was expected in the next day or two. Khrushchev then hastily drafted the emotional October 26 letter with terms more acceptable to the United States, and sent it instead. On the morning of October 25, as a way of confirming the intelligence report, Kornienko called the journalist and invited him to lunch. When he accepted the invitation, "it was immediately clear that he had not flown to Florida," Kornienko remarked. This new information was reported to Moscow and in combination with further intelligence that an invasion was not imminent, the Soviet leader dispatched the original October 25 letter to Kennedy.[45]

The Smell of Scorching Hangs in the Air

Khrushchev did not notify the Cubans about either letter in advance. Castro learned of the first one months after the crisis, and of the second one when it was released publicly on October 27. Late the night before, and into the early hours of October 27, he drafted a cable to Khrushchev warning the Soviet leader that an air strike or an invasion was likely in the next twenty-four to seventy-two hours. Castro estimated that an invasion was "less probable although possible." He then advised ominously that if the United States did invade Cuba

> the danger that that aggressive policy poses for humanity is so great that following that event the Soviet Union must never allow the circumstances in which the imperialists could launch the first nuclear strike against it . . . that would be the moment to eliminate such danger forever through an act of clear legitimate defense, however harsh and terrible the solution would be, for there is no other.[46]

There is still uncertainty about whether the letter had an impact on Khrushchev's decision to withdraw the missiles from Cuba. Though dated October 26, the letter was finished early in the morning of October 27, and the translated and encrypted version arrived at the Soviet Foreign Ministry only at 1:10 A.M. on October 28. Oleg Troyanovsky reported in 1992 that "the letter was read to Khrushchev over the phone and was circulated to the Politburo" prior to their meeting on the morning of October 28, during which they drafted Khrushchev's statement about withdrawing missiles. The Soviet leader's son, Sergei Khrushchev, recalled in 1991 that the letter did influence his father. "As a matter of fact," he said, "this letter worried Khrushchev . . . it confirmed his point of view . . . that the missiles should be withdrawn."[47] Indeed, Khrushchev advised Castro in a cable on October 28 "not to be carried away by sentiment and to show firmness. . . . But we mustn't allow ourselves to be carried away by provocations, because the Pentagon's unbridled militarists . . . are trying to frustrate the agreement and provoke you into actions that could be used against you."[48] And two days later he strongly disagreed with the October 26 letter, saying, "you proposed that we be the first to launch a nuclear strike against the territory of the enemy. You, of course, realize where that would have led. Rather than a simple strike, it would have been the start of a thermonuclear war."[49] Khrushchev also may have been influenced by the cable from Soviet Ambassador Alekseev, which summarized Castro's letter and arrived in advance of it.[50] Notably, an October 27 cable from Foreign Minister Andrei Gromyko to Ambassador Alekseev in Cuba refers to the ambassador's "communication" concerning a message from Castro and Cuban President Osvaldo Dorticós that indicated "an armed American intervention to Cuba is imminent."[51]

Years later, former Soviet officials still argued that "on the weekend of 27–28 October, there was no time for consultation with Havana."[52] Former Soviet Foreign Minister Gromyko remarked in 1989 that, ideally, the Soviets might have tried to extract more concessions from the United States to deal with "problems that interested Cuba. . . . But, all the same, it was necessary to preserve the ally of time."[53] Soviet officials, like their U.S. counterparts, feared the crisis was unraveling, getting out of control. It was as if, in Khrushchev's evocative phrase, the "smell of scorching hung in the air."[54] The incident that most provoked their anxiety was the shootdown of a U-2 reconnaissance plane over the eastern part of Cuba by a Soviet SAM.

The United States had been deploying the U-2s twice a day over Cuba since the discovery of the missiles, and there had been no Soviet attempt to fire on the planes.[55] But as tension increased by October 27, the Soviet military officers in Cuba believed that a U.S. attack was imminent. Former General Anatoli Gribkov captures the stress at the time by recalling that "I often saw our troops showering or swimming in the days after President Kennedy's speech" in keeping with "an old Russian military tradition [that] soldiers bathe themselves on the eve of battle."[56] In the face of an expected attack, Lt. Gen. Stepan Grechko, commander of the Soviet air defense in Cuba, requested permission from the Kremlin on October 26 to use "all available antiaircraft means" against U.S. forces. He had not received approval on the morning of October 27 when the U-2 flew again. Meanwhile Castro had ordered Cuban antiaircraft to open fire on any U.S. planes, though Cuban guns could not reach the U-2s, which flew at 70,000 feet. Soviet soldiers sensed the anticipated battle was commencing, and in the exhilaration of the moment Grechko ordered three SAMs to be fired at the U-2.[57]

As they sensed the fever pitch rising on the island, Soviet leaders realized they could no longer control events from Moscow. Two factors made this especially dangerous. First, the Soviet missiles were not configured with permissive action links, so local commanders could have disobeyed or misinterpreted orders—as they did with the U-2—and fired the ballistic missiles in the heat of battle. Second, unknown to the United States, the Soviets also had shipped tactical nuclear missiles to Cuba, with twelve warheads. The warheads had approximately one-quarter the destructive capability of the Hiroshima bomb. These battlefield weapons were intended to be used against invading forces, though Malinovsky had ordered on October 22 that they not be used with nuclear warheads, and the warheads were not mated with the missiles.[58] Still, the Soviet leaders feared that in the event of an invasion, Moscow's orders would be overruled, the more than 200,000 invading U.S. forces would suffer enormous casualties, and the brink of nuclear war might be breached. When Robert Kennedy informed Ambassador Dobrynin on October 27 that "time is of the essence"—because after the downing of the U-2 "there are many unreasonable heads among the generals, and not only among the generals, who are 'itching for a fight'"— the horror of these scenarios compelled Khrushchev to act quickly.[59]

On October 28 he was so anxious to convey his acceptance of Kennedy's terms for ending the crisis that he broadcast his response over the radio, so that it would be transmitted quickly and accurately.[60] Yet the decision to remove missiles had been made on the 25th. There would have been sufficient time to inform Castro about the change in the Soviets' position, and to consult with him about strategy. The Soviet fear of nuclear war was real, but lack of time was not the reason for failing to consult with the Cubans.

A more compelling explanation is that the Soviet leaders believed that if they involved Castro this would have made a resolution of the crisis more difficult. First, they believed the Cuban leader was unready to compromise. During the height of the crisis he addressed a crowd of 100,000 cheering people in Havana with a fiery oration.[61] He had ordered his forces to be on full alert, and he seemed to be eager to engage in battle. In this regard, whether or not Khrushchev's recollections about the way Castro's October 26 speech influenced him are accurate, they are a metaphor for the way in which the Soviet leader viewed the Cuban's spirit of defiance and desire for confrontation. He described Castro as "a young and hotheaded man."[62] Second, Soviet leaders believed if they had added Cuba's demands into the equation this would have complicated their negotiations with the United States, as Gromyko suggested.

In one sense, Gromyko's claim is an unassailable truism: It is more difficult for three parties to reach a compromise than two, and adding demands makes the resolution of any conflict more elaborate. But if the Soviet leaders had been less contemptuous of their Cuban allies, they might have found it relatively easy to include at least one of Cuba's demands in the compromise, that the United States be required to negotiate directly with Cuba.[63] Kennedy likely would not have rejected such a condition out of hand. It would have been difficult for him to justify launching an attack which could have led to nuclear war on the grounds that the United States was unwilling to talk to Cuba. But Cuba's "problems," in Gromyko's disparaging phrase, simply were not seen as serious, though these problems were nothing less than a well-founded fear of a U.S. desire to overthrow the Cuban government. Certainly other Cuban demands, such as the withdrawal of U.S. forces from Guantanamo naval base, would have been quite complicating. But a demand for direct negotiations between Cuba and the United States would have acknowledged that Cuba's conflict with the United States was the source of the crisis—as Khrushchev claimed it was—and that Cuba had the sovereign right to negotiate its own fate.

Khrushchev's unwillingness to consult Castro, therefore, might have reflected the Soviet fear of Armageddon and the desire to reach a speedy accommodation. But if this were so important, the Soviets would not have complicated matters themselves by demanding on October 27 that missiles in Turkey be removed. Thus it seems that superpower arrogance—the Soviets' desire to extract a U.S. promise not to invade Cuba without any Cuban participation in the deal—was evident here.

The Mikoyan Appeal

Cuba refused to permit verification on its soil. It had not been party to the Kennedy–Khrushchev agreement, and Castro insisted that Cuba had the sovereign right to reject any inspections. Frustrated by this Cuban stance, Khrushchev sent First Deputy Premier Anastas Mikoyan to Havana to talk to the Cuban leadership. He arrived in Havana on November 2 and remained there until November 26, 1962, despite the death of his wife during this period.[64] Mikoyan had been the first high-level official to visit Cuba after the Revolution—on a trade mission in February 1960. Inside the Kremlin, he was viewed as having a special relationship with the Cuban leadership. His son years later remarked that some saw Mikoyan as "Fidel's agent in the [Soviet] Politburo," which was a reputation the Cuban leadership appreciated. Castro joked in their first meeting, "we are aware . . . that N. S. Khrushchev once said: 'there is a Cuban in the CC CPSU [Central Committee, Communist Party of the Soviet Union] and this Cuban is A. I. Mikoyan.'"[65]

On his way to Havana, Mikoyan stopped in New York and met with U.S. officials at the United Nations. They gave him a note listing U.S. demands, and for the first time there was an explicit mention of IL-28 bombers.[66] Neither the Soviets nor the Cubans had anticipated that Kennedy would demand that anything besides the ballistic missiles be removed from Cuba.[67] Yet Khrushchev had provided a loophole for Kennedy to go after these planes. In his crude attempt to maintain the claim that the ballistic missiles were merely defensive, the Soviet leader referred to them as the "weapons you describe as offensive" in his October 28 speech announcing the end of the crisis.[68] Kennedy seized the opportunity afforded by this ambiguity and conditioned his agreement with Khrushchev upon the withdrawal of the IL-28s.

Mikoyan refused to accept the note and on November 5, in recounting to the Cuban leaders how he had rejected the new U.S. demands, he remarked: "I would like to mention, that the Americans are trying to broaden the list of weapons for evacuation. Such attempts have already been made, but we will not allow them to do so."[69] He continued to maintain this position for the next week. Meanwhile, Kennedy pressured Khrushchev to withdraw the bombers. On November 11 the Soviet leader bowed to the pressure and told the U.S. president, "We will not insist on permanently keeping those planes in Cuba."[70] Castro knew none of this. On November 12 Mikoyan encouraged the Cuban leader to give up the bombers, but indicated that the Soviet decision to withdraw them would depend on Cuban acquiescence.[71] The next day Khrushchev wrote to Kennedy that "I can assure the President that those planes will be removed from Cuba . . . in 2–3 months."[72] Khrushchev's anger over Castro's intransigence apparently led the Soviet leader and the Presidium to decide on November 16 to bow to Kennedy's insistence that the bombers be removed immediately. But Cuba learned of this decision only on about November 20.[73]

Khrushchev did continue to request, as Cuba had demanded, that the United States lift the quarantine announced on October 22 and end surveillance flights over Cuba. But on November 19 the Soviet leader meekly suggested that in light of the Soviet Union's willingness to remove the IL-28 bombers, "we presume that we have grounds to count on similar understanding on your part also in the questions of the flights of American planes over Cuba."[74] For the Soviets, the crisis ended on November 20 when Kennedy announced the lifting of the quarantine because the IL-28s would be removed from Cuba. The overflights continued.

Both Kennedy and Khrushchev personally appear to have come away from the crisis with important new lessons about nuclear crises and superpower confrontation. The fear both experienced forced them to reconsider deeply held attitudes about how each should relate to his main adversary, and encouraged them to work toward negotiations over arms control agreements.[75] Some of the American and Soviet officials—in looking at the way in which the crisis nearly went out of control—also came to believe that crises cannot be managed and that they must be prevented.[76]

But in the Kremlin, ultimately, the outcome was seen as a U.S. victory and a Soviet humiliation. As Raymond Garthoff observes, "in the longer run the outcome of the affair undoubtedly contributed to his [Khrushchev's] fall from power two years later."[77] Though Khrushchev continued to contend proudly that "The Caribbean crisis was a triumph of Soviet foreign policy and a personal triumph in my own career . . . ,"[78] Adam Ulam observes that "his successors chose publicly to emphasize his 'hare-brained schemes.'"[79] Securing Cuba was not deemed to be such an important achievement.

While the two superpowers at least may have taken from the crisis a better understanding of each other than they had had before, neither seemed to derive any empathy for the Cuban point of view. The crisis formally ended on January 7, 1963, with two letters to UN Acting Secretary-General U Thant. One was a joint letter from the United States and the Soviet Union. The other one was from Cuba alone.[80]

CUBA'S PERSPECTIVE: CONFLICT AVERTED BUT CRISIS ENDURES

Although the October Crisis was the one that brought Cuba closest to the brink of devastation—by way of either a nuclear conflagration or a U.S. invasion—it was one of many crises between Cuba and the United States in the first years of the Revolution. Though each actually does not have its own designation, Cubans say that they distinguish among them by reference to the date when they occurred; this one happened in October.[81] Their name for the crisis thus highlights Cuba's ongoing conflict with the United States, which they argue led to the confrontation over the missiles. But from the Cuban perspective, it was Soviet–U.S. interests that defined the terms by which an actual conflict was avoided. By serving their own interests and not addressing the Cuban–U.S. conflict, the two superpowers thus did not resolve the underlying causes of the missile crisis.[82]

Mongoose Presages the Crisis

Scholars have assigned many causes to the speedy deterioration in U.S.–Cuban relations after the January 1, 1959 triumph of the revolutionary forces. These include: the nature of the U.S. imperial state and the challenge posed to U.S. hegemony by a revolutionary government; the psychodynamics of the relationship, including the personalities of key officials in both countries and their expectations of how the other country would behave; Cuba's "internationalism," which threatened perceived U.S. interests; U.S. efforts to pressure and then subvert the Revolutionary government, which "pushed" Cuba into the Soviet camp and made Cuba a strategic threat to the United States; alleged secret ties of the Cuban leadership to the Soviet Union, which led the Cubans to view the United States as an enemy from the outset; Castro's calculation that an external enemy would enable him to consolidate and maintain the revolution by strengthening the Cubans' sense of nationalism and by justifying internal repression; Castro's ambition for Cuba to play a major role on the world stage; and the inevitable clash between a dependent country undergoing fundamental internal change, whose political and economic structures were dominated by economic interests that were displaced by Cuba's transformation, and the dominant country which absorbed the outcast rulers and beneficiaries of the old regime.[83] Regardless of the source, though, there is agreement that by April 17, 1961—the start of the Bay of Pigs invasion—the two countries had become enemies. The United States was seeking to overthrow the Cuban government, and Cuba assessed that it had to defend itself from a hostile United States.

Meanwhile, Cuba had begun to receive assistance from the Soviet Union, with which it established diplomatic relations in the spring of 1960. In the second half of that year the Soviet Union supplied some light arms, artillery and mortars, tanks, antiaircraft rockets, and technical assistance.[84] But only after the Bay of Pigs invasion did the Soviets begin to send sophisticated weapons and substantial assistance.[85] The Soviets anticipated, as Khrushchev asserts in his autobiography, "that the Americans would not let Cuba alone . . . and they wouldn't refuse a chance to repeat their aggression."[86] The Cubans believed this as well. Castro remarked in 1992:

> But Girón, the Bay of Pigs, was undoubtedly the prelude to the October crisis, because, for Kennedy, this was a severe political blow. He was very saddened and embittered by these events, and as of then, the Cuban issue had a different, special connotation for him. This was reflected in the relations between our two countries. . . . The idea was that in one way or another he [Kennedy] had to put an end to the revolutionary process in Cuba.[87]

Thus, Cuban officials perceived that all U.S. behavior concerning Cuba after the Bay of Pigs was directed to the one goal of destroying the Cuban revolution. In reality, they were not far from the mark, as the Kennedy administration decided within three weeks of the failed invasion to make a more determined effort to bring down the revolutionary government.[88] Then, in November 1961, Kennedy authorized Operation Mongoose, a multifaceted plan explicitly intended to overthrow the Cuban government.[89] Some analysts have focused on the counterrevolutionary and terrorist aspects of Mongoose and have argued that the Kennedy administration committed itself only half-heartedly to the goals of the plan because sabotage operations were conducted only sporadically.[90] But Mongoose is best understood as a four-part model for what later came to be described as "low-intensity conflict."[91] In addition to the development of counterrevolutionary forces and support for their activities, the overall Cuba Project also included economic warfare, military threats, and political demarches designed to isolate Cuba from potential supporters in the Third World, especially in Latin America.[92]

With their own experience of the September 11, 2001, terrorist attacks, Americans now may be better able to appreciate how repeated incidents against civilian targets can induce a sense of fear and anger in a population. Even if these actions were authorized unenthusiastically, and carried out lackadaisically, the first component of Mongoose did include the sabotage of tractors, factories, and machinery; the burning of fields; the contamination of sugar awaiting export; and the resupply of anti-Castro guerrillas who engaged in terror tactics throughout the island. They were intended to create the conditions for a successful invasion by U.S. forces, though Kennedy never authorized such an invasion. There was also an associated though independent operation to assassinate Fidel Castro.[93] The CIA station in Miami, out of which Operation Mongoose was run, cost $50 to $60 million a year, according to Sam Halpern, deputy to CIA deputy director for operations and the principal CIA official overseeing the operation. This figure, however, did not account for any funds spent by the more than thirty other agencies involved.[94] Mongoose was the largest CIA covert operation undertaken until that time.

While there is evidence that considerable terrorist activity did occur—in 1991 Gen. Fabian Escalante Font cited "5,700 acts of terrorism, sabotage, and murder" during 1962—it is not clear that all the guerrilla activities were actually directed by the CIA. There were independent counterrevolutionary groups operating within Cuba, as well as groups based outside, that also launched attacks. Cuban officials, nonetheless, perceived all of the terrorist acts as part of one plan directed by the U.S. government.[95] McNamara acknowledged years later that U.S. covert activities against Cuba certainly suggested a U.S. invasion was in the works, though he emphasized that Kennedy had not authorized an invasion plan. "I want to state quite frankly," he said at a conference on the missile crisis in 1989, "that with hindsight, if I had been a Cuban leader, I think I might have expected a U.S. invasion."[96]

The second facet of Operation Mongoose was economic, and in February 1962 the United States formalized its unilateral economic embargo while encouraging U.S. allies to cut their own trade with Cuba. The de facto embargo against Cuba began when the Eisenhower administration barred the sale of Cuban sugar to the United States in mid-1960. Sugar was Cuba's main means of earning hard currency, and the United States was its principal buyer. Most commerce between the two countries ended when the United States broke diplomatic relations with Cuba in January 1961. The formal embargo closed off all transactions, including those for food and medicine. Congress authorized the president to institute such an embargo against Cuba in 1961, and Kennedy relied on his authority under the 1917 Trading with the Enemy Act to impose the trade sanctions in 1962.[97]

The third component of Mongoose, military threats, was evident in naval exercises the United States conducted in the Caribbean. Most prominent were "Lantphiblex 1-62" and "Quick Kick," each of which involved approximately 40,000 troops. Lantphiblex included a practice invasion of Vieques, an island off the coast of Puerto Rico, with a force of 10,000 troops. Historian James Hershberg explains that these maneuvers "were designed to test procedures that would be used by CINCLANT during an actual invasion of Cuba."[98]

While the successful U.S. campaign to suspend Cuba's OAS membership was an integral element—the fourth, political component—of the larger plan to overthrow the revolutionary government, this particular effort also may have been a reaction to Cuba's support for revolutionary movements in the hemisphere. Castro has acknowledged that as early as 1959 Cuba supported insurrectionary efforts against the Trujillo dictatorship in the Dominican Republic. The Cuban government trained revolutionaries, allowed them to disembark from Cuba, and permitted Cuban volunteers to join the revolutionaries. There also have been charges that it supported revolutionaries against the Panamanian and Haitian governments, but Cuba has denied these allegations.[99] U.S. officials reportedly were most anxious about Venezuela. As historian Arthur Schlesinger, who served as an aide to Kennedy, recounted in 1991:

> We were particularly concerned about Fidel's support for guerrilla activity in Venezuela. This persuaded us that he saw the contest in the same terms that we did and that he regarded [Venezuelan President Rómulo] Betancourt as his main target— proving that Betancourt could not succeed would be the strongest way he could support the spread of the communist alternative.[100]

In 1992 Castro acknowledged that Cuba had supported efforts to oust Betancourt, but he noted that there was "very strong opposition from the left" within Venezuela against the president. "So we did not create the opposition, because we could not create it." However, Castro viewed the Venezuelan leader as "one of the most active enemies of the Cuban Revolution." As a consequence

> we did help the leftist forces in Venezuela. We helped the Communist Party, and all the other leftist organizations, and some of the military and people who were not communists in various sectors. . . . We really were not organizing the opposition to Rómulo Betancourt. What we did was support the opposition against Rómulo Betancourt. . . . We definitely supported that movement. But Cuba was not the only one that supported that movement.[101]

The Soviet Nuclear Umbrella

Whether the Cuban role in the Venezuelan guerrilla movement was perceived as a genuine threat to the hemisphere or was merely a pretext for the U.S. campaign against Cuba, Cuba's actions did provide the justification for a bare two-thirds majority of the OAS to suspend Cuba's membership.[102] Cuba's response came on February 4, 1962, in the Second Declaration of Havana, as Castro proclaimed:

> The duty of every revolutionary is to make the revolution. . . . Even if the Yankee imperialists prepare a bloody drama for America, they will not succeed in crushing the peoples' struggles, they will only arouse universal hatred against themselves. And such a drama will also mark the death of their greedy and carnivorous system.[103]

The speech confirmed U.S. fears of Cuba as a fomenter of trouble, though U.S. anxiety may have had a self-fulfilling quality because it was not until 1963 that Cuba began a serious effort against Venezuela, which resulted in the 1964 hemisphere-wide embargo against Cuba.[104]

It is, of course, impossible to know whether the United States still would have attempted to subvert the Cuban government in the absence of its revolutionary activities.[105] As we discuss in the epilogue, U.S. officials in 1962 also were concerned about Cuba's ties to the Soviet Union, its expropriation of property owned by U.S. citizens and corporations, the symbol of defiance to U.S. dictates that it represented, and the increasingly socialist character of the regime. Whatever the reason for the U.S. decision to overthrow the Cuban government, this goal was evident from U.S. actions after 1960.

Largely because of its perception of a U.S. threat, Cuba sought to be brought under the protection of the Soviet umbrella through membership in the Warsaw Pact. But the Soviets refused to admit Cuba. They feared it would not have been tenable to protect Cuba, given its proximity to the United States, and that it might even increase Cuban vulnerability.[106] Notably, Castro first characterized the Cuban revolution as socialist on the eve of the Bay of Pigs invasion, with the probable intention of drawing the Soviet Union into Cuba's defense.[107] Yet the Soviets did not fully acknowledge the socialist character of the Cuban revolution in 1961, in part because this would have implied the necessity of defending Cuba, and in part because a communist party did not rule Cuba.[108] In 1961 Castro had subsumed the old pro-Soviet Cuban communist party—the Popular Socialist Party (PSP)—under an amalgamated party, the Integrated Revolutionary Organizations (ORI). It included members of the PSP, the Students' Revolutionary Directorate, and his July 26th Movement.

However, by April 1962, the Soviets were ready to recognize Cuba as a "socialist" country. *Pravda* signaled this by declaring Cuba had "embarked on the path of socialist construction."[109] Two factors seem to have engendered the change. First, Castro announced that the Cuban revolution would follow a Marxist-Leninist path. "The reality of history has demonstrated fully, has confirmed, the doctrine of marxism-leninism," he declared on December 1, 1961.[110] Second, he forced Moscow to appreciate that in dealing with Cuba it would need to abandon any hope of working through its former allies in the PSP. The Cuban leader conveyed this message sharply in March 1962—with a foretaste of the January 1968 trial of the microfaction at which he gave the missile crisis speech—by purging Aníbal Escalante from the ORI.

Escalante had been a leader of the PSP, which was the most organized faction of the newly formed ORI, and he became organization secretary of the new party. In this capacity he recruited new members who took direction from him, and he used the PSP party cells (called "nuclei") to build a base of power within the ORI and over governmental administrators.[111] After exiling Escalante to Czechoslovakia, Castro then made his meaning clear in a strongly worded speech on March 26 that pointedly opened with a catch-all reference to Lenin:

> To begin with, I would like to refer to a saying of Lenin, that . . . the seriousness of pur-
> pose of a revolutionary party is measured, basically, by the attitude it takes towards its
> own errors. . . . One of the fundamental problems produced in the struggle against reac-
> tionary ideas, against conservative ideas, against the deserters, against those who wa-
> vered, against those with negative attitudes, was sectarianism. It may be said that was the
> fundamental error produced by the ideological struggle which was being waged. . . .
> What sectarianism? Well, the sectarianism of believing that the only revolutionaries, the
> only ones who could [sic] positions of trust, the only ones who could hold a post on a
> People's Farm, on a Cooperative, in the government, anywhere, had to be old Marxist
> militants. . . . The comrade who had the task . . . of working as the Organizing Secretary
> of the Integrated Revolutionary Organizations . . . most regrettably, fell into the errors we
> have been enumerating, was comrade Aníbal Escalante. . . . Comrade Aníbal Escalante
> is responsible for having promoted the sectarian spirit to its highest possible level, of
> having promoted an organization which he controlled. . . . He simply allowed himself to
> be blinded by personal ambition.[112]

A few weeks later, when the Soviets proposed placing missiles in Cuba, the Cuban leadership perceived this as an acknowledgment, finally, that the Soviet Union would protect Cuba. The Soviet Union had not placed nuclear missiles out-side of its territory before, and by doing so in Cuba it necessarily was extending its umbrella over the island.[113] Notably, Castro's explanation of why Cuba accepted the Soviet proposal—"In the first place . . . we believed that this was something that would buttress the defensive power of the entire socialist camp"[114]—focuses on Cuba's role within the family of socialist nations. This made it a de facto member of the Warsaw Pact, though unlike other members of the Pact, the Soviets had no formal obligation to defend Cuba if it were attacked.

A Conflict over Publicizing the Agreement

There were unquestionably risks for Cuba in housing the missiles. First, it became a U.S. strategic target. But from Cuba's perspective, the impending invasion was viewed as the equivalent of a nuclear holocaust—in the sense that it would have devastated the country—and the image of an invasion was more palpably frightening than the abstraction of being a nuclear target.[115] Second, there was the potential that Cuba would be perceived in Latin America as nothing more than an outpost of the Soviet Union.[116] "We armed ourselves against our own wishes," he told the Cuban public on October 23, 1962, "because we were forced to strengthen our military defenses on pain of endangering the sovereignty of our nation and the independence of our country."[117] But the associated benefit of the close collaboration with the Soviets was that the superpower would be seen, in effect, as endorsing Cuba's strategy of armed struggle in the hemisphere. Given Cuba's quarrels with Soviet-oriented Latin American communist parties, which opposed armed struggle, the placement of missiles on the island was a victory signal for Cuba and a tacit endorsement of the revolutionary program he advocated in the Second Declaration of Havana three months earlier.

The benefits of accepting the Soviet proposal thus outweighed the risks. Cuba would become the revolutionary leader of Latin America with Soviet blessing. It would secure a deterrent against a likely U.S. invasion. And it would become a full member of the Soviet socialist family of nations—the first Third World country to achieve this status.

It was for this last reason, in part, that the Cuban leadership wanted the Soviets to announce publicly the signing of the Soviet–Cuban military agreement under which the missiles went to Cuba. A public statement would verify Soviet acknowledgment of Cuba's status, and make any possible Soviet retraction difficult. Perhaps this is why Khrushchev rejected the Cuban request for an announcement. However, what he told Castro's emissaries, Che Guevara and Emilio Aragonés, was that revelation of the plan in advance would lead the United States to intervene.[118] The Soviet leader wanted to confront its adversary with a *fait accompli* that it could not successfully challenge.[119] Castro's counterargument focused on the benefits of a public announcement. He contended that

> If our conduct is legal, if it is moral, if it is correct, why should we do something that may give rise to a scandal? Why should it seem that we are doing something secretly, covertly, as if we were doing something wrong . . . ? We're giving *imperialism* the initiative, we're giving the *enemy* the initiative.[120]

But he acquiesced in the secrecy, no doubt because of Khrushchev's intransigence, though he said in 1968 that he had believed the Soviets "had a much better grasp of the overall situation than we did and therefore we left the decision to them."[121] Castro also sought to change the initial draft agreement so that its public version would provide a "clear political justification," which was that the agreement was between two sovereign nations and that its purpose was "to provide mutual military assistance" rather than "to save the Cuban revolution."[122]

As work on the missile sites progressed, though, the Cubans began to worry that it would be impossible to camouflage them any longer. Castro understood his northern neighbor better than his superpower rival did and was convinced that the United States would not respond well to a surprise discovery of the missiles. So he sought to reveal the secret publicly but opaquely. He directed Cuban President Osvaldo Dorticós to hint at their existence in an October 8 speech at the United Nations. Dorticós said there, "If . . . we are attacked, we will defend ourselves. I repeat we have sufficient means with which to defend ourselves; we have indeed our inevitable weapons, the weapons which we would have preferred not to acquire and which we do not wish to employ."[123]

The wonder is that this speech, delivered in New York, with a response from U.S. Ambassador to the UN Adlai Stevenson, seems to have had no impact at all on U.S. thinking as the crisis approached. Even though Dorticós virtually confirmed the presence of Soviet strategic nuclear forces in Cuba, Washington seems not to have noticed. Kennedy and his advisers were focused almost exclusively on Soviet statements and actions. The Cubans, in the telling phrase of a top-level Kennedy adviser, were regarded as mere "bit players" who had accidentally wandered onto the great stage of a superpower confrontation.[124]

Cuba Becomes "The Hinge of the World"

The Cuban leadership and the Cuban people approached the October 1962 missile crisis with supreme confidence that their new Soviet ally would stand by their side: it would deter a U.S. invasion of the island if possible, but if deterrence failed it would, the Cubans believed, use all its military resources—including its nuclear weapons in Cuba and in the Soviet Union—to make the United States and its allies pay the ultimate price for seeking to undermine the Cuban Revolution and overthrow the Cuban government. The alliance with the Soviets had brought nuclear weapons and tens of thousands of Soviet military personnel to the island in a matter of months. Suddenly, the small, beleaguered nation of Cuba became, in the apt phrase of William D. Rogers, "the hinge of the world."[125] It may be difficult now, forty years removed from those events, to appreciate the Cuban psychology of that moment. But their outlook was unmistakable: Cubans in October 1962 had no fear of the United States and no doubts about the total Soviet commitment to Cuban security. Castro believed that Khrushchev had made the protection of Cuba equivalent to defense of the Soviet motherland.

Still, once the United States discovered the missiles, Castro was far less accepting of supposedly superior Soviet tactical prowess than he had been earlier. Anticipating that Kennedy's October 22 address would be about Cuba, Castro ordered a rapid mobilization of the island's forces before the speech was delivered. "The Nation on a War Footing," was the headline emblazoned across the next day's *Revolucion*, the official government newspaper. As nearly 300,000 Cuban soldiers prepared for a U.S. invasion over the next few days, Castro counseled Soviet generals about the placement of SAMs and about the need for antiaircraft weapons to defend them.[126]

Castro recalled in 1992 that Khrushchev's letter to him on October 23 confirmed the judgment that war was imminent. In that letter, the Soviet leader also expressed what seemed like a commitment to fight with Cuba against the "piratical, perfidious and aggressive" actions of the United States.[127] Castro recalled telling his colleagues, "Well, it looks like war. I cannot conceive of any retreat." Reflectively, in 1992, he then mused that "the idea of retreating never entered my mind. We never thought it was possible."[128]

Castro's public response to Kennedy's speech was defiant, expressing a surreal confidence. His address was as poignant and eloquent as it was brimming with pride in being Cuban. At what must have seemed to him to be the most critical moment in Cuban history, perhaps in world history, he proclaimed:

> If the imperialists, against the most basic interest of mankind, force things to the point of unleashing a war very painful to mankind, the historic responsibility will be theirs. . . . We have the conviction of the cause we defend, of all the justice and the justification on our side . . . these risks our people are running are . . . because our people have unfurled a banner of justice, . . . they know how to look ahead calmly. All of us, men and women, young and old, we are all united in this hour of danger, and ours, the fate of all the revolutionaries and the patriots, will be the same fate, and the victory will belong to all.[129]

Embedded in this statement are several messages for the Cuban people: their beloved "Cubita" (little Cuba) would be the hinge around which events would swirl. The United States may not take seriously the Soviet–Cuban alliance and its unshakable commitment to Cuba's security. If, as a result, war comes, then all Cuban citizens should understand that they will perform a sacred duty. Together with their Soviet brothers, they will at least remove the United States, the embodiment of imperialism, as the obstacle to the global struggle for freedom.

And so the Cubans and Soviets on the island prepared for a war they believed could be very destructive, especially in Cuba. This expectation was shared by most people on the island at the time, not only the leaders in Havana. Many older Cubans still recall that each night during the climactic days of the crisis, they silently said "goodbye" to their sleeping children. They imagined that they would never see them again, that all might likely perish in a nuclear holocaust of which Cuba would be the epicenter, the "Hiroshima" of the Cold War.[130]

The profound awareness that Cuba was on the front line of what could be the first nuclear war engendered seemingly contradictory emotions. On the one hand, there was a feeling of defiant pride and courage. On the other, there was a sense of the coming apocalypse. For example, while counterrevolutionary bands had been rounded up and jailed prior to the 1961 Bay of Pigs invasion, there was little concern about them in October 1962. Their threat paled in comparison to nuclear war. One Cuban official tried to convey the strange atmosphere created by this duality in recounting that Havana's famous Tropicana night club was open for business each night, and that it was packed with customers, mostly Cubans. He recalled questioning two colleagues about that. "Why should it be closed?" one asked rhetorically. "If the Yankees get the message and understand that this time they had better leave us alone, then why not dance? Or else they don't get the message, then Cuba will probably be the first to go up in a big mushroom cloud, but so will the Americans, then why not dance?"[131]

On October 26 Castro wrote his now controversial letter to Khrushchev. When Sergei Khrushchev first revealed its existence in 1989, and subsequently when Nikita Khrushchev's revised memoirs were published, much was made of the Soviet leader's view that Castro was suggesting the Soviets launch a preemptive nuclear attack.[132] In fact, Castro's letter did not make such a proposal. It predicted that there would be a U.S. attack in the next twenty-four to seventy-two hours, and that it was likely to be an air attack. But, he said, there was also the slight possibility it might be a full-scale invasion. As his own explanation to Khrushchev on October 31, 1962, makes clear, the Cuban leader was offering the Kremlin the same sort of tactical advice he was giving Soviet generals in Cuba. He wrote:

> I was aware while writing my letter that the words contained within could be misunderstood by you and so they were. . . . I did not suggest to you, comrade Khrushchev, that the USSR become the aggressor. . . . What was said was that at the moment that imperialist forces attacked Cuba—and, in Cuba, the armed forces of the USSR, deployed there to help us in our defenses if attacked from abroad—making the imperialists the de facto aggressors against Cuba and against the USSR, then they be responded with an annihilating counter-strike. . . . I did not suggest to you, comrade Khrushchev, that in the midst of the crisis the USSR attack, but rather that in the aftermath of an imperialist attack, the USSR act without vacillation and certainly not commit the error of allowing the enemy's chance to discharge against her a nuclear first strike. . . . I [raised this delicate topic] because of our concern that she [Soviet Union] never again find herself victim of the treachery and betrayal of the aggressor as occurred in 1941.[133]

The misunderstanding over Castro's letter contributed to the anger that he felt toward the Soviets. While its contribution was small, it exemplified for the Cuban leadership that Khrushchev lacked an appreciation and respect for Cuba. Even more galling as a matter of personal humiliation was the Soviet leader's failure to consult with Castro about the removal of the missiles, or even to notify him in advance of the October 28 announcement. An October 27 cable from Foreign Minister Gromyko to Ambassador Alekseev reveals the imperious way in which the Soviet Union treated Cuba during the crisis. Gromyko ordered Alekseev to meet with Castro and to

> say the following: "It is considered in Moscow that comrade Fidel Castro should urgently make a statement in support of the proposals of the Soviet government listed in the message from N. S. Khrushchev to President Kennedy of October 27 [regarding the removal of Soviet missiles in exchange for a noninvasion pledge and the removal of U.S. missiles from Turkey]."[134]

Castro did not find the Soviet excuse credible, that he was not consulted because there was a lack of time given the urgency of the situation. On November 4 he sternly told Soviet Deputy Premier Anastas Mikoyan that "The principle of agreement [between Kennedy and Khrushchev] had already been found [on October 27]. It seems to me that there was available time for consultations."[135]

Soviet Betrayal

Thus, at that moment when most of the rest of the world finally breathed a sigh of relief that the crisis was over, the Cuban leadership and Cuban people were furious. Castro recalled in 1992:

> Not only was this decision taken without *consulting* us, several steps were taken without *informing* us. . . . We heard over the radio on the 28th [of October] that there had been an agreement. So we were humiliated. . . . [T]he reaction of our nation was of profound indignation, not relief; of all the peoples, all of our cadres.[136]

The historical facts are consistent with Castro's recollection. Pro-Soviet posters and billboards were ripped down spontaneously all over the island by roving bands of angry young people. Castro's own anger was publicly evident shortly after the crisis ended. Early in November 1962, at a University of Havana meeting, he described Khrushchev as lacking *cojones* (testicles), and he encouraged the crowd to repeat a chant that had become quite popular: "*Nikita, mariquita, lo que se da no se quita!*" (Nikita, you little homosexual, what is given should not be taken back!)[137] But his wrath was rooted less in personal pique than in national insult about the way in which Khrushchev cavalierly ignored Cuban sovereignty when he accepted Kennedy's demand for international inspection of the missiles being removed. Neither the United States nor the Soviet Union had asked Cuba for permission to do the inspections on Cuban territory.

Meanwhile, the United States continued surveillance flights in Cuban airspace. Castro's insistence that the flights cease was one of five points he addressed to U Thant, acting secretary general of the United Nations on October 28. Taken together Castro's demands were an expression of Cuba's position on what was necessary to end the crisis.[138] U Thant went to Havana on October 30 to seek Cuba's permission for verification that the missiles were being removed. But Castro refused, charging that U Thant was legitimating a double standard by not requiring verification of the U.S. pledge that it would refrain from invading Cuba.[139]

Such was the circumstance when Mikoyan arrived in Cuba. He initially had two purposes in meeting with the Cuban leadership. First, he hoped to convince them that the Soviets had acted with Cuba's best interests in mind, and that the Soviets appreciated Cuba's views and respected Cuba's sovereignty. That is, it was a mission to assuage Cuban anger, especially in the face of Chinese accusations of Soviet weakness and perfidy. Recall that the Cuban leadership appreciated Mikoyan's reputation as the person inside the Kremlin who was their advocate. The deputy premier also hoped to achieve Cuban acquiescence in some form of international inspection, because that had become an obstacle to concluding the crisis. On this issue Castro was absolutely unyielding. He resolutely told Mikoyan on November 4, "We cannot take that step. If we agree to an inspection, then it is as if we permit the United States of America to determine what we can or cannot do in foreign policy. That hurts our sovereignty."[140]

As we noted earlier, a third reason for Mikoyan's trip emerged while he was on route—the removal of the IL-28 bombers. Castro's memory, in his secret 1968 speech, of the way in which the issue was broached in Havana deviates from the documentary record. But it captures the essence of what happened, and his account provides a sense of how the Cubans came to distrust Soviet promises. He recalled that

> after we explained to him [Mikoyan] our standpoints, we had him clarify what was going to happen with the IL-28 planes, and he vouched that no, the IL-28s would not leave Cuba. Then, if I remember correctly, I asked him, "But if they demand their withdrawal, what will you do?" He answered, "Then to hell with the imperialists, to hell with the imperialists." Then some 24, or at most 48 hours later, he arrived at the meeting—those famous meetings at the Palace of the Revolution—Mikoyan arrived bearing the sad news that the IL-28 planes would also have to be returned.

A Soviet "memorandum of conversation" shows that it was Mikoyan who raised the issue of the IL-28s on November 5. He explained that just prior to leaving New

York, U.S. Ambassador to the United Nations Adlai E. Stevenson handed a letter to the Soviet deputy foreign minister (Vasili Kuznetsov)—claiming he forgot to show it to him at dinner the night before—in which the United States listed several other weapons it considered "offensive" besides the ballistic missiles. Reading the list to the Cuban leaders, Mikoyan exclaimed, "There are mentioned: bombers, 'Komar' patrol boats, 'air-to-surface' bombs and missiles, 'sea-to-surface' and 'surface-to-surface' projectiles. The Americans are impertinently continuing their attempts to complicate the situation."[141] But behind Mikoyan's back, the Kremlin impertinently agreed to the U.S. demands.

Peace Was Not Achieved

The issue of verification was never resolved to the satisfaction of the United States, and Kennedy used it as a basis for qualifying his no-invasion pledge so significantly that he effectively vitiated it. In his November 20, 1962 press conference announcing that the Soviets would be removing the IL-28s and that the U.S. would be lifting the quarantine, the president declared that the U.S. pledge had been contingent on adequate verification, which Cuba had stymied, and on an end to Cuban subversive activities in Latin America.[142]

The Soviet retreat on the IL-28s, despite a firm Soviet promise to Cuba that they would not be removed, was the final confirmation of Soviet treachery. Five years later Castro explained to the Central Committee in the secret 1968 speech:

A new stage in our relations with the Soviet Union began, characterized by the special circumstance of having in [sic] before us an aggressive and emboldened enemy, an ally on the retreat and our desire to keep the weapons, as well as our resolve to prevent relations with that ally from deteriorating to the point of rupture.

No longer trusting Soviet guarantees, and having no faith in U.S. promises, Cuba attempted to codify the Kennedy–Khrushchev agreement in a UN Security Council protocol that also would have addressed Cuba's desire to end the U.S. economic embargo and to engage the United States in negotiations over the Guantanamo naval base.[143] On November 1, in a meeting with Stevenson, Mikoyan had "raised the question that it was necessary to write down in the form of a protocol the important provisions that are contained in the exchange of messages between N. S. Khrushchev and Kennedy, taking into account the statement by Fidel Castro."[144] But the United States refused to consider negotiating the proposed protocol seriously, and the Soviets did not insist on it.

Thus for Cuba, the crisis was never fully resolved. "An international conflict was avoided," Castro observed in 1992, "but peace had not been achieved. For our country, there was no peace."[145] Cuba viewed the U.S. threat of attack as the source of the missile crisis and vested no hope in the qualified U.S. pledge against inva-sion. In fact, while the U.S. honored the pledge not to invade, it did resort to nu-merous other tactics intended to destabilize the Cuban government. For Cuba, the missile crisis became one of many it endured with the United States. It was the one in October.

LESSONS OF THE MISSILE CRISIS

The most frequently chanted lesson of the missile crisis is derived from the tradi-tional U.S. perspective: superior military capability combined with the firm resolve to use that capability will deter aggression and repel an aggressor. Raymond Garthoff, at the time an intelligence analyst in the State Department, summarized this guideline well in a memo for the Under Secretary of State on October 29, 1962, writing:

> If we have learned anything from this experience, it is that weakness, even only appar-ent weakness, invites Soviet transgression. At the same time, firmness in the last analy-sis will force the Soviets to back away from rash initiatives.[146]

U.S. military superiority was seen as the "decisive factor" in bringing the crisis to a peaceful and successful conclusion.[147] The metaphor of the two superpowers go-ing eyeball to eyeball, as if in a *macho* game of "chicken," dominated post-crisis evaluations. Success became a matter of "guts," of proving resolve, because it was assumed that Khrushchev placed the missiles in Cuba in order to test Kennedy's re-solve.[148] "As a result of the crisis," James Nathan astutely observes, "force and toughness became enshrined as instruments of policy."[149]

A Shared U.S.–Soviet Understanding

In reality, Kennedy was both more flexible than the early postmortems suggested and more sensitive to the Soviet need to salvage something positive from the crisis. In order to buy some time and avoid a direct confrontation with the Soviets, on Oc-tober 25 he permitted a Soviet tanker (the *Bucharest*) to proceed through the quar-antine.[150] On October 28 the president instructed the ExComm members, as Robert Kennedy recalled, "that no interview should be given, no statement made which would claim any kind of victory. [President Kennedy] respected Khrushchev for properly determining what was in his own country's interest and what was in the interest of mankind."[151] Perhaps most importantly, he offered up removal of the U.S. missiles in Turkey and was prepared to accept a public trade of the missiles if that were necessary to prevent a conflagration.[152] The appropriate lesson that should have been drawn from this behavior, then, is that flexibility, compromise, and respect for an adversary's calculus of its vulnerability is essential for the peaceful outcome of a crisis. Instead, the traditional view of what is needed in a crisis—toughness and inflexibility—seemingly has guided U.S. officials for decades, in confrontations from Vietnam to Iraq.[153]

A second lesson of the crisis emerged from the plaudits given to Kennedy for the way he handled the crisis. Arthur Schlesinger captured this lesson—that crises can be managed—in his effusive observation that the world escaped a nuclear war and the United States achieved it aims because of the president's "combination of toughness and restraint, of will, nerve, and wisdom, so brilliantly controlled, so matchlessly calibrated."[154] A clearer way of stating this lesson, though, might be that nuclear crises can be managed only when several unlikely conditions are present: leaders have sufficient time away from the glare of the media to learn about each other's positions and interests; good fortune at that moment provides each of the adversaries with leaders who have adroit political skills, the political will to limit their objectives, and sufficient self-confidence to reject advice from forceful advisers; and unforseen events and unanticipated behavior by any of the thousands of people involved does not set off an uncontrollable chain reaction.[155]

Since then, there have been many critiques of the view that the United States can act with a blithe confidence that nuclear crises can be managed, though none is more poignant than the one articulated by Robert McNamara, who originally had embraced the traditional view. He noted that, had the Soviets launched any of their nuclear weapons in 1962, "the damage to our own [country] would have been disastrous." Then he added,

> But human beings are fallible. We know we all make mistakes. In our daily lives, mistakes are costly, but we try to learn from them. In conventional war, they cost lives, sometimes thousands of lives. But if mistakes were to affect decisions related to the use of nuclear forces, there would be no learning period. They would result in the destruction of entire nations. Therefore, I strongly believe that the indefinite combination of human fallibility and nuclear weapons carries a very high risk of a potential nuclear catastrophe.[156]

Notably, this was the lesson the Soviets took away from the crisis. For them, it was not the threat of force that ended the crisis. They saw U.S. threats—in the form of Gilpatric's speech and seeming plans to invade Cuba—as the cause of the crisis. Though some in the Kremlin may have derived a lesson similar to U.S. policymakers—that superior U.S. force led to a humiliating withdrawal that they would avoid in the future by building up their military forces[157]—the Soviet leadership believed the crisis ended because both Soviet and U.S. officials realized they were at the brink and that the crisis was threatening to destroy humankind. They did not fear only for their immediate safety and were not worried merely about losing a battle in Cuba. That kind of fear is of a personal nature, where one's own safety is at risk. That is the kind of fear evoked by the image of leaders going eyeball to eyeball. But a leader whose decisions may result in the deaths of thousands of others may experience a second kind of fear that is not common, the fear of deciding the fate of so many others, even civilization itself.[158] Leaders in the United States and the Soviet Union experienced the second kind of fear during the missile crisis, which in fact was what enabled them to reach a peaceful solution.[159]

In contrast to the Americans, the Soviets did not leave this episode with a belief that crises could be managed. They emphasized that crises must be prevented. Hard-liners argued that this could be achieved by building up Soviet military forces, to discourage U.S. aggressive tendencies. But Soviet concerns about losing control over their nuclear weapons also led them to resolve never again to place nuclear missiles in a country so far away from their home territory. Mark Kramer explains, "By underscoring how easily control could be lost, the crisis inevitably bolstered Moscow's determination to ensure strict centralized command over all nuclear operations."[160] The crisis taught others that political "means must govern international politics and be used to prevent or resolve conflicts."[161] In this vein, they sought ways to improve communications between U.S. and Soviet leaders, to avoid the sorts of misunderstanding that occurred during the missile crisis that could escalate a confrontation unintentionally. Both countries embraced the installation of a "hot line" to facilitate the rapid and direct exchange of information between heads of state.

Cuba Learns a Different Lesson

But what would Kennedy have said to Fidel Castro if such a hot line had existed before the crisis? Imagine the conversation in which the U.S. president explained to the Cuban leader that "we are trying to assassinate you, but you shouldn't take it personally." From the Cuban perspective, the lessons of the crisis were not about the inability to control events due to misjudgment and miscalculation. Cuban leaders accurately perceived that the United States was trying to overthrow their government. In the first instance, crisis prevention for them meant that a superpower should treat *all* countries—not just another superpower—with equal respect. They believed Cuba's sovereignty should be accorded as much deference as the United States demanded for itself.

Cuba viewed the crisis from the vantage point of a small power, for whom an invasion by conventional means would be as threatening as a nuclear confrontation would be to a superpower. The Kennedy–Khrushchev agreement seemed to place Cuba in a perilous situation. It had been transformed into a strategic U.S. target when the Soviet Union placed missiles there. But then Soviet withdrawal of the missiles in the face of U.S. pressure made Cuba even more vulnerable. The Soviet Union's acquiescence suggested that it would not come to Cuba's assistance were the United States to attack the island. The Soviet posture, in Cuba's view, had created a new set of conditions that would encourage hard-liners in the United States to press for an invasion.[162]

The Soviets did not seem to comprehend this perspective, and so they did not appreciate fully why the removal of the IL-28 bombers was so significant to the Cubans. Mikoyan tried to explain to Castro that the Soviets were leaving other weapons in Cuba that were superior to the IL-28s.[163] But the Cuban leader saw the withdrawal of the bombers as tantamount to inviting a U.S. invasion, because it demonstrated to the United States that the Soviet Union would not stand with Cuba in the face of U.S. threats. "We realized," Castro explained to the 1968 Central Committee, "how alone we would be in the event of a war." In the same mode, he described the Soviet decision to remove all but 3,000 of its 42,000 military personnel from Cuba as "a freely granted concession to top off the concession of the withdrawal of the strategic missiles."[164]

The primary lesson Cuba drew, then, was that neither superpower could be trusted. It viewed U.S. guarantees as ploys and Soviet promises as hollow. Both countries ignored Cuba during the crisis, and Castro's suspicion that the Soviets were treating Cuba as a bargaining chip were confirmed early in 1963 during his trip to the Soviet Union. He learned inadvertently then about the secret agreement between Kennedy and Khrushchev to exchange U.S. missiles in Turkey for Soviet ones in Cuba.[165]

Though the United States posed the immediate menace to Cuba in 1962, Castro was as concerned about Cuba's relationship with the other superpower. Given the Soviet arrogance and lack of concern about Cuba's fundamental rights, joining the Soviet camp as a subservient member posed a potential long-term threat to Cuban sovereignty and independence. And so, in the six years immediately after the October Crisis, Cuba was as worried about the threat posed by its friendship with the Soviet Union as it was about the danger arising from its enmity with the United States.

And we were defending those rockets with amazing fervor and love. For the first time we were participating in a certain state of equality with an enemy that had been attacking and provoking us incessantly, and we were really enjoying such a different and new situation, we were intoxicated with that extraordinary spirit of proletarian internationalism, as we dreamed it would be, backed up by that letter so full of resolution, principles and rights.

—Fidel Castro, January 25, 1968

Cuba was not in any crisis when, considering it an international duty, agreed to the deployment of one thousand missiles here; Cuba did not agree with the way the issue was handled; it stated the need to approach the problem from different, more drastic, more revolutionary and even more legal positions; and it totally disagreed with the way in which the situation was terminated. However, the argument "Cuba lives" . . . For goodness sakes, we have been alive since our mothers brought each one of us into the world, and that has nothing whatsoever to do with the Soviet missiles!

—Fidel Castro, January 26, 1968

As we began to lose faith in the Soviet policy, we began to change our tactics. While at a given moment we had struggled to have the planes stay, we had struggled to have the troops stay—bearing in mind that Kennedy demanded their withdrawal every day—we later decided that in a situation such as that, with an ally that was in out-and-out retreat or even more than retreat, in open flight, we had to at least try to save some things. We realized how alone we would be in the event of a war; we also realized how stupid it was to withdraw those troops in the face of an enemy that demanded it, and that would, in future years, further aggravate our perilous situation. Under those circumstances, we abandoned the objective of trying to keep the troops and practically resigned ourselves to focusing on keeping at least the weapons.

—Fidel Castro, January 26, 1968

2

FIDEL CASTRO'S SECRET SPEECH

"That Cuba lives has nothing to do with Soviet Missiles"

AUTHORS' INTRODUCTION

On January 23, 1968, Raul Castro, Minister of the Armed Forces and the Cuban Communist Party's Second Secretary, convened the first plenary meeting of the party's Central Committee. Nearly two and a half years already had passed since the establishment of the Cuban Communist Party in October 1965. The main purpose of the session was to conduct a "trial" of 37 members of the party, who were labeled the "microfaction." Though the designation "micro" was meant to diminish their significance, there was little doubt that the attack against them was filled with high drama and potentially high stakes for the Cuban revolution. All of the proceedings, except Fidel Castro's speech, were reprinted in the Cuban Communist Party newspaper Granma.

Most prominent among the thirty-seven was Aníbal Escalante, a figure well known in Cuba. The leader of the Popular Socialist Party (PSP) before 1959, he also headed the Integrated Revolutionary Organizations in 1961, which was the party created to mesh Castro's July 26th Movement, the Revolutionary Directorate, and the PSP into one unit. (The PSP had been Cuba's communist party before the 1959 Revolution.) What made the attack on Escalante and his cohorts especially dramatic was that they were charged with smearing the Cuban Communist Party with criticisms that had been voiced by Moscow-directed communist parties in Latin America. Moreover, the microfaction was accused of meeting with officials in the Soviet embassy, of providing these officials (one of whom was allegedly the KGB station chief) with false information about Cuba, and of encouraging the Soviet Union to apply economic sanctions against Cuba. Their crime, then, was not characterized merely as ideological deviation.

It was treason, because if the microfaction had succeeded, it was asserted, they would have subordinated Cuba's sovereignty to Soviet dictates.

Following Castro's speech, the Central Committee removed the microfaction from the Communist Party, and Escalante subsequently was prosecuted for treason. The purge was a clear message to the Soviet Union, to back off from trying to influence Cuba's internal affairs.

If sending that message was one of the reasons for the purge, why then would Castro keep his harshly critical review of Cuban–Soviet relations secret. (Despite our repeated requests, the bulk of the speech is still secret, and the only portion that has been declassified is the portion pertaining to the missile crisis.) After all, the microfaction trial itself was well publicized. Interviews we conducted in Havana with former officials make clear that Castro had three motives in keeping his speech from the public.

First, there was a concern that the United States would interpret such direct Cuban criticism of the Soviet Union as a visible sign of rupture between Cuba and its benefactor. Cuban leaders, quite mindful of the 1965 U.S. invasion of the Dominican Republic, did not want to encourage U.S. hawks to attempt military attacks against Cuba. The microfaction trial, after all, focused on allegedly errant individuals and avoided implicating the Soviet Union directly.

Cuban leaders also were worried about internal disunity. On the one hand, they did not want to encourage the Cuban public to seize on the speech as a sign that Cuba disavowed all aspects of Soviet socialism. There was considerable cultural ferment in Cuba at the time, and Cuban leaders were feeling besieged by increasing criticism from the artistic community. This was also a period when Havana was awash in graffiti and juvenile vandalism, which leaders associated with a growing "hippie" movement.

Still, Castro believed he had to "educate" the Central Committee about the errors of the microfaction, and to demonstrate to party leaders that the purge was warranted. He could not be certain how popular Escalante was with the 100 members of the Central Committee, because it was such a nascent and diverse group. He thus sought to avoid party disunity by convincing the leaders that the microfaction ouster was necessary to protect Cuban nationalism. Castro did this, one former official remarked, by explaining that "the platform of the microfaction would in fact turn us into a Soviet satellite." Such a move not only would have subverted Cuban national identity, but would have threatened the very survival of the Revolution, because—as Castro argues in the section of the speech on the missile crisis—the Soviet Union fundamentally was untrustworthy.

Third, by keeping the speech secret, Castro sent a message to the Soviet Union that while Cuba profoundly disagreed with it over several issues, there was still the possibility of accommodation. Had the Cuban head of state made his criticisms public, it would have been far more difficult to overcome the tensions with the Soviet Union.

These tensions were reaching their peak in January 1968. In a public speech on January 2, the Cuban leader blamed the Soviet Union for an inadequate delivery of fuel that he asserted would require a stricter rationing of gasoline. What the Soviets had done was to increase supplies only modestly from the previous year, and well below what the Cubans needed to pursue their ambitious plan of producing a ten-million-ton sugar harvest by 1970. That plan was critical to the success of Cuba's larger goal: achieving economic independence from the Soviet Union.

The Soviet action was a stark way of delivering a message to Cuba that it had been repeating for four years: Cuba had to stop supporting revolutionary guerrilla movements in Latin America. Cuba's support for these movements had been a source of friction between the two countries for most of the period after the missile crisis. Armed struggle was the antithesis of the Soviet model for developing socialism in the region, which emphasized peaceful coexistence and the "ripening" of the proletariat through educational efforts by the communist party in each Latin American country. The Soviets were not prepared to mess around with countries in the U.S. sphere of influence. Cuba's approach thus threatened Latin American communist parties, which had been slavishly loyal to the Soviet line opposing armed struggle, as it challenged the Soviet Union's self-proclaimed leadership of the Third World.

Fidel Castro started his speech about the October Crisis on January 25. By the end of the day he had not finished telling the Central Committee members everything he thought they should know, and he returned on January 26 to conclude his twelve-hour account. The version here is the official English translation, produced by the Translation Department of the Council of State. The text here reproduces the punctuation used in the official translation.

* * *

And now we must begin with the October Crisis,1 something that must be understood by the comrades. How the decisions were made. For some time we had been raising the issue of the need to take measures that would guarantee the country's safety.[2] In that period we had tremendous faith in the Soviet Union. I think perhaps too much. Many things were dealt with, we were not demanding papers or things.

And right about then a Soviet military delegation, headed by a Field Marshal, showed up and asked us how we thought the aggression business might be avoided.[3] We responded that this could be achieved by taking measures that would serve as a clear indicator to imperialism that any onslaught against Cuba would mean a war that would not be limited to Cuba alone. But as the man had obviously come with his ideas already formulated, he said: "But concretely, how? Concrete action is needed to evidence that."

He had already been given the mission of proposing to us the deployment of strategic missiles and was perhaps a little apprehensive that we would not accept them. We could have considered the following: well, by deploying the missiles here, we would probably become the target of criticism and campaigns against the Revolution in the rest of Latin America, but we had no doubts at all.[4] In the first place, when we were approached with the matter of the missiles at that moment, we believed it to be something that would bolster consolidation of the defensive potential of the entire socialist community, something that would contribute to that purpose; we were not thinking of our own problems.[5] Subsequently, it would be equivalent to our own defense. In all truth, the comrades that participated, the members of the Secretariat,[6] met to analyze this question and make a decision. How did we see it? We saw it as a means of strengthening the socialist community . . . and if we were proposing that the entire socialist community be prepared to go to war to defend any socialist country, then we had absolutely no right to raise any questions about something that could represent a potential danger. We considered the problem of propaganda, and we also saw the real danger that any crisis would represent. Nonetheless, without hesitation, and in all earnest, in a truly internationalist spirit, all of the comrades involved agreed to give an immediate answer. In view of our affirmative response, and given our immense confidence, seeing them as a country with great experience in many international questions, including war, we raised the convenience of signing a military pact.

Well, then they sent a draft agreement that would be published when it was opportunely announced at a future date, after the missiles had been deployed. And really, if there is anything I regret it is not having kept that document, because it was one of the shoddiest things ever written . . . we returned it at their request, they sent it by courier and everything. So what did we do? We wrote out an agreement that contained all the main elements, but one that was publishable. It was the work of feeble-minded bureaucrats, totally apolitical that type of agreement. So we wrote another out, here it is in my own handwriting, the agreement that was later sent to the Soviet Union and signed, although they never sent us a copy of the signed document.[7]

COMMANDER RAUL CASTRO: The original idea was that I go—remember—and sign it with Malinovsky.[8] But at that point Khrushchev said that it was so important that he would come to Cuba in December[9] and that you and he could sign it here and make it public, and that Malinovsky and I should just initial and validate it. And since they had to bring it for you to sign . . .

COMMANDER FIDEL CASTRO: And our boundless confidence was the innocent victim of all those subtle particulars that we never dreamed a Party or revolutionary leadership could be capable of.

That document reads thus:

"Agreement between the Government of the Republic of Cuba and the Government of the Union of Soviet Socialist Republics on military cooperation in the defense of the national territory of Cuba in case of aggression."

I suggested two titles: this one, or "Agreement between the Government of the Republic of Cuba and the Government of the Union of Soviet Socialist Republics on military cooperation and mutual defense. . . ." In other words, a commitment by both parties. Not just because theirs concentrated on Cuba. If there had been a war over there, then, what? Did anyone really believe that in such a case we would be left untouched over here? Ridiculous! Isn't it? Let's talk about it, let's deal with this issue on that basis.

And finally, "Agreement between the Government of the Republic of Cuba and the Government of the Union of Soviet Socialist Republics on Soviet military support in the defense of the national territory of Cuba in case of aggression. . . ." We proposed that one of these titles be adopted. Any of the three aforementioned titles were suggested, but we expressed our preference for one of these, I do not remember whether it was the first or the second.

"The Government of the Republic of Cuba and the Government of the Union of Soviet Socialist Republics, guided by the principles and objectives of the Statutes of the United Nations, reiterating their desire to live in peace with all States and peoples, determined to make every possible effort to contribute to the maintaining and strengthening of world peace, anxious to establish and develop friendship, collaboration, and mutual assistance among all peoples under the principle of respect for the sovereignty and independence of all States, as well as the noninterference in their internal affairs, faithful to a principled policy based on friendship and solidarity among peoples that defend a common cause, the fundamental pillars of which are peaceful coexistence among States with different social systems. . . ."

We were going to arm ourselves with strategic thermonuclear missiles, and really, in that type of peaceful coexistence, all countries well armed and protected, it is a different kind of peaceful coexistence, one in which the imperialists have no right to repression or reprisals on whatever scale they want, whenever they want.

"The legitimate defense in response to aggression, the right of each people to choose the form of government deemed to be the most convenient for pursuing its goals of well-being and progress, to live in peace without being perturbed or assaulted from abroad, in the recognition of each nation's historical prerogative to break the chains that tie it to any form of domination or economic exploitation whenever it so chooses. . . ."

Some of the terms in this document, such as *peaceful coexistence*, which I hardly ever use, and a couple of others, were included because the original document used them and it would not have been polite to eliminate them. But all the basics, the concepts that gave this agreement a political and principled content, are there.

"Determined to take whatever steps necessary to jointly defend such a legitimate right of the Cuban people [and I suggested that it might also read "of the peoples of Cuba and the Soviet Union"] . . . taking into account, furthermore, the urgency with which measures must be taken to assure a mutual defense in response to a potential aggression against the Republic of Cuba and the USSR, in our desire to settle all questions regarding the support that the Soviet Armed Forces will provide in the defense of the national territory of Cuba in the event of an aggression, have arrived at the following Agreement:

"Article 1: The Soviet Union shall send to the Republic of Cuba armed forces with which to strengthen its defenses given the danger of foreign aggression and thus contribute to the preservation of world peace. The type of Soviet troops and the areas in which they shall be stationed in the territory of the Republic of Cuba shall be established by the bylaws included under Article 11 of this Agreement.

"Article 2: In the event of an aggression against the Republic of Cuba or against the Soviet forces stationed in Cuban territory, the Government of the Union of Soviet Socialist Republics and the Government of Cuba, in exercise of their right to individual or collective self-defense defined by Article 51 of the United Nations Statutes,[10] shall take all necessary measures to repel the aggressor.

"All information referring to any case of aggression and to actions taken in fulfillment of this Article shall be presented before the Security Council as stipulated by the United Nations Statutes. The aforementioned actions shall be suspended once the Security Council has taken the necessary measures to reestablish and preserve world peace.

"Article 3: The Soviet Armed Forces stationed in the territory of the Republic of Cuba shall fully respect that country's sovereignty; they and their family members shall show the same respect for the laws of the Republic of Cuba.

"Article 4: The Government of the Union of Soviet Socialist Republics shall be responsible for the expenses associated with maintaining the Soviet Armed Forces stationed in the territory of the Republic of Cuba under the terms of this Agreement.

"Article 5: In order not to affect the supplies of the Cuban population, the consumer items, assorted materials, machinery, devices and other goods destined for the Soviet Armed Forces shall be supplied from the Soviet Union. Said supplies, plus the equipment and munitions destined for the Soviet Armed Forces, as well as the ships used to transport them, shall have free entry to the territory of Cuba.

"Article 6: The Government of the Republic of Cuba, in agreement with the Government of the Union of Soviet Socialist Republics, asserts to render their armed forces all necessary facilities for their emplacement and stationing, communications and mobility. The transportation of Soviet Armed Forces personnel, the use of electric energy and means of communication, as well as all public services and other conveniences afforded the Soviet Armed Forces shall be paid for by them according to the rates applied to the armed forces of the Republic of Cuba. The buildings and grounds shall be supplied by the Republic of Cuba free of charge; their remodeling and care taking to be the responsibility of the Soviet Armed Forces.

"Article 7: In those areas assigned to the Soviet Armed Forces, the construction of buildings, air bases, roads, bridges, permanent radio-communications installations or any other type of facility shall be carried out using means and materials belonging to the Soviet Armed Forces following coordination with the competent authority of the Republic of Cuba.

"Article 8: Military barracks, air bases and other constructions and permanent military facilities that cease to be used by the Soviet Armed Forces shall be ceded to the Government of the Republic of Cuba without compensation."

Compensation was mentioned here, I understand that it was proposed by them; meaning that it would be returned without charge.

"Article 9: All question of jurisdiction pertaining to the presence of the Soviet Armed Forces personnel in the territory of the Republic of Cuba shall be regulated by separate covenants based on the principles set forward in Article 3 of this Agreement."

It is the one that says that they shall fully respect the laws.

"Article 10: Both Parties agree that the military units of each nation be subordinated to the commands of their respective Governments, which, in a coordinated manner, shall determine what responsibilities to assign to their corresponding forces in repelling foreign aggression and restoring peace.

"Article 11: In order to adequately regulate those questions stemming from the presence of the Soviet Armed Forces in territory of the Republic of Cuba, the Government of the Republic of Cuba and the Government of the USSR shall each designate their respective representatives.

"Article 12: This Agreement shall be subject to ratification by the respective Governments and shall come into force on the day that letters of ratification are exchanged, which shall take place in. . . ." The date was left in blank.

"Article 13: This Agreement is valid for a period of five (5) years. Either Party may terminate this Agreement by notifying the other Party of such a decision one year prior to the date of expiry. If the five (5) year validity period concludes and neither Party has expressed a desire to annul it, this Agreement shall be considered valid for a consecutive five (5) year period.

"Article 14: Upon the expiration of this Agreement, the Soviet Armed Forces shall abandon the territory of the Republic of Cuba. The Soviet Party to this Agreement reserves the right to evacuate from the Republic of Cuba any materials, munitions, equipment, machinery, weaponry or other goods that are property of the Soviet Armed Forces. . . ."

The military facilities were to be left to us.

"The Government of the Republic of Cuba shall offer every assistance in the withdrawal of the Soviet Armed Forces from the territory of the Republic of Cuba.

"This Agreement, of which there are two copies—one in the Russian language and the other in the Spanish language—of equal validity, has been drawn up on the _____ day of _____ of 1962.[11]

"In certification of the above, the Heads of Government of both States signed and sealed this Agreement. Prime Minister of the Republic of Cuba and President and Minister of the Union of Soviet Socialist Republics, Khrushchev. . . ."

And a copy was taken there, legalized and endorsed by both Ministers of the Armed Forces,[12] leaving the formal ceremony to be held at a later date; but the Agreement was valid immediately, because the entire affair of bringing and installing that equipment plus the related political negotiations was set into motion.

As we considered that they had a greater grasp of the overall situation regarding the correlation of strength with the enemy, we left the initiative on that issue up to them and we prepared to cooperate to our utmost. We called in the first comrades that began to work on the project—and here I must point out that the discretion of the Cubans was as phenomenal as that of the Soviets was poor. We became extinguishers of continual spot fires as a constant stream of people would come up to us and say: "Hey, lock me away because I know about this, that and the other. This Soviet guy so-and-so told me . . ." There are endless stories that could be told.

COMMANDER RAUL CASTRO: We were holding a bunch of our officers prisoner at their own request.

COMMANDER FIDEL CASTRO: Self-interned prisoners.

COMMANDER RAUL CASTRO: We left them their weapons and we explained the situation to them, but we had them concentrated at the Club in Cacahual.[13]

COMMANDER FIDEL CASTRO: At the same time, we were under the impression that the first installations would be the so-called *palm emplacements*[14] to shake off aerial espionage, and that these would then be followed by the missiles themselves.

Our comrades worked arduously in relocating farmers and solving all such problems associated with the installations.

The first ground-to-air rockets began to arrive, supposedly for use in preventing the missiles from being photographed.

And gentlemen, those are the inconceivable things, such are the vacillations and the indecisive modus operandi, the vacillations that lead to problems. We did not know the faintest thing about these rockets, not even their size, where they would have to be installed or where they were shot from, because, frankly, if we had known these things about the rockets and had been approached with the question of camouflaging it all, it would have been so easy for us to make decisions. Or to make the decision to shoot down the U-2s, set up the radars among the palm trees, which was elemental, or, if the decision was to not down the U-2s, then to have taken steps to camouflage that weaponry.[15] In a country so full of construction projects, with so many chicken farms and things everywhere, it would have been the easiest thing in the world for us to build those emplacements under the guise of something totally different and they would have never been discovered.

The amazing thing was that they weren't discovered earlier. They were discovered just a few days before the crisis. And what's also inconceivable is that the U-2s were overflying us, yet they neither shot down the U-2s nor hid the missiles. It was absurd that some people were asking themselves if perhaps it was being done on purpose, and I can guarantee you that such was not the case—it was a question of carelessness, lack of foresight.

It was incredible because that wasn't the only detail; because when the crisis ignited, we remember going to a meeting, to offer our cooperation—we were at maximum alert—and that was when we found out about those ground-to-air missiles. . . . We met with a Field Marshal or a General . . .

COMMANDER RAUL CASTRO: An Army General.[16]

COMMANDER FIDEL CASTRO: The first thing we did when we realized that those planes only carried two insignificant guns as antiaircraft weapons and fired from a thousand meters, and that the stuff could be destroyed in a matter of minutes on low flying missions, and I have absolutely no doubt in my mind that the imperialists could have destroyed all those rockets in a couple of minutes had they used their B-26s, they would not even have needed jets—what we did was deploy all our antiaircraft batteries, including 50 out of the reserve, and we put them next to the strategic missile and the antiaircraft emplacements.

It must be said that some batteries fired when the order was given. People here drove themselves hard and took everything very seriously.

It was my impression that, had their own security, prevention and defense measures continued to prevail, not one strategic base, one ground-to-air rocket, not one rocket launching boat, nothing at all would have survived. The Americans are quite smart, they use their means, they are no fools, and they knew of these weaknesses. So the defense of all those emplacements with an artillery capable of representing at least some level of protection was something that fell to us from the very beginning of the crisis.[17] That history is well known, and it is known how the crisis began, as well as it is known that there was a whole series of symptoms, Council meetings and everything, and how—long before the Declaration[18]—we called a nationwide military alert because we knew there was a crisis in the making.

But in the meanwhile, more or less around the month of July, we saw that the United States was creating an atmosphere of hysteria and aggression, and it was a campaign that was being carried out with all impunity.[19] In the light of this we thought the correct thing to do was to adopt a different position, not to get into that policy of lies: "we are sending Cuba defensive weapons."[20] And in response to the imperialist's position, the second weakness (or the first weakness) was not to stand up and respond that Cuba had every right to own whatever weapons it saw fit—which was always our position at the United Nations and everywhere else—but rather to adopt a policy of concessions, claiming that the weapons were defensive. In other words, to lie, to resort to lies which in effect meant to waive a basic right and a principle.

Because we believe that the whole problem should have been dealt with in a different manner: Cuba is a sovereign, independent country, and has a right to own the weapons that it deems necessary, and the USSR to send them there, in the same light that the United States has felt that it has the right to make agreements with dozens of countries and to send them the weapons that they see fit, without the Soviet Union ever considering that it had a right to intercede. From the very outset it was a capitulation, an erosion of our sovereignty and our right to respond to that campaign.[21] We sent a delegation to the Soviet Union—I believe comrades Aragonés and Che[22] went on that occasion—to state our position, that of facing the campaign head on and declaring that line and even publishing the Agreement if necessary; but that, naturally, they had a much better grasp of the overall situation than we did and therefore we left the decision to them, but that we suggested such an approach.

Khrushchev received them, spoke and said: "No problem, no, I'll send the Baltic Fleet in October, and I'll send over a letter to Kennedy 24 hours before, and the rockets are there." . . . The Baltic Fleet! Meanwhile the affair was heating up in the United States, the campaign was being fed, a joint resolution[23] was agreed upon: an entire series of events. And when we were actually on the brink of the crisis, we realized what it was all about many hours in advance, the whole thing was aimed at Cuba, so we immediately and energetically—because the Revolution has never been slow or lazy in the face of danger—when the news reached us. . . .

COMMANDER RAUL CASTRO: Excuse me, let me interrupt. To stress what you were saying: we foresaw that, we foresaw it. When we went over there we didn't know anything about rockets or how big they were, as Fidel has explained. Field Marshal Viriusov,[24] at that time head of Soviet rocketry and later Chief of the Soviet General Staff, who died later in that airplane accident in Yugoslavia; and Rashidov,[25] a candidate to or alternate member of the Political Bureau, both came here. Immediately after reaching the Agreement we went on a nationwide strategic exploration to see where we would situate the things. Then after they had left and we were here—I had already asked him for data, because we had accumulated some experience in dealing with the surveillance of enemy agents and the fact that of the few things that we received in our country, we would often be immediately informed by our counter-intelligence and security forces that the data on it had been sent out of the country, it is rare that a ship enter any of our ports without being instantly spotted by some agent or other. Then I found out that the rockets were 20 meters long. Keeping in mind our previous experience and aware of the thousands of people that would be coming, I reported this to Fidel and we were analyzing the situation.

And Fidel reasoned as follows: They are the ones that know, they are the ones with experience, etc. But Fidel, I said: "Well, ask them what's happening" . . . with our experience . . . what was going on . . . because that was July, the interview was in June, the Agreement was in July and was to be made public in December or January, with Khrushchev here.

COMMANDER FIDEL CASTRO: No, it was going to be done in November.

COMMANDER RAUL CASTRO: In November or December, during Khrushchev's visit here.

DR. OSVALDO DORTICOS[26]: In November.

COMMANDER RAUL CASTRO: In November, while Khrushchev was visiting.

Then we asked ourselves: well, if they find out about every little thing we receive here, how are we supposed to unload 20-meter-long rockets and thousands of soldiers without enemy intelligence getting wind of it before November? Then Fidel agreed that the only question to ask Khrushchev was the following: "Khrushchev, this is the situation, what happens if the yanquis, if Kennedy, finds out before the agreement is made public?" And that was the only question that Fidel authorized me to personally ask Khrushchev.

All of this was dealt with in such utmost secrecy that Fidel's letter, the arrangement, was translated at the Soviet General Staff building by Alejandro,[27] our ambassador, and myself—me reading to him in Spanish since I do not speak Russian, and him searching through the dictionary and trying to put it together—with such secrecy that not even our translators knew about it, absolutely no one! Then later, when I was with Khrushchev at his farm, with Alejandro (the ambassador) acting as interpreter, I posed the situation to him. Khrushchev, who had a very foul mouth, said: "Don't worry, I am going to grab Kennedy by the testicles" (he used a different word). "Oh no," he told me, " don't you worry. If that problem arises I will send you a message —and because we were not even trusting the use of coded messages— a conventional phrase within the text of a coded communication, and that will be signal for you to invite the Baltic Fleet to visit Cuba, just in case they find out beforehand."

And we sent Che and Aragones over there, as agreed with Khrushchev, to warn that the news was going to get out because our security forces had already collected an entire bag of letters from vulgar *gusanos*[28] on the streets who would see the rockets go by and were beginning to comment and to harangue against the United States, saying things like: "These sons of bitches are ruining us by filling this place with rockets and the Americans are not doing a damned thing to help us" . . . and so forth.[29]

Gentlemen, we had to build roads to skirt towns because the rockets would not fit through some places.

That is what I wanted to clear up. Excuse me: the last phrase. When I told Khrushchev that, he responded with: "Don't worry, I'm going to grab Kennedy by the testicles and he will just have to come and talk it over because, after all, they have our country surrounded by bases, in Turkey, here, there, everywhere."[30] I told you all this and you said to me; "Ah!" and continued to ponder the problem. Alright . . .

So then . . . I have my own impression of the whole situation. And that is why they had absolutely no interest in concealing it, none whatsoever! And afterwards the blame was put on Viriusov, that Viriusov deceived him and told him that the rockets could be hidden among the palm trees—that he told Carlos this.[31]

COMMANDER FIDEL CASTRO: They wanted to camouflage the rockets! Why, from all points of view it would have been strategically formidable for the socialist community. In response to the whole defense system, the radars, the presence of the rockets here would have enormously strengthened the Soviet position. If only a thousand rockets could have been emplaced! And that is what I told Viriusov: a thousand rockets. I said to him: "Look, if this is convenient for the interests and the defense of the entire socialist community, then we are willing to receive a thousand rockets." When they told me that the number of rockets to be emplaced was 80 ... no? ... I do not remember the exact number of the first ones, around 40 strategic rockets.[32]

COMMANDER RAUL CASTRO: I think the first lot was 40. Land-based, because the submarines were also going to carry rockets and they were to resupply at Mariel. ... [33]

COMMANDER FIDEL CASTRO: Of course, because the submarines had rockets.

When we foresaw the problem, we counseled and we exhorted that it not be dealt with from such a position of renunciation and lies. We went to the United Nations and there we at least stood our ground and offered no excuses. The speeches are on record! There is the address by comrade Dorticós, made at that forum, never wavering from our position.[34] We did not grant imperialism any right to decide what type of arms we should or should not have in Cuba.

By the time the crisis broke out, we had been at full alert for a while: we had mobilized the reserves, we had mobilized everything.[35] And then we receive the first letter from Khrushchev. It said:

"Dear Comrade Castro: The Soviet Government has just received from President Kennedy of the United States, the following document, of which we are enclosing a copy" —It was Kennedy's declaration, that insolent piece.—[36]

"We consider this declaration by the Government of the United States, as well as Kennedy's address on October 22, to be a brazen interference into the affairs of the Republic of Cuba, a violation of the norms of International Law and of the elementary codes that govern relations among States, it is also considered to be a flagrant provocation against the Soviet Union. The Republic of Cuba, just as any other sovereign nation, has every right to defend itself and to select its allies according to its own criteria. We reject the North American government's insolent demands to control arms shipments to Cuba, and their endeavor to determine what type of weapons the Republic of Cuba may possess." [Every valid argument that could have been used in response to the campaign.]

"The Government of the U.S.A. knows perfectly well that no sovereign State would ever allow another country to meddle in their relations with third nations, nor would it tender accounts about measures taken toward strengthening its national defense.

"In response to Kennedy's interference, the Soviet Government issues a declaration in which it expresses a most decided protest against the piratical actions of the

U.S. Government, and brands such actions as perfidious and aggressive regarding sovereign States, declaring its decision to struggle actively against such acts.

"We sent out instructions to our representative at the Security Council[37] to the effect that he urgently bring before the Council the issue of the U.S. violation of the norms of International Law and of the United Nations Charter, and declare a strong protest against the aggressive and treacherous actions of U.S. imperialism.[38]

"Because of the situation created, we have given the Soviet military representatives stationed in Cuba instructions to take all necessary measures and to be fully alert.

"We are certain that the actions undertaken by the U.S. imperialists, that tend to deny the Republic of Cuba its legitimate right to strengthen its defenses and to protect itself, will stir up outraged protests from all peace-loving peoples, who will promote a broad-based movement in defense of revolutionary Cuba's just cause.

"We send you, comrade Castro, and all your comrades-in-arms, our warmest greetings and we express our complete assurance that the aggressive plans of the U.S. imperialists are doomed to failure.

"October 25, 1962."

Right then we dedicated ourselves, as everyone recalls, one hundred percent of our manpower, everyone, involved in the mobilization, setting our units into place.[39] And when, incidentally, I found out about that preposterous lack of foresight and the virtual absence of protection for those rockets in general, we sent the 50 reserve batteries to defend those emplacements. Our calculations included the possibility that they would attempt bombing raids, destruction, and we even met with the representatives, the Chief of Staff,[40] and, with all the maps and the officers there, one by one the outpost commanders called in and reported: the ground-to-air rockets, ready; ready also those medium–range rockets; the air force was ready, and so was everything else, including some of the strategic missiles. There were also tactical rockets, tactical nuclear weapons.[41]

So I explained to them that we had to be very prepared and extremely alert—the low altitude overflights had already begun,[42] and that we could not allow them to fly over us at low altitudes, that we—I was reading all the cables, and, knowing the Americans as we do—had to take extreme measures, not allow them to fly over, and foreseeing that they could feasibly destroy some of those rockets and get their way, we could even remove some of the strategic missiles from their emplacements and hide them in some other place so that even after a bombing we would have a supply of strategic rockets, based on the thesis that they were going to bomb us, an air strike to destroy the rockets. And we were defending those rockets with amazing fervor and love. For the first time we were participating in a certain state of equality with an enemy that had been attacking and provoking us incessantly, and we were really enjoying such a different and new situation, we were intoxicated with that extraordinary spirit of proletarian internationalism, as we dreamed it would be, backed up by that letter so full of resolution, principles and rights.

In other words, when we began to look at the possibility that they would attack us by air, we go over and convince those people to deploy everything, even the low altitude radars so that we could defend ourselves from low flying planes, we also asked them what they were going to do in the event of an attack. We spoke of the strategic weapons, we spoke of the tactical weapons—it was always taken for granted that any use of the strategic weapons could only be ordered from the Soviet Union. I asked about the tactical weapons and if they were planning to use them in the event we were invaded, and he led me to believe that yes, they were, that if it became necessary, the tactical nuclear weapons would be used to turn back an invasion.[43]

Not very convinced of the combat preparedness and efficiency of the situation, though it was all very clear on paper and on the maps, given our knowledge of the weaknesses of that type of weapon in responding to massive air attacks, we convinced him not to deploy all the arms if he was not doing to use them, to only deploy the ones he thought plausible, so that those not in use would not be destroyed in an attack. I believe that they did just that. Besides, everything else had already been done.

And I remember, it was about the third day, when things were red hot, when we, together with the Soviets, told them that—I don't remember clearly if it was in agreement with the Soviets or just on our own, but it was based on the information that we gave them and the measures that we had asked them to take, which they did, of uncovering the radars. And we gave all our antiaircraft batteries the order to fire on any plane overflying us at a low altitude. In other words, as of the morning of the following day we would oppose those low flying planes, because we could not accept—to do so would have been taking the stance of an ostrich or some other nonsense—giving the enemy a free hand to buzz a mere 50 meters over the heads of our installations, the soldiers, and the entire country.

COMMANDER RAUL CASTRO: They told us not to open fire. That was later, when you said: "Well, what is happening?"

COMMANDER FIDEL CASTRO: No, that was later. We opened fire early in the morning over near Candelaria[44] and all those other places on the day that the U-2 was downed.[45]

It was at night and all the measures had been taken, a tremendous, incredible mobilization. I began to ask myself what was left to be done and what I should do, what I had not done. I do not remember if I consulted these things with you or not. And then I said: "I am going to write Khrushchev a letter of encouragement. I am worried that these people might make an historical error." I was remembering how, when the Soviet Union was invaded by the Nazis and the first shots rang out, they responded: "Don't shoot back, it is a provocation" . . . and all that story. I perceived that our situation could not be settled without confrontation. I saw very little room for backing out of the affair. It was necessary to hold our ground at all costs, so I decided to write a letter to Nikita, to encourage him and exhort him not to waver (LAUGHTER).

It was a short letter really, I am not very fond of the epistolary method, but at that moment I said to myself: I will write a letter.[46]

It reads: "Havana, October 26, 1962 . . ." I went with Alejandro and I dictated it there. Afterwards I've had to reconstruct it, I had the news and I asked him for a copy.

It reads: "Dear Comrade Khrushchev" . . . Comrade Khrushchev and I always treated each other as "dear comrade" as did his successors, until one day I mistakenly put an "esteemed" and they misunderstand over there and continued with the "esteemed," so the condition is at "esteemed" now.

"Dear Comrade Khrushchev: From the analysis of the situation and the reports that we have received, I believe that the aggression is imminent within the next 24 to 72 hours.

"There are two possible variations, the first and most probable is an air strike against certain targets with the limited objective of destroying them."

Terms such as *limited retaliation* and so on had not been coined yet.

"The second, less probable but not to be ruled out, is an invasion. I understand that to carry out this variant would require the use of numerable forces, and it is also the most repulsive type of aggression, which may inhibit them."

In other words . . . they would try to solve the issue with a bombing and not by invading.

"You may be sure that we will firmly and decidedly resist the attack, however it comes."

All the while, I was writing this letter with the utmost care and scruples because what I was about to say was so audacious and daring that I had to present it well.

I continued: "The Cuban people's morale is extremely high, as is its decision to face the aggressor heroically. At this time I wish to briefly express my personal opinion. If the second variation occurs . . . [meaning the invasion] . . . if the second variation occurs. . . ."

And there I was thinking, well, what could be done? If the second variation comes it will have to be destroyed. And it is incredible. Of course we could never present our country as the aggressor or anything like that, but my opinion was that if they invaded we would have to open fire on them with a complete and total round of nuclear rockets. With the total conviction that in a situation such as that, whoever struck first would have a 99 percent advantage. It would not have been a surprise attack, but only in the case of a concrete invasion, which would have involved the Soviet troops stationed here, and, since they would not have just stood by and watched them die here, what would they have waited for to settle the problem.

Keep in mind that back then there was not the unlimited supply of rockets that there is today. The Americans did not have too many rockets then, and we knew the speed of their planes and those things.

"If the second variation occurs and the imperialists invade Cuba with the objective of occupying it, the danger that such an aggressive policy represents to humanity is so great that after such an act the Soviet Union should never allow circumstances in which the imperialists could send against it a first nuclear strike . . ."

So as you see, I did not say to him: attack. I said that if they attack and invade they would be creating a situation so dangerous and unsolvable that he would have no time to lose or fool around and give the enemy the chance to strike first.[47]

"I tell you this because I believe that the imperialist's aggressiveness has became extremely dangerous and if they carry out so brutal, illegal and universally immoral an action as invading Cuba, then that would be the moment to permanently remove such a hazard in an act of the most legitimate self-defense, though a hard and terrible solution, there is no other. . . ."

This opinion was influenced by seeing how this aggressive policy evolved, how the imperialists, with total disregard for world opinion, oblivious to principles and rights, blockaded the seas, violated our air space and prepared an invasion, while on the other hand blocking all possibility of negotiation even though they were fully aware of the seriousness of the situation.

"You have been . . ."

At this point I offered a sort of condolence, actually, because he was mixed up in that mess, and I said to myself that he must have been feeling very sad.

"You have been and continue to be a tireless defender of peace. I understand how bitter these hours must be, seeing the results of your superhuman efforts so seriously imperilled [sic]. Nonetheless, up to the last moment we will keep up our hope that peace may be saved and to that end we are willing to contribute all that is within our power. But at the same time we are preparing ourselves serenely to face an eventuality that we see as very real and very close at hand.

"Once more I express the infinite gratefulness and the recognition of our people to the Soviet people, who has stood by us with such generosity and fraternity, and our deep gratitude and admiration for you, and wish you success in the enormous tasks and great responsibilities that rest in you lie ahead.

"Fraternally, Fidel Castro."

I even thanked him. In those moments, in which we should have been thinking that we could all be killed, we honestly did not assume the idea that we could vanish. OK, it had fallen on us to make them pay that price, but at least the world would have rid itself of imperialism if such a serious and unsolvable act as an invasion were to occur, which could only have led to all-out warfare. And if that was the inevitable result, I was worried that they would pussyfoot around, because he was always saying that he would never strike first and all that. But if the enemy were to launch that type of attack under circumstances such as those, there would not be any alternative.

Afterwards, this is a letter from Khrushchev and this one from Fidel.

It says: 28 . . . this is dreadful.

"Dear Comrade Fidel Castro: Our message to President Kennedy on October 27 allows for the situation to be settled in your favor, to defend Cuba against invasion and the outbreak of war. Kennedy's response, of which you are also apparently aware, offers assurances that the United States will not invade Cuba, not only with its own forces but will also keep any of its allies from invading. With this the President of the United States replies positively to my messages of the 26 and 27 of October of 1962. . . ."

Of course that all seemed to me to be such an indication of a bad case of nerves, that first response in which they began to talk about the rockets in Turkey and in Italy, all so confused, and afterwards they started talking about something else, when all the while he could have put him on the spot in such an easy and honorable manner just by saying: OK, we are willing to withdraw our forces if you give us guarantees that you will satisfy Cuba; they should have forced the yanquis to dialogue directly with us and they would have put them in the most super uncomfortable situation that they would have ever found themselves in, because they would have had to talk at length with us and that would have eased the tension. And the results would have been different and at least honorable and within principles and the most elemental sense of consideration for our country and the agreements undertaken with a people that did not for an instant hesitate in that critical hour. I am sure that the place where the people were calmest was right here, there is no doubt about it. An interesting detail, seeing that we were on the brink of nuclear holocaust, is that people were making jokes here. Korda was going around saying that he wanted to know where to stand to get the best shot of the mushroom when it went up and stuff like that.[48] And of course we knew that our role would be to do the dying, but we were willing to do that.

Then he said: "We just finished preparing our response to the President's message. I will not go into it here because you will hear the text when it is transmitted on the radio." [We heard it on the radio!] "Therefore, we would like to recommend that in this moment of change in the crisis, you not let yourselves be carried away by your feelings and that you show determination.

"We must say that we understand your indignation resulting from the aggressive actions and the violations of the most elemental standards of International Law undertaken by the United States. But what is in force now is not so much rights as the folly of the Pentagon militarists. Now that an understanding is at hand, the Pentagon is looking for excuses to thwart this agreement. . . ."

The Pentagon, those crazymen, those outlaws, wanted war. And in the Pentagon they might have been shaking from fear, shaking from fear. But with that idea, that theory of wanting war at any cost. That is blackmail, this is blackmail.

"This is why they have organized the provocative overflights by their planes."

Why? What had happened? When we gave the order to shoot, the firing started over near Candelaria and that entire region as soon as the first planes showed up in the morning, and was it ever hot! However, it is still not known exactly how the downing of the plane happened, whether it was the result of the previous morning's meeting, that decision, if it was the operations officer of the ground-to-air rockets, if it was the contagion of all our antiaircraft batteries bashing away, but the fact is that someone hit the U-2 and knocked it down. But on that particular day fire was opened on planes flying low and they made themselves scarce.

"This is why they have organized . . ."

"But what is in force now is not so much right as the folly of the Pentagon militarists. Now that an understanding is at hand, the Pentagon is looking for excuses to thwart this agreement. This is why they have organized the provocative overflights by their planes. Yesterday you shot one of them down, whilst before you would not shoot at them when they overflew your territory. . . ."

We were not able to shoot down U-2s, but no one had ever overflown us, and we would not have tolerated it.

"The aggressors will use that for their own purposes.

"Therefore, we wish to offer some friendly advice: be patient and steady, and ever more steady. It goes without saying that if there is an invasion it must be turned back by any means. . . ."

Friends, nothing could be more obvious! An invasion must be turned back!

"But do not allow yourselves to be suckered in by the provocations, because now, when it seems that the end of the conflict is near, and has worked out to your advantage while creating a guarantee against an invasion of Cuba, the unbridled Pentagon militarists want to sabotage the agreement and provoke you into acts that they can use against you. We ask that you not give any pretext.

"On our part, we will do everything possible to stabilize Cuba's situation, defend Cuba from invasion and assure you the possibility of building a socialist society in peace.

"We send you our regards and extend them to your entire leadership collective."

"October 28, 1962. Mister Nikita Khrushchev, Prime Minister of the Soviet Union and of the Union of Soviet Socialist Republics. Dear Comrade Khrushchev: I have just received your letter. Our Government's position regarding the content of your communication is included in the declaration issued on this date, the text of which you are surely familiar: the Five Points.[49]

"I wish to clear up something regarding the antiaircraft measures that we adopted. You say: 'Yesterday you shot one of them down, whilst before you would not shoot at them when they overflew your territory.'

"Before now, isolated violations were committed without any particular military objective or without there being any real danger attached to such flights."

In other words, we were not supposed to do anything about the U-2 and other flights. When he says, "you shot one down," I guess that means we are included among the antiaircraft battery personnel, because they were the ones who shot it down.[50]

"This was not the case now. There existed a real danger of a surprise strike against certain military installations. We decided that we should not refrain from taking action, because in a surprise attack, with our detection radar turned off while the potentially aggressor planes flew at will over targets that could be totally destroyed. We did not believe that we should allow such a thing after all the expense and effort involved, not to mention the fact that it would tremendously weaken us militarily and in morale. That is why the Cuban forces scrambled 50 antiaircraft batteries, our entire reserve, on October 24. It was done to protect the Soviet troop positions. If our objective was to prevent their being hit by a surprise attack, then it was mandatory that the gunners have orders to open fire. The Soviet military command can fill you in on the events surrounding the downed plane.

"Before, violations of our air space were actually done in a surreptitious manner. Yesterday the U.S. Government tried to officialize the right to violate our airspace at any hour of the day or night. This is something we cannot accept because it is tantamount to abdicating our sovereignty. However, we are agreed to avoiding an incident at this time, as it could seriously damage negotiations. So we will instruct the Cuban batteries not to shoot, but only for the duration of the negotiations and without revoking yesterday's declaration on our decision to defend our airspace. It must also be taken into consideration that given the current level of tension, accidental incidents are likely to occur.

"I also wish to inform you that we are, on principle, opposed to inspection of our territory.[51]

"I deeply appreciate your efforts to preserve peace and we coincide completely on the need to struggle toward that objective. If this goal is met in a just, solid and lasting manner, it will be a priceless service to humanity.

"Fraternally,"

That is, questioning . . .

"We have received your letter dated October 29 and the communications on the conversations held between yourself, and also President Dorticós, and our ambassador.

"We understand your situation and take into account the difficulties that you are facing now in the first transitory stage following the elimination of the maximum tension created by the U.S. imperialist threat that you expected from one moment to the next if . . ."

Now listen to what this gentleman says:

"We understand that certain difficulties have been created for you as a result of our promise to the United States Government to withdraw the missile base on the grounds that it is an offensive weapon, in exchange for the United States' promise to drop its plans to invade Cuba using its own troops or those of its Western allies, and to raise the so-called quarantine or, in other words, put an end to the blockade against Cuba.

"This led to the elimination of the conflict in the Caribbean, a situation well understood to be pregnant with the clash of two mighty powers and its transformation into Thermonuclear World War.

"We have learned from our ambassador that some Cubans share the opinion that the Cuban people would have desired a declaration with different characteristics, or, in any case, no declaration at all, just the withdrawal of the rockets.

"It is possible that such a feeling exist among the people: but we, political and State personalities, are the leaders of the people who do not and cannot immediately grasp the entire scope within which their leaders must act. Therefore we must be at the head of the people and then the people will follow us and respect us.

"If we, yielding to the people's sentiment, had allowed ourselves to be swayed by certain electrified sectors of the population and had refused to reach a reasonable agreement with the Government of the United States, then, there would have probably been a war in which millions of persons would have lost their lives, and the survivors would have blamed the leadership, for not having taken the necessary measures to put a stop to this war of annihilation.

"Prevention in Cuba and an attack on Cuba did not only depend on the measures adopted by our Government, but also on the calculation of the possible actions of the enemy forces situated near you; therefore, the situation had to be considered as a whole.

"There are also opinions that we and you did not carry out consultation over these questions before adopting the position of which you are aware. On this particular, we believe that we have consulted with you, dear Fidel Castro, receiving the cables—some more alarming than others—and the last, on October 27, in which you affirmed to be almost certain that the attack on Cuba would be consummated. You believed that it would only be a question of time before the attack, between 24 and 72 hours. Upon receiving this utterly alarming cable from you, aware of your personal valor, we were of the opinion that the alarm was totally reliable."

It has occurred to this gentleman to try and alter the meaning of that letter, presenting it as an alarmist letter. Wasn't this the purpose of his consultations with us? And you have all read that letter word for word, its content and its meaning.

"We have interpreted this cable as a signal of extreme alarm. . . . Why, under the circumstances created, keeping in mind also the information that the group of unbridled U.S. warmongerers was trying to use the situation to carry out an attack against Cuba, if we had continued the consultations, we would have lost precious time and the strike would have been approved.

"We have formed the opinion that our strategic missiles in Cuba became a magnet for the imperialists. They were frightened. And because of the fear that the rockets would be used, they were willing to destroy them via bombing raids or an invasion of Cuba. And it must be said that they could have put us out of combat."

And here is the other, also distorted:

"Your cable on October 27 proposed that we be the first to send a nuclear strike against enemy territory. You, naturally, understand what that would have led to: it would not have been a simple strike, it would have been the beginning of thermonuclear or global warfare.

"Dear Comrade Fidel Castro: I consider that proposal to have been incorrect, even though I understand your reasons. We have lived the most serious moment in which global thermonuclear war could have been unleashed."

On top of it all, all this problem, this demoralizing situation. . . . The masses were not mobilized. . . . They exploited their lies to the utmost, they exploited to the utmost that ostrich-like, rights-abdicating defense policy, and even promoted the creation of crisis conditions within the United States. There is not the slightest doubt that not having faced the situation from a politically correct position gave rise to the crisis.

"Obviously, in such an event the United States would suffer enormous losses, but the Soviet Union and socialist community would also have suffered greatly.

"As regards Cuba, the Cuban people, it is hard to say what their fate would be in such an event."

Yes. In the first place, Cuba would have burned in the fire of war. There is no doubt that the Cuban people would have struggled valiantly, but would perish. Of this there is no doubt either.

"But we do not struggle against imperialism in order to die, but rather to fulfill our possibilities to their utmost, to lose less in this struggle and gain more, to triumph and win the victory of communism."

That was the entire thesis, like Hitler. . . . And it continues in a similar fashion.

Here, of course, we made concessions, we accepted the compromise, we made pacts based on the principle of concession at the cost of concession. The United States also made concessions, assumed before the world, . . . etc.

"October 31, 1962.
Mister Nikita Khrushchev,
Prime Minister of the Soviet Union,
USSR.

"Dear Comrade Khrushchev: I received your letter dated October 30. As you understand it, we were consulted prior to adopting the decision to withdraw the strategic missiles. Your understanding is based on the alarming news that reached you from Cuba and lastly my cable dated October 27.

"I do not know what news you received; I only respond for the message that I sent on the night of October 26, and that you received on the 27th.

"What we did given the circumstances, comrade Khrushchev, was prepare and ready ourselves to fight. There was only one class of alarm in Cuba: the combat alarm. When we understood that the imperialist attack was impending, I thought that I should inform you and alert the Soviet Government as well as the Army General Staff, given that there were Soviet forces sworn to fight by our side to defend the Republic of Cuba from foreign aggression, of the possibility of an attack that would not be within our power to prevent, only to resist.

"I explained to you that our people's morale was very high and that the aggression would be heroically resisted.

"At the end of that message I reiterated that we would await the events serenely. Danger could no longer impress us because we have felt it gravitate over our country for a long time now, and to some extent we have grown accustomed to it.

"The Soviet men that have been here with us know just how admirable our people's attitude has been during the crisis and how deep a bond was forged between our peoples in the decisive hours.

"Many eyes of Cuban and Soviet men who had been willing to give their lives with sublime dignity filled with tears when the surprising, sudden and practically unconditional decision to withdraw the arms was announced.

"Perhaps you are unaware of the extent to which the Cuban people had prepared themselves to fulfill their duty to their country and to humanity.

"I was aware while writing my letter that the words contained within could be misunderstood by you, and so they were, perhaps because you did not read it carefully, maybe because of the translation, it is possible that I tried to express too much in too few lines. Nonetheless, I did not hesitate to do it.

"Do you believe, comrade Khrushchev, that we were thinking selfishly of ourselves, of our generous people prepared to sacrifice itself, and not, might I add, unconsciously, but with a total understanding of the risks involved? No, comrade Khrushchev, few times in history, if ever—given that there has never been such a danger pending over the head of any other people—has a people prepared to struggle and to die with such a universal sense of duty.

"We knew—do not presume that we did not—that we would be exterminated, as your letter insinuates, in the event of thermonuclear war. Nonetheless, we did not ask you to withdraw the missiles, we did not ask that you give in. Do you, perhaps, believe that we desired that war? But how could it have been avoided if they had invaded? The whole idea was that this was a plausible scenario, and that imperialism was blocking all possible solutions and their demands were—from our point of view—totally unacceptable for the USSR and for Cuba.

"And if it happened . . . what could be done with the deranged forces that unleashed war?"

Because he refers to the deranged.

"What could be done with the deranged forces that unleashed war? You yourself have stated that under today's conditions any war would inevitably, and rapidly, turn into thermonuclear war.

"I understand that once the aggression had been unleashed, the aggressors should not be given the additional privilege of choosing when to use its nuclear weapons. The destructive power of this weapon is so great, as is the speed of delivering it, that it would represent a considerable initial advantage for the aggressor.

"And I did not suggest to you, comrade Khrushchev, that the USSR become the aggressor, because that would be more than incorrect, it would be immoral and contemptible on my part. What was said was that at the moment that imperialist forces attacked Cuba and, in Cuba, the armed forces of the USSR, deployed there to help us in our defenses if attacked from abroad, it would make the imperialists the aggressors against Cuba and against the USSR, then they would be answered back with an annihilating counterstrike.

"Each has his own opinions, and I maintain mine regarding the dangerousness of the Pentagon's aggressive circles and their tendency for preventive strikes.

"I did not suggest to you, comrade Khrushchev, that in the midst of the crisis the USSR attack, but rather that in the aftermath of an imperialist attack, the USSR act without vacillation and certainly not commit the error of allowing the enemy a chance to discharge against her a nuclear first strike. It is in this sense, comrade Khrushchev, that I defend my opinion, as I understand it to be a real and just evaluation of a given situation.

"You may be able to convince me that I am wrong, but you cannot tell me that I am wrong without trying to convince me.

"I realized that this is such a delicate topic that it could only be discussed under circumstances such as these and in a very personal message. You might ask yourself what right I had to do so. I did so without consideration for the thorniness of the topic, following the dictates of my conscience, as a revolutionary duty, and inspired in the most selfless feelings of affection and admiration for the Soviet Union and what she represents for the future of humanity. I did so because of our concern that she never again find herself victim of the treachery and betrayal of the aggressor, as occurred in 1941, which cost so many millions of lives and so much destruction.[52] Besides, the person addressing you was not some instigator but a combatant in the trenches under the greatest danger.

"I cannot see how you can affirm that we were consulted on the decision you made. There is nothing I would like more at this moment than to be mistaken. I wish you were the only one who is right. It is not 'some Cubans,' as you were informed, but the majority of Cubans that are currently experiencing unspeakable bitterness and sadness. The imperialists have again begun to speak of invading our country, a demonstration of how short-lived and untrustworthy their promises are. Our people, however, maintain their indestructible will to resist the aggressors, and, perhaps now more than ever, needs to trust in themselves and this will to struggle.

"We will struggle against adverse circumstances, we will overcome the current difficulties and get ahead, and nothing will destroy our feelings of friendship and eternal gratitude toward the USSR.

"Fraternally,

"Fidel Castro."

He responded with a long, endless letter.[53] And a letter was written by the leadership in response that supported the aforementioned points of view.

There are more documents. It might even be convenient.... And this has to continue to be explained so that you are all aware of the nuances and details of the events, allowing you to have full knowledge of the antecedents, motives and actions that are the basis of our attitude and our policy. But I believe that it would be better, given the importance and the interest that there is in this, if we did not mistreat the subject, and continue after we have rested a little. We will convene again for another half day or so to cover this issue. You are all aware of the importance of these documents and the need to analyze them carefully, without rush and fully rested.

Have breakfast and come back at 11 A.M.

BLAS ROCA: (unintelligible)

COMMANDER FIDEL CASTRO: Begin to draft the decision and declaration on Korea, and tomorrow when you come it can be presented and everything; I proposed that we be commissioned to draw up that declaration.

COMMANDER RAUL CASTRO: It is decided then, tomorrow at 11 A.M.

MEETING OF THE CENTRAL COMMITTEE OF THE COMMUNIST PARTY OF CUBA

PALACE OF THE REVOLUTION, HAVANA

JANUARY 26, 1968—YEAR OF THE HEROIC GUERRILLA

MORNING SESSION

COMMANDER FIDEL CASTRO: In the early hours of the morning we stopped while on the topic of the reply sent to the Soviet Government in response to their letter attempting to find justifications in alleged alarms, and purporting insinuations of a nuclear strike in the sense that we had advised the USSR to attack the United States.

These issues were made perfectly clear in that letter. Later there was another long letter containing the same points of view, and though couched in more diplomatic terms, so to speak, answering each of the items in Khrushchev's letter one by one.

At that time Mikoyan's visit occurred.[54] Mikoyan's visit was also taken down. . . . No, Mikoyan's visit was not taken down in shorthand; there were notes on Mikoyan's visit.[55] U Thant's visit was the one that was taken down in shorthand.[56] It is a real pity that the discussions with Mikoyan were not taken down in shorthand, because they were bitter; some of the incidents during the meetings were like anecdotes.

Initially, after we explained to him our standpoints, we had him clarify what was going to happen with the IL-28 planes, and he vouched that no, the IL-28s would not leave Cuba.[57] Then, if I remember correctly, I asked him, "But if they demand their withdrawal, what will you do?" He answered, "Then to hell with the imperialists, to hell with the imperialists!"[58]

Then some 24, or at most 48 hours later, he arrived at the meeting—those famous meetings at the Palace of the Revolution—Mikoyan arrived bearing the sad news that the IL-28 planes would also have to be returned.[59]

That was really unpleasant, but the situation was such that, with the missiles withdrawn, we were on the verge of another problem over the planes. It would have made sense to have had it out over the missiles but not over the IL-28 planes—they were useful planes; it is possible that had we possessed IL-28s, the Central American bases might not have been organized, not because we would have bombed the bases, but of their fear that we might.[60] What we were most concerned about then was avoiding a new impact on public opinion as regards a new blow, a new concession.

We recall perfectly well how we assumed the always unpleasant initiative of making a statement—at my suggestion—that would create the right atmosphere, trying to justify the action by saying that the planes were obsolete, etc. All of which was done in consideration for public opinion, to protect the people from the trauma of another blow of that nature, since we were seriously concerned—and, in our view, rightly so given those circumstances—over the pernicious effects of a chain of such blows on the confidence and the consciousness of the people. And, I repeat, given that under the circumstances we were profoundly incensed, we saw that action as a mistake, in our opinion there had been a series of mistakes, but the extent of our overall confidence, and that deposited in the Soviet Union and its policies, was still considerable.

So the planes went too. Together with the planes—and that is something that they had requested, the issue of the missiles—they requested the withdrawal of the Soviet mechanized infantry brigades stationed in Cuba. Let me add here, in case anyone is unaware of it, that at the time of the missile issue, there were 40,000 Soviet troops stationed in Cuba. The imperialists must also have known that, but they never declared the amount, they limited themselves to speculative figures, which revealed their interest in reducing the amount, perhaps due to possible effects on public opinion.[61]

In fact, anyone who reads Kennedy's statements, his demands, will notice that he did not include those divisions, which were not offensive or strategic weapons, or anything of the sort. We must note that the withdrawal of the mechanized brigades was a freely granted concession to top off the concession of the withdrawal of the strategic missiles.

We argued heatedly, firmly, we were against this. He said that it would not be carried out immediately but gradually, and we reiterated that we were against it and insisted on our opposition. I am explaining all this because of subsequent events, so that you can understand how all this fits into the history of our relations with the Soviet Union. We flatly rejected the inspection issue. That was something we would never agree to. We told him what we thought about that gross, insolent arbitrary measure, contrary to all principles, of taking upon themselves the faculty of deciding on matters under our jurisdiction. And when it was remarked that the agreement would fall flat—an agreement that we were completely at odds with—we said that we could not care less and that there would simply be no inspection.

That gave rise to endless arguing and counter-arguing, and they actually found themselves in a very difficult situation. I think that at this point Raul made a joke that caused quite a commotion in the atmosphere of that meeting. I think it was when we were discussing formulas. Do you remember exactly? Was it the Red Cross thing?[62]

CARLOS RAFAEL RODRIGUEZ: He went to the extreme of proposing that the international vessel be brought to Mariel, saying that because it was an international vessel it would no longer be Cuban territory, and the UN inspectors could be on board the vessel and could supervise the operation. It was then that Raul woke up and said, "Look, why don't you dress them up in little sailor suits?" (LAUGHTER), referring to the international inspectors.

COMMANDER RAUL CASTRO: These people think that I said that because I had been dozing; I actually woke up at that point and came out with that, have them bring those people on their vessel, dressed up as Soviet sailors, but leaving us out of the whole mess. It is true that I was falling asleep, but I was not that far gone.

COMMANDER FIDEL CASTRO: That was it.

COMMANDER FIDEL CASTRO: We had problems with the translators and there were occasions when some of the things we said were badly translated and there was even one point when poor Mikoyan got furious. It was over some phrase or other.

Anyway, those deliberations—as well as some of the others—were characterized by total and complete disagreement. Needless to say, we have the highest opinion of Mikoyan as an individual, as a person, and he was always favorably inclined toward Cuba, he was Cuba's friend, and I think he still is a friend of Cuba; I mean, he did quite a bit for us. That is why he always received from us a high personal regard.

It was during those days that it gradually became evident that we were totally correct—as was, unfortunately, so often the case throughout that whole process—

about the imperialists' attitude vis-à-vis the concessions. This could be seen as low-flying aircraft increased their constant and unnecessary daily flights over our bases, military facilities, airports, antiaircraft batteries, each time more accentuated; they harbored the hope, after the October Crisis, of demoralizing the Revolution and they fell on us, hammer and tongs, with all their arsenal of propaganda and with everything that might demoralize our people and our army.

We had agreed not to shoot; we agreed to revoke the order to fire on the planes while the talks were under way; but made it clear that we did not consider those talks conclusive at all. I believe we were totally right on that; had we acted differently, we would still have their aircraft flying low over us and—as we would sometimes say—we would not even be able to play baseball here.

The demoralizing effect began to manifest itself in the fact that the anti-aircraft gunners and the crews at the air bases had begun to draw caricatures reflecting their mood and their situation, in which they depicted the planes flying above them, the yanquis sticking their tongues out at them, their planes and guns covered with cobwebs. And we realized once again to what extent the men who were supposed to be very experienced in struggling against the imperialists were oblivious to the psychology of imperialists, the psychology of revolutionaries, our people's mentality, and the extremely demoralizing effects of such a passive—more than passive, cowardly—attitude.

So we warned Mikoyan that we were going to open fire on the low-flying planes. We even did him that favor, since there still were ground-to-air missiles and we were interested in preserving them. We visited some emplacements and asked that they be moved given that they were not going to shoot and we did not want them destroyed, because we were planning to open fire on the planes.

We recall those days because of the bitter decisions that had to be made.

Every day at 10:00 A.M., two American planes flew over the San Antonio base. And when we took all the steps, mobilized all the antiaircraft batteries and issued the order, I remember. . . . We were going through a really bitter moment due to it all, the whole situation pained me. I thought of the planes that were going to be shot down and that we would have to face a reprisal attack, that very likely there would be many fatalities. I remember that the mood I was in led me to go to the San Antonio base early and be there. I wanted to be there when they shot at the planes, and if people were going to be killed; I wanted to run the risk of being among the dead, not because I was thinking of suicide or anything like that, but because, really, in that situation, in an air raid. . . . We know that an air raid takes a toll in lives and everything.

So we spent the whole morning there waiting for the planes to come and it was the first day that the imperialists did not send them.[63] Evidently, they did not send the planes because they were convinced that we were going to shoot and they were more than satisfied with the gains they had already obtained, and on that day they showed signs of good sense by suspending the flights.[64]

During those days, some flew near the coasts of Havana City and all the batteries and anti-aircraft emplacements along there shot at the planes. So of course the planes began to fly higher, in the stratosphere, where they could not be reached by our anti-aircraft fire. But we managed to rid ourselves of something that would have become a habit in just a few days, habits which—like the Guantánamo base and the U-2 flights—once established by the imperialists as a right, become very difficult to break.

And thanks to the resolve of the Revolution, following its line, following its attitude, following what it deemed most proper, we staved off that evil.

It is perhaps impossible for anyone to imagine the disastrous effects that allowing the enemy to fly over our heads with impunity every day would have had for the morale of the Revolution. No revolutionary, no soldier, no one can get used to such infamy, such passivity; in that case, it's better to throw down your weapons and quit being a revolutionary soldier, abandon everything. I don't think that any nation with an iota of dignity would be willing to accept such humiliation. And we were face to face with the terrible reality of their total obliviousness to these truths and circumstances.

The planes stopped their low overflights and began to fly where no one could see them or even realize that they were up there. Then we started a training period for the personnel manning our antiaircraft, ground-to-air rocket, and other weapons.

This was important because, as we began to lose faith in the Soviet policy, we began to change our tactics. While at a given moment we had struggled to have the planes stay, we had struggled to have the troops stay—bearing in mind that Kennedy demanded their withdrawal every day—we later decided that in a situation such as that, with an ally that was in out-and-out retreat or even more than retreat, in open flight, we had to at least try to save some things. We realized how alone we would be in the event of a war; we also realized how stupid it was to withdraw those troops in the face of an enemy that demanded it, and that would, in future years, further aggravate our perilous situation. Under those circumstances, we abandoned the objective of trying to keep the troops and, practically resigned, ourselves to focusing on keeping at least the weapons.

That is why, at a given moment, and faced with the prospect of their taking away all the weapons, we agreed in principle to allow some, though not all, the troops to leave.[65]

That is, we had begun to strive to keep the weapons here, in our hands, so that, in the event of an attack, they would be used. I am not saying that the Soviet soldiers would not have used them; I am sure the Soviet soldiers would have fought here bravely, but I am not certain that they would have been given the order to fight. Maybe, after half of them died, the order might have come.

A new stage in our relations with the Soviet Union began, characterized by the special circumstance of having in before us an aggressive and emboldened enemy, an ally on the retreat and our desire to keep the weapons, as well as our resolve to prevent relations with that ally from deteriorating to the point of rupture.

Consequently, a new stage began in which we exercised a policy of great effort to prevent further deterioration in our relations with the USSR, considering our concrete strategic situation and also considering that since our main enemy, our greatest enemy, was right there in front of us, we had to dissemble, contain, hold back our indignation, our outrage and prevent any sustained deterioration in those relations from affecting our primary problem: fighting imperialism.

From the very first we contended that there was a military agreement, and that this agreement had been violated, that our country was being left without any kind of guarantees, and that it was necessary to devise other means which would serve as an effective warning or some sort of alternative guarantee to the missile agreement, given the evident intentions of the Yanqui imperialists. Different variants were discussed.

One of the solutions that we liked was keeping the troops, even reinforcing the troops here, based on the idea that the presence of Soviet units would at least indicate certain a Soviet resolve to fight in the event of an invasion of Cuba; or a bilateral military agreement; that is, something similar to our participation in the Warsaw Pact. In other words, we offered them a choice of variants, and, above all, it was made clear that the need to search for a substitute to the unilaterally violated military agreement was inexcusable.

Days later . . . no, not days, a few months later, Nikita—who was not what we would call an inept politician; he was an intelligent and sharp man who was occasionally skillful we might add——undertook efforts to assuage, to improve, to try to reach a better understanding with us. Some months had elapsed since the crisis. It was January 31, 1963. He wrote a 27-page long letter, which I will not read fully because of its length, an extremely affable letter, trying to explain—because all those things had actually remained unanswered, all our demands, all our accusations. So he wrote an extremely warm letter. I am not going to read all of it, only a few paragraphs:[66]

"Dear comrade Fidel Castro:

"I have long been nurturing the idea of writing you this letter. Now, on my way to Moscow from Berlin, where I attended the Congress of the Unified Socialist Party of Germany, I am writing to you. Our train is crossing the fields and forests of Soviet Byelorussia, and I suddenly thought how nice it would be if, during this season, on such a sunny day, you could see the land covered with snow and the forest all silvery with frost."

It was a bucolic letter, poetic in many ways.

"You, a man of the South . . ."

He was trying to find an explanation, I am not sure whether climatic, ethnic, or what, for the attitudes adopted by the Revolution.

"You, a man of the South, perhaps have never seen this other than in paintings. It is probably difficult for you to imagine the land carpeted with snow and the forest covered with white frost. It wouldn't be a bad idea for you to visit our country during each season of the year, since each of them—spring, summer, fall and winter—has its own charm.

"Cuba is a country where summer is eternal. I remember that during our conversation in New York we reacted differently to the climate of that city: I was suffocating from the heat and you said you were cold.[67]

"However, all these reflections on nature should not distract us from the central topic of this letter. The main thing is the enormous desire I and my comrades have of meeting with you and conversing, talking with open hearts. We must talk. We would like this meeting, this talk, not to be put off for too long. We would like the meeting to be as soon as possible.

"Why? Because we have gone through a very important period, one which will be a landmark in the development of Cuba, the Soviet Union and the rest of the socialist countries. For the first time since World War II we were close, very close to war. Cuba has been at the vortex of severe crisis in the Caribbean area.

"We realize that today the extreme severity of the crisis no longer exists, but the danger of a clash is not over. You understand that very well and we fully share your concern and assess the situation in the same way.

"But, what is the main thing now? Why should we meet and talk frankly?

"The seriousness of the crisis created by U.S. imperialism in the Caribbean has disappeared. But it seems to me that the crisis has left a certain imprint, vague though it may be, on the relations between our States—Cuba and the Soviet Union—and on our personal relations. Strictly speaking, they are no longer what they were before the crisis. I will not deny that this saddens and worries us. And I am inclined to believe that the development of our relations may, to a large extent, depend on our meeting. At present, impersonal communications such as mail are no longer satisfactory. Nothing can replace a personal conversation. It is in precisely such a setting that we can most easily and rapidly overcome any misunderstanding resulting from our respective positions and comprehend one another.

"That is why people, aside from using technical means, etc. . . .

"We too should have an interview. During the Caribbean crisis our viewpoints did not always coincide, we didn't see the various stages of the crisis in the same light. It became evident that we also had different approaches to the various methods of defusing it. After our well-known statement, you even said publicly that during the development of the crisis there had arisen several discrepancies between the Soviet Government and the Cuban Government.[68] As you may well realize, that did not fill us with joy. And now that tension has abated and we have entered another phase in relations between Cuba and the Soviet Union on the one hand, and with the United States on the other, our relations with Cuba present certain crevices whose depths are difficult to determine. . . ."

And so on and so forth. He continued his analysis in that very affable, very friendly tone, he conveyed a very serious concern, a wish to find some formula for an understanding.

In keeping with our line, which as we previously explained was that of doing all we could to prevent our relations from deteriorating further to the point of posing a danger, as I stated, to our main objective, we, in accordance with that strategy, decided to take advantage of that opportunity and traveled to the Soviet Union; although as a rule we are not fond of traveling, I mean, we are not overenthused by official trips, much less knowing that such trips, particularly to some of the socialist countries given that their habits and customs usually imply constant drinking, constant eating and constant "protocoling" to which I am somewhat allergic.

Also, at that time, I was not feeling too well due to other allergies, intestinal allergies. But, in spite of everything, we agreed to the trip. It was a long, tiring trip.[69] It must be said that during that trip we came to realize something which later became part of the things we highly appreciated and considered proper to preserve: the attitude of the Soviet people. You should have seen how deeply the question of the Cuban Revolution had penetrated the feelings of the Soviet people.[70] Although it is true that we were no longer confident in the Soviet leaders, we simply could not begin to understand how they would be able to face the enormous impact, the explosive and unrestrainable impact that news of a U.S. invasion of Cuba would have on the Soviet people.

On the other hand, there was a certain positive sign. It was the fact that they did not try to dampen that emotional state, that feeling of love in the people; in fact, they had launched an enormous and intense propaganda campaign based on it.

Perhaps now this can be better understood because at that time the problem of the Caribbean crisis, the problem of Cuba, had begun to be an issue in Soviet domestic policy, and the domestic problems perhaps justified or explained, more than anything else that propaganda campaign around our visit, more so than any attitude consistent with that of the Soviet people and their feelings toward the Cuban Revolution.

In any case, that factor began to be taken into account. It's true that they were extremely attentive, and it is also true that Khrushchev spoke very candidly, or, at least, in a very friendly tone, making efforts to explain. And he showed us a whole series of communications that had been exchanged. Among them, there was one which had been written in really strong terms, during an exchange of notes with Kennedy, when Kennedy insisted in one of his letters, saying, . . . well, this and that—I do not remember just which incident it was about—and "something is going to happen," or one of the sentences insinuated that something was going to happen, to which he replied in very strong terms, in a very harsh letter he sent to Kennedy through his embassy—through contacts via one Thompson,[71] and at the time, contacts with Kennedy's brother and the Soviet ambassador[72]—that is how the letters were exchanged. In one of those letters he gave a very strong reply, like someone who was tired of being of annoyed. He replied harshly, and regarding the fact that "something is going to happen," he said verbatim: "Yes, something is going to happen, but something incredible!" That is, to the insinuation by the other that something might happen, he insinuated that something even worse might happen; he said verbatim: "Something is going to happen, but something incredible!"[73]

That letter was a really strong reply. We noted and assessed all that evidence. But particularly and above all, we assessed the attitude of the Soviet people.

But at the same time, there was something very curious and that very few comrades know about—the comrades of the Bureau know about it—and it was a certain piece of information that I picked up on that occasion, during the reading of the letters. The Russian I know does not even total ten words, and the letters were in Russian and the ones he received had been translated into Russian. I remember, by the way, that regarding the strong letter which he believed had some impact on the United States, Kennedy's brother had complained that it was a very harsh letter and that, out of respect for his brother, he would not show it to him, etc.—this was the reply that Thompson, or the ambassador, or whoever, had given Nikita. But the fact was that the letter got there and had an impact. The Americans are very calculating in all such things: they calculate each comma, each word, the implications, everything they do, and then you discover from their books what their philosophy for action is, with their great practical sense, calculating everything, measuring everything.

But regarding those letters Nikita was reading, a translator translated them. And in those letters. . . . (It sometimes happens. . . . We were reading here . . . in the report that Raul was reading yesterday, there was a paragraph he didn't want to read because it said something unpleasant about a comrade, and inadvertently he read it.) So Nikita was reading the letter to the translator, he had been reading the pages and on one of them the Americans said: "For our part, we have abided by all the agreements and have withdrawn the ballistic missiles from Turkey and Italy." And I said, "How's that? Repeat that part." Then Nikita realized he had read a paragraph by mistake—he had not given the letter to the translator to read—and he laughed the way he does, showing his teeth, and I did not insist. He had read enough. I then realized that secretly . . . and, of course, the reason why I never discussed this before today is that if you really have to discuss with different governments very, very serious things, you feel compelled to a special discretion, as a standard procedure; otherwise, you might lose the necessary confidence when some things have to be said. Although this is becoming something practically historical, I do not think it is possible to tell the Central Committee the story of these relations without mentioning this deed, because it reveals that in the middle of this whole affair was an agreement that must have been a great satisfaction to him over there, a compensation. It consisted of an American commitment to withdraw the ballistic missiles from Turkey and Italy, something that happened almost immediately after the October crisis, under the pretext that those weapons were no longer as important now that intercontinental ballistic missiles, planes, Polaris rockets, etc. existed. In actual fact, they gave up weapons which had been deployed in specific locations, and this was a secret concession made by the United States that nobody ever learned about;[74] the ones to save face in the eyes of U.S. public opinion and the others to save face domestically, they made mutual concessions. They made this trade and we were never informed of it, the only reason we learned of it at all was entirely by chance, totally by accident, as I explained, but we took careful note of it, *very* careful note!

That long and exhausting trip finally came to an end, a trip in which, I repeat, the most interesting aspect for us was the chance to gauge the feeling of solidarity of the Soviet people, so much so that, in our opinion, in the event of an onslaught against Cuba, they would have been very difficult to control.

And that is one of the factors that we have always attributed great importance to whenever we have been faced with the possibility of a public dispute with the Soviet Party, so as not to give rise to it being used to undermine the Soviet people's profound feeling of love and solidarity toward the Cuban Revolution, a feeling of love and solidarity that revealed the human stature of the Soviet people, and I for one was really impressed by it. We sincerely believe that whatever the mistakes made by the Russian Revolution, for a long period of time it has instilled in the Soviet people a profound spirit of solidarity, stoicism, a spirit of work, and we do not know how long it would hold up under the impact of new circumstances and new events.

We have also seen it, in general, in the men who have worked here in this country. We saw it during the October Crisis; we saw when the general who was stationed here as an advisor cried on the infamous day that we heard of the withdrawal of the missiles; we saw it in the attitude of the soldiers; we saw it in the attitude of so many, many excellent and friendly people, the Soviet technicians and citizens who have worked here, despite the actions of some individuals, for which I am sincerely convinced that the Soviet Party bears great responsibility in what happened and acted in a totally disloyal manner in its relations with us.

Thousands of soldiers, thousands of technicians, thousands of Soviet students have come here and there has never been a single instance, not a single instance, of a man of this Revolution trying to approach any one of those technicians, soldiers, never! That never happened. If there has been any conflict or situation of another kind at a given moment, it has been over an argument about something, but never has there been a policy of trying to influence, of trying to create a state of opinion, of winning over, of sounding out, of recruiting a Soviet technician, citizen or worker.[75]

If some have been labeled pro-Cuban, it has been simply because of the kind of treatment and friendship we have always extended to them. Similarly, never have our security agencies, our intelligence and counterintelligence services carried out that sort of activity in any country of the socialist block, an activity which, in our view, is an intolerable and ill-advised practice—the practice implemented by the socialist countries in Europe of carrying out intelligence activities inside other socialist countries.

Immediately after our return from the Soviet Union, the new imperialist tactics began to take shape. We caught on right away because the constant presence of a nearby enemy has forced us to get to know it well. And so the period of pirate bases in Central America and pirate raids on our coasts was ushered in.[76] This was a flagrant, public, extremely irritating activity because the moral damage of those attacks was far greater, the indignation they awakened, the irritation against all that Soviet foreign policy; the attacks carried out with impunity by vessels equipped with all the most modern electronic devices, all the navigation equipment, against a country with 2 or 3 thousand km of coasts, vessels based in Central America. Systematic attacks were launched against the refineries, ports, sugar warehouses, fuel deposits. They even sent frogmen to place a bomb and sink a naval unit stationed at the Isle of Pines base, leaving behind another powerful bomb in the channel to take lives, and which would have taken many more had it not been detected in time. There were attacks on facilities, on ships that traded with Cuba. It was the most unabashed and flagrant piracy, and it took place right in the middle of the twentieth century. So, in the great and extraordinary era of proletarian internationalism and intercontinental missiles, we were forced to go back to the time of the Dutch pirates, Drake, Jacques de Sores, and all those gentlemen whose exploits we have read about in history books.

Modern pirates, with radars, U-2 spy flights, with full cognizance of where our units were deployed, and with all the necessary means to carry our their treacherous attacks. You may well imagine that we would have had to have ice-water in our veins to suffer that with resignation and favorably accept that policy as good, great, marvelous, wonderful. Kennedy, however, had demanded the withdrawal of the IL-28s, the same IL-28 planes that would have allowed us to intimidate, the IL-28 planes that would have allowed us pursue the pirate ships out into the ocean, particularly the mother ships; the IL-28s would have allowed us to fly over their bases, and if bad came to worse, also to give the pirate bases a taste of our bombs, and rightly so. But there was the impunity factor: withdraw such and such a weapon, they constitute a danger to the security of the United States. Immediately the pirate bases were organized and the Soviet Union, however, was not even in a position to threaten to supply us with the IL-28 planes if the attacks were not stopped.

Those standards, those internationalist practices are very difficult to understand. The problem of the U-2 flights over our territory was still pending. Together with the pirate attacks and the U-2 flights, incidents began to flare up at the Guantánamo base. The same Guantánamo base which, we are certain, would have been dismantled had there been a modicum of serenity and firmness during the October crisis. Had they had the presence of mind to have posed the demand correctly from a principled standpoint, had they said that they would withdraw the missiles if satisfactory guarantees were given to Cuba, had they let Cuba negotiate, the crisis might even have been turned into a political victory. We would have been able to say, "All right, you have to take the base away, you have to do this and that," and we would have set the terms ourselves. That episode was an evident defeat for the socialist community and for the revolutionary movement.

All the rest are euphemisms of different kinds: Cuba was saved, Cuba lives. But Cuba had been alive and Cuba had been living, and Cuba did not want to live at the expense of humiliation or surrender; for that, you do not have to be a revolutionary. Revolutionaries are not just concerned with living, but how one lives, living most of all with dignity, living with a cause, living for a cause.

Every time the trite expression "Cuba was saved"—quite honestly, the respect I feel for all these expressions is the same "respect" I feel for Mr. Bofill's story—has been used.[77] But Cuba was not in any crisis when, considering it an international duty, agreed to the deployment of one thousand missiles here; Cuba did not agree with the way the issue was handled; it stated the need to approach the problem from different, more drastic, more revolutionary and even more legal positions; and it totally disagreed with the way in which the situation was terminated. However, the argument "Cuba lives" . . . for goodness sakes, we have been alive since our mothers brought each one of us into the world, and that has nothing whatsoever to do with the Soviet missiles!

There is the habit of not searching for the reasons, of not analyzing, and instead trying to solve everything with a catch phrase.

Daily provocations were stepped up at the Guantánamo base, a legacy that has remained, a byproduct that might have been extirpated victoriously and without a war then, we are absolutely sure of that. If they wanted to yield—because it honestly never crossed our minds to yield and there is no way we could have yielded when dealing with an issue that would affect the socialist bloc as a whole—but since they were willing to yield in one way or another, it opened up the responsibility of doing it in such a way that the enemy would be forced to yield also; not just giving and getting nothing. If they gave in secretly and withdraw the missiles, what position did that leave us in?

Little by little, against our all out resistance, they were withdrawing, and with them, the mechanized troops. During the visit to the Soviet Union, we stated all our views regarding the matter.

As I was saying, then came the period of the pirate attacks, the stepping up of actions at Guantánamo base. A soldier was killed in Guantánamo, another soldier was wounded in Guantánamo, soldiers were shot at in Guantánamo, another soldier dead. It even became necessary to do something as contrary to our practice of avoiding incidents as pulling our men back some hundreds of meters and setting up fortified positions. However, in light of all that was happening, we realized that any day there would be an incident that they could use as a pretext to invade our country, to orchestrate a clash, and that, if the clash was unavoidable, it served no purpose for us to act like ostriches.

It was on one such occasion that we declared that the U-2 flights had to end or we would start shooting the U-2s down. If we were going to become involved in a conflict, we, not they, would choose when.

On that occasion there was a mobilization of planes and all that, blackmailers in Florida, but what actually solved the problem were not the planes going to Florida; what actually solved the problem then, when they were going to deliver the missiles, was a message from the Soviet Union. I cannot remember now whether it was verbal or in writing; I haven't been able to look for all the data in such an enormous amount of documents. . . .

COMMANDER RAUL CASTRO: It was verbal and the answer came only a few minutes before your address on May Day.

OSVALDO DORTICOS: The answer was delivered almost at the podium.

COMMANDER FIDEL CASTRO: They said that, being the situation what it was, they would not turn over the ground-to-air missiles to us if we intended to use them to bring down the U-2s. There again we were faced with a problem. Of course, the fact that they were not going to deliver the missiles was something we could decide by ourselves and, ultimately, we could seize them from them. But, naturally, we did not think that should be the solution and much less our attitude toward the men who would be guarding those missiles. We did not think it was essential, imperative nor unavoidable to create a problem under those circumstances. And once again, concerned over preventing greater mistrust and frustration among the people, something that we were trying to dispel and not foster, we told them we thought that theirs was a disastrous decision, that, in the face of such circumstances they should trust us and turn over the missiles, that we would use those weapons only in an extreme situation, such as in the event of an attack against us.

And, under those circumstances, they showed some degree of confidence, and just as the May Day rally was about to begin, the news was conveyed to us in the stand by the ambassador that delivery of the ground-to-air missiles was about to begin.

[Five pages excised]

So it became necessary to respond again. It was, of course, a letter in keeping with the situation. It included mention of other topics, the combines, and all those things. But by page 3 we had advanced to the U-2 spy flights. I explained: "On this issue we will abide strictly by the agreement arrived at with the ambassador in late April.

"We were very pleased with the decision to continue turning over the ground-to-air missiles to the Cuban personnel. We agree with the opinion contained in the letter. I don't remember what this was about, but it was in keeping.

"The problem sharpened because of the preposterous provocations carried out at the land access to Guantánamo Naval base on April 19.[78] The gross actions by yanqui guards that day led us to believe that it was done with the definite purpose of provoking a conflict. As you may recall, days later the Secretary of State spoke to the Soviet ambassador in a way which seemed to convey the wish of the United States Administration to avoid a serious problem with Cuba during the election campaign. However, several days later, on June 9, there was a new incident at the base: a yanqui guard shot at one our soldiers and wounded him. Barely two weeks later, on the 25th, another of our soldiers was more seriously wounded in a similar incident.

"These three incidents occurred in the midst of an evident exacerbation of their daily provocations, and it would seem that they are deliberate and planned actions.

"Every time we issue an official protest, the U.S. Administration systematically claims its innocence while counter-charging that we are the ones who are carrying out provocations against their guards.

"After the last incident, I contacted a person in the United States who had shown an interest in improving relations between the U.S. and Cuba in some way, and who has connections with liberal and influential political personalities in the party in house. I asked that person to give us an insight into what might be behind these events.

"These personalities, as well as President Johnson himself," we were told, "were surprised to hear of the events and declared that they had no intention of creating such conflicts at the base and that they would order a thorough investigation.

"So far, however, provocations continue unabated and are so notorious that they cannot go unnoticed by the commanders of that military facility.

"I can assure you that such provocations as hurling stones for several minutes, aiming their guns at our outposts and yelling insults, occur by the dozens daily.

"Our soldiers, who to a certain extent have become used to these acts of hostility, have borne all this with serenity. But these provocations change in nature and become more serious when men start to fall wounded by the shots. That is why we have decided to build a fortified line several hundred meters from the perimeter of the base and bring our men back to those positions. This work will take some 3 months. Moreover, faced with the threat of an air raid against our military facilities whenever there is talk of taking steps against the U-2s, we are adopting measures to protect our military equipment against a surprise air attack. These are also necessary measures for our defense under any circumstances. The bombing of Vietnam had not yet begun at the point.[79]

"As you may perhaps recall, comrade Malinovsky once said that Cuba would not be able to resist a U.S. attack for more than 72 hours using conventional weapons." The views of a "doddering" old marshal, may he rest in peace.[80]

"We sincerely do not think so. If the military equipment we have is not destroyed in a massive surprise attack, and if it is used rationally, the occupation of Cuba would not be a matter of days.

"We are not specialists." —They are always harping on about specialists and super-specialists—but as a people and as revolutionary fighters, we are, in a certain way, inured to the enemy we are facing and we know that if we make good use of the resources we have, we can present a long and stubborn resistance. Until now, for example, it was customary for our tanks, planes, heavy artillery and other equipment to be kept at their respective facilities, one next to the other in perfect rows." This is a subtle allusion to our advisors, who arranged the planes and everything else just like the Sinai desert." All our facilities and equipment were constantly being photographed. I do not doubt that the American strategists are convinced that it can all be destroyed in a matter of minutes.

"We also know that in the event of an attack against our country, hundreds of enemy planes would be flying over our troops constantly; that our air force, which proved extremely effective in countering attacks such as the one at the Bay of Pigs,[81] would be completely neutralized within a few hours of the direct attack. The ground-to-air missiles themselves are very vulnerable under our conditions, and we are examining ways of simultaneously defending them while using them efficiently. These concrete circumstances must condition our concept of defense. Very soon our tanks, of which there are more than a few, the artillery brigades, the *Katiushka* groups[82] and other weapons will be underground. Some will be in natural shelters and others in man-made shelters. The U-2 planes and other observation means will no longer be able to watch our most important troops. Our infantry, tanks and other units will also need to have as many antiaircraft batteries as possible to put up a defense against the tactical air force. Moreover, we know that in the event of a direct assault, during the first few hours we would have to fight the airborne troops. As we have been able to learn, during the October crisis one of the senior officers of the airborne troops was appointed commander of the forces that would be used in the attack on Cuba.

"Our military units were somewhat disperse [sic] in our effort to simultaneously defend all our coasts at once. We are now deploying them so that all the key and vital positions will be covered by whatever is needed for an efficient defense. The need to consider these problems has to do with the fact that when the last Soviet units are withdrawn from Cuba, which have acted like a dam against the temptation of plotting an attack against Cuba since the October crisis, this will not act in our favor.

"Just imagine for a second that the Pentagon also believe that Cuba could be occupied in three days.[83] They might entertain the thought of such an operation as an alternative without great war risks, since they would not be clashing with Soviet soldiers and might also show the world a fait accompli, in just three days. I have always wondered why they insist so vehemently on the withdrawal of the Soviet military personnel, and yet, on the other hand, have shown no signs of attempting to reduce tension toward us and, indeed, maintain an intransigent position vis-à-vis our demands for the most elementary guarantees.

"Our concern over these things and our efforts to prevent the enemy from making a military and political mistake, are also an attempt on our part to preserve peace as far as we can.

"Without a doubt, they have undertaken the commitment with the Soviet Union not to invade Cuba, but I always keep your saying in mind; that the imperialists do not follow legal or moral considerations, instead, in each case they abide by reality, by the balance of forces and the risks implicit in each of their actions."

It is indeed incredible that a country 90 miles away from the United States, and ready to fight that enemy, should have to hear the views of their senior specialists telling it that it would only be able to resist for 72 hours. If this is not an insinuation to surrender, if this is not a suggestion of impotence, if this is proletarian internationalism, if this is the correct method, if this is their way of guiding and encouraging the revolutionary movements, then it is no wonder that the Arabs in the UAR got stomped in a matter of hours! That was a reflection of this, what was written here in 1964 or '63 . . .

COMMANDER RAUL CASTRO: Late '63 or early '64.

COMMANDER FIDEL CASTRO: July 3, 1964.

Of course the Arab issue is explained by the other thing. We have taken all the possible precautions. And today I'm sure that it would not be easy, but the Americans have much more military equipment than the Israelis to launch a blitzkrieg against us. So then, that was the opinion of the senior specialists: Cuba would only be able to resist for 72 hours in the event of an onslaught.

"That is why we believe it is our duty to do everything possible so that they never consider invading and occupying Cuba an easy task from a military point of view. This, together with the well-known and firm Soviet position will add greater force to the commitment.

[END.]

[W]e must walk by the path of liberation even when it may cost millions of atomic victims, because in the struggle to the death between two systems the only thing that can be considered is the definitive victory of socialism or its retrogression under the nuclear victory of imperialist aggression.

—Che Guevara[1]

[The Soviets were] feeble-minded bureaucrats. . . . And our boundless confidence was the innocent victim of all those subtle particulars that we never dreamed a Party or revolutionary leadership could be capable of.

—Fidel Castro, January 25, 1968

OCTOBER/NOVEMBER 1962:
THE SHADOW OF THE MISSLE CRISIS
DESCENDS ON HAVANA AND MOSCOW

"It influenced Cuban–Soviet relations for years."[2]

THE BETRAYAL

When UN Acting Secretary General U Thant traveled to Cuba on October 30 to seek permission for international verification that the missiles were being removed, Castro rejected his entreaties. He argued that such an inspection would violate Cuba's sovereignty, and that U Thant had used a double standard in not requiring a similar verification of the U.S. pledge to refrain from invading Cuba.[3] Early in 1963 Castro emphasized this position in summarizing how he understood the causes and resolution of the missile crisis. In a speech commemorating the fourth anniversary of the Revolution, he asserted that the missiles were intended to defend Cuba against U.S. aggression and to fortify the "socialist camp." Cuba, he argued, had the sovereign right to accept the missiles. Sovereignty was the essence of independence, he explained. It provided the freedom to set one's own course and not follow the dictates of the United States.[4] This dogged determination to secure Cuba's sovereignty and independence lay at the core of its distrust of the Soviet Union. The socialist superpower neither appreciated nor respected the importance Cuba attached to these fundamental matters. As a result, Castro told Italian journalist Gianni Minà in 1987, the way that the missile crisis was resolved "influenced Cuban–Soviet relations for years."[5]

"The First Cut Is the Deepest"

When the crisis began, the Cuban leaders were pleased and impressed by Khrushchev's strong response to Kennedy. Castro's confidence in Soviet fidelity was clear in his public remarks the day after Kennedy announced the quarantine. Speaking in radio and television interviews, the Cuban leader said,

> Against that policy of provocation and violence, our position is to be firm and calm and to defend ourselves. The position of the Soviet Union? . . . Firm, calm, full of arguments, full of reasons that reduce the aggressive policy of Mr. Kennedy to its skeleton. And history will have to mark all this down, the position of one camp and the other, the position of the defenders of peace, of those who struggle to avoid for the world the tragedy of a war.[6]

Imagine the Cubans' shock, therefore, when they awoke five days later to discover that their Soviet partner had backed down, that the Americans had won a great victory without firing a shot, and that Cuba, humiliated by the Soviet collapse, was now in danger of extinction due to Soviet cowardice. On October 28, the Soviets began to make their ignominious exit, leaving Cuba fully exposed to a U.S. attack.

Literally overnight, the Cuban perception of the Soviets shifted from that of savior to traitor. Just as Judas had betrayed Jesus ironically with a kiss, the Soviets had betrayed Cuba, with equal irony, with their bogus offer of a boundless fraternal commitment to Cuba's security. In any relationship, according to a popular song of the late 1960s, "the first cut is the deepest."[7] In the October 1962 missile crisis, the Cubans felt that the Soviets, with whom they believed they had recently established a close and mutually respectful relationship, had cut them to the bone—had betrayed them, had treated them condescendingly, and had shocked them into the unwelcome recognition that when the chips were down, the Soviets cared little or nothing about Cuba's security interests. The Cubans were absolutely stunned at what they saw in the crisis as Soviet ineptitude, spinelessness, and callous disregard for the fate of the Cubans and their revolution.

The shock to the Cubans can hardly be overemphasized. This cut went very deep; the Cubans would never fully trust the Soviets again for the security of their island. This was the first psychological scar left in Cuban memory by the missile crisis. The second was that the outcome of the crisis crushed their idealistic hopes for the success of an immediate world revolution, along the lines of the Cuban Revolution.[8] This was the essence of the trauma for the Cubans: Having dreamed of a Soviet umbrella of protection for their island, and of Soviet backing for Cuban leadership of worldwide socialist revolution, they suddenly, on October 28, 1962, found that on both points they were shockingly and absolutely *alone*. The leader of the socialist world had showed starkly that is was not interested in sticking its neck out either for Cuba or for Cuba's crusade on behalf of the victims of imperialism around the world.

In contrast, Cubans had been prepared to lay down their lives for "the whole socialist camp," Castro angrily told Soviet Deputy Premier Anastas Mikoyan. Despite impending attacks on the capital, "we decided to weaken the antiaircraft defense of Havana, but at the same time strengthen the defense of the missile locations."[9] And in return for such loyalty the Soviets seemed to offer only treachery. The Soviets had betrayed Cuba, its leaders felt, and the socialist dream.

The Affront Was Political, Not Personal

When Soviet Deputy Premier Anastas Mikoyan arrived in Havana to placate the Cuban leader, Castro immediately made clear that his concern was political, not personal. The Cuban leader testily compared Khrushchev's willingness to permit inspections to the 1901 Platt Amendment, which he reminded Mikoyan gave the United States the right to intervene unilaterally in Cuban internal affairs. The United States had demanded Cuba add the amendment to its constitution as a condition for the withdrawal of U.S. occupation forces after the so-called Spanish–American War.[10]

In fact, on the very day the Great Power deal to end the crisis was announced, the Cuban government made clear in admirably concise language the substantive reasons for Cuba's anger. What Cuba had obtained from the agreement was worse than nothing at all. The Kennedy–Khrushchev agreement seemed to place Cuba in a more perilous situation than it had been in before. The missiles had transformed it into a strategic U.S. target. Soviet withdrawal of the missiles—in the face of U.S. pressure—indicated that Cuba had lost its protector in the event of a U.S. attack. Castro parsed his righteous rage at the Soviets into five brief points and sent them to UN Acting Secretary General U Thant. He demanded:

- First: An end to the economic blockade and all economic and trade measures throughout the world by the United States against Cuba.
- Second: An end to all subversive activities, drops of weapons and explosives by air and by sea, organization of mercenary invasions, infiltrations of spies and saboteurs—actions all carried out from U.S. territory and from some accomplice countries.
- Third: An end to pirate attacks from bases in the United States and Puerto Rico.
- Fourth: An end to all violations of Cuban sea and airspace by American aircraft and naval craft.
- Fifth: Withdrawal from the naval base in Guantánamo, and return of the territory occupied by the United States.[11]

These were the central issues to the Cubans and, from their point of view, what the crisis was really about. All involve what they considered to be acts of war carried out by U.S. forces, or U.S.-backed operatives, and all related to activities that began before the missile crisis. The United States at the time was, in fact, endeavoring to starve, subvert, terrorize, and intimidate the Cuban revolutionary government. Singly, or in combination, these policies could have resulted in the destruction of the Cuban Revolution, if they were pursued with tenacity and the Soviets did not threaten a countervailing response. The Cubans had been willing to accept the risk of placing Soviet missiles on their territory, because of their calculation that this would certify their mettle in the Socialist Bloc and would enhance socialism globally, and because the Soviet presence in turn might force the United States to forego its dream of overthrowing the Cuban government.

The Soviets' failure to make the fulfillment or even negotiation of *any* of the Five Points a requirement for ending the missile crisis shocked the Cubans into the recognition that the Soviets were quite different from the kind of partner with whom the Cubans believed they had contracted. Soviet leaders either were woefully naive about the Americans (if they really believed Kennedy's pledge not to invade or attack Cuba) or, worse, they simply didn't care about Cuban security and were content to escape the crisis in any way they could, the Cubans be damned.

From this point forward—after October 28—the Cubans' public statements became increasingly intransigent and implicitly directed at their putative ally. The most famous and telling example may be Castro's November 15, 1962 letter to U Thant (included in full in appendix B). The conclusion to the letter is a masterpiece of vitriolic allusion to the anger and humiliation the Cubans felt at the hands of the Soviets—feelings that are only slightly disguised in a document that is ostensibly a diatribe against U.S. imperialism. But read as a warning to the Soviets, it is a powerful statement of a small, proud, and betrayed country that refuses to go quietly when bidden to do so by its Great Power benefactor.

In the letter Castro first refuses resolutely to accept any on-site inspection in Cuba, and then threatens to shoot down U.S. planes, supposedly on missions to inspect the missile sites, flying in Cuban airspace. Finally, he articulates Cuba's view of itself as a defender of all small countries:

> We are sounding the alarm for the defense of world peace, we are defending the right of small countries to be considered on a footing of equality, we are telling all the peoples of the earth that before the imperialist enemy there can be no weakening. . . . Our right to live is something that cannot be discussed by anyone.
>
> But if our right to live is made conditional upon an obligation to fall to our knees, our reply once again is that we will not accept it. We believe in the right to defend the

liberty, the sovereignty, and the dignity of this country, and we shall continue to exercise that right to the last man, woman, and child capable of holding a weapon in this territory.[12]

This stance must have angered and even frightened the Soviets. Even as the world was still balanced precariously at the brink of destruction—the U.S. nuclear alert remained at DefCon 2 (the highest state of readiness before nuclear war) and U.S. strategic forces were kept at a hair trigger—the Cubans were ready to engage in acts of war against the United States. While the Cubans did not want war, they were saying, neither were they willing to withdraw peacefully until they had obtained tangible and important concessions from the Americans. And what if the Americans refused, and the crisis stretched out intolerably and became more dangerous? That would not be Cuba's doing, Castro believed, because to give in might mean the end of the Cuban Revolution. It was too much to ask of a small country, when all it sought was acknowledgment of the threat it faced. This new crisis would be the consequence of the Soviets' cowardly, undignified surrender to the United States at Cuba's expense. Between the lines of this anti-imperialist screed, then, the Cubans pointedly were asking the Soviets: Where is your courage? Where is your dignity? Where is your sense of responsibility to your smaller and vulnerable fraternal ally? Where, in a word that would become a point of contention in the succeeding years, is the Soviets' socialist *internationalism*?

THE CLASH

The Soviets had no need to divine Cuba's message, to read between the lines of the public statements made by Cuban leaders in late October and November 1962. Mikoyan heard it directly from the Cuban leadership as soon as he arrived in Havana. He began the first conversation graciously, by telling Castro that he understood some issues were "unclear" to "the Cuban comrades" and that he was there to answer their questions. Castro quickly moved to the heart of the matter, asking some sharp questions and also explaining to the Soviet leader why the Cubans were so angry. "Why," Castro asked,

was that decision made unilaterally, why are the missiles being taken away from us? And will all the weapons be taken back?—these were the questions disturbing all the people. In some 48 hours that feeling of bitterness and pain spread among all the people. Events were rapidly following one another. The offer to withdraw weapons from Cuba under the condition of liquidating bases in Turkey was advanced on 27 October. On 28 October there came the order to dismantle the missiles and the consent to an inspection. . . . At the same time the insolent flights of American planes into Cuban airspace became more frequent, and we were asked not to open fire on them. All of this generated a strong demoralizing influence. . . . The decision was made without consultation, without coordinating it with our government. Nobody had the slightest wish to believe it, everyone thought it was a lie.[13]

The seeming Soviet contempt for Cuba was dangerous, Castro continued, because "[p]sychologically our people were not prepared for that. A feeling of deep disappointment, bitterness and pain has appeared, as if we were deprived of not only the missiles, but of the very symbol of solidarity." In turn those feelings could encourage counterrevolution and perhaps even challenges to his leadership.[14]

Mikoyan and the Cuban Leadership Talk Past Each Other

Though Mikoyan tried to be empathetic with the Cuban concerns, he kept returning to the goals of his mission. As a result, there was a palpable tension in his meetings with the Cuban leaders from the very start, despite the positive predisposition toward him in Havana. By the third day Castro had become so frustrated with the Soviet leader that he refused to meet with him for another week, claiming he had to inspect agricultural projects. Sergo Mikoyan, the son of the deputy premier and a leading Soviet scholar on Latin America, accompanied his father to Cuba. He recalled in 1989 that the Cuban leader left his father to "walk the corridors" in order to demonstrate displeasure.[15]

The deputy premier, who had been characterized as "Fidel's agent" in the Kremlin, was clueless about what he had said to offend Castro. He confided later in the day to Carlos Rafael Rodríguez—whom the Soviets trusted because he was one of the only Cuban leaders who had been a member of Cuba's communist party (which was called the Peoples Socialist Party) before the Revolution—that "Perhaps I let some clumsiness show, spoke in some kind of tone?" No, he concluded. He had simply become a "victim" of Castro's sharp tongue, "evidently because I extemporaneously put forth my idea. An old man, I have the shortcomings of the young."[16] In fact, the Soviet analysis of the Cuban anger reflected an attitude of condescension verging on racism. The Cubans were displaying what the Soviet leadership believed was typical Latin emotionalism. Mikoyan remarked in a cable to Khrushchev from Havana that "these are good people, but of a difficult character, expansive, emotional, nervous, high-strung, quick to explode in anger, and unhealthily apt to concentrate on trivialities." Often, Mikoyan said, the Cubans' "bitter feelings overcome reason."[17] Such an observation about the Cubans would have reinforced Khrushchev's own judgment.

In his memoirs, the Soviet first secretary described Castro as "a young and hot-headed man."[18] During the November crisis, as Cuba refused to give up the IL-28 bombers that the United States demanded be removed, Khrushchev contemptuously described Castro's assertion of principle in the November 15 letter to U Thant as "just shouting," and he sent a blistering cable to Mikoyan, saying, "We . . . consider that the position of our Cuban friends can never be considered reasonable." He added that "they must show greater flexibility."[19]

Mikoyan understood the Cuban leaders were unhappy because they were neither consulted nor informed about the removal of the missiles; they had to learn about the Kennedy–Khrushchev agreement over the radio, rather than through proper diplomatic channels. But what seemed so odd to the Soviets was how the Cubans dwelled on this diplomatic slight instead of the good news that a nuclear holocaust had been averted. So, on November 5 Guevara tried to help Mikoyan see the Cuban point of view by stating it without diplomatic gloss.

> I think that the Soviet policy had two weak sides. You didn't understand the significance of the psychological factor for Cuban conditions. This thought was expressed in an original way by Fidel Castro: "The USA wanted to destroy us physically, but the Soviet Union with Khrushchev's letter destroyed us legally [iuridicheskii]."

Taken aback, Mikoyan answered, "But we thought that you would be satisfied by our act. We did everything so that Cuba would not be destroyed." Guevara shot back:

> To a certain extent you are right. You offended our feelings by not consulting us. But the main danger is in the second weak side of the Soviet policy. The thing is, you as [much] recognized the right of the USA to violate international law. This is great damage done to your policy. This fact really worries us. It may cause difficulties for maintaining the unity of the socialist countries. It seems to us that there already are cracks in the unity of the socialist camp.[20]

On November 19 Castro tried again to explain to Mikoyan the peculiarity and extremity of the Cuban situation in the crisis:

> It is hard to feel the emotional impact in the Soviet Union, at a distance. Imagine, our soldiers were crying in the trenches because they weren't allowed to shoot at the planes. This had a terrible effect on their morale, and you must bear in mind that the enemy will threaten us for a long time yet. Cubans do not want war. They understand how dangerous it is. However, the people's hatred for the imperialists is so great that it is as if they would prefer even death.

ive thought the Soviet visitor could have empathized with Castro. Af-
r million Soviets had died defending the homeland from the German
World War II. But Castro's point was not merely about patriotism. It
involved an even greater passion about imperialism and what that represented to a
small country like Cuba. So Mikoyan ignored Castro's point and instead asked him,
in effect, to find a way to argue the *Soviet* position to the Cuban people: "You enjoy such great authority and trust that you will be able to bring about the desired
change in the people's mood." Exasperated, Castro replied, "No, I myself am to
blame for the situation that has been created. . . . Cuba cannot be conquered, it can
only be destroyed."[21]

This way of thinking went beyond Mikoyan's frame of reference. Two weeks earlier the Soviet leader had told the Cuban leaders "we will always be with you," by
which he meant that the Soviet state would be ready to provide aid to Cuba. But the
Cuban leadership expected far more, as Che Guevara's caustic and skeptical re-
joinder to Mikoyan revealed. "To the last day?" he asked rhetorically. He and the
Cubans were in a life-and-death struggle. The Soviets clearly wanted no part of it.

For the Cubans, imperialism was not just a slogan or an idea. They had lived under American domination before the Revolution, when the U.S. Congress determined whether Cuban families could eat depending on how the legislators set the
sugar quota. Defense of the homeland did not focus merely on military threats. It
involved securing and preserving Cuba's independence. Powerful countries do not
worry about such a threat; it typically does not even enter into their frame of reference. Their very strength gives them considerable freedom to maneuver. But small
countries must take into account economic, political, and cultural domination as
well as military vulnerability. For Cubans who had recently gained what they believed was their freedom for the first time, the promise of Soviet socialism was that
it would counter U.S. imperialism.

They had believed, until October 28, that the Soviets would feel as they did, because the Soviet Union was the leader of global socialism. They would be willing
to defend Cuba to the death out of a moral obligation as fellow revolutionaries, and
because Cuba represented the future of the movement. Now Mikoyan was explaining that they had deluded themselves about the Soviet Union. He advised them to
"let our enemies die. We must live and live. Live like communists. . . . A maneuver
is not the same as a defeat. . . . We will show our enemies. But we do not want to die
beautifully." But this was not a choice the Cubans felt they had. The Soviet Union
was a large country, a great power. It could absorb defeats. "Sometimes, in order to
take two steps forward," Mikoyan advised, "it is necessary to take a step back."[22]
But for a little country, a defeat by the other superpower could mean annihilation.

Toward the end of the November crisis, Mikoyan decided to see whether Castro
had absorbed the dual message that the Kremlin had wanted him to understand:

the Soviets would give the Cubans the means to defend themselves, but the Soviets would not go to war with the United States over Cuba, or any other issues. "You know Comrade Fidel," Mikoyan said,

> that we have done and shall do all that is necessary for the defense of Cuba. We shall give you people, equipment, weapons, without reckoning the cost. But you must know that we cannot go to nuclear war—that is a line we cannot cross. . . . For Cuba would cease to exist. Many millions of people would perish. The survivors would never forgive the communist leadership for not using all opportunities to avoid war. In that event communism would lose its appeal in people's eyes.[23]

Castro reluctantly accepted this limited offer, but he had little choice at that point. He knew that Kennedy had called a press conference for the next day, and the expectation was that the president was going to announce air strikes against Cuba unless the matter of the IL-28s was settled. In fact he used the press conference to announce that the Soviets had agreed to withdraw the bombers and that he was lifting the naval quarantine imposed at the start of the crisis, six weeks earlier.[24]

Mikoyan had achieved most of his purposes in Cuba. He had prevented Castro from provoking a war, and he had made clear to the Cuban leaders the basis of the Cuban–Soviet relationship. But he would not be able to bring back a clear appreciation of what animated this seemingly unpredictable and irascible ally. In a candid admission to Guevara, the deputy premier said, "I would like to exchange some thoughts with you. . . . Every meeting is very useful for me. . . . When I return to Moscow, I should have the right to say that I understood the Cubans, but I am afraid that when I return I will say that I don't know them, and in fact I will not know them."[25] He was correct. Neither he nor any of the Soviet leaders at the time could comprehend what socialism and independence meant for a little country. Undoubtedly, had any of them been asked, they would not have been able to explain Guevara's comment to a friend two years later, just after Khrushchev's fall from power. "I will never forgive Khrushchev," Guevara said, "for the way he resolved the missile crisis."[26]

The Duty of Every Revolutionary Is to Make Revolution

There could be a temptation to see Guevara as the romantic of the Cuban revolution, an apocalyptic rebel who would rather go down in flames than secure a partial victory.[27] This was clearly Mikoyan's view of him, as someone who wanted "to die beautifully." Guevara's writings provide ample evidence to support this view. One of his most famous statements was the "Message to the Tricontinental," written in Havana just prior to his departure for the Congo in 1965, though not made

public until April 1967, when he was in Bolivia, where he would be killed six
month later. The message almost seems as if it is that of a death foretold:

> How close and bright would the future appear if two, three, many Vietnams, flowered
> on the face of the globe, with their daily quota of death and immense tragedies, with
> their daily heroism, with their repeated blows against imperialism, obliging it to dis-
> perse under the lash of growing hate of the people of the world!
> ... [W]e feel proud at having learned from the Cuban Revolution and its great main
> leader the great lessons to be drawn from Cuba's attitude in this part of the world:
> "What difference the dangers to a man or a people, or the sacrifices they make, when
> what is at stake is the destiny of humanity?" Our every action is a call for war against
> imperialism and a cry for the unity of the peoples against the great enemy of the hu-
> man species: the United States of North America. Wherever death may surprise us, let
> it be welcome if our battle cry has reached even one receptive ear, and another hand
> reaches out to take up our arms, and other men come forward to join in our funeral
> dirge with the chattering of machine guns and new calls for battle and for victory.[28]

Yet Guevara also spoke eloquently about life. This is perhaps most evident in an
essay on "man and socialism in Cuba" that he wrote as a letter to the editor of a
Uruguayan magazine:

> Let me say, with the risk of appearing ridiculous, that the true revolutionary is guided
> by strong feelings of love. It is impossible to think of an authentic revolutionary with-
> out this quality. . . . Revolutionary leaders must have a large dose of humanity, a large
> dose of a sense of justice and truth, to avoid falling into dogmatic extremes, into cold
> scholasticism, into isolation from the masses. They must struggle every day so that
> their love of living humanity is transformed into concrete deeds. . . .[29]

The contrast between the two works seems enormous, which is only to say that
Guevara was an enormously complex person. People with whom he worked in
Cuba have described to us a gentle, generous, forgiving, humorous, and intense
man, a disciplined scientist who was also a poet. Yet Castro has criticized Guevara
for being "reckless" about his own life.[30] Such criticism has led to the supposition
that Guevara and Castro were a kind of "yin" and "yang" of the Cuban Revolution,
with Guevara as the devil-may-care Don Quixote and Castro as the pragmatic man-
ager. In fact, Castro could sound at times as apocalyptic and furious as Guevara, as
damning of imperialism and as fervent about revolution. In the Second Declaration
of Havana, written in response to Cuba's ouster from the OAS in 1962, he asserted:

> The duty of every revolutionary is to make the revolution. It is known that the revolu-
> tion will triumph in America and throughout the world. But it is not for revolutionar-
> ies to sit in the doorways of their houses waiting for the corpse of imperialism to pass

by. The role of Job doesn't suit a revolutionary. . . . But now from one end of the continent to the other they are signaling with clarity that the hour has come—the hour of
their redemption. Now this anonymous mass, this America of color, somber, taciturn
America, which all over the continent sings with the same sadness and disillusion-
ment, now this mass is beginning to enter conclusively into its own history, is beginning to write with its own blood, is beginning to suffer and die for it. . . . For this great
humanity has said "enough" and has begun to march. And their giant march will not
be halted until they conquer true independence—for which they have vainly died
more than once.[31]

Certainly there were differences between Castro and Guevara, but their analysis
of the circumstances in which Cuba found itself, and what it was necessary for
Cuba to do, was remarkably similar. Both were revolutionaries, as were many of the
other Cuban leaders, who envisioned a world in which poor people could aspire to
dignity and independence.[32] Socialism seemed to them the only way to achieve that
goal. But their socialism—especially Castro's—was not learned principally from
books.[33] The language of Marxism, of socialism, was merely a vehicle for expressing their vision. Castro especially also was more concerned about how to achieve
his political goals than about the tidiness of his ideology. "The key to victory" that
Castro had learned from his careful study of prior struggles, historian and filmmaker Saul Landau insightfully explains,

> was national unity, a formula that coincided with Marxism-Leninism as practiced by
> the Soviet leaders. The fact that he was a Marxist and a Leninist, however, did not
> make him different from most other Third World nationalist revolutionaries. . . . This
> revolutionary ideology offered not only the mobilizing rhetoric for anti-imperial cam-
> paigns, but a language for achieving social and economic justice within the emerging
> new system.[34]

Experience also convinced the revolutionaries that their natural enemy was aggressive Western capitalism, which they called imperialism, headquartered in the
United States. Cuba's embrace and incipient leadership of a global socialist movement, they concluded, is what made the small country a threat to the United States.
Resisting this threat thus became a patriotic and moral mission, because if they
were successful, they would enable Cuba to be sovereign and independent and at
the same time make their contribution to the march of international socialism.

In this sense, resistance has been the leitmotif of the Cuban Revolution since
1959, expressed by Cuban leaders thousands of times over the past four decades.
The expression is *"resistir"—to resist*, to stand firm, to dig in the heels, to refuse to
give an inch where matters of moral principle are deemed to be centrally involved,
or when Cuba's security seems to be at risk. Recall that Castro's immediate reaction

to Kennedy's October 22 speech was to call on the Cuban people to *resist*. "If they blockade our country," he said the day following Kennedy's announcement of the quarantine, "they will exalt our nation, because we will *resist*."[35] Cuba's new Soviet allies were doubtless impressed during and after the crisis by this remarkable Cuban capacity to summon the courage to resist, rather than to capitulate or conciliate, even when confronted by what must have seemed like hopeless odds against them.

In fact, the mark of being a Cuban revolutionary has long been similar to that of a resistance fighter, an opponent of tyrannical power. That was one of the distinguishing qualities of José Martí, Cuba's "Apostle of Freedom" who is universally revered for his uncompromising resistance to Spanish rule at the end of the nineteenth century. Castro often appeals to this Cuban sensibility by invoking Martí's name and refers to Martí more than to any other Cuban.[36] Before he was killed in 1895 during Cuba's war for independence, Martí had written about the day when Cuba would face its greatest challenge as an independent nation—resisting "the monster" to the north, avoiding its tentacles and its desire to swallow smaller countries. "The scorn of our formidable neighbor who does not know us," Martí wrote, "is Our America's greatest danger."[37] In fact, following Cuban independence, Cuba *was* more or less "conquered" economically by U.S. business interests. And though it remained nominally independent throughout the first half of the twentieth century, the preponderance of U.S. influence on Cuban affairs was such that Castro's frequent characterization of the period as that of the Cuban "pseudorepublic" is a reasonable one.

In his 1965 "Farewell Letter" to Castro, Guevara underscores his genuine affection for Castro and their shared conception of revolution. He then recalls "the sad and luminous days of the Caribbean crisis."[38] Why the sadness that tinges every memory of those October days? Because that was the shocking moment of truth about the Soviet Union, that its leaders lacked the vision and courage Guevara shared with Castro, and the revolutionary commitment to struggle to the very end, "to the last day," as Guevara said to Mikoyan. The Soviets could not bring themselves to share in the luminosity of the moment, a brilliance that emanated from comrades facing possible death together in a glorious battle. The October Crisis was the moment when the dream that one of the superpowers might help to foster a global revolution disappeared.

COMPETING LESSONS FROM THE CRISIS

This is how it looked from the island of Cuba in November 1962: The Cubans could not fathom that the Soviets believed Kennedy's pledge was even worth the paper on which it was printed. Nevertheless, the Cubans relented over the IL-28 bombers because they had no realistic alternative to doing so. They needed Soviet assistance after the missile crisis more than ever. And the Soviets, under severe criticism from the Chinese and from others in the socialist camp who were aghast at their having backed down in the missile crisis, could ill afford to give the further impression that they were now going to altogether abandon the Cubans to their fate.

And so it went, with the Cubans traumatized by the missile crisis into the unshakable belief that the Soviets were mostly over-the-hill bureaucrats lacking the courage of their supposed convictions, and who could not be trusted either to protect Cuban interests or to promote the kind of world revolution to which the Cubans were devoted. The Soviets, on the other hand, were traumatized by the missile crisis into an equally unshakable belief that the Cubans were a bunch of intransigent, irrational, possibly suicidal wild men who had recklessly helped bring the Soviets and the world to the brink of nuclear extinction, and who, unbelievably, seemed upset that the Soviets had not pushed the world even closer to the brink of nuclear oblivion on behalf of so-called Cuban interests.

The two countries had experienced this one event in remarkably different ways. Understandably, then, the message each derived from it also diverged. These lessons reflected how Cuba and the Soviet Union assessed their own threats and calculated their individual strategies for overcoming these dangers; the value each assigned to revolutionary struggle; and how each hoped to manage the relationship between them, which had become troublesome for both.

Cuba's Lessons from the October Crisis: The Logic of Armed Struggle

1. *Cuban Security*. Cuba's dilemma was daunting. It faced a giant to the north whose power was unparalleled in history. Never before had the United States come so close to imagining its own devastation, and Cuba was the locus for the U.S. trauma. Cuba's military had been much improved between the April 1961 Bay of Pigs invasion and November 1962, and there were nearly 300,000 people who could be placed under arms by drawing on civilian militias. But it still lacked a meaningful air force and navy, and anti-aircraft weaponry. It did not even have the obsolete IL-28s the Soviets retrieved in response to Kennedy's demands, and which Cuba hoped to use against repeated terrorist expeditions. The Soviet betrayal had left the physical continuance of the Castro-led government very much in doubt at the end of 1962, a fact that is easy to overlook now, more than forty years since it came to power.

Meanwhile the Cuban economy was reeling from the shock of losing the United States as its principal trading partner. The entire infrastructure was organized with

U.S. equipment, and the new U.S. embargo was having an impact on the purchase of spare parts. Buses could not run, electrical generators broke down, and even small chores of daily life were becoming monstrous tasks. Trade with the Soviets might provide some relief, but it was far from sufficient to enable Cuba to remake its whole economy.

2. *Soviet Lack of Empathy.* The Cubans concluded—correctly, as it turned out—that the Soviet inability to empathize with Cuba's unique security dilemma—so close to U.S. danger, so far from the Soviet Union—was endemic and irremediable. The Soviet Union, they believed, would never empathize with Cuba's uniquely vulnerable position. It was a Third World country with a limping economy, a population only one-twentieth that of the giant, and a land mass only one-eighty-seventh as large as the continental United States. Cuba had become a declared mortal enemy of the United States, ninety miles from Florida in the very heart of the traditional sphere of U.S. hegemony. In such circumstances, the Cubans understood that they must never appear weak to the United States, because weakness would stimulate the U.S. impulse to try to bring Cuba to heel. The Soviets, who sought both an ally in Cuba and détente with the more powerful Americans, had now demonstrated that in a crunch, they cared a great deal more about their relationship with their superpower adversary than they did about their small socialist ally. This realization was perhaps more shocking to Cubans than any other aspect of the missile crisis. They found that the Soviets were more comfortable, more understanding, more at home, with the American imperialists than with the Cuban socialists.

That recognition had important implications for the way Cuba assessed it could relate to communist parties in Latin America. Since the Soviets preferred to operate internationally almost exclusively via communist parties set up to receive Soviet wisdom and dispense Soviet influence, the Cubans regarded such parties with indifference or even suspicion. As the Soviet Union had demonstrated that it was a status quo power, so parties under its influence and control could hardly be expected to favor armed struggle as the road to revolution. To the entire Cuban revolutionary leadership, but especially to Guevara, membership in a communist party sanctioned by Moscow was to be trusted no more than was their Soviet patron.

3. *Cuban Strategy.* The Soviet betrayal and abandonment of Cuba in the heat of the October Crisis, and their refusal to admit Cuba into the Warsaw Pact, meant that Cuba had to rethink its previous strategy for protecting itself, albeit buttressed now by the promise of newer Soviet arms and expertise. Cuba had to adopt its own variant of what has been called the "strategy of the weak"—in which a relatively less powerful country tries to deter aggression by raising the costs for the aggressor to an unacceptable level in terms of both blood and treasure.[39] Subsequently this

strategy came to be known as "the Cuban style of deterrence."[40] The Cubans sought to convince the United States that any attempt to replace the revolutionary government in Havana would result in "another Vietnam," a protracted guerrilla war that the United States could not "win" without resorting to a level of violence approaching genocide.[41]

At the same time, Cuba would attempt to reduce the capacity—essentially in terms of its political will—of the aggressor to engage the revolutionary government in a sustained campaign. This may have been why Castro seemed eager to respond positively to an intriguing opportunity in 1963 to restore normal relations with the United States.[42] Despite his contempt for the Soviet strategy of peaceful coexistence, peace with the United States would give Cuba time to fashion an independent course of development, one that allowed it to diversify its dependency, reducing the leverage of any single power, and thereby securing Cuba's sovereignty. Normal relations would weaken the justification, and thus the political capacity, for an attack on Cuba. The stillborn attempt at normalization occurred over a six-month period, involved minor celebrities such as ABC reporter Lisa Howard, and ended dramatically with Kennedy's assassination—the news of which Castro heard on the radio as he met with Jean Daniel, a French journalist who carried a message from Kennedy to Castro encouraging the process to continue.[43]

Cuba's strategy of the weak was one of the three reasons it intensified the support for armed struggle in Latin America (later in Africa) after the missile crisis. By fanning the flames of revolution in a wide variety of locations, Cuba would force the Americans to "overextend" themselves in order to suppress the insurrections.[44] The giant's resources for attacking the island would thus be diluted, and its attention would be distracted away from Cuba.

The second reason for armed struggle was psychological: It would raise morale on the island. Cuba would be engaged in an historic mission, fulfilling its destiny, as Martí had envisioned, of bringing independence to the Americas. It would be carrying out the "duty" Castro had proclaimed in the Second Declaration of Havana on February 4, 1962, "to make the revolution."[45]

The third reason emerged out of Cuba's increased understanding that it own internal development was compromised by the dual threat of U.S. aggression and Soviet lack of empathy. It needed an alternative that did not depend on either superpower, which meant that finding allies in the Third World took on greater urgency.[46] This was the same inspiration that had led to the creation of the Non-Aligned Movement (NAM) in 1961.[47] Spearheaded by Yugoslavia, India, Indonesia, and Egypt, twenty-five relatively poor countries feeling trapped in the middle of the U.S.–Soviet Cold War believed that they could create some "space" for themselves if they banded with others in a similar circumstance to provide mutual assistance, or at least political support. Cuba was the only Latin American country to send a full delegation to the first NAM meeting, but it could not rely on the NAM alone. Cuba needed allies who saw the world as it did, who forged their identity in struggle, and shared a commitment to revolution. The support for armed struggle in Asia and Africa, as well as Latin America, could help to foster the emergence of such countries and enable Cuba to develop an alliance on which it might build a new world order uncontrolled by either superpower.[48]

The Cuban Revolution would become the model on which to base all future armed struggles. These would be led by a *foco*, a small guerrilla vanguard that would launch an armed rebellion in the countryside where poverty was experienced most profoundly, and its success would spark others to bring down the illegitimate oligarchs who ruled many of the Latin American countries in a way that served their own narrow interests. This was the mythology of how the Cuban revolutionaries succeeded in removing Fulgencia Batista from power only two years after Castro and Guevara returned from exile to begin the guerrilla struggle in the Sierra Maestre mountains. (In reality, a well-developed urban movement supported the guerrillas, and Cubans had developed a revolutionary tradition dating back at least to the 1933 insurrection, if not as far back as 1868.[49]) The *foco* would invoke the spirit of the Cuban revolution to inspire the whole country to rise up. As Castro argued, "the virus of revolution is not carried in submarines or in ships. It is wafted instead on ethereal waves of ideas. . . . The power of Cuba is the power of its revolutionary ideas, the power of its example."[50]

At the same time Cuba had to consider that activities in Latin America could exacerbate its security dilemma. It would give the United States even more reason to attack the island, and would also be a source of friction with the Soviets, who did not want to play around in the U.S. sphere of influence while they pursued improved relations with the United States. Cuban support for armed struggle in the region would likely increase Soviet pressure on Cuba. Meanwhile, as the United States poured increasing amounts of economic and military assistance into the region to prevent "more Cubas," insurrection became that much more difficult. The multiple reasons for pursuing armed struggle coincided with the decreased attractiveness of Latin America by 1964 and led Cuba to focus its attention on Africa, which is where it devoted considerable energy after 1964, though it neither ended its campaign in the Western Hemisphere nor toned down its rhetoric.[51]

Soviet Lessons from the Missile Crisis: Never Lose Control

In chapter 1 we reviewed some lessons the Soviets derived from the missile crisis about the danger of nuclear war, and what this taught them about how they should relate to the United States. The Caribbean crisis, as they called it, also taught them how they needed to deal with partners whom they believed were subordinate. These can be inferred by examining recently declassified Russian documents from the October 1964 special plenum of the Central Committee of the Communist Party of the Soviet Union, which removed Nikita Khrushchev from power. Of particular interest are the notes for the prosecution regarding the missile crisis, prepared by Central Committee staff member Dmitry Polyanski. The following is a synopsis of what went wrong, according to those implementing the bloodless coup against Khrushchev, along with the lessons to be drawn from Khrushchev's mistakes.[52]

1. *The Missile Crisis Was Too Dangerous.* The missile gambit, far from being the great victory claimed by Khrushchev, was actually the worst humiliation suffered heretofore in the Cold War by the Soviet Union. "Not having any way out," reads the anti-Khrushchev brief, "we had to accept every demand and condition dictated by the United States."[53] One of Khrushchev's principal errors—his so-called adventurism—was going around party procedures in both the Soviet Union and in Cuba and cutting what amounted to a personal deal with Castro and his colleagues in Cuba. The operation was insane from beginning to end: deploying ballistic missiles to America's back door, at a time when the Soviets were so inferior to the United States in deliverable nuclear weapons, was much too dangerous. Khrushchev's claim that the endeavor was successful in reality was hollow; Kennedy's pledge not to invade Cuba was empty and worthless. It was stupid and nearly treasonous to rely so heavily on Castro, who had to be regarded as a loose cannon and who might in the future lead the Soviets into other dangerous adventures. From then on, Castro had to be kept on a much tighter rein, in order to prevent the Cubans from raising the risk of another dangerous confrontation with the United States.

2. *Soviet Interests Paramount.* Khrushchev (and by implication, Castro and his colleagues) simply forgot that within the world socialist movement, Soviet security interests must always be paramount. If the Soviet Union, the historic and acknowledged leader of the movement, were threatened with extinction, as it was in the missile crisis, then the movement itself is also threatened with extinction. What is good for the Soviet Union is, therefore, good for all allies of the Soviet Union, but *not* vice versa. In his wild enthusiasm for supporting national liberation movements, especially those of interest to the Cubans in Latin America, Khrushchev had forgotten this fundamental wisdom, according to the brief against the Soviet leader. It asserted that "any one of our marshals or generals . . . will tell you that plans for 'military penetration' of South America were gibberish, fraught with enormous danger of war."[54] So: forget about liberation movements and their fiery Castroist allies, and deal with these areas on a party-to-party basis only, with control lodged firmly within the International Department of the Communist Party of the Soviet Union— that is, under the direction of those who understand that the paramount Soviet

interest is not raising hell in the Third World, but first and foremost avoiding dangerous confrontations with the other superpower.

3. *The Soviet Line Must Be Cuba's Line.* If Cuba is to remain within the Soviet sphere of influence and control, while inextricably deep in the heart of the traditional U.S. sphere of influence, then the Cubans must be made to adhere absolutely to a line laid down in Moscow. Any other course, as the missile crisis demonstrated conclusively, was simply too dangerous—too threatening to the Soviet Union itself, and thus to the worldwide movement which it led. Quoting Lenin, the anti-Khrushchev brief stated, "we must exhibit stable and peaceful moods, because the imperialists will exploit every possibility to launch a war"—a prophecy that seemed to be confirmed by the missile crisis.[55] So, no more Cuban adventures, no more risky schemes with doubtful payoffs. And by implication, if Castro and his colleagues cannot play by these rules, then either the Soviets must abandon their Cuban investment or, less embarrassingly, perhaps a Cuban with good communist credentials could be found who could lead his country in a manner more to the liking of Cuba's Soviet patron.

In fact such a Cuban was waiting in the wings. Aníbal Escalante had been a leader of the Popular Socialist Party (PSP), the communist party in prerevolutionary Cuba. Castro had subsumed the PSP under an amalgamated party, the Integrated Revolutionary Organizations (ORI) in 1961. The ORI included members of the PSP, the Students' Revolutionary Directorate, and Castro's July 26th Movement. Escalante became organization secretary of the new party, and in this capacity he recruited new members who took direction from him, using PSP party cells (called "nuclei") to build a base of power within the ORI and over governmental administrators.[56]

Castro saw the threat this development posed to his own power fairly late, after it had gone a considerable distance. When he did recognize it, in March 1962, he ousted Escalante and his followers—the so-called sectarians—from the ORI leadership and exiled Escalante to the Soviet Union, via Prague. This group obviously had to lay low after that, and its views of the missile crisis certainly were not publicized at the time. Yet Escalante would return to Cuba in 1964, and would in 1967–68 try again to challenge Castro's leadership by pushing a pro-Soviet program among the party members, and by working to promote within the party those inclined to pro-Soviet views. Recall that Escalante's effort was the proximate reason for the Central Committee to meet in January 1968, when Castro made his secret speech on the October Crisis.

There is every reason to believe that Escalante embraced the Soviet analysis of the missile crisis and fully endorsed the Soviet lessons, and that he saw himself as the one Cuban communist who might conceivably lead Cuba into the path of "true" communism—that is, to a relationship with the Soviet Union similar to the Czech or East German, in which there was rarely a failure to adhere closely to the Soviet line. Escalante was in Moscow during the missile crisis. According to at least one highly placed Cuban source, he began lobbying the Soviets even before the crisis was over, possibly when the Cubans dug in their heels in November 1962, creating a new crisis for the Soviets by refusing to accept American dictates. Fabio Grobart, a close associate of Castro, told American journalist Tad Szulc in 1985 that Escalante was a "saboteur" who, while in Moscow in 1962 and after, "tried to make himself appear as a friend of the Soviet Union, and to throw garbage and mud at the Revolution, saying, 'You know, they [Castro and his associates] are anti-Soviet,' and so on. . . . He tried to present himself as the true defender of the Soviet Union. . . ."[57]

Having thus found like-minded comrades in Moscow during and immediately after the missile crisis, Escalante returned to Cuba in 1964, following Castro's visit to Moscow in January. His brother, Cesar Escalante, a faithful and much honored Cuban communist, had recently died of cancer, and the trip home ostensibly was intended to handle his deceased brother's affairs. That Escalante was allowed to return to Cuba at all would seem to indicate a certain amount of Soviet leverage in the matter.

The Missile Crisis Shadow after October/November 1962

Both the Cubans and the Soviets vowed after the crisis never to allow anything like it to happen again. But rather than bringing them together around a common objective, their discrepant memories of the crisis made the management of their relationship after October 1962 mightily challenging, to say the least. The main strands of the incommensurable memories in the Cuban–Soviet relationship after the trauma of the October missile crisis were these: when the Cubans remembered the missile crisis and thought "never again," they vowed never again to trust the Soviets, never to let the stolid, spineless Soviets control events that affected them centrally; when the Soviets remembered the crisis and thought "never again," they vowed never again to let the meteoric, irrational Cubans draw them into policies or situations that put Soviet national interests at risk, or risked a serious breach in Soviet relations with the United States. These incommensurable memories of the crisis—the Cuban memory and the Soviet memory—provided the essential tension which characterized their relations thereafter.[58]

There is something almost breathtaking about the audacity of Cuba's response to what they regarded as Soviet betrayal and abandonment during the missile crisis. Left starkly alone at the moment of truth, the Cubans did not seek to ameliorate their situation by placating the United States (except for the brief flirtation with normalization) and U.S.-backed governments in Latin America, or by promising the Soviets that they would be more obedient in the future. Instead, Cuba defied both superpowers, in effect, daring the United States in word and deed to go ahead and try to remove the Castro government and replace it with another "puppet" regime; and challenging the Soviets at every opportunity to change their stolid, sclerotic, party-oriented ways and join the true revolutionaries of the 1960s—the Cubans. They were driven by a primal-like force, a determination to be free from both superpowers, each of which demanded its own kind of subservience as the price for peace. Superficially, Cuba's relations with the two giants seemed diametrically opposed. The United States and Cuba were enemies, and the Soviet Union and Cuba were nominally partners. But Cuba regarded both with the wary eye of the hunted.

Of course, the Soviets wished to aid Cuba and to keep it firmly in the Soviet camp. Despite the challenges Cuba threw at the Soviets, the "Siberian Communists" (as some Cubans called them) did provide the "Caribbean communists" with the materials necessary for protecting the island from U.S. aggression, for building itself domestically, and even for promoting and assisting revolutions—revolutions that the Soviets often assessed would create more risks than any potential gains. Cuba's need to accept Soviet largesse, and its fear that the aid would be used to control Cuba, produced one set of strains in the relationship. The Soviet's frustration, in not being able to secure more control as a result of the aid, generated another.

This stress in Cuban–Soviet relations after the missile crisis provided Cuba and the Soviet Union with its essential joint task: managing the relationship in such a way as to prevent the tension from becoming so taut that the ties would snap. Virtually every issue, every episode, every negotiation, every exchange of views could suddenly become tense, trying, and difficult for both sides. Every discussion, no matter what the subject, stood a chance of exploding into a confrontation. In this way the shadow of the missile crisis, etched indelibly in their minds and hearts, drove everything. October 1962, everyone on both sides believed, was the moment when each came within a hair's breadth of ceasing to exist, of being destroyed forever. The Soviets laid the blame for the close call with oblivion on the Cubans' lack of caution and common sense. The Cubans held the Soviets accountable for their near demise due to a lack of courage and basic honesty. Each thereby held the other *responsible* for the indelible horror of October 1962, and each was hypervigilant thereafter about the possibility of something like it happening again. In this way, the shadow of the missile crisis descended on the Cuban–Soviet relationship, its presence often unacknowledged, but its intensity and pivotal significance never forgotten.

What Nikita Khrushchev and his colleagues in the Soviet leadership clearly did not foresee was the degree to which the Cuban tradition of resisting attempts by outside countries or organizations to impose their will on Cuba would also apply to *them*—to Cuba's Soviet ally. In October and November 1962, the Cubans, in the

Soviets' way of thinking, resisted with almost pathological obstinacy attempts by Khrushchev in Moscow, and Mikoyan in Havana, to obtain Cuban acquiescence to the deal that Khrushchev and Kennedy had agreed to without either consulting or even adequately informing the Cuban leadership. As the Soviets were to discover throughout the 1960s, this pattern would recur, and each time the Cubans felt every bit as exalted in resisting the Soviets as they did in resisting the Americans.

Political scientist Jorge Domínguez argues convincingly that the history of Cuban–Soviet relations between 1962 and 1968 can be seen as the often unsuccessful effort by each side to "to manage the debris of the November 1962 crisis."[59] As Castro told his colleagues in the Cuban leadership in his secret speech of January 1968, dealing with the Soviets was in some ways more difficult than dealing with the Americans. The struggle with the Americans entailed clear expectations and the fist of the Cuban "David" could be shaken at the U.S. "Goliath" publicly, with gusto, in front of millions of cheering Cubans.[60] But beginning with the missile crisis, as Castro explained to the Cuban leadership in January 1968, a herculean effort had to be made by Cuba to build "our resolve to prevent relations with that ally from deteriorating to the point of rupture. . . . [W]e had to dissemble, contain, hold back our indignation, our outrage."

Cuban Resistance to Soviet "Imperialism"

But what *was* it about the Soviets that required constant suppression of the urge to publicly rage against them? Why did the Cubans privately and regularly refuse to go along with conditions the Soviets established for the assistance they gave to Cuba? In particular, what was the Cubans' perception of the Soviets in the critical period of 1962–1968, when each side was engaged in "managing the debris of the November 1962 crisis"? What was all that pent-up Cuban anger *about*? Cuban officials almost never discussed this issue in any detail publicly during the Cold War, and for the same reason they gave into Mikoyan in Havana in November 1962, because to do otherwise was, the Cubans were convinced, to invite another betrayal and abandonment by the Soviets, which might in turn embolden the United States to move quickly to apply all its power to eliminate the Castro government and destroy the Cuban Revolution.

With the demise of the Soviet Union, however, some Cuban officials who worked with the Soviets throughout the nearly three decades of their relationship have been willing to reveal their impressions. Jorge Pollo worked for nearly thirty years with East Bloc countries, including the Soviets, as a senior staff member of the Central Committee of the Cuban Communist Party. During the course of an interview with us in Havana, he remarked ironically that "history has yet to record whether Cuba has suffered more from U.S. imperialism or Soviet friendship." When we laughed in response, he added that he was serious. We asked him to tell us what led him to this conclusion.

> In the end, we usually achieved most of the objectives that we set for ourselves in our negotiations with Soviet leaders. But almost never without a struggle, without moments in which our whole relationship with them came close to a complete rupture. This was especially true between 1962 and 1968—between the October missile crisis and the Czech invasion in August 1968. All through this period, our relationship with the Soviets was very, very tense. What caused all the tension, all the difficulties? You have to recognize that in the Soviet Union the psychology of the Great Power dominated. That is a historical fact. Russia was a Great Power. Russia was an imperial power. So obviously, if you are a Great Power, your psychology—the psychology of the strong, of the victor—is not the same as the psychology of a vanquished or colonized country. Russian political culture was thoroughly imperialist, no more or less so than the United States, as we unfortunately had to learn in the 1960s. Now, if you are an imperialist, you may be able to animate political ideas—essentially socialist ideas—that are more or less progressive from the social point of view—I mean in your own country, in Russia. But you see, your psychology, your history, and your culture all will induce you to believe, maybe even unconsciously, that you have a right to impose that idea on me, on a small, relatively weak former colony like Cuba. That is the imperialist logic. But it is not my logic, not the logic of a victim of imperialist occupation and exploitation, especially a country like Cuba which is still in danger of being recolonized [by the United States]. Not at all. No matter how benevolent may be the purpose of the imperial power, I believe—everyone in Cuba believes—that you have absolutely no right to impose your belief on me. You may in time be able to convince me that I should, of my own accord, adopt your program, your idea. But you cannot impose it on me, and I will resist all of your attempts to do so. And this was what the Russians had to learn about us in the 1960s. In this way the Russians, in dealing with Cuba over the past thirty years—but especially between 1962 and 1968—were victims of their own imperialist psychology. They were also victims of their own ignorance. Being an imperial power, the Russians usually did not think it was necessary to try to fully understand why Cuba took the positions it took. Being an imperial power, they had no clue what it was like for us to continue to resist and exist in the shadow of the United States—why we could not and did not ever show weakness of any kind, for fear that the United States would take it as a signal that they could now try to destroy our revolution, once and for all. Yes, that period between 1962 and 1968, that was a difficult period. There were so many instances when our relations with the Russians hung by a slender thread.[61]

Now we understood Pollo's enigmatical remark: that Cuba had suffered greatly from both Soviet friendship and U.S. imperialism. In his view, which we believe was (and remains) the dominant view in Cuba, Soviet friendship and Soviet imperialism were essentially the same thing. Or to put it another way: the price of Soviet friendship was having to resist when possible, and reluctantly to endure when necessary, the arrogance, paternalism, and condescension typical of any imperial power.

The day after our interview with Pollo, riding from the Hotel Nacional in the Vedado section of Havana to José Martí Airport, we encountered several billboards that read: *"Everything on this island is 100% Cuban!"* This was a bit of postmodern wisdom that, while apparently at variance from the physical facts, still revealed something psychologically true about the Cubans' own sense of their relations with the Russians over the previous thirty years, something the Soviets, encased in the bell jar of their imperial mindset, never grasped, at least not to the extent that would have been required to elicit trust from the Cubans.

As the Cubans saw it, therefore, the Soviets learned essentially nothing about their new Cuban ally from the missile crisis. For Cuba had, at a moment of tremendous tension and danger, defied the Soviets utterly. How then could they have failed to notice, as Jorge Pollo said in the same interview, "that Cuba was not Hungary, that Cuba was not Romania, that Cuba was not Poland"?[62] He got his answer, he said, on a vacation in East Germany (his first visit to Eastern Europe), back in the 1960s. "It was immediately clear to me," he recalled, "that I had landed in an *occupied* country, a country in complete subjugation to the imperial Soviet Union."[63] He mentioned this to his wife, who became frightened, he said, that someone would hear him and that they would not be allowed to return to Cuba. She made him promise not to utter the words again, until their return flight had landed in Havana—a promise he said he kept.

The Soviets, in other words, simply could not, from the Cuban perspective, break their old "imperial" habits. They did not grasp the full significance of Cuba's uniqueness: that Cuban socialism was homegrown, rather than imposed by the Soviets at the point of a gun; and that *because* it was not a country that was occupied by the Red Army, yet was a mere ninety miles from the United States, its security was always precarious, and required a total commitment to resisting any and all attempts by the United States to intimidate or destroy it. But that kind of total commitment is exactly what the Cubans believed the Soviets had pledged to Cuba when it had accepted the nuclear missiles in 1962, fully aware that it was transforming itself into a target for U.S. nuclear missiles. Instead, in the Great Betrayal of October 1962, the Soviet imperialists rescinded their pledge to their fraternal socialist ally in return for a pledge from the other imperialist superpower, the United States, not to attack or invade Cuba.

Thus, as Jorge Pollo emphasized, the abandonment of Cuba in the missile crisis was only one-half of the Cuban prosecutory brief against the Soviets. The other half was equally revealing and significant to the Cubans: the Soviets were not only unfaithful and unreliable, they were imperialists. Just imagine the Cuban mindset at

that moment, having realized all this *and* also having concluded that without massive and continuing Soviet assistance, the Cuban Revolution might in fact be
doomed. This revelation must have arrived in October and November 1962 with
the force of a bucket of cold water in the face; the missile crisis revealed Cuba and
its Revolution to be trapped in a kind of pincer movement between two global superpowers, one of which was determined to destroy it economically, politically, and
(possibly) militarily, while the other wanted, in effect, to dilute, trivialize, and ultimately control a people and revolution that they did not understand, nor—as the
Cubans believed—did they want to understand.

The Heart of the Matter: Peaceful Coexistence versus Armed Struggle

The significance of the Cuban proclivity to resist any and all attempts by their
new "imperial" ally to control them after the missile crisis was this: the activity that
the Soviets most sought to control—Cuban involvement in and support for national
liberation movements—was precisely the activity the Cubans viewed as central to
their own security. This was the fundamental contradiction between what the Soviets believed they needed to enhance their own security vis-à-vis the United States,
and what the Cubans believed they needed to enhance their security, also vis-à-vis
the United States.

The Soviets after the missile crisis eagerly sought rapprochement with the
United States via the establishment of ongoing arms control negotiations and agreements, and also by trying to clamp down on national liberation movements (a key
demand made by the United States). In many ways, the mutual U.S.–Soviet pursuit
of what came to be called "peaceful coexistence" can be traced to the nuclear
endgame of the Cuban missile crisis. The Cubans, on the other hand, realized that
they needed Soviet arms, know-how, and materiel to deter a U.S. attack and invasion. So a wholesale repudiation of the Soviets was, as Castro emphasized at length
to the Cuban leadership in his secret speech of January 1968, simply out of the
question. They desperately needed the Soviets to give them the means to defend
and develop themselves.

But "peaceful coexistence" was absolutely anathema to Cuba after the missile crisis.
To the Cubans, the term simply meant collusion between the two imperialist superpowers and deals made at the expense of the small, the weak, the poor—countries such
as Cuba—exactly as Americans and Soviets had done in October 1962. It meant accepting U.S. domination of at least the Western Hemisphere. Even though Castro
sought to normalize relations with the United States, he would not have accepted it ultimately at the price of Cuban principles, if it had meant acquiescing in U.S. imperialism. In other words, the Cubans resisted the very idea of "peaceful coexistence" upon
which U.S.–Soviet relations were to become based after the missile crisis.

But in addition to the obvious security implications for such countries and peoples, Castro's ferocious attack on "peaceful existence" allowed him adroitly to usurp the moral high ground of the socialist movement from the Soviets from the very early days after the triumph of the Revolution. Castro hurled his thunderbolts of *moral* outrage as if Havana were some Third World Olympus, and he did so on behalf of countries and peoples that had been exploited as Cuba had been exploited. And not only moral outrage, but a call to arms to follow Cuba and take up the armed struggle immediately as a right and duty of oppressed peoples, the Great Powers—including the Russian Great Power leading the socialist bloc—be damned.

As we emphasized earlier in this chapter, Castro characterized "peaceful coexistence"—and the socialist passivity it implied—as an accommodation with a mortal enemy. His charge in the "Second Declaration of Havana"—that "the duty of every revolutionary is to make the revolution"—came just two months after Castro declared that he would "be a Marxist-Leninist until the day I die" and three months before the Soviets made their fateful offer to deploy nuclear missiles in Cuba.[64] As Jorge Pollo notes, the "imperial" Soviets often seemed to him not to believe they needed to understand their new Caribbean ally. Had the Soviets felt the need for empathy with the Cubans, and had they read carefully the text of a document like the "Second Declaration of Havana," they might have had second thoughts about getting involved with these Caribbean radicals.

Perhaps they did not believe that Castro and the Cubans believed what they said. Or maybe the Russians thought that the Cubans could in time be brought around to relinquishing such incendiary views—views which, if acted upon within the context of a Soviet–Cuban alliance, would greatly inhibit Soviet attempts at rapprochement with the United States. After all, they may have convinced themselves that Mikoyan, the "old Bolshevik," had brought the Cubans around in November 1962.

U.S. Senator J. William Fulbright (D-AR) once remarked that while Castro's anti-imperialist fulminations, and Cuba's actions, were a thorn in the side of the United States, they were far from being a dagger in its heart.[65] But in light of Jorge Pollo's summary of Cuba's analysis of its "imperial" Soviet ally, it is obvious that Castro's unqualified endorsement of armed struggle, on the Cuban model, may well have felt to the Russians more like a dagger struck at the heart of the world socialist movement, which they presumed to lead, rather than a mere thorn in the flesh. For after the missile crisis, Castro became ever bolder, ever more critical of what he almost always called "the socialist bloc" (rather than naming the Soviets directly) for its alleged abandonment of the oppressed of the world, in favor of better relations with its imperialist cousin, the United States. From the Cuban perspective, the history of international relations *after* the missile crisis was in danger of becoming the missile crisis writ very large—on a hemispheric, or even a global scale.

There were other dimensions of the dysfunctional Cuban–Soviet relationship as well. These included: Soviet pressure on Cuba to "rationalize" what seemed to the Soviets as chaotic and inefficient economic arrangements; Castro's ideological heresies, regarded by the Soviets as hopelessly naive and anarchic; and the Cuban leadership's hostility to old-line, Soviet-trained communists in Cuba, and to Soviet-controlled communist parties throughout Latin America.

But there is no doubt that the issue—the piece of missile crisis "debris"—these new allies had the most difficulty in managing was the irreconcilable contradiction at the very core of their relationship: the Russians, deeply sobered, even frightened by their evident inferiority to U.S. power in the missile crisis, sought above all else to improve their relations with the Americans; while the Cubans were deeply sobered too, they were also angry about how the Soviets betrayed and abandoned them in the crisis. Henceforth the Cubans would increasingly follow their own instincts regarding Cuban security. They would begin by fanning the flames of revolution whether the Americans (or Soviets) liked it or not, and they would do so both for reasons of state security and reasons of moral principle.

A BRIEF HISTORY OF TIME (SPENT RESISTING THE RUSSIANS): JANUARY 1963–APRIL 1967

It is not our intention here to provide anything like a comprehensive history of this most combative period of an always difficult relationship. This history has been well told from several different perspectives.[66] But we can suggest something of the tone and substance of the downward trajectory of the relationship in the years immediately after the missile crisis.

In the beginning of their joint effort to manage the "debris" of the missile crisis, Cuban resistance was directed at what Havana saw as Soviet errors of *commission*, such as Castro's discovery in May 1963 that missiles in Cuba had been "traded" for NATO missiles in Turkey, and the U.S.–Soviet Limited Test Ban Treaty of 1963. After that, however, the Cubans became increasingly bold in their public critique of Soviet errors of *omission*, mainly what they took to be Soviet passivity, even timidity, in the face of increasing U.S. actions in Vietnam and elsewhere.

The latter form of Cuban resistance to the Russian "line," to alleged Soviet errors of omission, became increasingly blatant, caustic, and thus ever harder for the Soviets to tolerate in silence. Cuba, in public statements by both Castro and Guevara (and occasionally by others as well), issued regularly with increasingly transparent accusations against their Soviet patron. The Cuban critique might be summarized this way: The Soviet Union had forsaken its radical Leninist roots and become a flaccid and cowardly Stalinist fortress. The Cubans viewed the Soviets as interested in little more than the safety of the national borders of the Soviet Union, and in retaining control over communist parties elsewhere, which the Soviets' sought, in the Cubans' view, to mold in their own pitiful image.

In spite of the way he had treated Cuba in the resolution of the missile crisis, Khrushchev was, as a longtime Soviet Cuba hand Karen Brutents said in an interview, "an original person—what in Russia is called 'a man from the earth.' He loved the excitement of the Cuban 'experiment.' He had a good relationship with Fidel."[67] Sergo Mikoyan, son of Anastas Mikoyan and for many years the editor of *Latinskaya amerika* (the official Soviet journal of Latin American affairs), agrees. According to Mikoyan:

> Khrushchev was a romantic. For the post-Khrushchev leadership [of Leonid Brezhnev and Aleksei Kosygin], the idea of revolution was a fantasy of their fathers. They were also more calculating and didn't like the financial side of the relationship. They couldn't really say "no" to Cuba, but they didn't like it. They couldn't say "no" because Cuba was important in the Third World, and they couldn't risk looking like a traitor to Cuba.[68]

The Cuban critique of the Soviets in fact became especially virulent and unrelenting after Khrushchev was deposed in October 1964 and replaced by Leonid Brezhnev as general secretary (he changed the title from first secretary) and Aleksei Kosygin as premier.[69] These thunderous and defiant Cuban pronouncements transformed Castro and Cuba, in the minds of the new Soviet leadership, from something like a socialist thorn in their side into a dagger poised to strike at the heart of their presumption to lead a worldwide movement claiming to be governed by Marxist-Leninist principles. By the spring of 1967, what Jorge Pollo called the "slender thread" holding together the Soviets' relationship with the Cubans was in this fashion stretched nearly to the breaking point.

The following annotated chronology lists some of the key moments of Cuban resistance to Soviet "imperial" admonitions, policy, or preferences. They represent some of the more notable episodes in the downward spiral of Cuban–Soviet relations after the missile crisis. Suffice it to say that this "sampler" of Cuban resistance to the Soviets could be greatly expanded.

- *Castro in Moscow, April–May 1963*. Castro visited the Soviet Union for the first time in 1963. He was lavishly and enthusiastically received. Yet Castro's principal recollection of that visit seems to have been his discovery, due to a slip of the tongue by Khrushchev, of yet another dimension to Soviet duplicity and betrayal in the missile crisis. He learned that in a secret protocol, the

Soviets "traded" missiles with the United States: the Soviets agreeing to re-move theirs from Cuba, and the United States agreeing to remove NATO mis-siles from Turkey and Italy. Castro still bristles at the thought of Cuba having been used as a kind of "bargaining chip" in the resolution of the missile crisis. Khrushchev had written a long letter to the Cuban leader in January 1963, in which he acknowledged Castro's anger and extended the invitation for the trip.[70] Castro was able to parlay the Soviet leader's effort to appease him into a significant increase in Soviet aid and, quite reluctantly, acquiescence in Cas-tro's demand that some Soviet troops remain in Cuba to act as a trip wire. Still, as a result of learning about the Turkish missile trade, he returned to Cuba with an even greater appreciation of the extent and dimensions of the Soviet abandonment of Cuba the previous autumn, and was determined not to let the Soviets control the manner in which Cuba pursued its own security interests.

- *Cuba Rejects Arms Control Treaties, September–October 1963*. On September 28, Castro announced that Cuba's situation, so near to a hostile and powerful United States—that is, living "in the neighborhood of Yankee imperialism"—required that Cuba refuse to sign the Limited Test Ban Treaty the Soviets had just negotiated with the Kennedy administration—the first significant arms control agreement of the nuclear era.[71] Then, on October 7, Carlos Lechuga, the Cuban ambassador to the UN, announced that Cuba would not endorse a Mexican resolution declaring Latin America a nuclear-free zone, which was supported by both the United States and Soviet Union.[72] (This initiative led to the 1967 Treaty of Tlateloco.) Thus, as the Soviet effort to develop a work-ing relationship with the United States in arms control began to succeed, Cuba, already the Soviet Union's most voluble and unruly ally, formally repu-diated all of it as antithetical to Cuban security. Cuba did participate in subse-quent Tlatelolco treaty meetings as an observer, but claimed that given the U.S. nuclear threat (and implicitly the Soviet unwillingness to shield Cuba with its nuclear umbrella), Cuba would not foreclose any options that might bring it added security from U.S. pressure or outright aggression.[73]

- *Intensified U.S. Covert Action against Cuba, 1963–1965*. In mid-1963, the Kennedy administration decided to renew support for efforts to destabilize the Cuban government via covert action. The operation was based in several Central American countries and continued the efforts that were begun before the missile crisis, under the code name *Mongoose*.[74] At the same time the CIA continued to pursue its campaign to assassinate Castro.[75] These activities readily recalled for Cubans U.S. preparations for a seeming invasion in 1962. In fact, Cuban intelligence learned of a plan that was initiated in late 1964 to launch a second invasion of the island using Cuban exiles headquartered in

Costa Rica and Nicaragua. According to Tad Szulc, who broke the story in 1974, the plan was scuttled when civil war broke out in the Dominican Republic in April 1965, which led to U.S. intervention there.[76] Taken together, the disparate efforts reinforced the Cubans' conviction that the United States was a mortal enemy and that Moscow's efforts to placate Washington were antithetical to Cuban interests.

- *Cuba Rejects Soviet "Formalistic" Communism, January 2, 1965.* On this, the sixth anniversary of the triumph of the Cuban Revolution, Castro delivered a blistering critique of what he called the "exclusively formal or formalistic character" of Soviet communism. He warned his fellow Cubans that the day might come, perhaps sooner rather than later when, due to irreconcilable differences between Cuba and "the socialist camp," Cuba would be forced to rely entirely on its own resources to defend itself from "the threat of imperialist aggression" and also to meet its domestic needs. In short, Castro concluded, the Soviet Union had gone astray in its interpretation of Marx and Lenin, and the sclerotic bureaucrats in charge in Moscow had lost touch with the needs of their own people, and socialist nations worldwide. This would not happen in Cuba, Castro argued. Instead, Cuba "must find solutions which bring about the unity of form and substance, and not the divorce between form and substance."[77] Translation: the Cubans would resist all attempts by Moscow to "sovietize" Cuban institutions. This would be an important aspect of Cuba's never-ending struggle to retain its independence, even if the Russians should—as Castro warned they might—pull out of Cuba altogether.

- *Guevara in Algiers, February 26, 1965.* According to Guevara, "There are no boundaries in this struggle to the death. . . . The development of countries now starting out on the road to liberation should be paid for by the socialist countries. . . . The socialist countries have the moral duty of liquidating their tacit complicity with the exploiting countries of the West."[78] This was a frontal attack on the Soviet Union. In effect, Guevara, speaking on behalf of the Cuban government, indicted the Soviets not only for having regressive ideological views, but also for their moral culpability in having any commerce at all with the West—for not directing all their energy and resources toward liberation movements. The Russians complained bitterly about Guevara's remarks to Cuban Defense Minister Raul Castro, who was in Moscow. But *Revolución*, the official newspaper, reprinted Guevara's speech, remarking that it was "very important." Castro symbolically embraced this view by going to the airport to welcome Guevara home. The day before, on March 13, 1965, Castro delivered an equally tough attack against the Soviets declaring "We're no one's satellite and never will be."[79]

- *U.S. Interventions in Vietnam and the Dominican Republic, February–April 1965.* The events of early 1965 offered further confirmation of the main lesson the Cubans had drawn from the missile crisis: that despite massive Soviet aid and assistance, they stood essentially alone with regard to the threat from the United States. First, on February 7, the United States began the bombing program that would soon grow into an expanded campaign against North Vietnam known as *Rolling Thunder*, the relentless, three-year air war against North Vietnam. In late March, the first U.S. Marines waded ashore at Danang, in northern South Vietnam, the first step toward the Americanization of the ground war in Southeast Asia. And on April 28, 4,500 U.S. troops intervened in the Dominican Republic, inevitably raising the specter in Havana that Cuba might be next.[80]

  All of this, as Castro emphasized in speeches on May 1 and 13, was done without the allegedly fraternal and unified socialist camp (i.e., the Soviet Union) lifting a finger to oppose the United States. On May 1, he lambasted the Soviets in all but name for allowing the invasion and occupation of the Dominican Republic by U.S. troops. In a manner recalling his stance in the missile crisis, he urged the Soviets to threaten the United States with nuclear annihilation, as a way to "cut off the hands of the imperialists."[81] But this is of course what Khrushchev had unwittingly threatened in October 1962 and, given the results, no Soviet leader would ever do it again. In a speech on March 13, Castro contrasted Cuban courage in accepting the missiles, at tremendous risk, with the Soviets' cowardly retreat when the United States applied pressure. In drawing the analogy to Vietnam, he asserted: "Who benefits from this [inaction]? The imperialists. Who are the victims? The Vietnamese. And what suffers? The prestige of socialism. . . ."[82]

- *Guevara's "Farewell Letter" Made Public, October 3, 1965.* The "Farewell Letter" of Che Guevara was delivered to Castro in April 1965. The Cuban leader revealed its contents publicly in early October, reading it aloud during a Cuban television program announcing the installation of the newly established Cuban Communist Party. Recalling the missile crisis, Guevara told Castro: "I felt at your side the pride of belonging to our people in the sad and luminous days of the Caribbean crisis."[83] But in a key passage, Guevara wrote: "Other nations of the world call for my modest efforts. I can do that which is denied you because of your responsibility as the head of Cuba, and the time has come for us to part . . . to fight against imperialism wherever it may be."[84] At the moment the letter was revealed, Guevara was already deeply involved in an odyssey that would result in a failed effort to foment revolution in the Congo and conclude with the failed effort in Bolivia, where he was killed, along with all but three of his compatriots. Guevara's letter and Castro's enthusiastic endorsement of its stated intent represented a flagrant flaunting of established Soviet policy toward the Third World, which was to establish a party they could control, which might gain in stature and power surreptitiously, so as not to compromise the top Soviet priority—good relations with the United States. In case the Russians missed the point, Castro shoved it in their faces by declaring during his presentation: "We aspire not only to a communist society but to a communist world in which all nations will have equal rights," he asserted. "We aspire to a free society of free nations in which all the countries, large and small, will have equal rights. We will defend our points of view as we have defended them up to now. . . . This revolution was not imported from anywhere. . . . Nobody told us how we must carry it out. . . . And nobody will have to tell us how me must continue to carry it out."[85]

• *The "Tricontinental Conference," Havana, January 3–15, 1966.* This conference, attended by more than 500 delegates from the "tricontinent" of Africa, Asia, and Latin America, represented Cuba's attempt to seize the institutional initiative away from the Soviets, and to begin to organize (with Cuban leadership) an alternative to the moribund, Soviet-controlled system of communist parties on each of the three constituents of the "tricontinent." The Tricontinental, as an organization, was dedicated to carrying out armed struggle everywhere it seemed possible to do so. Until this meeting, the Soviets believed they had papered over its differences with Cuba on the matter of armed struggle by resolving at a December 1964 meeting of Latin American communist parties that while armed struggle was a valid means of achieving socialism, the appropriate means were to be assessed by each communist party. Cuba, moreover, had agreed to deal only with the established communist parties in Latin America.[86] While the Tricontinental Conference was fully endorsed by the Soviet Union, which hoped the conference would undermine China's influence with revolutionary movements (and which it apparently did), the Soviets were taken aback by the barely veiled criticisms of its allegedly weak support for North Vietnam. The conference also created a new organization, headquartered in Havana, to support armed revolutionary activity throughout the world, and the organization's executive secretariat had only three representatives from communist parties—Cuba, North Vietnam, and North Korea, all of whom were critical of the Soviet Union.[87] In a call for armed struggle in every Latin American country, Castro concluded the conference (which included a hapless Soviet delegation led by Candidate Politburo member Sharaf Rashidov) by fervently criticizing the Latin American communist parties: "if there is less of resolutions and possibilities and dilemmas and it is understood . . . that sooner or later all or almost all people will have to take up arms to liberate themselves, then the hour of liberation for this continent will be advanced.[88] The editors of the U.S.

Marxist journal *Monthly Review*, while praising Castro's initiative and his closing speech to the conference, added prophetically: "There is a real contradiction here: . . . Fidel is passionately advocating the very policies of armed
national liberation struggle which the Soviets would like to abandon in the interests of a deal with the United States."[89]

- *Castro Attacks Communist Parties in Latin America, March 13, 1967.* In response to accusations by leaders of the Venezuelan Communist Party that
  Cuba had a hand in the kidnapping and murder of the brother of the Venezuelan foreign minister, Castro struck back in a speech attacking the entire system
  of Soviet-backed parties in Latin America. In so doing, Castro broke publicly
  and (apparently) irrevocably with a long-standing and fundamental principle of
  Soviet foreign policy. Rather than adopting the "line" laid down by the various
  parties (and, by implication, by Moscow), Castro said, "Our stand regarding
  communist parties will be based strictly on revolutionary principles. . . . And if
  in any country those who call themselves communists do not know how to fulfill their duty, we will support those who, without calling themselves communists, conduct themselves like real communists in action and in a struggle."[90]
  So henceforth, according to Castro, it would be perfectly possible, even ex-
  pectable, for Cuba to support groups or movements that were struggling
  against forces supported by the official, Soviet-backed communist party in that
  country. Cuba would make up its own mind as to who it would support and
  what kind of support it would give, not excluding military support. In his concluding remarks, Castro in fact lumped the communists and their parties together with a litany of undesirables. "This Revolution," he thundered, "is a
  Revolution—understand this well all puppets, oligarchs, shilly-shalliers, and
  pseudo-revolutionaries of all stripes . . . this Revolution will maintain its position of absolute independence."[91]

- *Guevara's Message to the Tricontinental.* In mid-April 1967, the official Cuban
  news service, *Prensa Latina*, published a message by Guevara "from somewhere in the world" to the Organization of the Solidarity of the Peoples of
  Africa, Asia, and Latin America, the formal name of the Tricontinental. (Guevara was in fact already fighting in Bolivia, having arrived there on November
  4, 1966; the message was written before he left Cuba.)[92] The message, which
  was widely noted throughout the world when it appeared, was, as Guevara biographer Jon Lee Anderson has written, apocalyptic, implacable, chilling, and
  dramatic.[93] Everyone reading it knew he was "somewhere" putting into practice his uncompromising emphasis on armed struggle as the only valid path to
  liberation in the Third World. As we have seen, Castro, in his veiled anti-
  Soviet jeremiads, had come to repudiate what he saw as the inert, sclerotic
  Soviet-led array of communist parties in Latin America and elsewhere. Castro

almost always concluded these speeches with a rousing defense of armed struggle as the only road to revolution. By April 1967 he had all but burned his bridges with the Russians on this issue.

But Guevara went even further, much further, in fact, than Castro. He went further in two senses. *Psychologically*, Guevara spelled out what armed struggle really meant, really felt like to those like himself who were acting on their beliefs. For example, in his "message" Guevara emphasized the central importance of *hate* "as a factor in the struggle, intransigent hate for the enemy, which takes one beyond the natural limitations of a human being and converts one into an effective, violent, single-minded killing machine."[94] So hate is the correct attitude. The objective: "eliminating . . . the imperialist domain of the United States of North America."[95] The means: igniting a world war of "two, three, many Vietnams," more or less as Guevara was attempting to do in Bolivia at the moment his message was published.

Guevara also went further than Castro *politically*, by ceasing to argue any longer with the Soviets and their do-nothing local parties. He simply ignored them and set out personally to refute everything the Soviet Union's policy of "peaceful coexistence" stood for. At a time when the Soviet Union was desperately trying to rein in its North Vietnamese ally and bring it to the negotiating table with the Americans, Guevara was in South America endeavoring to ignite "Vietnams" all over the Western Hemisphere.

"Stretching the Cloth, Watching Carefully to See When It Will Rip"

The inflamed rhetoric in this period came only from Havana. There was nothing approaching a response in kind from the Soviet Union. Instead, Moscow was mostly silent about its heretical and outspoken Caribbean ally. Were the Soviets concerned? Were they angry? Was there a limit to how much heresy and abuse they would take from the Cubans?

The answer to all three queries is: yes, absolutely! Over the past several years, we have interviewed many former Cuban and Soviet officials—in Havana, in Moscow, and at various locations in the United States—who dealt with one another during this turbulent period. Our purpose was to try to discover what this volatile relationship really felt like—what it felt like to be dealing with one another in an atmosphere as highly charged, and with as much at stake, as was the case with the Cubans and Russians in the 1960s. In the course of carrying out these interviews, it became quite clear that this struggle between the Soviets and Cubans was often very bitter behind the scenes.

But the bitterness is perhaps not so surprising, in light of what was already known publicly, a partial sample of which one can get simply by scanning the chronology in the previous section. What surprised us in the interviews was the extent to which each side found it virtually impossible to empathize with the situation of the other. The more contact the Cubans and Russians had, at all levels, the more they seemed to resent each other, to conclude that those on the other side were really guilty of thinly disguised blackmail. If we had not come to the interviews already well aware that the Cubans and Soviets were allies, not declared enemies, during this period we might have concluded, on the basis of what we were told, that in the 1960s the Soviet Union was Cuba's principal adversary, and that Cuba was a major nemesis of the Soviet Union.

Moreover, very little of the material we gathered would have made any sense at all if we had not come to it from a study of their mutual perceptions of the way the October 1962 missile crisis was resolved. The shadow of the missile crisis haunted virtually all aspects of the Cuban–Soviet relationship. It was the event that proved to the Cubans that the Soviets were cowardly imperialists at heart, and from which the Soviets concluded that the Cubans were naive, emotional troublemakers. In short, due to the crisis and with regard to one another, both remained empathetically challenged, so to speak, from that point forward.

Kiva Maidanik spent three decades in several Soviet institutes working on Latin America in various capacities, much of it on Cuba. According to Maidanik, the Soviets watched Cuba after the missile crisis with both fear and loathing, though they dared not express either sentiment publicly for fear of provoking still more extreme behavior from the Cubans. If this happened, then—this was what Maidanik called "the fear of fears"—Cuba could gravitate toward China, which would be perhaps the final nail in the coffin of the Soviet Union's claims to lead the socialist movement in developing countries.[96] The fear went back to Stalin's time, in Maidanik's view:

> Our tradition, going all the way back to Stalin, and continuing after him, was that we could have no more dangerous adversary than an adversary on the *left*. The Soviet leadership believed you could always negotiate with those on the right of you, but those on the left, like Trotsky, Mao, and now Fidel, were perceived almost as anti-Soviet agents.[97]

Maidanik summarized the Soviet view in an arresting metaphor: "We, like a hedgehog, pointed our ideological needles in the direction of Cuba."[98]

As for the loathing, there seems to have been plenty of that as well. It was fed by the need to pretend that relations with Cuba were always excellent—by the prohibition on responding in kind to Cuban attacks on the Soviets. "I don't know how much the Cubans really knew about that," Maidanik says, "but of course they felt it, no doubt."[99] They were made to feel it in a quite personal way in March 1966 at the 23rd Congress of the Communist Party of the Soviet Union, the first since

Khrushchev had been ousted in October 1964 in a bloodless coup led by Leonid Brezhnev and Aleksei Kosygin. This was the moment when the full force of the shift in the Soviet leadership was felt for the first time. Emblematic for many of what was to come was a resolution pushed through by Brezhnev changing the name of his position from "First Secretary" of the party, which had been Khrushchev's title, to "General Secretary," which had been the name of the party leader under Stalin.

Leading the Cuban delegation to the 23rd Party Congress was education minister and longtime confidant of Castro's Armando Hart. Hart gave a plenary address to the delegates and Kiva Maidanik, as a top Soviet specialist on Cuba, was of course very interested in what the Cuban leader had to say, and in the response to it from his Soviet colleagues. Maidanik recalls that Armando Hart gave "a very emotional speech devoted to only one subject—it was an urgent call to help Vietnam." Maidanik said he will never forget the reaction in the hall to Hart's passionate request for help on behalf of a fraternal socialist ally being attacked, even as he spoke, by the United States. "There was no response," he said, "just ice-cold, estranged, and totally indifferent silence." Hart was stunned, recalls Maidanik, and went about afterward among some Soviet friends, including Maidanik, asking for an explanation.[100]

The public Soviet stance toward the litany of Cuban provocations listed in the previous section was to endure them in silence. But the silence was difficult to interpret. In fact, Cuban–Soviet relations were generally believed by the world at large, certainly by many in the United States, to be at least comfortable, and probably more than comfortable. After all, the Soviet aid package to Cuba was unprecedented, and continued to grow. But the silent treatment given to Armando Hart had only one interpretation, and neither Hart nor his colleagues in the Cuban leadership really needed to ask what that was: The Soviets were absolutely furious with the Cubans for their unqualified and unrestrained advocacy of armed struggle as the only true path to liberation in the Third World. The significant unanswered question by March 1966 was how much more ideological heresy, how much more verbal abuse of their principles and of their allied communist parties in the Third World—how much more extortion and blackmail—would the Soviets tolerate before they began to turn the screw on Cuba, before they would try to bring the Cubans to heel? That question would be answered a year later, in the spring of 1967.

The psychological dissonance is immense between the famous bear hug between Khrushchev and Castro at their first meeting, in New York in the autumn of 1960, on the one hand; and, on the other, the post–missile crisis, anti-Soviet diatribes of Castro and Guevara, to say nothing of the stone-cold treatment given to Hart in Moscow in March 1966. As Castro emphasized in his secret speech to the Cuban leadership in January 1968, the "original sin," so to speak, of the Soviets was the betrayal and abandonment of Cuba in the resolution of the missile crisis. That was the moment of great awakening for the Cubans. That was when the seed of mistrust was planted in the hearts and minds of the Cubans. And like any form of "original sin," it can only be disguised with more or less success. It can never be eliminated from one's nature because it resides at the core of one's character, or in this case, as the Cubans saw it, at the core of the Soviet national character.

Yet, as it turns out, the Soviets were suspicious of the Cubans even before the missile crisis. Kiva Maidanik recalls many meetings in his department at the Institute of World Economy and International Relations (IMEMO) in the spring of 1961 regarding Castro's sudden announcement on April 16 that the Cuban Revolution was a socialist revolution. According to Maidanik:

> Of course, we were all glad to see the Americans embarrassed—that this thing could happen right under their noses. We enjoyed that. But in that statement of Fidel's lies all future difficulties between Cuba and us. Because without even thinking about it, he attacked the very basis of our legitimacy, our claim to be a Marxist-Leninist state and society, and the leader of the entire bloc, as well as the legitimacy of all the other parties we supported throughout the world. This was something very, very radical and troubling. This was not even like Vietnam, or like China—which also gave us a lot of trouble. No, Cuba was even worse. All of a sudden, these guys in green fatigues say they are *communists*, and they are even *leaders* of world communism. And we don't even know who they are. To us, this is an impossible concept, because *we* decide who is and is not a communist. And of course, there is no "leader" other than ourselves. From that moment, we regarded them with suspicion, as heretics who can turn to other heresies at any moment, as people highly susceptible, in principle, to what we were already in 1961 calling the "Chinese virus"—the advocacy of armed struggle as practically the only qualification allowed for a "real" communist.[101]

The principal audience for Castro's April 16 embrace of socialism seems to have been the Russians. As it happened, the signal that he meant to send—"we in Cuba are like you, we are fellow communists"—was not the message that was received. According to Kiva Maidanik, the message received in official Moscow might be summed up as: "they are troublemakers of the worst sort, probably the Chinese sort."

Sergo Mikoyan agrees with Maidanik's assessment. All through the turbulent period after the missile crisis, according to Mikoyan, it was obvious in Moscow that "Fidel wasn't a real communist in the Soviet sense. He was expedient. His dream was to be a twentieth-century Jose Martí or Simón Bolívar." Like Castro's April 16, 1961, embrace of socialism, Mikoyan remembers another effort by the Cuban leader that, he believes, was probably supposed to soothe feelings in Moscow toward Cuba, but did not.

One of the oddities about Cuban communism until October 1965 was that it had few of the trappings of Soviet communism. For example, until October 1965 it did not even have a party that called itself "communist," nor obviously did it have a Central Committee, which in other communist countries was the principal decisionmaking body of the party, hence of the state itself, if the party was in power. Whatever Castro's reason for choosing that particular moment (October 3, 1965) for beginning to institutionalize Cuban communism, Mikoyan recalls that in Moscow, the belief was that "in creating the PCC [*Partido Communista de Cuba*, or Cuban Communist Party] in 1965, Fidel was merely trying to stop attempts by other Latin American communist parties from characterizing him as—many called him this at the time—a 'petty bourgeois adventurer.' The Soviet leadership was not impressed by this."[102]

Mikoyan also vividly recalls that the January 1966 Tricontinental Conference in Havana did that rarest of things: It united all the officials in the International Department of the Communist Party of the Soviet Union, the Foreign Ministry, and in the academic institutes—everyone, according to Mikoyan, who had anything to do with Cuba. The Tricontinental was read universally in Moscow, he said, as a brazen attempt by Cuba to exclude the Soviets from the leadership role in the Third World that they felt was rightfully theirs. There was also concern, he said, that maybe this was the beginning of some kind of rapprochement between Cuba and China. The latter, by 1966, was fast becoming a mortal enemy of the Soviet Union. Ironically, Mikoyan now muses, there was no need to worry about Cuba falling under the domination of the Chinese. Why? Because "China was like the Soviet Union. It didn't like competitors or people who did not obey. And Fidel—he didn't obey *anybody!*"[103]

The Soviet officials in this period who had by far the most contact with the Cuban leadership were Aleksandr Alekseev, the Soviet ambassador in Havana from June 1962 through January 1968; and Oleg Darusenkov, the director of Cuban affairs in the International Department of the Central Committee of the Communist Party of the Soviet Union. Both may justly be described as "pro-Cuban," in the sense that each had a deep understanding of the language, history, culture, and peculiar situation in which the Cuban revolutionary government found itself, and each was very fond of Cuba and Cubans. Darusenkov arrived in Cuba for the first time in May 1961, just after the failed Bay of Pigs invasion, and immediately went to work as an aide to Guevara. He remained Guevara's closest Soviet friend until Guevara's death in Bolivia in October 1967. Darusenkov's complete fluency in Spanish meant that he often acted as interpreter for Soviet officials, both in Havana and in Moscow. Alekseev also spoke fluent Spanish and became very close to Castro himself. He was the ideal man to represent Khrushchev in Havana. Alekseev shared Khrushchev's earthy enthusiasm for the young Caribbean revolutionaries. As Alekseev said in an interview, "I was in love with Fidel, and at first I had complete freedom as ambassador. Khrushchev trusted me."[104] This, like so much else related to the Soviet Union's relations with Cuba, would change drastically after Khrushchev's ouster in October 1964.

In fact, Alekseev told us that by early 1966 he could read the handwriting on the wall. In February 1966, just before the 23rd Party Congress in Moscow, Alekseev wrote a memorandum to the Presidium of the Congress asking that he be removed from the embassy in Havana. According to Alekseev:

> I was going to support Fidel all the way to the end. I would not abandon Fidel. Everybody knew that. But some people in my embassy did not support Fidel—were even anti-Fidel, I would say. In my memorandum, I said our relations with Cuba should be based not on personal friendship, as was the case in Havana, but on considerations governing normal state-to-state relations. This was the way I put it. But of course, what I was really saying was that I disagreed with our policy toward Cuba—that I could no longer support it.
>
> And what happened? They sent me back to Cuba for another year or more, knowing I would disagree personally—very personally—with most of what I would be ordered to say to Fidel. I hated it. More than that. I was supposed to be elected to the Central Committee at the 23rd Party Congress. But I was not. After the Congress, [Yuri] Andropov [then the head of the Department of Fraternal Relations in the International Department of the Party] asked me: "what have you done to yourself, asking to leave Cuba?" That was the way it was: I had to choose—Fidel or my bosses in Moscow, and I had chosen Fidel. But first they made me suffer through another year in Havana as my punishment.[105]

Such was the personal impact on one Soviet official of the behind-the-scenes warfare between Cuba and the Soviet Union in the mid-1960s.

Although Oleg Darusenkov was also highly sympathetic to the Cuban cause, his role as head of Cuban affairs in the Central Committee of the party gave him a very different perspective from that of Alekseev.[106] For he was in the center of the policymaking process with regard to all Cuban matters, and thus usually found himself in the role of a broker between what the Cubans wanted and what the Soviet leadership was willing to provide, and with what conditions, if any. A key difference, of course, was that whereas Alekseev was in Havana where his principal interlocutor was Castro, Darusenkov was usually located in Moscow, where he had to answer daily to Soviet officials whose view of Castro was, to say the least, less uncritically enthusiastic than was Alekseev's.

Darusenkov recalls that by late 1966, or early 1967 at the latest, the relentless and increasing radicalism of the Cubans had, in effect, made *his* job almost impossible. "Our government was sick and tired of Fidel Castro's criticism," he said in an interview. "It was the worst moment in our relationship. There was a real potential for a fight."[107] Darusenkov was ideally situated, in fact, to see deeply into why both sides held their respective attitudes. He had worked as an interpreter in the Soviet embassy in Havana during the missile crisis and had been Mikoyan's interpreter in his difficult talks with the Cubans in November 1962. But he also knew keenly that by early 1967, the patience with Cuba by his superiors in Moscow had grown exceedingly thin. According to Darusenkov:

> From Fidel's point of view, I can see why he lost confidence in the Soviet Union after the October missile crisis. After that, he no longer believed that the USSR would protect Cuba from U.S. aggression. He was always pushing the Soviet Union to change, to take views that he thought would protect Cuba's security. I believe he was always testing our limits, [gestures dramatically, as if trying to tear something in half] like stretching the cloth, watching carefully to see when it will rip. That was from Fidel's point of view. But from our point of view, we could only stand so much. Our people said privately: "why do we let Fidel Castro blackmail us? If he wants to attack us, well then fine, but let's not reward him for it." In other words, there was growing sentiment to think seriously about reducing the level of our material support to Cuba. Fidel's opponents in Moscow had a way of talking about his strategy. They said: "Fidel sucked the Soviet tit, but at the same time he bit it."[108]

Sticking with Darusenkov's metaphor, though one that is somewhat less physiological, it is clear that by early 1967 there was growing sentiment in the Soviet leadership that the time had come for Moscow to assume its role as the stern "parent" in this relationship and begin to discipline this exceedingly rebellious Cuban "child."

It seemed to us in our interviews with former Cuban officials that the Cubans, in fact, sensed early on that the *Russians* took the parent–child metaphor seriously—that the Soviet demeanor toward the Cubans was one of condescension, often augmented with expressions of indignation because the Cubans seemed insufficiently grateful for all the favors the Soviets, in their fraternal generosity, had done for Cuba. What seems to have particularly offended the Cubans was that it was so patently obvious that, in return for the Russians having become Cuba's "savior" and benefactor (so they seemed to believe), they expected the Cubans to respond as obedient children might: obsequiously, unquestioningly, radiating nothing but gratitude, at least in their public remarks.

The missile crisis proved this irrefutably to Castro. In his January 1968 secret speech to the Cuban leadership, he voiced special resentment at what, in his mind, was a Soviet attitude that was completely at variance with the facts—that the Soviet

Union had "saved" Cuba in the missile crisis and had continued to "save" Cuba ever since. According to a retrospectively irate Castro:

> Every time the trite expression "Cuba was saved"—quite honestly . . . [or] "Cuba lives" . . . for goodness sakes, we have been alive since our mothers brought each one of us into the world, and that had nothing whatsoever to do with the Soviet missiles.[109]

Clearly exasperated, Castro then goes on to make a more general point about the Soviet attitude toward Cuba and Cubans. The Soviets, he said, have "this habit of not searching for the reasons, of not analyzing, and instead trying to solve everything with a catch phrase."[110] This is precisely the attitude taken by many parents, of course, when they are weary of explaining "why" to their children. Confrontations of this sort are usually resolved with what Castro calls a "catch phrase": the parent simply says to the child, "because I said so," and that is the end of it. But the Cubans did not accept this—did not stop arguing, questioning, pushing for answers—either in the missile crisis or thereafter. They totally rejected the implicit assumption on which they believed Soviet behavior toward them was based: that they should act more or less like grateful and respectful children.

Faure Chomón was Cuba's first ambassador to the Soviet Union, occupying that post from 1960 to 1962. He was heavily involved in all aspects of Cuba's dealings with the Russians thereafter. As he said in an interview, he was thought by the Chinese to be pro-Soviet, even though, as a Cuban official, he would have found it almost impossible really to be "pro-Soviet" in the insulting sense intended by the Chinese. Echoing the views of Jorge Pollo, the basic problem, according to Chomón, was that:

> the Soviets did not understand the Cuban character or our historical process. Because of this, they never really, deep down, recognized Cuban independence in the sense that Cubans felt and meant that term, and they also didn't appreciate, or maybe even understand, why were are so protective of our sovereignty.[111]

In fact, as Faure Chomón recalls, the Cubans could have been a lot *more* critical of the Russians than they actually were—a recollection that would no doubt have amazed his Soviet interlocutors. Like the Soviets, the Cubans detected at a very early point in their relationship that their new ally would be difficult to deal with. Chomón remembers a conversation he had in 1961 with Carlos Rafael Rodríguez (always referred to in Cuba simply as "Carlos Rafael"), one of the few senior old-line Cuban communists who went to the Sierra Maestra Mountains to join Castro's movement in the 1950s. In the period immediately after the triumph of the Revolution, Rodríguez was one of the few people close to Castro who had *any* significant experience with the Soviets. He would eventually become Cuba's vice president. According to Chomón:

> We knew there were deep problems in the Soviet Union, and we hoped these problems would be resolved. But we could not speak out publicly to criticize the Russians because we needed to maintain solidarity in the international socialist movement. Already in 1961 Carlos Rafael said to me that he had defended Stalin [in the 1940s and 1950s], but all he was really defending was a bag of shit. The basic problem was that the Soviets acted like an imperialist country. It was the only way they knew how to act toward small countries like Cuba.[112]

Imagine what those in the Cuban leadership must have been thinking, therefore, when in March 1966 Leonid Brezhnev asked for and received permission from the Soviet Party leaders to be called the "General Secretary" of the Party, the title that had been eliminated by Khrushchev, but that Stalin—the "bag of shit" referred to by the Cuban most knowledgeable about the Soviets—had used.

It was stunning to us that so many Cubans who dealt with the Soviets recall that from the very outset of their relationship, there were big problems, most having to do with the issue of *control*. The experience of the missile crisis was decisive in that thereafter the Cuban leadership would not permit the Soviets to control anything that they regarded as integral to Cuban security and independence. But the feeling that the Soviets wanted to put the Cubans in a straitjacket was, the Cubans felt, there from the start, even before the missile crisis.

Manuel Piñeiro felt this intensely. Piñeiro, known throughout Cuba as *"Barbarroja,"* or "Red Beard," was, after 1960, director of the Cuban DGI (*Direccion General Inteligencia*, or General Intelligence Directorate).[113] This was Cuba's chief external intelligence and counterintelligence body, which in the beginning relied very heavily on Soviet advice.[114] In an interview, Piñeiro recalled that from the outset of Soviet involvement with his Cuban intelligence service, "I felt they [the Soviets] did not merely want to help Cuba, but to lead, to tell us what to do."[115] A former subordinate of Piñeiro's in the DGI agrees. The missile crisis, according to Domingo Amuchastegui, made things even worse. "After October 27, 1962," he asserts, "Soviet, Czech and East German intelligence dramatically reduced the flow of information and assessments that they shared with Cuban intelligence. This was the beginning of a trend that would last until 1968, and which was only partially reversed thereafter."[116] Piñeiro also recalled that the Soviet-led effort to control the Cuban intelligence service not only involved withholding information. In addition, the Russians, said Piñeiro, "wanted details from us like names, but we never gave them a name. The effort to control us was my basic disagreement with the Soviets."[117]

The Cuban perception of the Soviets as, above all else, bent on controlling Cuba and its Revolution is one of the sources of Jorge Pollo's comment, referred to earlier: that the Cubans felt it was very important to impress on the Soviets that "Cuba was not Hungary, that Cuba was not Romania, that Cuba was not Poland." That is, Cuba did not join the socialist camp just so it could receive orders from its "parent" in Moscow. In fact, after the missile crisis, Cuba not only did not take orders from the Soviets, they didn't even trust them, as Manuel Piñeiro's remarks attest. The Cubans felt they should be treated as *equal* to the Soviets in the socialist bloc. It is possible that Nikita Khrushchev may have been able to accept this, in principle. But the way he chose to resolve the missile crisis demonstrated to the Cubans that even a Soviet leader with good intentions—who was at heart a real revolutionary—could not translate the belief in Cuban equality into appropriate action when the chips were down. And those leaders who ousted Khrushchev in October 1964 appear never even to have entertained the thought that Cuba was, in any relevant sense, the equal of the Soviet Union.

A CORE CONFLICT

The late British political philosopher Sir Isaiah Berlin has written that there are two prerequisites required for people from one culture, tradition, location, and situation who wish to understand those from very different circumstances. First, according to Berlin, one must accept, in principle, "the equal validity of incommensurable cultures."[118] This requires a kind of intellectual commitment to be vigilant in avoiding ethnocentric attitudes and positions. The second step is more difficult, Berlin has written, because it requires more than an intellectual grasp of the "differentness" of others. It requires an emotional commitment of actually trying to enter that other perceptual world. In other words, it requires *empathy*—not sympathy, not agreement, not acceptance—but instead, seeing and feeling the world as others see and feel it. "[To] understand them," Berlin writes, "one must perform an imaginative act of 'empathy' into their essence, understand them 'from within' as far as possible, and see the world through their eyes—be [as] 'a shepherd among shepherds' with the ancient Hebrews."[119] Or, we might add, "be a Cuban among the Cuban revolutionaries of the 1960s"—a task at which the Americans famously failed but which, as we now know, also one at which the Soviets, despite many protestations to the contrary, failed dismally as well. And of course, the Cubans failed, so it seems, to empathize with either superpower.

Why did they all fail? In particular, why did the Russians fail—why did they fail to anticipate the Cubans' response in the missile crisis; and why did they fail to understand the Cuban sensitivity about losing their independence to their Soviet ally, even though significant Soviet assistance was deemed necessary to survive various threats by their U.S. adversary? Here again, Isaiah Berlin is helpful in elucidating why empathy would have been in such short supply in Havana and Moscow in the 1960s. In a word, the Soviets did not, perhaps because they could not, comprehend anything as foreign to them as Cuban *nationalism*. In a passage that demonstrates Berlin's considerable ability to practice empathy himself, as well as recommend its virtues to others, he wrote:

> [N]ationalism . . . is a pathological form of self-protective *resistance* . . . [by] groups which feel humiliated or oppressed, to whom nationalism represents the straightening of bent backs, the recovery of a freedom they may never have had (it is all a matter of ideas in men's heads), revenge for their insulted humanity. . . . It animates revolts . . . for it expresses the inflamed desire of the insufficiently regarded to count for something among the cultures of the world.[120]

If there is a more succinct and eloquent description of the core psychological characteristics of the "inflamed" nationalism that ignited and sustained the Cuban Revolution, we are unaware of it.

Of course the Soviets could not empathize with the Cubans. In a very real sense that the Cubans felt keenly, the Soviets did not seem interested in providing opportunities for the Cubans to straighten their theretofore "bent backs." Rather, the Russians seemed to prefer that the Cubans' backs stay bent—but in the direction of Moscow. Whether the Soviets "meant" to convey this impression to the Cubans is much less important than is the undeniable fact that this is how the Cubans perceived them, and that the Soviets were singularly unable to alter this impression, possibly because they lacked sufficient interest in trying to doing so. And this is after all why the Cubans resisted them with all the energy, if not quite all the public rancor, that they brought to bear in their fierce resistance to the U.S. economic embargo, U.S.-backed covert action programs carried out in Cuba, and the U.S. effort to isolate Cuba politically in the hemisphere and beyond.

Strategies of Conflict in Havana and Moscow

In order to further illuminate the core conflictual nature of the Cuban–Soviet relationship, and to examine some of its implications, it is instructive to notice how snugly the post–missile crisis Cuban–Soviet relationship fits within the framework of what the former Harvard economist Thomas Schelling famously referred to as "the strategy of conflict."[121] Schelling was interested in the ways in which adversaries in conflict *deter* one another from attacking each other's interests. As is well known, the most influential application of Schelling's ideas was to the U.S.–Soviet relationship during the Cold War, particularly to the *nuclear* aspect of the relationship—to nuclear deterrence.

Here then were the two superpower adversaries, two radically different world views, two incompatible systems of domestic arrangements, two nuclear arsenals targeted on one another. The two giants were certainly in conflict, but of a sort that required each to make "threats which leave something to chance," as they proceeded with what Schelling called a kind of "bargaining" that constituted their "competition in risk-taking."[122] In this kind of conflict, according to Schelling, the "combat" must become more psychological than physical, more about manipulating the cost–benefit calculations of the adversary than it is about manipulating guns and soldiers and supplies. Why is this the case? Simply because actually going to war—an all-out nuclear war, in the paradigmatic case that concerned Schelling and those he influenced—carried with it an unacceptable risk of committing mutual national suicide, or *mutual assured destruction* (MAD), to use the term coined to describe this situation. And of course, should the United States and Soviet Union destroy each other in a nuclear war, the fate of the rest of the world would also be highly precarious, at best.

Two common features link U.S.–Soviet nuclear deterrence and the strategies employed by the Cubans and Soviets with regard to each other. First, neither the Cubans nor the Soviets felt they could walk away from the relationship; thus to sever relations, no matter which side initiated the split, risked a political form of mutual assured destruction (for the Soviets), and possibly something even worse for the Cubans—their annihilation by the United States. Second, this particular relationship, as we have seen, was immensely aggravating for both sides, and for reasons described by Schelling who, as it happens (perhaps because he and his wife raised four boys), was fascinated by the role of deterrence in parent–child relationships.[123]

Schelling pointed out that a basic prerequisite for the employment of a strategy of conflict—of deterrence, whether between individuals or nations—is a significant degree of *mistrust*. The effort to deter another from committing a certain act is necessary, Schelling wrote, "when trust and good faith do not exist and cannot be made to by acting as though they did."[124] As Schelling knew from experience, and as generations of his readers have acknowledged, parents and their children can also become locked in a relationship that cannot be terminated by either side, but can be decidedly hellish for both parents and children a great deal of the time. After the missile crisis, we now know, trust and good faith were often absent from the Cuban–Soviet relationship, and one way to explain the fierceness of Cuban resistance to the Russian line in the period is this: The Cubans felt the Soviets, in their efforts to micromanage the trajectory of the Cuban Revolution, were treating them like children.

Schelling's analysis applies to the Cuban–Soviet relationship with a comprehensiveness that is both surprising and revealing:

Some aspects of deterrence stand out vividly in child discipline: the importance of rationality and self-discipline on the part of the person to be deterred; of his ability to comprehend the threat if he hears it and to hear it through the din and the noise, of the threatener's determination to fulfill the threat if need be—and more important, of the threatened party's conviction that the threat will be carried out . . . [and] . . . the important possibility that the threatened punishment will hurt the threatener as much as it will the one threatened, perhaps more.[125]

Once a threat has been issued and heard, threats and counterthreats become the axis around which the relationship revolves until the underlying conflict is resolved, one way or the other.

"There is an analogy," Schelling noted, "between a parent's threat to a child and the threat that a wealthy paternalistic nation makes to the weak and disorganized government of a poor nation in, say, extending foreign aid and demanding 'sound' economic policies or cooperative military policies in return."[126] The canonical parent–child case described by Schelling contains many of the issues the Soviets would have to resolve, to their own satisfaction, before they could tell the Cubans to shape up, or they, the Soviets, would ship out. For example:

- Would the Cubans respond *rationally*—a subject that concerned several generations of Soviet leaders, and U.S. leaders as well?
- Could the Cubans actually *comprehend* the threat the Russians might make, in the din of their own overheated rhetoric and hypersensitivity (so it seemed in Moscow) to every suggestion made to them by outside parties?
- Are the Soviets, as a party and government, really willing to *fulfill* the threat to break with the Cubans, with all the uncertainty and unintended consequences of what might follow, not excluding the destruction of the Cuban Revolution?
- If the Soviets resolve to make the threat and carry it out, will the Cubans actually *believe* them and alter their behavior accordingly?
- If the threat is made, and if the Cubans continue to resist in their customary fashion, and if the threat is therefore executed with finality, is it possible that the action will actually *hurt the Soviets* more than the Cubans?

These items were surely among those at the top of the Soviet agenda when the time finally arrived to face the Cuban dilemma squarely, as it evidently did in the spring of 1967. As the list of relevant uncertainties associated with Schelling's analogy indicates, the Soviets had a good deal to discuss and plenty of reason to feel anxious about the outcome.

As our Cuban and Soviet interviewees emphasized, and as one might surmise from the chronological "sampler" in a previous section, by the spring of 1967 relations seemed to both sides to be approaching the breaking point. Both sides seem to have reached the end of their forbearance and patience with one another. The Soviets could not impart the discipline on the Cubans they felt was necessary if they were to obtain a respectable return on their continued massive and multifaceted investment in Cuba. Nor could the Cubans expect to build their communist society at home and "make the revolution" abroad without that Soviet support, yet both objectives, but particularly the latter, led to exactly the kind of Cuban behavior that, from the Soviets' perspective, put the entire relationship at risk.

Let us, then, within this framework, summarize the Soviet and Cuban prosecutory briefs against one another by early 1967. This is where things between them had come to by the spring of 1967:

From the Soviet Perspective. These are the perverse uses to which the Cubans are putting Soviet resources:

1. Threatening nascent and absolutely essential movement toward U.S.–Soviet rapprochement, by continually inciting and assisting anti-U.S. forces in the Third World.
2. Undermining Soviet relations with Latin America, especially the national Latin American communist parties, in which the Soviets had a huge investment historically, financially, and psychologically.
3. Undertaking costly and irrational economic experiments, chiefly by utopian attempts to eliminate material incentives altogether and instantly leap to a mature communist society.

The key question for the Soviet leadership thus became: How to discipline Castro and Cuba without placing the massive economic, political, and psychological Soviet investment in Cuba at risk? In particular, how should the Soviets begin to apply gradual pressure on Cuba, using "threats [to cut off Cuba] that leave something to chance," giving the Cubans an opportunity to rein in their unacceptable behavior before it is too late.

From the Cuban Perspective. The Soviet efforts to control Cuba, using their aid to Cuba as leverage, are unacceptable threats to Cuba's sovereignty and independence, and must continue to be resisted. The following factors need to be considered in responding to any attempts by the Soviets to apply pressure on Cuba to conform to their commands.

1. Cuba has enormous geopolitical value to the Soviet Union, which is Cuba's best insurance that continued resistance will not lead to a break with Moscow.
2. Yet Castro and his colleagues in the Cuban leadership are rational, and they realize there must be limits to Cuba's ability to extort or blackmail the Soviets indefinitely, although it is difficult to determine what those limits are.

The key question for the Cuban leadership thus became: How far can the Soviets be pushed by Cuban "threats [to leave the Soviet fold] that leave something to chance" before they will seriously contemplate breaking with Havana?

This situation was clearly unsustainable. Something had to give. Given the trajectory of the strategies of conflict being deployed by the Cubans and Soviets, their mutual competition in risk-taking threatened at any moment to create a deep crisis. In fact, the Cubans and Soviets were heading toward something like their very own "Cuban missile crisis," in this sense: a showdown was in the offing in which the entire relationship would be at stake; a false move by either side could mean disaster for both. As in the missile crisis itself, it would be the Soviets who made the decisive move that led directly to the crisis.

A new stage in our relations with the Soviet Union began, characterized by the special circumstances of having before us an aggressive enemy, an ally on the retreat and our desire to keep the weapons, as well as our resolve to prevent relations with that ally from deteriorating to the point of rupture. . . . [W]e had to dissemble, contain, hold back our indignation, our outrage.

—Fidel Castro, January 26, 1968

The great fear was that the Prague Spring would lead to an "American Autumn." There is a connection between the events of October 1962 and August 1968. As in the October crisis, the Cuban people had a very strong negative reaction to the Soviets—then to withdrawing the missiles, now to the occupation of Czechoslovakia. Once again, Fidel had a lot of explaining to do.

—Felix Pita, former editor of *Rebel Youth* newspaper, April 29, 1995[1]

4

JUNE 1967–AUGUST 1968:
FROM THE SHADOW OF THE MISSLE CRISIS
TO THE SHADOW OF THE FUTURE

"Bitter necessity called for the sending of those forces into Czechoslovakia."

DEJA VU, NOVEMBER '62? KOSYGIN IN HAVANA, JUNE 26–28, 1967

Sometime in October or November 1966, the Soviets learned that Che Guevara and his band of fighters were already operating in Bolivia, with the intention of using Bolivia as a base of operations from which to ignite revolutions across all of South America. Soviet General Secretary Leonid Brezhnev was told this either by Cuban Defense Minister Raul Castro on a visit to Moscow in October or by Bolivian Communist Party boss Mario Monje during a November visit to Moscow, or by both. In a stunning reversal of roles from their shared primal experience of October 1962, the Cubans did not consult the Soviets about this momentous development (though they informed them after the fact).[2]

Brezhnev's discovery that the Cubans were actually following through on their incendiary calls to armed revolution in Latin America apparently led him and his colleagues in the Soviet leadership to what journalist Malcolm Gladwell has recently called a "tipping point."[3] As Gladwell has emphasized, while trends can build gradually, seeming to move slowly over time, they often explode suddenly. All of a sudden, that which was hazy, complex, and uncertain seems crystal clear and straightforward, and the action needed is obvious. This is what Gladwell says happens, for example, when a disease that has been growing in frequency incrementally, thus controllably, "becomes" an epidemic, grabs the attention of everyone, and ignites efforts (often quite late in its development) to cope with it.

Something like this seems to have happened in the minds of Soviet leaders with regard to their Cuban "disease" when they learned that Guevara was in Bolivia.

Suddenly, everything seemed clear, with regard to the Cubans. Before they learned of the Guevara mission, the Soviets had been personally angered but publicly silent or equivocal about Cuban resistance to their "line," in part because a good deal, though by no means all, of the Cuban resistance was rhetorical. It was now clear to the leadership, however, that the Cuban apostasy had reached epidemic proportions and had to be stopped. The time had arrived for decisive action, something Castro often declared or implied in his speeches to be a capability the Soviets lacked altogether.

So sometime in late 1966 or in very early 1967, the Soviet leadership agreed on a strategy for bringing the Cubans into line. There was simply too much at stake in the budding Soviet rapprochement with the United States, on which the Soviets under Brezhnev hoped at last to gain the status—not just in their own eyes, but also in the eyes of the United States—of "the other superpower." The Cubans were not going to be allowed to prevent the Soviets from achieving this objective. In the minds of the Brezhnev leadership, the Cubans, with their wild-eyed advocacy of world revolution, had suddenly become an unacceptable nuisance.

In a message sent by the Soviet leadership, probably via the Cuban ambassador in Moscow, the Cubans were told that they had provoked the United States repeatedly and that, should the United States decide to move militarily against Cuba (as well they might), the Cubans should not expect the Russians to lift a finger on their behalf. This message thus conformed to a pattern of Soviet behavior that began in the very early 1960s, by means of which the Soviets, seeking to gain greater control over various Cuban activities, exaggerated the U.S. threat to the island.[4] The Cubans were also told point blank: Stop fooling around in Latin America or grave consequences will arise between the Cubans and the Soviets. On March 13, as noted in chapter 3, Castro issued forth with a vehement attack on "all puppets, oligarchs, shilly-shalliers, and pseudo-revolutionaries of all stripes."[5] The Soviet-backed Venezuelan Communist Party was Castro's specific target on that occasion. Its members stood accused of being the "puppets" of the "pseudo-revolutionaries" in Moscow.

Later in the spring—we are not certain of the date—Brezhnev sent a message to Castro in preparation for a late-June meeting in Havana between Soviet Prime Minister Aleksei Kosygin and the Cuban leadership. Brezhnev told Castro that in endeavoring to foment armed revolution in Latin America—the Soviets found the Guevara mission in Bolivia especially offensive—Cuba stood in violation of a number of accords involving the communist parties in Latin America. Brezhnev also expressed regret that Cuba had apparently decided on this course of action without consultation with Moscow. And Brezhnev reiterated the message sent through the Cuban ambassador in January: Should the United States decide to move militarily against Cuba, the Cubans would be on their own. The Cubans replied in a message that accused the USSR of subverting the cause of revolution in Latin America and elsewhere. The Cubans expressed resentment at the Russians for having evidently instructed the Bolivian Communist Party not to assist Guevara and his group. Cuban–Soviet relations thus entered a glacial period of mutual recrimination as the June 26–28 visit to Havana of Kosygin approached.

There were several features of the context of the Castro–Kosygin meetings in late June 1967 that should be emphasized. First, when Kosygin arrived in Havana on June 16, the Six-Day War in the Middle East had just occurred (June 6–12). It was a disaster for the Soviets' Middle East policy, of which Aleksei Kosygin was a principal architect. The Cuban interpretation of what had occurred in part reflected their own experience with the Russians in the missile crisis. They accused the Soviets of "capitulationism," having agreed to a cease-fire without securing Israeli withdrawal from the occupied territories. What they saw as the Soviet abandonment of the Arabs reminded them vividly of their own abandonment in October 1962.[6]

Yet Cuba's views on the Six-Day War were not an expression of either anti-Israel or even pro-Arab sentiment. All of the Warsaw Pact countries except Romania had broken diplomatic relations with Israel during the war, on June 10. Cuba did not follow the pack. While it had begun to develop a relationship with the Palestine Liberation Organization, which was founded in 1964, the Six-Day War was not about the Israeli–Palestinian struggle. The Arab countries had not done much more than give lip service to the Palestinian quest for a homeland. The war was about the Arab–Israeli struggle, and in this Castro also found common cause with the Jewish state. He told Shlomo Lvav, Israel's first ambassador to Cuba after the triumph of the Revolution, that he could see a parallel between Israel's struggle to survive in their hostile environment and Cuba's similar struggle with a U.S. adversary that wanted to destroy it.[7] Here was yet another issue on which the Cubans refused to toe the Soviet line. Cuban sources leaked a story while Kosygin was in Havana that the Russians had pressed Castro to break relations with Israel. Castro's reply: First the Russians must break relations with the United States.[8]

The Six-Day War thus had multiple meanings for Cuba. It was one more example of Soviet weakness and unwillingness to support allies in a time of need. This is what Castro emphasized to Kosygin. But in maintaining diplomatic relations with Israel, Cuba could assert that it supported Israel's right to exist, and also could demonstrate its independence from the Soviet Union.

A second feature of the Havana summit was that it occurred immediately following a summit in Glassboro, New Jersey, between Kosygin and President Lyndon Johnson. Their discussions were dominated officially by three issues: the Middle East War; the nascent launching of the era of U.S.–Soviet arms-control negotiations, beginning with the limitation on antiballistic missile systems; and the Vietnam War, which had just entered a particularly bloody phase. Yet we now know that Johnson also pressed Kosygin to get control of the Cubans and rein them in. The declassified notes of the U.S. interpreter, Alexander Akalovsky, reveal the following appeal by Johnson to Kosygin in their meeting on the afternoon of June 25.

> The President then said he wished to inform Mr. Kosygin of an extremely important matter. He said we had direct evidence of Cuba's encouragement of guerrilla operations in seven Latin American countries. This was a form of aggression and a threat to peace in the Hemisphere as well as the world at large. . . . The President emphasized that he therefore strongly felt that Castro should be convinced to stop what he was doing.[9]

The notes report that "Mr. Kosygin did not comment on the statement."[10] But later that evening Johnson told former president Eisenhower in a telephone conversation that Kosygin had responded that "he couldn't comment now but he was leaving for Cuba tomorrow and he would bear these things in mind in talking to them." According to Johnson, "[Kosygin] acted like he was a little upset with Castro."[11]

In any case, Kosygin seems not to have objected in any way to Johnson's characterization of Cuba's activities in Latin America. And we know why: because Kosygin agreed with Johnson completely, even though it was impossible for him to say so in a face-to-face meeting with the American president. We now know that the Soviets had also decided that Castro had to be "convinced to stop what he was doing," as Johnson put it. This unenviable task fell to Kosygin, beginning the following day when his plane landed in Havana.

The Cubans believed they knew exactly what the Glassboro summit had been about: It was another fateful step, they were convinced, toward the institutionalizing of "peaceful coexistence" as the new slogan of the Cold War. And this is why the Cubans hated it. While they may not have been privy to the details of the discussions in Glassboro, they knew that their interests in those discussions would be under attack from both the United States and the Soviet Union. So having had a cordial set of discussions with the leaders of his superpower adversary in Glassboro, Kosygin girded up his loins to do battle in Havana with his Caribbean ally.

Kosygin knew that his mission was as necessary as it would be disagreeable. In many ways, it was deja vu, '62. Just as Anastas Mikoyan had arrived in Havana in November 1962 to inform the Cubans that Soviet missiles, planes, and troops had to be removed from the island, so Aleksei Kosygin arrived in Havana in June 1967 to inform the Cubans that their forces had to be removed from other Latin American countries and that henceforth, as Johnson had told Kosygin, Castro had to "stop what he was doing." Like Mikoyan in 1962, Kosygin was treated with all the disrespect the Cubans felt was due the representative of a spineless ally that had sold Cuba down the river yet again. Castro refused to meet Kosygin at the airport, just as he had refused at first to meet Mikoyan.

Oleg Darusenkov was the Soviet interpreter for the Castro–Kosygin summit in Havana. In an interview, he recalled:

> The Kosygin visit was bad from the start. He was badly received. There was no mass rally. The Cubans told Kosygin that they believed he did not want one. But that was a pretext Kosygin did not accept. It was common for there to be mass rallies for major state visitors.
>
> Kosygin and Fidel talked for seven hours without a break, though there were others present with Fidel. The conversation was *very* hard. Fidel was critical of Soviet policies across a large panorama of issues—for example, he accused us of abandoning the Arabs in the Middle East War. Kosygin then asked Fidel to stop the support of liberation movements in Latin America. The Soviet Union, he said, did not approve of these activities. Then Kosygin and Fidel had a tough argument over whether real revolution has to emerge from the lower levels—from the armed struggle. Kosygin expressed the view that revolution cannot be exported as the Cubans were evidently attempting to do. He said these efforts are not only doomed to failure, but they inevitably bring undesirable reactions.[12]

This was a prime example of what former Soviet–Cuba hand (later Russian ambassador to Cuba) Arnold Kalinin described in an interview as the ongoing Soviet effort to make "the Cubans understand that they had to interpret events more profoundly, in terms of global affairs."[13] But of course, this was precisely the kind of Russian pedagogical exercise that most infuriated the Cubans. To the Cubans, so close to the United States and so far from the Soviet Union, what mattered was not Soviet calculations about "global affairs," but the much more concrete possibility that the United States might at any time try to crush the Cuban Revolution. After all, were they not, at the very moment of Kosygin's visit, seeking to crush Cuba's North Vietnamese ally? So why not Cuba?

Castro, recalls Darusenkov, was greatly incensed by the discussion with Kosygin. In the end, according to Darusenkov, "Fidel expressed strong criticism of the Soviet Union for going too far in making concessions to imperialism in its efforts to foster détente."[14] The exchanges were especially bitter, according to Darusenkov, when the mission of Guevara in Bolivia was discussed.[15]

Darusenkov's account tends to confirm his judgment that Kosygin delivered a "virtual ultimatum" to the Cubans in Havana.[16] Darusenkov's believes that the message Kosygin intended to convey in Havana was this: cease and desist from trying to foment revolution in Latin America or suffer the consequences.

As in their November 1962 negotiations with Mikoyan, the Cubans knew they had no realistic option other than to go along with the Soviets. But they also knew—as they did *not* in 1962—that they had a good deal of leverage over the Soviets because by June 1967, the Soviet investment in Cuba was, per capita, larger than their involvement anywhere else on Earth outside the Soviet Union itself.

And the investment had political, psychological, and ideological dimensions, in addition to the more purely economic sunk costs of the Soviets on the island.

Thus, whereas in 1962 Mikoyan left the island with Cuban agreement on every proposition he argued for, Kosygin left with nothing other than the memory of his icy reception and the long, heated discussions with a very angry Castro. This time the "agreement" would obviously take a lot longer to work out. There would be nothing in June 1967 like the moment during the negotiations with Mikoyan when Castro said, in effect, all right, take everything—the missiles, the planes, the troops—everything, the hell with it.[17] This time, however, the Russians were not asking for the return of what was essentially Soviet property but for a fundamental reversal of Cuban foreign policy, a policy that reflected some of the most deeply held beliefs of the Cuban leadership. And so, rather than concluding an agreement, Kosygin's visit signaled the beginning of the bargaining to determine what the Cubans would get from the Soviets in exchange for acceding to their demands.

The similarities to November 1962 were eerie. Even the atmospherics of the Kosygin visit were reminiscent of those surrounding the Mikoyan mission. Just as Mikoyan had arrived, pro-Soviet posters were ripped down in Havana and some Soviet citizens were jeered publicly. Just after Kosygin left Havana at the end of June 1967, Havana cafés and streets were full of "revisionist" jokes—*revisionists* being a code word for the Soviets, who had "revised" Leninist principles so as to promote peaceful coexistence with the imperialists as the highest virtue of socialism. French journalist K. S. Karol, who arrived in Havana in early July, recalls that he was told on his first day in the city to take note that "revisionist trucks" were of extremely poor quality and that were he to use "revisionist razor blades," he need not invest in shaving cream, because his tears would suffice for lubrication.[18]

AFTER KOSYGIN: THE BEGINNING OF A NEW APPROACH

Kosygin had been the ideal Soviet official to deliver the "virtual ultimatum" to Castro. Kosygin was the very opposite of Castro—at least the caricatured Castro of lore, the Castro that many people, especially in the United States, think of when his name comes up—he of the flashing eyes, threatening gestures, and inflammatory rhetoric. Kosygin, on the other hand, was reserved, cautious, a technocrat who had served in Stalin's retinue for a dozen years and thus knew the value of keeping his emotions under control and his personal thoughts to himself. Unlike the "old Bolshevik," Mikoyan, who seems to have been genuinely affected by the young Cuban revolutionaries with whom he had to deal in November 1962, Kosygin approached his task, as always, dispassionately. He told Castro the new facts of life for Cuba, that is, if it wished to stay allied with the Soviet Union—if it wished, therefore, to continue to receive extraordinarily favorable terms in its dealings with Moscow. And when he had finished giving Castro the message he intended to deliver, and after listening quietly to Castro's (no doubt) much lengthier responses, Kosygin did not offer to amend his message. When he was convinced that Castro had gotten the message, he left for the airport.

Castro did not accompany Kosygin to the airport following their discussions on June 28, 1967. There is no reason to doubt that the anger Oleg Darusenkov remembers seeing in Castro during the discussions with Kosygin was anything but real and deeply felt. Yet, though undoubtedly angry and frustrated, he did not rush out and call a rally to denounce the Soviets—not yet, anyway. In fact, the caricature of Castro as a leader ruled by his emotions, rather than one who typically has them under firm control, is fallacious.[19] Just to state the obvious: he has been in power since Dwight Eisenhower was president of United States; he has survived dozens, perhaps hundreds of attempts on his life; he has outwitted U.S. administrations at every turn; and Cuba has, as a consequence, survived more than forty years of U.S. attempts to isolate it and bring down Castro and his government. It is unlikely, to say the least, that an emotional, irrational person could accomplish anything like this.[20] Behind his well-cultivated reputation for emotionalism, obstinacy, and irrationality is instead a leader who, no matter what else one may think of him, is a master at considering his options and playing the odds. Of course, he takes risks, but not, we believe, without carefully considering the probable consequences.

What were his options after receiving the "virtual ultimatum" from Kosygin? Three broad courses of action were open to him, each of which had its pros and cons.

1. *Condemn the Soviets.* He could take the gloves off, cease to criticize the Soviets via attacks on proxies (like the Venezuelan Communist Party, as he had the previous March), attack the Soviets by name, and in effect push both the Soviet Union and Cuba to the brink of a schism by making a whole series of threats that might, given his reputation, seem plausible. He could even couple a denunciation of the Soviets with an overture to China. The obvious drawback: Were he to take this route, he might miscalculate as to how far the Soviets could be pushed and, were he to go too far and the Soviets pulled out of Cuba, his people and his government would face unprecedented shortages without the available resources to deal with the situation. Moreover, even if the Chinese were to look favorably on an overture, it was unlikely they could meet Cuba's needs in either the short or long term.

2. *Cave In to the Soviets.* He could, in principle, inform the Soviets that after discussing Kosygin's message with his Cuban comrades in the leadership, they had decided that the Soviets were correct, that Cuba had lost its way and would henceforth try much harder to be a loyal follower of its Soviet leader, acknowledging

Soviet hegemony at all relevant points. In effect, Cuba would become the East Germany of the Caribbean. Were the Soviet leaders given to political fantasies (to which they seem to have been more or less immune), it is still unlikely that anything this fantastic would have occurred to them. Castro was not the type for docile subservience, nor were the Cuban people, for that matter, as the Russians had first discovered during the missile crisis. In fact, it is highly unlikely that Brezhnev, Kosygin, and their colleagues in Moscow thought it remotely possible that Cuba would become something like the East Germany of the Caribbean, marching in lock-step with Moscow's every whim. Still, if the Soviets had really wanted to bring Cuba to its knees, by 1967 they certainly had the power to do so, and Castro knew it. So a capitulation by the Cubans, while it would be wildly out of character, was at least a theoretical possibility.

3. *Seek Independence (while waiting for Guevara's success, but preparing to resist).* There were two tracks of the Cuban pursuit of independence and space to maneuver, even if it meant openly opposing the Soviet line. First, in foreign policy, support revolutions in the Third World, which of course was what Che Guevara's mission was all about. Carry on publicly, for the time being, as if Kosygin had never come to Havana, keeping all available options open while awaiting for the results of Che Guevara's mission in Bolivia. It was, by late June 1967, still possible that Guevara and his fighters could ignite a substantial revolt in Bolivia, perhaps even elsewhere, spreading the "spark of revolution" throughout the Andes and beyond. Unfortunately, one implication of keeping all options open was that mounting a large Cuban effort to buttress Guevara's small band was not feasible. To do so, after having been told unequivocally by Kosygin that the Soviets were deeply offended by Guevara's presence and mission in Bolivia, might in fact have been received in Moscow as the last straw—as a response so defiant as to leave no Soviet option other than to pull out of Cuba. So all that could be done about Che's mission in Bolivia was wait and hope for the best. Meanwhile, Cuba must prepare to resist inevitable Soviet pressure to conform, especially if Che were to meet with disaster.

A second track concerned Cuba's domestic policy, in which Cuba would by means of moral incentives seek to build its own brand of communist society (at a time when the Russians were embracing material incentives with increasing fervor). The pinnacle of this policy—in many ways the symbolic equivalent of Guevara's mission in Bolivia—was the pursuit of a ten-million-ton sugar harvest by 1970. Both turned out to be chimerical, but at the time—in the summer of 1967—it seemed to the Cubans at least an open question as to whether they would succeed.

Castro and his colleagues chose the third option. They would wait and hope for good news from Bolivia, even though the outlook was bleak, and they would continue to mobilize Cuban society on something like a war footing in pursuit of the ten-million-ton harvest. If Che pulled off a miracle in Bolivia, many things might be possible, not excluding a private expression of forgiveness from the Soviets, who might even wish to take some of the credit for the success. Castro, meanwhile, had already begun to plan his program of *resistir*—resistance to pressure from the Soviets that would, as he saw it, compromise Cuba's revolution and reduce Cuba's room to maneuver independently.

In fact, Kosygin's visit had made a highly uncertain situation for Cuba even more complex, for Castro understood perfectly well by the time Kosygin had left for the airport on June 28 that the Cuban–Soviet relationship was entering a new phase. The "virtual ultimatum" was of course an important piece of new information that needed to be taken into account. The Russians, in other words, intended to put pressure on Cuba of a kind, and to an extent, that would likely far exceed the private requests and occasional public expressions of disapproval to which their protests about Cuban positions and behavior had theretofore been limited. Another factor was the terribly depressing news arriving daily about Guevara's deteriorating situation. But so too was the generally unfavorable trend in the Latin American political situation, which increasingly found the Cuban-backed, rural guerrillas faring poorly, sometimes due in part to alleged "betrayals" by local communist parties (reminiscent of Guevara's situation in Bolivia). Latin America was, in fact, just on the verge of several right-wing military coups (in Uruguay and Argentina) in which Cuban-backed rebels would be ferociously crushed. Castro, of course, was well aware of all these ominous developments and signs.

Castro gave himself a little less than two months to react publicly to the impending crisis created by the confluence of these factors. For he was due to give the closing address, on August 10, 1967, to the conference in Havana of the Organization of Latin American Solidarity (OLAS), the specifically Latin American sequel to the broader initiative begun with the Tricontinental meeting the previous year. It was a major, hemisphere-wide forum, the perfect occasion for Castro to state Cuba's position on a host of controversial issues.

Even the organization of the conference was guaranteed to embarrass and enrage the Russians. Cuba arranged for nearly all of the delegations to be dominated by noncommunist revolutionary movements.[21] Castro's closing address to the OLAS meeting was unusually fiery and provocative, even by his standards. But it is now possible to see quite clearly with the benefit of hindsight that the speech contains all the essential elements of the emerging Cuban strategy of resistance to the Soviet "virtual ultimatum" (the existence of which, at that point, would have been known only to the Cuban and Soviet leaders). It laid out a kind of "game plan" that Cuba would follow in the months ahead, a three-part program of resistance and defiance of the Russians and virtually everything the Cubans believed

Moscow stood for. He concluded his OLAS address with three messages: one to the Russians, one to the Cuban people, and one to the Cuban leadership and Communist Party.

- *To the Soviets.* Castro defiantly declared a state of ideological war to exist "between those who want to make revolution and those who do not want to make it. It is the conflict," he said, "between those who want to make it and those who want to curb it."[22] And he was savage and unremitting in his critique of the Venezuelan Communist Party, begun the previous March. He declared that the Soviet-backed Venezuelan party was led by immoral "rightist" forces who had unforgivably betrayed the Cuban-backed guerrillas fighting in the rural areas. He claimed that these traitors to the revolutionary cause had now "completely unmasked themselves, and said 'let's have an election,' and they became electoralists."[23] *The message to the Soviets was this: Cuba will continue to make revolution even to the point of engaging in conflict with Soviet-supported entities that oppose it.*
- *To the Cuban People.* Castro told his people that while the Revolution does not seek conflict for its own sake, "neither will they see the Revolution hesitating, the Revolution giving up; they'll never see the Revolution yielding one iota of its principles." There will be no turning back, no watering down of Cuba's sacred mission to resist imperialism by making revolution. "For 'Patria o Muerte' . . . means being revolutionaries until death, it means being a proud people until death."[24] This remark was heavy with significance for Cubans by August 1967. In an expression that had already taken on a kind of canonical significance, Castro had said on many occasions: "within the Revolution, anything is possible; outside the Revolution, nothing is possible." *The message to the Cuban people was this: You will be called on to continue to make revolution, to continue to aspire to the ethical standard of Che Guevara, until death. Anything else is "outside the Revolution."*
- *To the Cuban Communist Party and Leadership.* Castro made it clear that the *unity* of the party would remain inviolable. His particular target in the speech was the group headed by Aníbal Escalante, some of whom had been purged from the leadership in March 1962 as "sectarians"—as old-line, pro-Soviet communists who sought to oust Castro and his colleagues, assume control in Cuba, and take a line with the Russians that closely resembled that of the Eastern European countries. Castro now referred to Escalante—who had returned from exile in the Soviet Union in 1964—and his group with the belittling term *microfaction.* According to Castro, "they have never believed in Revolution, they haven't learned in eight years, nor in ten years, and they will never learn."[25] Moreover, Castro asserted, the members of the microfaction committed the original sin: they agreed

with the Soviets in the missile crisis. "They were the ones," he said angrily, "who ... at the time of the October crisis thought that we should have let Yankee imperialism inspect us, search us from head to foot, let the planes fly over low, in fact everything." Indeed, Castro told his audience, they are traitors. He asserted: the microfaction group "constitutes a new form of counter-revolutionary activity ... the same as McNamara, Johnson and all those people."[26] *The message to the party and leadership was his conclusion to the speech: "this little island will always be a revolutionary wall of granite and against it all conspiracies, all intrigues, and all aggressions will be smashed."*[27]

These, then, would be the three pillars of Cuban resistance in the months ahead. There would be no caving in to the Soviet demand for moderation in Cuban international behavior, no let-up in the relentless pursuit of the selfless communist ideal, exemplified by Che Guevara, and no toleration of pro-Soviet dissidents within the party. The wagons were circled. The Cubans had dug in. The threats implied in the Soviet "virtual ultimatum" had been answered. The "answer" was to meet the perceived threat in a way that by 1967 had become the favored Cuban riposte: with counterthreats to resist any outside effort to divert Cuba from its chosen revolutionary path.

Underlying these "three pillars" was the objective that buttressed Cuban policy throughout this period: an independent policy that met what the Cubans believed were *Cuba's* security needs, no matter what "line" was being given out in Moscow at the time. The Cubans had seen all too clearly in October and November of 1962 that if they did not look out for their security interests and left this task to the Soviets (as was the case in Eastern Europe, for example), Cuba could once again be betrayed and abandoned. In his speech to OLAS, Castro had said, in effect, to the Soviets: We're in charge, Escalante et al. are not running this or any other show; we have our own foreign policy, centrally involving support for revolution in the Third World; and we are also running our own show in domestic affairs, and the ten-million-ton harvest in 1970 will prove that we can do so successfully.

"SEREMOS COMO EL CHE"

In the early autumn, word reached Havana that Che Guevara and his guerrillas had met with disaster. Guevara was captured on October 8, 1967, executed at a schoolhouse in the mountain town of La Higuera, Bolivia, and his force was destroyed. The French philosopher and activist Regis Debray was a confidant of both Castro and Guevara. Recalling the moment, Debray has written that Guevara's death was "like a cold shower to those living in the euphoria of this exceptional period," after which "the rural guerrilla's curve turned downward, ineluctably, irreversibly."[28]

Castro biographer Tad Szulc is eloquent on the far-reaching impact of the death of Che Guevara:

> The death of Ernesto Che Guevara in the Bolivian jungle on October 8, 1967, climaxing the destruction of his guerrilla movement there, was the central drama in the history of the Cuban revolution in the decade of the 1960s. . . . His ultimate disappearance had a profound impact on the evolution of Fidel Castro's domestic and international policies. It even helped Castro to settle his disputes with the Soviet Union, festering since the 1962 missile crisis.[29]

Guevara's personal demise, together with the utter lack of any "chain reaction" the Cubans hoped his mission might have in Latin America, spelled the end of that particular dream. It died with Guevara.

As to banishing the shadow of the missile crisis from the relationship, there would be some tough bargaining ahead—threats and counterthreats which left plenty to chance—before it was laid aside, at least for the time being. The shadow was never really banished with finality because in essence it derived from the extreme asymmetry of interests, power, and resources of Cuba and the Soviet Union, and from the almost antithetical trajectories of the relations of each with the United States. The shadow of the missile crisis past would periodically haunt the Cubans and Soviets up to, and even a little beyond, the demise of the USSR.

On October 18, 1967, Castro delivered a eulogy for Guevara in Havana before a million grieving Cubans.[30] In his speech, Castro began a process of portraying Guevara as what today might be called a "role model." "Che," Castro said, "has become a model of what men should be, not only for our people but also for people everywhere in Latin America. Che carried to its highest expression revolutionary stoicism, the revolutionary spirit of sacrifice, revolutionary combativeness, the revolutionary spirit of work."[31] Cuban children would henceforth recite daily: *"Seremos como el Che"* ("We will be like Che").[32] Moreover, the "cult of Che" spread instantly and seemingly everywhere after his demise. The following spring and summer, during the student demonstrations in Paris and elsewhere, Guevara's image was ubiquitous on T-shirts and posters, along with slogans such as "Be realistic, demand the impossible," that did indeed reflect the philosophy behind the life and death of this remarkable man.

As the autumn of 1967 gave way to winter, the cold war between the Soviets and Cubans continued unabated. Neither Fidel nor Raul Castro chose to attend the celebration of the fiftieth anniversary of the Great October Revolution in Moscow. Shortly thereafter, Cuba pointedly chose to absent itself from a Soviet-organized preparatory meeting of world communist parties in Budapest.[33]

But no longer would the Soviets sit by idly and tolerate this behavior. Cuba finally had gone too far. In October the Cuban foreign trade minister learned in

Moscow that the Soviets would not raise the level of fuel deliveries to Cuba at a rate commensurate with the growing Cuban need for petroleum. In his annual January 2 address celebrating the anniversary of the triumph of the Revolution, Castro announced the necessity for gasoline rationing and ordered sugar mills to begin to use alternative fuels. At the time, Cuba depended on the Soviets for approximately 98 percent of its petroleum. In that speech, Castro told his audience that the dignity of the revolution did not permit Cuba to beg the Soviets for oil.[34] Kosygin, it seems, had not been bluffing. The Soviets had begun to turn the screw on vulnerable, oil-needy Cuba. Castro retaliated rhetorically on January 13 in a speech to the International Cultural Congress in Havana, in which he alluded transparently to the Soviets as "Marxist fossils" and a "pseudo-revolutionary church."[35]

A few days later, the Soviets announced that they were replacing their longtime, pro-Cuban ambassador in Havana, Aleksander Alekseev, with Aleksander Soldatov, whose most recent post had been as ambassador to Great Britain. The message the Cubans received in the withdrawal of Alekseev and his replacement with Soldatov was this: no more "sweetheart deals" favoring Cuba; no more overlooking Cuba's inefficient use of the massive Soviet support it was receiving; Cuba would henceforth be held to the same rational standards as other countries with whom the Soviet Union had significant political and economic ties. To the Cubans, this was just one more example of the betrayal by the Soviets of the very meaning of the phrase "fraternal comrades."

By late January 1968, therefore, this was the situation in the escalating conflict between Cuba and the Soviet Union. The Soviets had followed the tough line laid down by Kosygin with concrete actions that the Cubans were forced to accept: not meeting the Cuban requirements for petroleum; withdrawing the popular Alekseev and replacing him with Soldatov, a tough diplomat known to have an Anglo–U.S. bias; and stalling on the overall Cuban–Soviet trade agreement, which was still unsigned and might conceivably remained unsigned—yet another threat by the Soviets leaving something to chance. So far, however, the Cuban response had been almost entirely rhetorical, consisting of attacks on Soviet-backed parties and regimes, and hortatory calls to the Cubans to hunker down, to "be like Che," in the event that the Soviets cut Cuba off altogether, creating a domestic crisis in Cuba of potentially catastrophic proportions. It was tough Soviet action versus tough Cuban talk, so far.

"TREASONABLE AND COUNTERREVOLUTIONARY ACTIVITIES"

When the Cubans finally acted, they did it with flair and creativity—a virtuoso performance even by the highly theatrical standards on the island. A visitor to Cuba at the time, French journalist K. S. Karol recalls that on January 23 or January 24, he was to have been picked up by Fidel Castro and taken to visit an experimental farm. Castro did not show up, a not altogether unexpected event, given his helter-skelter schedule in those days. Suddenly, however:

> On January 24, 1968, all the most important Cuban leaders suddenly disappeared. I learned that the Central Committee of the Communist Party was meeting in plenary session. The conference was to last three days and was to be held *in camera* [behind closed doors]. Friends who were present merely reported that Fidel had delivered a remarkable ten-hour speech, one of the longest of his career, but they absolutely refused to tell me what about. At the time, the strangest rumors were circulating in Havana, especially at the Havana Libre [Hotel], where I was staying. Some claimed there would be a rupture with the USSR. . . . In any case, the suspense increased as the hours ticked by.[36]

Karol expressed his amazement that he could not get any of his high-ranking friends in the Cuban government to tell him even what the ten-hour speech of Castro was *about*, let alone what he had said. Secrets tended not to last long in Cuba, but this one proved impenetrable to Karol's efforts to find out anything about Castro's speech.

Finally at noon on Sunday, January 28, some answers were forthcoming, initially over Radio Havana. It was announced that Aníbal Escalante and a group of coconspirators had been convicted of traitorous activities also involving officials from the Soviet embassy. They had been expelled from the party and given prison sentences—Escalante's term was for fifteen years. And on February 4, the official organ of the party, *Granma*, gave over the entire issue to the trial that had just concluded. On the front page above the fold, a huge picture appeared of Fidel Castro speaking to the Central Committee, just in front and to his left of a large photograph of Che Guevara. The headline read: "MICROFACTION UNMASKED: Aníbal Escalante and Other Traitors Remanded to Revolutionary Tribunals." The summary on page 1 by *Granma* director Jorge Enrique Mendoza went straight to the main points: Escalante and his people had been put on trial; and Raul Castro had stated the case for the prosecution, indicting the Escalante microfaction for "treasonable and counterrevolutionary activities."[37]

Mendoza concluded his summary of the secret proceedings with the following cryptic statement:

> On the third and last day of the meeting, First Secretary of our Party and Prime Minister of the Revolutionary Government, Major Fidel Castro, began his remarkable report at 12:20 P.M., which, brief recesses intervening, he concluded after midnight.[38]

There was a good deal of speculation at the time about the precise nature of Castro's secret speech. Many assumed Fidel Castro had merely elucidated his brother's presentation in some way that put the blame for the affair overtly on the Soviets. As one scholar who was in Cuba at the time put it: "The presumption was that he [Fidel Castro] had dotted the 'i's' and crossed the 't's' of Raul's exposure of Soviet complicity with the microfaction," which, if made public, "could have forced the Kremlin to risk an open and severe reprimand of the Castro Regime, or even a break in relations."[39] That speech, Castro's personal analysis of the Cuban missile crisis, is now published for the first time, nearly thirty-five years after it was given, as chapter 2 of this book.

In other words, two separate but interconnected events had occurred behind closed doors, each of which found one of the Castro brothers acting in the role of prosecutor on an aspect of Cuba's relations with the Soviet Union. First, Raul Castro had accused the Escalante microfaction of conspiring with officials from the Soviet embassy to provide false and viciously anti-Castro reports to Soviet officials in Havana. The ultimate objective, according to Raul Castro's report, had been a Soviet-backed removal, in some fashion left to the imagination of the reader, of the present Cuban government and its leaders, and its replacement by the group led by Aníbal Escalante—in effect, a coup against Fidel Castro, Raul Castro, and their colleagues, presumably with the blessing, if not the active participation, of the Russians. By early February, these proceedings were published in great detail in *Granma*. In Castro's secret speech, we now know, he prosecuted (and convicted) the Soviets of all manner of misconduct in the missile crisis of October 1962. Thus, Raul Castro *publicly* attacked the pro-Soviet element within the Cuban Communist Party and got rid of it once and for all. Castro, on the other hand, *privately* attacked the Soviets themselves and rid his colleagues in the leadership of any remaining illusions they might have had about the reliability of the Soviets and their commitment to Cuba's security interests. It was an amazing accusatory duet, clever in its conception and forceful in its implementation, with the accusations backed up in each case by a plethora of empirical evidence.

In this joint three-day exercise, the Cuban leadership had at last acted on the points laid out in Castro's August 10, 1967, OLAS address. These, in sum, were the messages sent to the various intended audiences by the results of the trial of the microfaction and the secret speech of January 24–26, 1968:

- *To the Soviets.* The key message sent to the Soviets may have been stronger than was necessary, but the Cubans had no way of knowing how seriously leaders in Moscow had taken the anti-Castro messages passed on through the embassy in Havana or, indeed, whether Brezhnev, Kosygin et al. were even aware of what had been going on. Still, the Cubans felt that in dealing with the Soviet "imperialists" they should apply the rule they always followed in dealing with the U.S. imperialists: never appear weak; assume the worst case is the most probable and act accordingly; don't take any chances by underestimating the threat. The worst case? Some kind of coup against Castro. Indeed, a rumor had circulated in Havana just before the events of late January 1968 that the KGB might try to eliminate Fidel Castro and replace him with Raul Castro, who was thought to be close to the Soviets personally and ideologically.[40] But Raul had been the prosecutor of the microfaction. And Carlos Rafael Rodríguez, a former leader of the old-line communists, spoke voluminously at the trial against the microfaction. *The message to the Soviets was this: You have no anti-Castro allies in Cuba who matter any more; those you might have counted on to lead a pro-Soviet Cuba in a post-Castro government are in prison and no longer available. A coup of any kind, bloodless or bloody, is thus doomed to failure. So forget about it.*

- *To the Cuban People.* The publication in *Granma* of all the minute details of the trial of the microfaction served to reinforce in a very effective way what lay "within the Revolution," and what was therefore an acceptable view to take, and what lay "outside the Revolution," and was thus unacceptable. For example, members of the microfaction were said to have told Soviet and East German interlocutors that the goal of a ten-million-ton sugar harvest for 1970 "is almost impossible." They condemned the use of "moral incentives, with absolute disregard of material incentives." One went so far as to tell the political commissar of a Soviet fishing vessel that "There is a leftist, adventurist deviation . . . running the country." Finally, there were personal attacks on Fidel Castro himself. One defendant was reported to have said that "Fidel wants . . . to rise to a higher stature . . . than that of Marx, Engels and Lenin. Policy is decided by one man, Fidel Castro." Perhaps the most radical departure from what was "within the Revolution" was made by a member of the microfaction who, according to Raul Castro's brief, had said, "Che had crippled the economy. . . . The best thing he did was to leave Cuba"—which was pure sacrilege in the Cuba of early 1968—which on January 2, Fidel Castro had declared to be "the year of the heroic guerrilla," in Guevara's honor.[41] *The message to the Cuban people was this: None of these presumably pro-Soviet sentiments were acceptable "within the Revolution"—this was the clear message in the lines just quoted and many more besides; but the message between the lines was that the Soviets' views on the way Cuba should conduct itself should be discounted. The Soviets have not, do not, and will not run Cuba.*

- *To the Cuban Communist Party and Leadership.* Castro's attack on the Soviets' behavior in the missile crisis in his secret speech is chapter 2 of this book. His attack was blistering, unrelenting, sometimes ironical, often dismissive and damning in the extreme, especially since extensive documentation was provided along with Castro's memories of the events. To summarize Castro's brief against the Soviets in the missile crisis: the Soviets rejected the Cubans' advice in at least seven crucial aspects of the operation. Against the advice of the Cubans, according to Castro, the Soviets: (1) refused to make a public announcement of the missile deployment; (2) refused properly to camouflage the sites where the missiles were to be deployed; (3) refused to publicize (what the Cubans regarded as) a legal and binding treaty between the two countries that defined the terms of the deployment; (4) refused on all occasions to challenge the United States—at the blockade line, on overflights, and so on; (5) refused to consider in the resolution of the crisis any of the "five points" that Cuba considered critical to its own security; (6) refused to consult with, or even properly to inform, the Cubans of the Soviet decision to terminate the crisis (and the deployment); and (7) refused to leave all but a faint residue of a trip wire to deter a U.S. invasion (in the form of Soviet combat troops) or the means to combat attacks by CIA-backed Cuban exile groups operating out of Central America (in the form of Ilyushin planes). *The message to the party and leadership was this: Although we need Soviet assistance and support, do not ever depend upon them in a crisis involving Cuba's security; they are fundamentally imperialists seeking deals with the U.S., they are cowards, and they are supremely unreliable. Never again will Cuba trust its security to them.*

Thus did Fidel Castro, Raul Castro, and their colleagues in the Cuban leadership act on the principles first coherently laid out publicly in Castro's August 10, 1967, speech to OLAS. It is difficult to imagine sending such signals any more clearly than they were sent, and still not provoking the Soviet Union into a complete schism with Havana.

A FATEFUL SEVEN MONTHS

So the Soviets had delivered their "virtual ultimatum" and had begun to turn the screw on the Cubans. The Cubans responded in such a way as to show their extreme displeasure, and also to lay down some rough ground rules for a rapprochement. Just in case the Soviets were contemplating getting rid of Castro, they now knew there were no real alternatives. Just in case they were thinking of breaking off ties with Cuba, they now knew that the Cubans did not want to go this far. How did they know this? Because the secret speech remained *secret*. Oleg Darusenkov said in an interview that the Soviets were aware of it, were aware of its drift, perhaps even some of its content. But the fact that it was secret and meant to remain so was correctly perceived in Moscow as something of an olive branch.[42] This, in spite of the fact that Cubans with long experience in Cuban affairs, including Oleg Darusenkov and Kiva

Maidanik, believed the microfaction trial to be a travesty along the lines of Stalin's show trials of the 1930s—much ideological ado about little or nothing of consequence.[43] However that may have been, the Soviets understood the events of late January 1968 more or less in the way the Cubans intended: It was time to stop fighting, time for rapprochement on terms acceptable to both sides.

It was still not all smooth sailing, however. Castro's March 13 speech in which he proposed to move willy-nilly to a fully communist society via a "profound revolutionary offensive," totally devoid of material incentives, did nothing to calm the nerves of those in Moscow who wondered about the wisdom of continuing the current relationship with Cuba.[44] "Gentlemen," said Castro, "we did not make a Revolution here to establish the right to trade."[45] Then referring to the Soviets so that all present could identify them, but without mentioning them by name, he added:

> [It] must be said very clearly—and it goes without saying that the Revolution is not out to make enemies for the fun of it, but neither is it afraid of making enemies when necessary—it must be said that private trade, self-employment, private industry, or anything like it will not have any future in this country.[46]

What if such "enemies" as Cuba might make decided to discontinue assistance to Cuba because Cuba took such a radical path domestically? Then Cuba would become truly independent economically, according to Castro, via the projected ten-million-ton sugar harvest in 1970. "A sugar harvest of ten million tons," he said defiantly, "has become something more than an economic goal; it is something that has been converted into a point of honor for this Revolution."[47]

Soviet displeasure with that speech may have had something to do with both the timing and terms of the Soviet–Cuban Trade Protocol of 1968, which was initialed on March 22 (late by previous standards) and which called for only a 10 percent increase in the (in effect) Soviet subsidy, versus a 23 percent increase in 1967 over 1966. Meanwhile, talks behind the scenes in both Moscow and Havana suddenly became more productive and less vituperative.[48]

Castro made the nascent rapprochement more or less public in his annual speech on the July 26 commemorating the 1953 attack on the Moncada Barracks. He said nothing at all about Vietnam or about the Venezuelan Communist Party or, in fact, anything that might have been interpreted as anti-Soviet. And he said something that would have been unthinkable even six months before. "We do not claim," he said with theretofore rare modesty on the topic, "to be the most perfect revolutionaries . . . the most perfect interpreters of Marxist-Leninist ideas. But we do have our own form of interpreting these ideas."[49]

Here was the culmination of the tumultuous year since Kosygin had visited. The Cuban leadership, over the year, had fashioned a new set of terms on which Cuba could relate to the Soviet Union. Simply stated, the message from Castro's July 26 speech was this: Cuba was ready to live and let live with the Soviets, so long as the Soviets were willing to do the same. This was going to be a relationship based on mutual respect and reciprocal benefit, not a parent–child relationship. The Cubans therefore would expect the Soviets not to interfere with Cuban domestic politics: there would be no more Escalante affairs; Cuba would organize its economy in a way that it determined would be best for the Cuban people.

All that was left was a clarification about foreign policy. Cuba was willing to be a more gracious, less tendentious recipient of Soviet largesse. But it had not worked through yet how, in return, to show the Soviets that Cuba could serve Soviet interests. This was a delicate issue, because the Cuban leadership understood that a mutual, respectful relationship had to be built on reciprocal benefits. At the same time, it did not want to appear to be merely a Soviet lapdog.[50] As it happened, the opportunity to define the foreign policy terms of the relationship would occur less than a month after the July 26 speech.

AUGUST 23, 1968: FROM THE SHADOW OF THE MISSILE CRISIS TO THE SHADOW OF THE FUTURE

In the late summer of 1968, what was an already momentous year around the world became even more dramatic. On August 20 armored divisions of Soviet and other Warsaw Pact forces moved across Czechoslovakia, occupying Prague within hours. Thus the so-called Prague Spring, the attempt, led by Alexander Dubcek, to construct what he called "socialism with a human face," came to sudden and brutal end. While not entirely unexpected, the intervention still shocked the world, and none were more shocked than the socialist parties of Western Europe, many of which quickly condemned the Soviets and sided with the Czech liberal reformers.

In Havana, the developing crisis had gotten heavy coverage in the newspapers and on radio and television over the summer, almost all of it with a decidedly pro-Czech bias. And why not? Here was a small country trying, in the shadow of a great superpower, to carve out its own unique approach to the construction of a socialist society. But Cuban sympathy for the Czechs' aspirations was tempered by the recognition of how the West may have been trying to take advantage of the Prague Spring—in much the same way Cuban leaders imagined the United States would try to penetrate and control an "open" Cuban society.[51] This was one reason that Castro had railed against the counterculture movement in the United States, because it was becoming increasingly attractive in Cuba. Might Cuban youth demand an openness that would make Cuba vulnerable to penetration by U.S. operatives? Might they be attracted to the hedonism of the counterculture and demand the consumer goods Cuba could not afford? One purpose of his March 13, 1968, "revolutionary offensive" speech was to ward off such a possibility, by defining a revolutionary as someone who was motivated by moral incentives, not materialism.

Still, the Soviet-led invasion of August 20, 1968, shocked Havana. It bore little resemblance to the failed U.S-backed attempt to invade Cuba at the Bay of Pigs in April 1961. Tens of thousands of Warsaw Pact troops in full battle gear, carried across the Czech border by the largest tank force amassed in Europe since World War II, entered Prague unchallenged, occupied the city, and thereafter successfully intimidated those with any thought of resisting them. However, soon after the news of the invasion reached Havana, a virtual news blackout occurred regarding the events in Czechoslovakia. Except for a few obscure references to Soviet communiques claiming that the Warsaw Pact forces had been "called in" by anonymous comrades in Prague, nothing was forthcoming. Nevertheless, Cuban sentiment continued to run strongly in favor of the Czechs. For example, during the news blackout, Cuban onlookers gave their vocal support to a parade of Czech technicians marching through the Vedado section of downtown Havana. Shouts of *"Patria o muerte"* ("Fatherland or death") were heard from the crowds of Cubans as the technicians marched through the city.[52] Finally, on the afternoon of August 23, Radio Havana announced that Fidel Castro would address the nation on radio and television at 9:00 P.M. that evening. Nearly everyone expected Castro to lambast the Russians and express common cause with the Czechs.

One such person was Felix Pita, the young, energetic editor of *Juvenutud Rebelde* ("Rebel Youth"). In an interview in Havana, he vividly recalled the events of August 1968 from the perspective of a young, patriotic, politically aware Cuban:

> I think all Cubans' first reaction to the news of the Soviet invasion was one of revulsion at what the Soviets had done. That was our instinctual reaction. The invasion of a tiny country by its neighboring superpower—it is no mystery, just a few years after Playa Giron [i.e., the Bay of Pigs] why we should feel this way. This was my own immediate reaction. I was then the editor of *Juvenutud Rebelde* newspaper. After my staff and I heard the news, we worked through the night and produced an issue the following day [August 21] which contained the headline "Czechoslovakia Occupied." Then I got a call from someone in the leadership telling me to go home and stay at home until further notice. In effect, I was being put under house arrest. "Occupied," of course has a special meaning in Cuba. It is connected with the many times the U.S. has occupied our country since the War of Independence. I stayed there for three days—until Fidel made his speech. Then I got another call, from the same person, telling me I could go back to work at the newspaper. When I asked him why the change, he said that discussions within the leadership about how Fidel should respond to the Soviet invasion were very intense, very heated, and that a couple of people at the top agreed with the assessment alluded to in my headline, "Czechoslovakia Occupied."[53]

Felix Pita had followed his instincts and, like any good journalist, he wanted to get his story out first. The problem, to which he alludes, is that his story was the *wrong* story, the wrong interpretation, an interpretation at variance with the one for which Castro would argue in his speech of 9:00 P.M. on August 23, 1968. As Felix Pita said in the interview, when he got home and he began to think about what was happening, it dawned on him that Castro might actually be planning to *defend* the Soviet invasion. If it was true that he was going to back the Russians, said Pita, then the situation would mirror the immediate aftermath of the missile crisis, when Castro also went along with the Soviets' terms of resolving the crisis. "Once again," said Pita, "Fidel had a lot of explaining to do."[54]

And explain he did, more than sixty hours after the Soviet invasion, in one of the most difficult, complex, and pivotal speeches in his more-than-a-half-century career of making notable speeches. He sat down at a desk in the television studio, in front of a portrait of Che Guevara. Then he began in what was for him a remarkably somber, almost reluctant mood, as if perhaps he would rather not make this speech. "We are here tonight," he began, "to analyze the situation in Czechoslovakia." Then he gave fair warning of what was to come:

> Some of the things that we are going to state here will be, in some cases, in contradiction with the emotions of many: in other cases, in contradiction with our own interests; and, in others, they will constitute serious risks for our country.[55]

He then went on to say that "the Czechoslovak regime was heading toward capitalism and was inexorably heading toward imperialism. . . . We considered that Czechoslovakia was moving toward a counterrevolutionary situation."[56] That is, the liberal Dubcek reforms of the "Prague Spring" were leading in the direction of splintering the socialist bloc—with Czechoslovakia possibly leaving it. As one who emphasized unendingly the importance of the unity of the socialist world, this was unacceptable to Castro.

Because of the need for unity, and because the Czechs were moving toward breaking with the principles of the socialist bloc, Castro uttered the words that Cubans like Felix Pita never expected to hear from their "Maximum Leader." The following passage was the one most often quoted in the international press, in part because it was so surprising, and in part because it seemed to lead to the remarkable conclusion that the Soviets had finally "brought Castro and Cuba under control." Castro went on:

> The essential point to be accepted or not accepted is whether the socialist camp could allow a political situation to develop which would lead to the breaking away of a socialist country, to its falling into the arms of imperialism. And our point of view is that

the socialist camp has the right to prevent this one way or another. . . . We acknowledge the bitter necessity that called for the sending of those forces into Czechoslovakia; we do not condemn the socialist countries that made that decision.[57]

This "bitter necessity," Castro said, is in spite of the fact that "the sovereignty of the
Czechoslovak state was violated. . . . Not the slightest trace of legality exists. Frankly,
none whatever." The necessity of the intervention, he said, "can only be explained
from a political point of view"—that is, the need to maintain the unity of the socialist camp, no matter what.[58]

So the deed was done. Cuba did "not condemn" the invasion. But Castro's
analysis of these events was much more subtle and interesting than can be gleaned
from the single passage in which he refuses to condemn the invasion. He asked
throughout, for example, how such a situation could have developed, strongly im-
plying that the Soviets had been asleep at the wheel at least since January 5, 1968,
when the liberal forces had removed Antonin Novotny from his post as leader of the
Czech Communist Party and replaced him with Alexander Dubcek. He also asked
whether now might be the time for the "socialist camp" (i.e., the Soviets) to intervene in some of the Latin American countries in order to shape up the do-nothing,
"electoralist" communist parties—the very parties that opposed the true revolutionaries who had been backed by Cuba.

But he really hit his rhetorical stride when he got to the question of Cuba's security, and the security of those Cuba considered to be her sister states:

> We ask ourselves: Will the Warsaw Pact divisions also be sent to Vietnam if the Yan-
> kee imperialists step up their aggression against that country if the people of Vietnam
> request that aid? Will they send the divisions of the Warsaw Pact to the Democratic
> People's Republic of Korea if the Yankee imperialists attack that country? Will they
> send the divisions of the Warsaw Pact to Cuba if the Yankee imperialists attack our
> country, or even in the case of the threat of a Yankee imperialist attack on our country,
> if our country requests it?[59]

But of course, this "question" was not really a question, but an accusation. Castro knew that the "answer" to his question was "no," and he had known this
since October 28, 1962, when he heard over the radio that his Soviet ally had
decided to remove its missiles from Cuba in exchange for (what the Cubans saw
as) a worthless pledge from the Kennedy administration not to attack and invade
the island. What really must have galled him was that the Soviets would intervene next door in Czechoslovakia, essentially for reasons of state, while they had
left Cuba high and dry in 1962, proving that the phrase "socialist fraternalism"
was, when the chips were down and the Soviets were involved, an oxymoronic
expression.

In fact, this speech, far from being the "rubber stamp" for the Soviet invasion it is often misinterpreted to be, shows Castro at his empathetic best when describing the situation of the Czechs, a situation he could relate to with ease. "This experience and this action," he says, "constitute a bitter and tragic situation for the people of Czechoslovakia." This is because:

> An entire nation has been exposed to the truly traumatic situation of foreign occupation, albeit by socialist armies. Millions of people have been placed before this tragic alternative: they must either remain passive in the face of circumstances that recall certain episodes of the past, or else they must make common cause with pro-Yankee spies and agents, and with other enemies of socialism.[60]

The tragic circumstances of the Czechs, in fact, led him to deliver this complex and tortured speech, in which he tried to show that Cuba's position is also tragic in a sense analogous to that of Czechoslovakia. Castro had two options, both unacceptable. First, Castro could violate his own instincts as a citizen of a small and vulnerable country, and endorse the invasion of another small country by a neighboring superpower, but thereby join with his supposed allies in supporting the invasion. Or, second, he could follow his instincts and repudiate the invasion, but thereby join with his enemies, such as the United States, who also condemned the invasion. It was a no-win situation for Castro and Cuba.

Castro must have felt this tension profoundly. The American filmmaker and historian Saul Landau believes he did. Landau, who was in Cuba to make a documentary film, was the only foreigner in the studio in Havana in which Castro made his speech on August 23, 1968. He recalls that "Fidel was obviously uncomfortable making that speech. When he finished, he just rushed out."[61] But of course he couldn't play it straight from the heart, as was his habit, relying on his instincts, as Felix Pita had done when he heard the news. It was this that seems to give the speech such poignancy for anyone who understands its context and takes the time to read it.

In fact, Castro and Cuba were faced in this instance with a classic example of what the American philosopher Thomas Nagel has called a "moral blind alley." These arise in cases where ends and means seem to be morally at war with one another. In Castro's case, he knew that if he endorsed the invasion of Czechoslovakia, that decision would probably be far more beneficial to Cuba—due to the Soviets' "reward" for coming to their support—than if he were to repudiate it. Yet every fiber in his body no doubt led him to want to condemn such an act, on principle, no matter what the consequences because, to any Cuban, certainly to Castro, the invasion of a small country by a large one is simply wrong, is immoral, is unacceptable. As Nagel points out, "The moral dilemma in certain situations of crisis will be

acute" because it will "appear that every possible course of action or inaction is unacceptable for one reason or another."[62]

Notice that Nagel does not say that in such situations one chooses "the lesser
of two evils." He says there are situations in which all the available courses of action are in fact morally unacceptable to one faced with such a dilemma. In Castro's case, endorsing the invasion seems supremely immoral and hypocritical, and
a terrible precedent to set, especially for the leader of a country that is at risk of
just such an invasion. On the other hand, condemning the Soviets for the invasion seems irresponsible, even immoral. Global imperialism was Cuba's foremost
enemy and the enemy of all poor countries. International solidarity against imperialism was the only way it could be overcome, and the Czechs seemed to be undermining such unity.

Castro must also have felt tremendous resentment toward the Soviets for putting
him in this position. No doubt he recalled vividly Cuba's experience with the Soviets in the missile crisis. Nagel concludes that such situations prove that "it is naive
to suppose that there is a solution to every moral problem with which the world can
face us. We have always known the world is a bad place. It appears that it may be an
evil place as well."[63] One gathers that Castro, squirming uncharacteristically behind
the microphone in that Havana television studio on August 23, 1968, would have
had little difficulty confirming this conclusion from his own immediate experience.

"Power," the American theologian Reinhold Niebuhr wrote more than fifty years
ago, "cannot be wielded without guilt . . . even when it tries to subject itself to universal standards."[64] This is what makes Castro's speech on the Czech invasion such
a pivotal moment in the history of Cuba since the triumph of the Revolution. Having reached a rapprochement with the Soviets over the course of a year or more of
very hard bargaining, of threats and counterthreats that left a good deal to chance,
Castro found himself in a position of supreme moral ambiguity, even of anguish,
perhaps also of some embarrassment, at the position he had to enunciate when he
went on the air to make his speech. He no longer could espouse the moral purity of
the Cuban Revolution in a vacuum—he could not simply "be like Che." Instead, he
had to weigh the consequences of his action against the feeling of doing something
that must have felt perfectly awful—and he had to do it with the world watching.
This was the "simple twist of fate"—the Soviet invasion of Czechoslovakia just as
Cuba and the Soviet Union were redefining their relationship—that had Castro and
Cuba in its clutches.

Castro did not shrink from the dilemma and instead seized this opportunity to
lay down the foreign policy terms of the new Cuban–Soviet relationship. Though
he did not condemn the invasion itself, he criticized virtually everything else connected with it. The only justification for the invasion, he said, was to secure international socialism. Yet this would not be a worthy goal, not worth trampling on the

sovereignty of a small country, unless the socialist camp lived up to its ideals—which, Castro charged, it had not done. Here was the final basis of rapprochement. Cuba would define for itself what it meant to be internationalist even as it acknowledged Soviet leadership. Particular members of the socialist camp might have unique interests, but at base they would be expected to support each other in the active pursuit of international socialism.

Castro and Cuba had come a long way from the "sad and luminous days" of October–November 1962 when the Cubans raged at the Russians, like King Lear shaking his fists at the heavens. There was also quite a *psychological* distance between the secret January 1968 speech on the missile crisis and the August 1968 speech on the Czech invasion. This time there would be no need for the speech to be secret. What needed to be said had to be public. This time there would not be carping criticism of prior bad faith. Instead, Castro would emphasize positive principles on which Cuba and the Soviet Union could agree, principles that would enable them to build a future together. This was the turning point from which future Cuban–Soviet relations evolved.

In his landmark 1984 book, *The Evolution of Cooperation*, Robert Axelrod wrote that a revolution of sorts in a relationship can take place when the players cease to "take the strategic setting as given . . . [and] . . . promote cooperation by transforming the strategic setting itself—for example, by enlarging the shadow of the future."[65] Henceforth, there would be no "threats that leave something to chance," no more undeclared wars between supposed allies who suspected one another of believing they were dealing with Cuban "children" or Soviet "parents." Strategies of conflict would become, from August 1968 onward, strategies of cooperation, from which Cuba would benefit, but so would the Soviet Union. As emphasized by Axelrod, whenever this happens, "the shadow of the future" comes to outweigh the mutual suspicions derived from the past. For Cuba, as for the Soviet Union, this meant above everything else that the shadow of the Cuban missile crisis of October 1962 was, by late August 1968, superseded by the shadow of a future that they both agreed they would share.

The evolution of the relationship did not occur in quite the way the Cuban leadership had hoped. The Cubans never were able to move Soviets to the point where they could empathize with their weaker partner, and over the next quarter century there were numerous instances of Cuban disappointment and Soviet frustration. Yet Cubans and Soviets generally abided by the basic principles of the relationship forged in the year between Kosygin's visit and the Soviet invasion of Czechoslovakia. Without forgetting the past, they were able to look to the future.

We are not sovereign by the grace of the Yankees, but in our own right . . . in order to take away our sovereignty it will be necessary to wipe us off the face of the earth. . . . We have not abdicated and we do not intend to abdicate any of our sovereign prerogatives in favor of the United States.

—Fidel Castro, 1962[1]

No one can deny that terrorism is today a dangerous and ethically indefensible phenomenon . . . the human and psychological damage brought on the American people by the unexpected and shocking death of thousands of innocent people . . . have shaken the world. . . . Whatever happens, the territory of Cuba will never be used for terrorist actions against the American people. . . . Our independence, our principles and our social achievements we will defend with honor to the last drop of blood, if we are attacked! It will not be easy to fabricate pretexts to do it. They are already talking about a war using all the necessary weapons but it will be good recalling that not even that would be a new experience. Almost four decades ago, hundreds of strategic and tactical nuclear weapons were aimed at Cuba and nobody remembers anyone of our countrymen sleepless over that. We are the same sons and daughters of that heroic people, with a patriotic and revolutionary conscience that is higher than ever.

—Fidel Castro, 2001[2]

EPILOGUE: CUBA'S STRUGGLE WITH THE UNITED STATES AFTER THE MISSLE CRISIS— THE CASE FOR REALISTIC EMPATHY

"The United States is always inventing something new in connection with Cuba."[3]

Toward the end of 1989 the unthinkable happened to Cuba: the Soviet Union began to collapse and the socialist world began to shrink. In the early 1970s, Cuba had integrated its economy into the Soviet-led consortium of socialist countries, and 85 percent of Cuba's trade occurred within that sphere. But apart from the economic impact the collapse of that system would have on Cuba, it raised the specter once again of the possibility that the United States might choose this moment of extraordinary vulnerability to rid Cuba of the revolutionary regime once and for all. This was the context in which Castro announced in mid-1990 that Cuba had entered what he called the "Special Period in Time of Peace." It was to be a period of unknown duration, and of unknown severity, in which Cuba would operate on the peacetime equivalent of a war footing.[4]

It was also a period in which, almost from the outset, the Cuban leadership began to resurrect the missile crisis of October 1962, as a kind of prototype of Cuban defiance and independence in the face of abandonment by the Soviet Union. One year after the November 1989 seismic political events in Europe, the Cubans published the correspondence between Fidel Castro and Nikita Khrushchev to which Castro referred repeatedly in the secret January 1968 speech (in chapter 2).[5] Formally the revelation of the letters was intended to correct the public impression that in 1962 Castro had irresponsibly pressured Khrushchev to launch a preemptive nuclear attack on the United States.[6] He hadn't. What he recommended, as his reading from the letters in the January 1968 speech show, was much more complex. But the publication of the letters also served another purpose.

Consider that in 1968 Castro's purpose in recalling the letters was to teach the new Central Committee members about Russian arrogance and incompetence, which buttressed Castro's argument that Cuba had to find its own path and not rely exclusively on the Soviets. In 1990 it was to teach a new generation a different lesson.[7] Now the Russians all but disappear from the discussion, almost as totally as the Soviet Union would soon disappear. The focus was rather on "the pride of being Cuban," of having resisted during those "sad and luminous days" of October 1962.[8] To what end? To arouse during the Special Period "the same intransigence and courage [that] was needed to repulse those who wanted to humiliate us through the imposition of an inspection of our territory."[9] That is, the focus was almost entirely on Cuba's situation with regard to the United States.

The shadow of the missile crisis had returned. Cuba would once again stand firm, unintimidated by an impending threat, willing to resist to the end. And how would it resist? Toward what would its stubborn determination be directed? The Cubans answered in November 1990: the "five points" that constituted the Cubans' demands during the resolution of the crisis itself, demands which both the United States and the Soviet Union ignored at the time of the crisis and ever since: (1) end the embargo; (2) halt subversion; (3) end attacks by exile groups at sea; (4) cease to violate Cuban air and naval space; and (5) give back Guantanamo.[10]

Not only had the *shadow* of the missile crisis returned for the Cubans, but so had key psychological aspects of the crisis itself—with Cuba abandoned again by the Russians, its five points still on the table, and facing the U.S. threat alone. The message for Cubans, especially the majority born since the missile crisis, was: We got through this before and we can do it again.

THE OCTOBER CRISIS CONTINUES

Fidel Castro's assessment of how the missile crisis ended can be stated simply: War was avoided, but peace was not secured. His "peace" would not be only the absence of conflict. It would be one that diminished the threats to Cuba's security. From Cuba's perspective the crisis was not merely about the missiles—which was the problem that absorbed the two superpowers—because its genesis lay in the avowed U.S. goal to overthrow the Cuban Revolution. The route to a meaningful peace could be cleared only by removing the real obstacle, namely, the continuing U.S. threat to the Revolution's survival.

Two of the five points remain relevant to the U.S.–Cuban relationship today, four decades after they were proposed: (1) U.S. withdrawal from the Guantánamo Bay Naval Base, which covers 117 square miles of the eastern part of the island; and (2) lifting the U.S. economic embargo and ceasing pressure worldwide to restrict

Cuban trade. Cuba views the unwanted U.S. military presence on its territory as a violation of sovereignty that also recalls a one-hundred-year history during which the United States has attempted to impose its will on the island.[11] U.S. economic sanctions against Cuba are more stringent than those the United States imposes on even the three "axis of evil" states. Their goal is stated clearly in the congressional report that accompanies the most recent extension of the embargo, the 1996 Helms-Burton Act: The law is "aimed at liberating the Cuban people from the dictatorship of Fidel Castro."[12]

Cuban officials thus operate from the assumption that their gigantic neighbor has contempt for Cuban sovereignty and seeks to overthrow the Cuban government, just as it has for more than forty years. In 1963 Castro asserted:

> The Cuban Government has put forward a proposal . . . declaring that it is ready to hold discussions with all those who are prepared to work for the improvement of relations and with all countries including the United States. But their answer is: new aggression against our country, new aggressive schemes and activities and the adoption of a series of steps to set up war bases in Central America to carry out aggressive activities against Cuba. They do not want to live together with us, but we are here and we shall remain here.[13]

This U.S. hostility explains for them why the United States seems to move the goal posts further away every time Cuba has come close to meeting a U.S. demand. It does not want to improve relations with Cuba, because it has had a single-minded determination to overthrow the Cuban regime, regardless of how it has behaved.

The war on terrorism adds currency to Cuba's assessment that it is under attack, because the United States designates Cuba as one of seven countries on a list of "terrorist" states. Even Afghanistan never achieved that status, despite the protection it gave to al Qaeda terrorists.[14] Current U.S. officials also feed Cuba's perception that the United States maintains a single-minded determination to destroy the Cuban revolution. They unfailingly describe the Cuban government as a "corrupt, dictatorial, murderous regime," repeating a mantra that U.S. policy aims at bringing about "a free and democratic Cuba," which Cubans interpret as a euphemism for overthrowing the current regime.[15] Once again Cuba feels imperiled by its northern neighbor, as it has many times since the era of the missile crisis. For Cuba, the October Crisis continues.

Cubans accept the notion that the island is under siege as if it were a truism—a fact so self-evident it is almost worth not stating. They find it hard to believe that people in the United States really do not see the situation as they do. Yet U.S. officials and commentators regularly dismiss the Cuban fears as little more than self-serving rhetoric. Such a circumstance, when people on opposite sides of a conflict judge that the other side's point of view is not legitimate, makes constructive dialogue nearly im-

possible. Our purpose in this epilogue, then, is to examine what both sides are saying, to begin a process in which both might be able to empathize realistically. It is a
process that necessarily recalls the Cuban–Soviet relationship after the missile crisis,
when the absence of empathy governed the way events unfolded.

THE U.S. VIEW: MUCH ADO ABOUT NOTHING

From the vantage point of the United States, it may be easy to dismiss Cuban fears
about the looming U.S. menace. Many Americans trust that their country would
not commit aggression against Cuba. Others argue further that the United States
actually has had good reason to attack Cuba during the last four decades, because
of the way Cuba has harmed U.S. interests, and that the long history of U.S. restraint, despite such harm, is evidence that Cubans actually have little to fear from
the United States. Their anxiety, critics say, is much ado about nothing.

A Small Power That Acts Like a Great One

Cuba is larger than many people, and even some policymakers, imagine. Late in
1960, as casual suggestions of a U.S. invasion seemed to be moving toward more
serious consideration, General David M. Shoup, commandant of the Marine
Corps, realized that his colleagues envisioned Cuba as a small island, perhaps one
hundred miles long. Smartly he brought them back to reality by superimposing a
map of the "small island" over one of the United States. Cuba stretched nearly from
New York to Chicago.[16] In fact, it is the largest island in the Caribbean and has
more people than all other Caribbean countries combined.

Still, Cuba is small in comparison to powerful countries. Its land area of 43,305
square miles is slightly less than Pennsylvania's, and its population is a little over
eleven million people; in 1959 it was seven million. Even in the 1980s, when
Cuba's economy benefitted from Soviet assistance and marketing arrangements
with the Eastern Bloc's Council of Mutual Economic Assistance (CMEA), it was a
poor, Third World country. Yet Cuba has impacted global affairs in a way usually
reserved only for more powerful countries. "Cuba is a small country," political scientist Jorge Domínguez observed during the Cold War, "but it has the foreign policy of a big power." [17]

The revolutionary regime was able to do this, in part, because the Soviet Union
provided Cuba with military assistance and other resources necessary to extend itself overseas.[18] Cuba also developed an appeal in the Third World because it successfully resisted U.S. attacks, it promoted a message of resistance that resonated
among oppressed people, and it assisted other poor countries by sending them

EPILOGUE 151

teachers, health care professionals, construction workers, and even sports instructors. Its aid also highlighted Cuba's notable domestic achievements.[19]

Cuba's potential power troubled U.S. policymakers almost from the beginning of the Revolution. At that point, the concern was not about the Soviet Union, with which Cuba had neither diplomatic nor trade relations, but about Fidel Castro's charisma. Vice President Richard Nixon reported in a confidential memo, after his April 1959 meeting with Castro, that the Cuban leader

> has those indefinable qualities which make him a leader of men. Whatever we may think of him he is going to be a great factor in the development of Cuba and very possibly in Latin American affairs generally. . . . But because he has the power to lead to which I have referred we have no choice but at least to try to orient him in the right direction.[20]

Castro rejected U.S. "orientation," and by the end of the year the Central Intelligence Agency was developing plans to overthrow the Cuban government.[21]

Castro's defiance provided the initial justification for these efforts, because they indicated to U.S. officials that he was prepared to confront the United States. One piece of evidence for this was Cuba's alleged support for subversion in the Western Hemisphere, particularly against dictatorships in the Dominican Republic, Panama, and Nicaragua.[22] These expeditions implicitly challenged U.S. dominance in the region and the U.S. conception of itself as protector of the hemisphere, an idea nurtured since the 1823 Monroe Doctrine. In early November 1959, Secretary of State Christian Herter assessed why such deviance from U.S. discipline posed a threat to the United States. Writing to President Dwight Eisenhower, he observed that Castro "has veered towards a 'neutralist' anti-American foreign policy for Cuba which, if emulated by other Latin American countries, would have serious adverse effects on Free World support of our leadership."[23] In September 1960 Castro made the challenge to U.S. leadership explicit, openly proclaiming Cuba's duty to make revolution in the hemisphere.[24]

Cuba's rejection of U.S. hemispheric hegemony took on a special meaning in the context of the Cold War, because policymakers' *perceptions* of threats to U.S. power became more important than the reality of those threats.[25] These perceptions were guided by a set of ideological assumptions, established shortly after World War II, which divided the world into two hostile camps, the western one dominated by the United States and the eastern one dominated by the Soviet Union. Policymakers at the time believed that most global events could be tallied on a "zero-sum" balance sheet: a gain for the Soviet Union would necessarily be a loss for the United States, and vice-versa. Thus, they argued, U.S. policy toward a country should be guided by the single criterion of whether or not it stood with the United States against a global communism whose head lay in Moscow.[26] In this global war, all areas were of equal importance, as officials assumed that U.S. interests formed a seamless web. Just as a tear in a fish net will let the fish escape regardless of where the hole forms, so the resulting U.S. global containment strategy assumed that a defeat anywhere was a defeat everywhere.

This assumption rested on the view that global communism was monolithic and aggressive. If the United States did not defend supposed interests even in its own backyard, then Soviet agents might be encouraged to attack U.S. interests in Asia and Africa, or even in Europe. As the dominoes fell so would U.S. security.[27] Therefore, the United States needed to convince the enemy in advance that it would "pay any price" to deter aggression, and maintaining the credibility of such U.S. resolve was seen as the key to American security and power. Yet this assumption itself induced an element of insecurity, because credibility is an intangible attribute, always susceptible to erosion. As a result, constant vigilance was essential: The United States always needed to act unhesitatingly to eliminate any doubts about its readiness to defend any vital U.S. interest.[28]

Policymakers were thus primed to believe that Cuba's challenge would create the *perception* of U.S. weakness, regardless of whether the Soviet Union backed Cuba's initial forays in Latin America.[29] Once Cuba began to trade with the Soviet Union in early 1960, and soon after began to receive Soviet arms (although they were antiquated and limited in number), the potential loss of U.S. power became even more imaginable. If the Soviet Union could use Cuba to acquire allies in Latin America, this would not only damage U.S. credibility in general; it would be a major blow inflicted directly by the Soviet Union itself, and would certainly encourage Soviet adventurism elsewhere.[30] At that point, Cold War ideology took full control of U.S. policy toward Cuba, because the small island seemed to pose an enormous security problem, well beyond the harm it could inflict on particular U.S. interests in the hemisphere.[31]

The 1962 missile crisis confirmed the Kennedy administration's worst fears about how the Soviet–Cuban connection could undermine U.S. security. Afterwards, even though the Kennedy–Khrushchev agreement vitiated the nightmare scenario of the island becoming a Soviet military base, Cuba remained a serious threat because of its close ties to the other superpower.[32] U.S. officials were convinced that Cuba's actions inescapably served Soviet interests after 1962, whether or not the Kremlin controlled them—and, they believed, the Kremlin did control Cuba.[33] Shortly before he was killed, Kennedy told journalist Jean Daniel that Castro was a "Soviet agent in Latin America."[34] At about the same time, National Security Adviser McGeorge Bundy asserted in a top secret memorandum that the United States could improve relations with Cuba only if it ended its "submission to external Communist influence" and ceased its "determined campaign of subversion directed at the rest of the Hemisphere."[35]

Bundy's position remained at the core of U.S. policy for the next thirty years. The United States regarded Cuba as a continuing threat to significant interests in Africa and Latin America until the Soviet Union disintegrated at the end of 1991 and Castro announced that Cuba would no longer support revolutionary movements in Latin America in 1992. National security analyst Gregory Treverton summarized the prevailing view among policymakers as late as 1989, by observing that "Cuban actions both in and beyond Latin America inject that country to the center of East–West, and U.S.–Soviet, relations. Whatever the fact, it is impossible for Americans not to regard Cuba as a kind of Soviet 'hired gun' in the Third World."[36]

Several times during those thirty years, Cuba and the United States found themselves on opposite sides in a conflict.[37] Most Cuban operations were not intended necessarily to sabotage U.S. objectives, and usually were not determined by Soviet dictates. But Cuban motivations for their overseas military campaigns were less important for balance of power considerations than the effect of these operations, which tended to benefit the Soviet Union. Both the United States and the Soviet Union had decided that the Third World provided a surrogate battleground in the superpower contest for global domination, and both sought to bring many of these countries to their side. When this contest focused on a place such as Ethiopia, which also had geostrategic significance because it could create a "choke" on waterways used for transporting oil or vital military supplies, it became especially difficult to imagine that the Cuban military served any purpose other than Soviet strategic aims. Zbigniew Brzezinski captures his sense of how the Soviets used the Cubans as a stalking horse in Ethiopia when he wrote:

> as more Cuban troops went to Ethiopia, [Soviet Foreign Minister Andrei] Gromyko suggested the classic Soviet solution to regional disputes—a joint U.S.–Soviet mediation effort pointing to a condominium. I believed that would only legitimize the Soviet presence in the Horn.... Not only will access to Suez be threatened, and this involves the oil pipeline from Saudi Arabia and Iran, but there will be a serious and direct political threat to Saudi Arabia.[38]

At other times, especially in Central America and the Caribbean in the 1980s, Cuba did aim to weaken U.S. dominance. It supported the governments of Nicaragua and Grenada against U.S. subversion and gave assistance to the insurgents in El Salvador fighting against the U.S.-backed regime. In the 1960s it actively was involved in subversion against South American countries and may have continued to provide aid to guerrilla groups there into the 1980s.[39]

This pattern of overseas interference would have been annoying even if Cuba had not been tied closely to the Soviet Union. When U.S. officials viewed it through the lens of the East–West struggle, in which local struggles were either manifestations of U.S.–Soviet competition or ultimately could be used by the Soviet Union to weaken the United States, Washington elevated these annoyances to the status of national security threats.[40] Cuba had a worldwide presence, unlike any other Third World country. It sent more than 35,000 troops to Africa and military advisers to several countries in Africa and Asia; it had aid missions in dozens of countries; and it invited thousands of students from countries in Asia, Africa, and Latin America to study at schools on the Isle of Youth, which some U.S. analysts viewed as a training ground for future guerrilla operations.[41] Cuba seemed to act as if it were a global power, and in most cases it supported countries and organizations that were hostile to the United States.

U.S. "Restraint"

Regardless of whether U.S. policymakers were right or wrong about the danger Cuba posed for U.S. national security, there is abundant evidence that they believed Cuba was a deadly menace. That belief led them directly to the goal of overthrowing the Cuban government in the early 1960s. Yet, after the missile crisis, they did not seem to pursue this objective vigorously. One might even argue that U.S. policy toward Cuba during much of the Cold War provides evidence of extraordinary restraint, because the principal aim became merely to contain and isolate the Cuban Revolution, not to destroy it. While officials may have hoped that by containing Cuban overseas operations they might weaken the Revolution and thus cause its demise, U.S. efforts in that period never were committed fully to that end.[42]

Even the initial effort to overthrow the regime was timid. The 1961 Bay of Pigs invasion, in which 1,500 CIA-trained Cuban exiles were overcome in three days by Cuban forces, was so poorly conceived that it is known as "the perfect failure."[43] What might have made it successful was the collateral CIA plan to assassinate the Cuban leadership. But in order to provide U.S. officials with "plausible deniability" for the crime, the CIA developed circuitous plans involving organized crime bosses.[44] In early 1961 Washington had not yet developed an argument it felt could convince the world that Cuba was a serious threat, so they handled the problem in indirect ways.

By early 1962 the Kennedy administration was ready to take its case to the Organization of American States (OAS). It did so in conjunction with an ambitious program the president had approved on November 30 to overthrow the Cuban government, code-named Operation Mongoose.[45] Years later those involved with Mongoose argued it was a minor effort that generated little more than pinpricks for the Cuban government, even though at the time it was the largest operation ever undertaken by the CIA.[46] Ultimately there may have been fewer Mongoose terrorist attacks than the plans envisioned. But it is important to recognize, as we discussed in chapter 1, that the overall "Cuba Project" was a multifaceted program. It included—in addition to bombings; the sabotage of sugar mills, factories, and machinery; the burning of sugar fields; and the destruction of processed sugar—a concerted propaganda effort, an economic embargo, and pressure on countries that traded with Cuba to support U.S. sanctions, and attempts to isolate Cuba politically. Suspension of Cuba's OAS membership was central to this last goal.[47]

The OAS resolution, approved by a vote of 14–1 on January 31, 1962, echoed the Monroe Doctrine in asserting that the organization's principles required the "rejection of alliances and agreements that may lead to intervention in America by extracontinental powers." It then declared that "the present Government of Cuba, which has officially identified itself as a Marxist-Leninist government, is incompatible with the principles and objectives of the inter-American system."[48] By declaring, in effect, that the Cuban government was predatory and illegitimate, the decision could have paved the political way for a U.S. attack.

Former Kennedy administration officials have argued that the president never intended to launch an invasion. Arthur Schlesinger, for example, firmly asserted in 1991 there was "never any consideration nor any talk in the White House about sending an army to invade, to conquer Cuba." He noted that had Kennedy "wished to invade Cuba, Fidel Castro provided him with the perfect pretext when he accepted nuclear missiles."[49] But Kennedy's advisers have acknowledged that Cuba reasonably could have concluded otherwise, based on the OAS expulsion, Mongoose activities, and assassination attempts in 1962.[50] Perhaps Kennedy sought only to induce this fear, hoping to frighten Cuba into ending support for revolutionary movements. If that were the case, he certainly made a miscalculation of historic proportions, because the Soviets also interpreted these efforts as unmistakable evidence of an invasion plan.[51] The missiles followed soon after.

The claim that Kennedy never seriously considered overthrowing the Cuban government by force seems implausible, or at best exaggerated. First, the evidence for this contention—that he resisted pressure to do so at the time of the missile crisis—does not suggest a lack of prior intention. During the crisis the president was rightly worried that an invasion might lead to a nuclear war, or at least to a Soviet countermove at another location, such as Berlin. This fear pervaded ExComm deliberations, especially on October 27 when events seemed to be spiraling out of control.[52] Second, the Pentagon had developed serious invasion plans before the missile crisis. While there may be an abundance of such "scenarios" that have filled trash dumps, because generals try to anticipate every contingency, the Cuban attack plans were under active consideration.[53] Even after the missile crisis, in April 1963, Kennedy urged the Pentagon to "[strengthen] our Cuban contingency invasion plans."[54] At the same time, the U.S. Congress was encouraging the president to launch such an assault. In 1962 it authorized the use of "whatever means may be necessary, including the use of arms" to prevent Cuba from threatening U.S. and hemispheric security.[55]

Still, here we are forty years later without there having been an invasion since the Bay of Pigs. Certainly this abstinence has not been due to a lack of U.S. capability. Nor has it been because the United States was, in President Richard Nixon's famous characterization, a "pitiless, helpless giant." Rather U.S. policymakers have tended to feel more like Gulliver, who recalled with pride his own forbearance in not killing Lilliputians after he had freed one arm from its tethers: "I confess I was often tempted, while they were passing backwards and forwards on my Body, to seize Forty or Fifty of the first that came in my Reach, and dash them against the Ground."[56] Similarly, U.S. officials believe they have treated Cuba with an admirable self-restraint. Philip Bonsal, the last U.S. ambassador to Cuba, remarked in 1973:

> Since the Bay of Pigs and the Missile Crisis there have been considerable changes in American attitudes and policies towards Castro's Cuba . . . responsible American policy has never envisaged the use of American forces in Cuba except at the time of the Missile Crisis of 1962 when the confrontation was with Khrushchev and not with Castro. . . . Our current policy no longer contemplates the overthrow of whatever internal regime the people of Cuba may support.[57]

One might argue that U.S. officials were restrained by their concerns that Latin Americans might react negatively to an invasion.[58] The United States had been trying to overcome the legacy of "gunboat diplomacy" that had made the *yanqui* hegemon so unpopular in the hemisphere. Yet such qualms about Latin America's reaction did not deter either President Lyndon Johnson from sending 23,000 Marines into the Dominican Republic in 1965 to prevent "another Cuba" or President Ronald Reagan from sending an equally large force into Grenada in 1983 to topple a Cuban ally.

On the other hand, during the Cold War there were pressures to attack Cuba, from those in the government who wanted to respond to Cuban provocations, from some members of Congress, from a powerful Cuban American lobby (after 1981), and from presidents who were personally and ideologically antagonistic to Cuba. Henry Kissinger notes, for example, that "Cuba was a neuralgic problem for Nixon." Still in 1970 the president allowed Kissinger to reaffirm the 1962 Kennedy–Khrushchev agreement under which the United States pledged not to invade Cuba.[59] Similarly, Reagan had a visceral contempt for Cuba.[60] But he resisted Secretary of State Alexander Haig's prodding to invade the island and did not even close off Cuba's ability to trade with U.S. corporations in third countries, a relaxation of the embargo that President Gerald Ford had instituted only six years before Reagan took office.[61]

American policymakers thus assume the restraints against an invasion have been merely minor impediments. Like Gulliver even with one arm tied down, the United States easily could have chosen to destroy Cuba. Instead it has treated Cuba more gently than it deserved. This attitude was evident, for example, in 1984 remarks by the head of the State Department's Office of Cuban Affairs, when he said: "Cuba remains militant and prone to stimulate violent change. There remains, however, a willingness on our part to resolve those problems with Cuba . . . for which there is a reasonable basis for mutually satisfactory solutions."[62]

Officials also tend to belittle the harm that the United States has done to Cuba. In 1998 the head of the State Department's Cuba "desk" suggested that the island's economic problems stem largely from the fact that its "'investment climate' remains hostile to private enterprise." The embargo, he suggested, has more political than economic importance; it sends a "message on the need for fundamental, democratic, systemic change."[63] More recently, the State Department's 2001 human rights report deprecated the burden the embargo imposes on Cuba by ignoring it. The report found that the decline of the Cuban economy in the 1990s was wholly "due to the inefficiencies of the centrally controlled economic system; the loss of billions of dollars of annual Soviet bloc trade and Soviet subsidies; the ongoing deterioration of plants, equipment, and the transportation system; and the continued poor performance of the important sugar sector."[64]

Still, U.S. officials believe the embargo serves two purposes, neither of which is to overthrow the Cuban government. The first is as a statement about what kind of regime the United States would prefer in Cuba; that is, "one in which the people of Cuba can freely choose their leaders, can freely speak their minds, and can freely practice their faith. . . . It is a vision of a free Cuba that respects the civil and human rights of its people."[65] The second purpose is as a bargaining chip to pressure Cuba to pursue these goals, because "the current Cuban Government will not institute political and economic change unless it has to."[66]

Cuba Never Misses an Opportunity to Miss an Opportunity

Starting from the assumption that the United States has had good reason to attack Cuba, and has restrained itself for the most part over the last forty years, officials often have been frustrated that Castro does not trust their supposed good intentions. Privately they contend, as Abba Eban reputedly remarked about the Palestinians, that Cuba never misses an opportunity to miss an opportunity.[67] In 1974, for example, Kissinger initiated secret negotiations with Cuba aimed at what appeared to be a normalization of relations. The next year, as a signal of good faith, the United States voted with a majority of members in the OAS to lift the 1964 hemispheric embargo against Cuba. Supposedly as an added indication of positive

U.S. aims, Ford then significantly relaxed the U.S. embargo to permit subsidiaries of U.S. corporations in third countries to trade with Cuba.[68] But that same day Cuba introduced a resolution in the UN Committee on Colonialism calling for the independence of Puerto Rico, even though U.S. officials had warned Cuban emissaries with whom they had been negotiating that the United States strongly objected to Cuba's efforts.[69] Three months later, in November 1975, Cuba sent troops to Angola to support the new government there. Kissinger viewed this Cuban action as another direct affront, because the United States was supporting the forces attacking the new Angolan government. He had been patient with the Cubans, he recalls, during the year of discussions. But according to Kissinger, Ramón Sánchez-Parodi, Cuba's main emissary, resisted any step-by-step plan to negotiate U.S.–Cuban differences. He provided only "the classic Communist negotiating style—no concessions, innumerable attempts to turn proposals back against the proposer as an indictment of his country's behavior, constant *tu quoque* point-making."[70] In December 1975 Ford announced publicly that Cuba's Angola operation "destroys any opportunity for improvement of relations with the United States."[71]

President Bill Clinton seemed to meet a comparable response in 1999, when he challenged the seemingly impervious constraints of the 1996 Helms-Burton Act by authorizing new regulations to ease the embargo. These permitted: the sale of food to entities independent of the Cuban government, such as religious groups and private restaurants, and the sale of agricultural "inputs" to private farmers and farmers in cooperatives raising food for sale in private markets; charter flights to Cuba from New York and Los Angeles; coordination between U.S. and Cuban coast guards over drug enforcement; and an expansion of educational, cultural, humanitarian, religious, journalistic, and athletic exchanges.[72]

Several elements stand out on this seemingly insignificant list. First, even such a slight relaxation of the embargo went beyond what analysts had said would be possible under the 1996 Helms-Burton Act.[73] When asked whether the changes were consistent with the law, a senior National Security Council adviser asserted publicly that "Helms-Burton codified the embargo and at the same time, it codified the president's licensing power. That is, it codified a process by which there was an embargo to which exceptions could be granted on a case-by-case basis by the President."[74] Under this rubric, the door would have been open virtually to any license for trade with Cuba that a president would wish to make. Second, the changes were made unilaterally, without any demand that the Cuban government meet conditions or reciprocate. In contrast, Clinton's policy in his first term had called for "calibrated responses" by the United States in reaction to demands that the Cuban government improve its human rights record, and reciprocity had governed U.S. policy since the 1970s. The first evidence of the change in policy came in the spring of 1999, when the

Baltimore Orioles and a Cuban all-star baseball team played exhibition games in Havana and Camden Yards.

Yet Cuban officials resisted accepting even the baseball games, negotiations for which had been going on for three years.[75] They focused on Clinton's rhetoric, which emphasized that new regulations were "consistent with our policy of keeping pressure on the regime for democratic change . . . while finding ways to . . . help in developing civil society."[76] Ricardo Alarcon, president of the Cuban National Assembly and chief architect of Cuba's policy toward the United States, pointedly remarked in a radio broadcast that "the measures announced by the United States . . . have the purpose of subverting the Revolution." He described Clinton's announcement as a "new phase of the war against Cuba."[77] Castro then angrily denounced the U.S. initiative: "They have sought to deceive the world, saying they relaxed the blockade. Incredible! What they have done is strengthen the blockade."[78]

Continuing hostility did not seem inevitable to many policymakers and analysts during the quarter century between the 1975 collapse of Cuban–U.S. détente and the Clinton opening in 1999.[79] Normalization even seemed possible from 1977 to 1979, when the Carter administration quickly initiated negotiations with Cuba on fishing rights, and the two countries established diplomatic missions at their old embassies in Havana and Washington, staffed respectively by U.S. and Cuban diplomats. Yet each time there was a glimmer of light, it seemed to many U.S. officials that Cuba would challenge U.S. foreign policy interests. This is how they saw Cuba's response to the Carter rapprochement. For example, Cuba sent as many as 17,000 troops in 1978 to support the Soviet-backed Ethiopian government in its border dispute with Somalia, it accepted advanced Soviet MIG-23 fighter-bombers on the island (seeming to test the limits of the Kennedy–Khrushchev agreement on the introduction of offensive weapons to the island), and as the site of the 1979 Non-Aligned Movement Summit, Cuba fashioned an anti-imperialist (read as anti-American) draft declaration that the Third World nations used as the basis for the meeting.[80]

This pattern of behavior has led some to argue that Cuba does not want better relations with the United States. Surely, they contend, Cuban leaders are aware that U.S. politicians often must placate their domestic constituencies by criticizing Cuba, and that their harsh rhetoric is meant for a domestic audience.[81] This conclusion forms the base for Kissinger's explanation of why his 1975 effort to improve relations failed: "Castro needed the United States as an enemy to justify his totalitarian grip on the country. . . . Normalization of relations with the United States would have been difficult to reconcile with continued Communist rule."[82] From this perspective, Castro willfully ignores positive openings and craftily distorts the significance of inconsequential measures and hostile rhetoric. "Whenever Washington has lightened up," William Ratliffe and Roger Fontaine argue, "Castro has tightened up and effectively prevented further improvement."[83] He makes much ado about nothing, it is said, because he needs the existence of an alleged enemy to galvanize support for the government.

Such intransigence, some argue, is a double-edged sword that could be turned against the regime were it wielded deftly. If U.S. threats enable Castro to hold onto power, then the best way to promote change in Cuba would be to end the embargo and rob him of this convenient bogeyman. The sanctions, they say, provide an excuse for the failures of the Cuban economy and thus enable the regime to avoid unwanted reforms.[84] From this point of view, the problem with U.S. policy lies not so much in the real threats it poses to the Cuban revolution—those days are long past—but in how it *appears* to threaten Cuba.[85]

CUBA'S VIEW: A COUNTRY UNDER SIEGE

The United States has targeted Cuba for more than forty years, its officials believe, regardless of how Cuba has behaved. U.S. policy has not been shaped in response to Cuba's actions but has had a consistent theme of destroying the Cuban revolution. For example, in 1992 Castro remarked:

> The United States is always inventing something new in connection with Cuba. For a long time they said that as long as we had links with the Soviet Union, relations couldn't improve. So suddenly one day, the Soviet Union disappeared. For a long time they said that as long as we had troops in Angola, relations with Cuba could not improve. The moment came when that war was over . . . we withdrew. The Americans must know that it's easy to send troops, and hard to get them out. . . . Then you said that we had to get out of Nicaragua. When the political changes took place in Nicaragua, we withdrew our military advisers. . . . Then the question of subversion. The subversion issue changed . . . our "subversion" came to an end. So: "Break links with the USSR [Union of Soviet Socialist Republics]; leave Angola; leave Nicaragua"—there was always a reason. Now, the latest one is democratic reforms—I imagine along the lines of the United States—and the question of human rights. . . . Our relations never improve, and the U.S. invents new reasons again and again not to improve relations. You never know what the next reason is going to be. But these new issues are linked to the internal affairs of our country— to the sovereignty of our country.[86]

One constant has been the U.S. embargo against Cuba. Based initially on the 1917 Trading with the Enemy Act, its most recent major extension—the so-called Helms-Burton Act—maintains the claim that "the Cuban Government has posed and continues to pose a national security threat to the United States."[87] U.S. law thus establishes Cuba as a U.S. enemy and a threat. Cubans cannot imagine that the

United States is willing to tolerate an enemy ninety miles away. But they explain their own survival by arguing that the cost of a direct U.S. intervention has been too great even for the hovering giant. U.S. strategy to overthrow the Cuban government, they believe, has thus had to rely on indirect tactics. These have included support for terrorism against Cuba, pressure on U.S. allies to cut ties to Cuba, global propaganda offensives that seek to undermine Cuba's prestige, efforts to divide the Cuban people through support for self-proclaimed dissidents, and tightening of the embargo. Taken together, such tactics form a coherent plan to overthrow the Cuban regime, and they give Cuba good reason to feel under siege.

U.S. Support for Subversion

While the United States has not attempted an invasion of Cuba since 1961, it did not abandon efforts to destabilize the Cuban government after the missile crisis. The Kennedy administration renewed support for terrorist raids from bases in Central America and even South Florida, provided assistance to counterrevolutionaries located in the Escambray Mountains, and hired assassins to murder Cuba's leaders. Authorized attempts at subversion reportedly ended in the 1960s, but terrorist attacks do continue even today. The United States has denied responsibility for any of the assaults.[88] Cuba has blamed the United States for many of them, in part because of what they construe as tacit U.S. approval for the assaults against the island.[89]

Consider two issues that illustrate the more general problem: the 1976 terrorist bombing of a Cuban commercial airliner and assassination attempts against Castro.

- *Crime off Barbados*: On October 6, 1976, *Cubana* Flight 455, destined for Jamaica and Cuba, exploded nine minutes after taking off from Barbados. All seventy-three people on board died, including fifty-seven Cubans, eleven Guyanese, and five North Koreans. Among the Cubans were the twenty-four members of the national fencing team. The "crime off Barbados," as Cuban newspapers called it, was the work of at least two Cuban exiles—Freddy Lugo and Hernan Ricardo—who were convicted and jailed in Venezuela for the bombing. They worked for a third, Luis Posada Carriles, who was arrested and jailed for nine years but not convicted. A fourth, Orlando Bosch, was released from prison after being held as the mastermind of the plot.[90] The plane began its trip in Georgetown, Guyana; Lugo and Ricardo boarded it in Trinidad. They had booked passage to Jamaica, but left the flight in Barbados without their luggage.

    Cubans reacted with an outpouring of grief. At a mass funeral on October 15 Castro charged that the "CIA had directly organized the sabotage." He contended that the airline bombing had been the most recent in a series of terrorist acts against Cuban civilian targets—including others at airport facilities—and that terrorists "have unlimited financial resources. They use U.S. passports as naturalized citizens of that country or real or false documents of numerous countries. . . . Who else but the CIA . . . can carry out these acts?"[91] He then withdrew Cuba from a three-year-old antihijacking accord it had signed with the United States. In addition to provisions about hijacking, the agreement required both countries to "try with a view to severe punishment" any person who "conspires to promote, or prepares, or directs," or engages in "acts of violence or depredation against aircraft."[92] The U.S.–Cuba agreement had been seen as a harbinger of improved relations between the two countries.[93]

Secretary of State Kissinger denied any U.S. involvement in the *Cubana* bombing, decried the abrogation of the pact, and asserted that the United States would hold Cuba "strictly accountable for any encouragement of hijacking" in the future.[94] CIA support for the bombing has never been established. But it is clear that there had been prior CIA ties to the four terrorists. They had been trained by the CIA for the Bay of Pigs invasion and were involved in Operation Mongoose and the CIA-backed raids against Cuba in 1963 and 1964. Posada was in regular contact with the CIA while he worked for the Venezuelan secret police agency, DISIP, until the early 1970s and even until 1976.[95] Such evidence would be a slim reed on which to blame the United States. But it is U.S. behavior after the bombing that raises doubts about U.S. protestations of innocence.

Bosch was the leader of a violent anti-Castro network created in June 1976. The Co-ordinating Committee of United Revolutionary Organizations (or CORU for its Spanish name, *Coordinacion de Organizaciones Revolucionaires Unidas*), brought together representatives from the major Cuban-exile terrorist groups. The FBI subsequently blamed CORU operatives for numerous bombings. Bosch himself served two years in a U.S. prison for a 1968 bazooka attack against a Polish freighter docked in Miami. After his release from a Venezuelan jail, Bosch sought to return to the United States, despite the violation of his parole. Reportedly Otto Reich, then U.S. ambassador to Venezuela and now the assistant secretary of state for the Western Hemisphere, pressured Venezuelan authorities to give Bosch his freedom and advocated that he be granted a visa to return to the United States. The State Department denied the visa, on the basis of his "criminal history and involvement in terrorism." Bosch nonetheless entered the United States illegally in 1988. Despite the recommendation of the Justice Department, President George H. W. Bush paroled him in 1990. Once out, he publicly hailed the destruction of *Cubana* 455, saying, "It was a legitimate war action. . . . We are at war, aren't we?"[96]

Posada Carriles escaped from his Venezuelan jail in 1985 by bribing his captors with money he claims to have received from the brother of Cuban American National Foundation Director Jorge Mas Canosa.[97] He soon turned up in Central America, working for Felix Rodriguez, a CIA operative engaged in the *contra* war against Nicaragua.[98] With his background in explosives, Posada Carriles became the logistics chief for the illegal covert supply operation transporting weapons from El Salvador to Nicaragua directed by Lt. Col. Oliver North, a National Security Council aide.[99] Posada Carriles later worked as a security adviser for El Salvador's president, Jose Napoleon Duarte. In 1997 the *Miami Herald* identified Posada Carriles as the funding linchpin for a series of terrorist bombings that summer at tourist hotels in Havana.[100] Three years later Panamanian authorities arrested him for plotting to assassinate Castro, who was attending the Ibero-American Summit in Panama. Police found a briefcase filled with C-4 explosives in Posada Carriles' rental car.[101]

- *Assassination Attempts*: The plot against Castro in Panama indicates that assassination attempts on Castro did not end in the 1960s, though there is no evidence of direct U.S. involvement in any of the plots after 1965. Several of the earlier attempts have been well documented.[102] Perhaps the most famous involved Rolando Cubela, an agent whose code name was AM/LASH.[103] Cubela had been an officer in Castro's rebel army, and was number two in the Ministry of Interior when the CIA recruited him in 1961 to provide intelligence. By 1963 the CIA decided to use him as Castro's assassin, because the Cuban leader apparently trusted him. On November 22, 1963, possibly at the time Kennedy was assassinated in Dallas, two CIA officials handed Cubela a ballpoint pen specially fitted with a hypodermic needle and instructed him to fill it with a commonly available poison in order to kill Castro.[104] Cubela had wanted high power rifles, and refused to use the pen. In 1964 and 1965 the CIA did provide him with guns, but then allegedly broke off contact with him in June 1965. He was arrested later that year in Cuba.[105]

Cuban officials discount the U.S. claim that authorized assassination efforts ended in 1965. One difficulty in assessing the extent of official U.S. involvement in later plots is that after 1965 some of those involved in the earlier U.S.-orchestrated attempts may have continued to plan assassinations on their own, even while working with the CIA. Cuban analysts argue that the CIA keeps a close track on current and even former operatives, so they assume that if U.S. law enforcement agencies sought to apprehend plotters, they could do so easily.[106] Some even have documented ties to well-known anti-Castro activists in the United States. Consider a 1997 plan that was foiled accidentally by a U.S. Coast Guard crew which became curious about a forty-six-foot cabin cruiser anchored off the Puerto Rican coast. The boat turned out to contain sufficient fuel for a trip to Venezuela, where Castro was scheduled to attend a summit meeting, and to house an arsenal of weapons, including a powerful .50-caliber semiautomatic sniper rifle registered to CANF President Francisco J. (Pepe) Hernández. After the arrests, one of the crew confessed to authorities that they were on a mission to kill the Cuban leader.[107] Hernández was not deposed by prosecutors, and still serves as the CANF president.

   Both the "crime off Barbados" and the assassination attempts remain vivid for Cubans and continue to undermine Cuba's trust in the supposed good intentions of the United States. Even in 2002 *Granma* ran stories about the 1976 *Cubana* incident. Referring to it in 2001, Castro demanded "that justice be done, for these professional terrorists, acting from inside the very territory of the United States."[108] In light of the similar 1988 tragedy of Pan Am 103 over Lockerbie, Scotland, Americans can now appreciate why Cubans might still feel angry about the unconscionable murders of their countrymen more than a quarter century ago.

   The seeming impunity of alleged assassins convinces Cuban officials that the United States still retains assassination as a viable weapon against Cuba. Similarly, the respect U.S. politicians and government leaders accord terrorists reinforces the Cuban fear of assassination. The CANF connections to Posada Carriles, Bosch, and other terrorists, and to the 1997 assassination plot are quite public. Yet every U.S. president has proclaimed his support for the CANF since its founding in 1981.[109] In Miami, terrorism is a badge of honor.[110] For example, the person who supplied guns to AM/LASH for his assassination efforts was Manuel Artime, a Bay of Pigs ringleader who was active in CIA-backed sabotage efforts after the missile crisis.[111] After Artime died of cancer in 1977, a popular performing arts center, owned by the City of Miami in Little Havana, was named for him.

   When the Cuban media dwells on the close association between Assistant Secretary Reich and Bosch, it may seem as if it is engaged in propaganda ploys.[112] Such stories add to the impression that Castro does not want good relations with the United States. Yet the close relationship between assassination efforts and terrorist attacks over the last four decades—and the continuing ties between U.S. officials and those who have committed terrorist acts—raises the possibility that Cuba's denunciations actually could be animated by real fears. The case of Jose Basulto highlights how easily Americans can overlook the forty-year history.

Terror and the Helms-Burton Act

Basulto has become famous as founder and head of Brothers to the Rescue. Cuba's February 1996 shootdown of two of the group's planes led directly to the 1996 Helms-Burton Act. While the U.S. media generally described the organization's work as "humanitarian"—unquestionably it helped to save numerous lives— the Brothers also hoped it would fulfill their political ambition of weakening the Cuban government.

Basulto came to this humanitarian project late in life, claiming he had converted to nonviolence after engaging in militant actions for many years. One of the first members of Brigade 2506 (the name adopted by the group of Bay of Pigs invaders), he allegedly broke with the CIA in 1962 because he was frustrated with the slow pace of Operation Mongoose. In August of that year he orchestrated a spectacular terrorist raid on a Havana tourist hotel where Castro reputedly spent time, firing scores of rounds at the building from small cannons.[113] "We were pretty [lousy] terrorists, let me tell you," he is quoted saying to the *Washington Post* in 1997, "because somebody else would have got explosive ammunition." Still, he devoted the remainder of the 1960s to anti-Castro work with violent groups in South Florida, believing "that the only hope for the Cuban people lay in the physical elimination of Fidel Castro."[114] In the 1980s he again worked with the CIA, this time in support of the *contras*, helping to launch terrorist attacks against Nicaragua.[115]

In the early 1990s, as Cuba underwent severe economic distress, Basulto sought to highlight the island's difficulties by encouraging people to flee on rafts. He regularly spoke on Miami radio stations and on the U.S. government's propaganda outlet, Radio Marti, to inform Cubans that when they left the island, Brothers to the Rescue would be waiting to help them. The group, which Basulto created in 1991, did so by flying planes over the Florida Straits each day looking for rafters and then alerting the U.S. Coast Guard about their locations.

By early August 1994 the Cuban "rafter" exodus was reaching epidemic proportions. At that point Castro announced that people who sought to leave the island on the makeshift boats would not be restrained. The Clinton administration had refused to discourage their trips actively, and emigrés rescued at sea typically were brought to the United States. They would then claim political asylum, and after one year, under the terms of the 1966 Cuban Adjustment Act, were able to secure permanent resident status. But Cuba's decision to open the floodgates prompted the Clinton administration to change normal procedures. Two weeks later the administration announced that Cubans picked up in international waters would be detained at Guantánamo Naval Base and at a U.S. facility in Panama. In September the United States and Cuba signed a new immigration accord permitting 20,000 Cubans to emigrate legally each year.[116] When the Guantánamo detainees seemed poised to riot in April 1995, the administration quickly worked out a new plan with Cuba that enabled those at the naval base to enter the United States. But henceforth, the U.S. government declared, the Coast Guard would return rafters directly to Cuba.

The new policy enraged hard-line anti-Castro exiles. They called it "Bay of Pigs—Part II" and believed Clinton's decision was a response to business groups calling for trade between the two countries.[117] "The long-term implication," the conservative *Wall Street Journal* noted in a May 16 editorial about the impact of the immigration accord, "is that one of the most intractable U.S. foreign policy problems in the postwar period is ripe for a fundamental rethinking." Basulto seems to have judged that the only way to stop this slow movement toward improved U.S.–Cuban relations would be to provoke a confrontation.[118]

On July 13, 1995, he made his first foray over Havana in a small private plane. Taking with him a cameraman from the Miami NBC affiliate, Basulto flew a few hundred feet over the Malecon, a roadway along Havana's waterfront, dropping religious medals and bumper stickers.[119] On subsequent flights he dropped leaflets advocating that Cubans rise up against their government. Cuba protested the flights officially to U.S. authorities on at least four occasions.[120] It did so informally as well, notably to Congressman Bill Richardson (D-NM), a confidant of Clinton's who traveled to Cuba on January 17, 1996. Cuban officials also conveyed their distress about the flights to a group of former high-ranking U.S. military officers with whom they met in early February. This group then reported to the National Security Council that Cuba was likely to shoot at future flights that violated Cuban airspace.[121] This was the backdrop to the Cuban shootdown of two Brothers to the Rescue planes on February 24, 1996, which killed four people.

Cuba still claims that three Brothers to the Rescue planes entered Cuban airspace that day and were over Cuban territory when Cuban fighter jets fired at two of them (Basulto was in the third plane). U.S. air traffic control tracking data indicates that the two planes were over international waters at the time of the shootdown, though Basulto's plane may have crossed into Cuban space. Even if this were the case, Cuba certainly might have reacted in a less aggressive way, for example by firing warning shots at the civilian planes. Both the UN Security Council and the Council of the International Civil Aviation Organization deplored Cuba's action. But, as Wayne Smith notes, their resolutions were less than "the United States had hoped" and were tempered by the "history of earlier violations of Cuban airspace which the United States had done nothing to prevent."[122]

The Cuban perspective about this incident may be easier for Americans to consider after September 11, 2001, than in 1996. Today, if a passenger even stands up on a plane thirty minutes before it is scheduled to arrive at Washington's Reagan National Airport, the flight may be diverted away from the city. Security precautions now are based on scenarios of terrorist plots that seemed unimaginable in 1996. But then they seemed quite probable to Cubans who had endured terrorist attacks. Is it conceivable today that U.S. officials would believe that an avowed enemy of the United States—a person who had attempted to assassinate a U.S. president and had a history of violence—had become a nonviolent humanitarian who sought merely to disseminate propaganda from his plane? If he could drop leaflets with impunity, might he drop anthrax the next time? And if he were warned by air traffic controllers that his flight trajectory was placing him in danger and he responded that he would ignore the warning—as Basulto did on February 24 in answering Cuban controllers—would U.S. defenses allow such a terrorist to proceed?[123] From Cuba's perspective, the civilian appearance of Basulto's planes merely camouflaged their military mission.[124]

Yet the Cubans did not make the decision lightly to shoot down the planes. They allowed the incursions to go on for several months, during which time they conveyed to high U.S. officials, through several channels, their growing impatience. Cuban military advisers were pressing for some retaliatory action, in part because of genuine worry generated by the prior terrorist history of the people in Brothers, and because the incursions undercut morale among the armed forces. But the Cuban leadership undoubtedly took into consideration the impact any retaliation might have in the United States. During this period different versions of the Helms-Burton law already had passed the House and Senate, but they had not yet been reconciled. Clinton provided the main uncertainty about whether they would become enacted. He opposed the bills publicly because their extraterritorial impact created tension with U.S. allies. But backers of the legislation heard vacillation in his remarks and believed that electoral considerations ultimately would lead him to approve some version.[125] If Castro also believed Clinton would approve some version of Helms-Burton, he would have had that much less incentive to spurn the warnings of his generals.

Political calculations, therefore, probably did play a role in the decision to attack the planes. But the debate in Cuba was not only between hard-liners who rigidly opposed better relations with the United States and soft-liners who favored a rapprochement. It focused on the trade-offs between maintaining Cuban security and achieving a political goal of reaching out to the United States. The security issue was a serious one, because the combination of Basulto's own history, the repeated provocations, and Clinton's unwillingness or inability to stop the incursions did seem to pose a threat to Cuba.

Given these circumstances, Cuba was somewhat taken aback by the inflammatory U.S. condemnation of the shootdown and then the quick passage of the Helms-Burton Act. Cubans had expected there would be some recognition of the context in which the incident occurred, and even some acknowledgment of

Cuba's efforts to resolve the problem peacefully. Castro hinted at the Cuban surprise in an interview with CBS's Dan Rather shortly after the shootdown, when
he said, "So our mistake was having trusted the assurances that we were given
by the U.S. administration."[126] Instead, in the very first title of the Helms-
Burton law, the Congress "condemns" the Cuban government for the February
24 attack against "unarmed and defenseless planes" on a "humanitarian" mission and "urges the President to seek, in the International Court of Justice, indictment for this act of terrorism by Fidel Castro."[127]

Such a condemnation seemed not only unfair to Cubans, because it embodied a
moral standard to which the United States itself has not adhered consistently. More
troubling to Cuban officials is the honor that the law accords to the Brothers' mission. That carries with it an implicit U.S. endorsement of terrorist acts against
Cuba.[128] Whether or not the president or Congress intended that message, the
Helms-Burton law reinforces the belief of Cuban leaders that they must maintain
constant vigilance against potential attacks. They assume that the U.S. government
cannot be trusted to restrain those who have tried to destroy the revolutionary
regime since 1959.

Deterrence Provides Security

The Cubans' lack of trust endures despite repeated assertions that the United
States has abandoned its early Cold War goal of trying to overthrow the Cuban government. As we reviewed earlier, U.S. officials contend that American behavior during the last thirty years has demonstrated considerable self-restraint, which should
have convinced Cuba that it really has little to fear from the United States. But
Cubans whom we have interviewed offer an alternate explanation for the seeming
U.S. restraint, that the cost of direct U.S. intervention against Cuba simply was too
great.

They note that the Cuban government had broad support on the island, and
that U.S. forces would have faced an inhospitable if not hostile citizenry. U.S. invaders also would have confronted much better military defenses than the Bay of
Pigs exiles encountered. By 1963 Cuba had developed its armed forces to the
point where an invasion would have entailed the loss of many American lives. A
continuing U.S. presence—which would have been necessary in order to maintain a friendly government in power—would have meant ongoing battles with a
guerrilla army in the Cuban mountains, which is where U.S. analysts expected
Castro would retreat.[129] Thus a Cuban invasion would not have been a cakewalk.
(In contrast, the Dominican Republic was in turmoil when Johnson intervened in
1965; Grenada's total population was only 110,000 in 1983 when Reagan sent
23,000 troops there.)

Cuban officials believe the country's military capability has been the most important element in deterring a direct U.S. attack. In the 1960s Cuba may have had as many as 300,000 soldiers in its armed forces, and in the 1970s about 120,000. Another 90,000 generally were in the military reserves.[130] Perhaps as important, Cuban leaders understood that the likelihood of a protracted war, involving what they call a "war of all the people" (*guerra de todo el pueblo*), could provide a deterrent against even the most aggressive U.S. antagonists.[131]

Their assessments may have been accurate. In 1981, Reagan administration officials publicly threatened to go to "the immediate source of the problem" in El Salvador, which Haig identified as Cuba.[132] Within the councils of government, he repeatedly pressed for military action against Cuba, and the administration did take initial steps to create a blockade while rattling sabers in the Caribbean with NATO exercises. But most of Reagan's advisers ultimately prevailed in stopping further plans, William LeoGrande reports, by pointing out "that the large and well-trained Cuban army would turn the country into another Vietnam."[133] Not taking such rationality for granted, though, Cuban leaders responded to the new threat by quickly implementing a plan for a 500,000-person civilian force—the Territorial Troop Militias—to defend the island and make an invasion that much more costly. Cuba also increased the size of the regular armed forces by 30 percent.[134]

But with the breakup of the Council on Mutual Economic Assistance (CMEA), the socialist trading bloc on which Cuba depended for 85 percent of its international trade, and the termination of Soviet assistance, Cuba underwent severe economic turmoil in the 1990s. This had a noticeable impact on its military strength. Oil shortages and a lack of hard currency for spare parts vitiated the capability of its air force and navy. Pilots were unable to meet minimum requirements for monthly flight training because of insufficient fuel. The number of active duty members of the armed forces was reduced by more than 100,000. A 1997 Defense Department study estimated that Cuban Armed Forces have been transformed "into a stay-at-home force that has minimal conventional fighting ability."[135]

Until a decade ago, the second important deterrent to a U.S. attack was the presence of Soviet soldiers and technicians. At the end of the missile crisis, Khrushchev finally agreed to leave a brigade of about 3,000 in Cuba, and there were perhaps as many as 30,000 additional Soviet technical advisers and assistants on the island in the 1970s and 1980s. These people became a kind of "trip wire," so that the United States needed to consider that an invasion of Cuba would likely kill Soviets and thus trigger a Soviet response.[136] Fear of a direct confrontation with the Soviet Union thus increased the limits on how the United States believed it could react to perceived Cuban "threat." In contrast the United States did not feel such restraints in other places where it perceived there were threats, such as in the Dominican Republic, Grenada, or even South Vietnam.[137]

Cuba thus interprets the history of U.S. restraint since the missile crisis as a consequence of limits imposed on the United States, not as evidence of good intentions. Cuban officials see little reason either to alter their assumption that the United States is a predator, ready to pounce if given the opportunity, or to lower Cuba's guard. On the contrary, when the Soviets withdrew their military forces from the island in 1991, and thereby removed the trip wire, an increase in vigilance seemed to offer the only hope of deterring U.S. aggression.

The Track II Threat

Without the Soviet trip wire, and with its military weakened, Cuba ultimately has had to depend for its security on the willingness of many Cubans to fight a peoples' war.[138] At a minimum, Cuban officials seem to believe, Cuba must appear united in order to deter U.S. aggression. They have feared that even a small crack in the facade could lead to fissures, which would invite U.S. intervention. At the same time they have assumed that the United States has pursued "Track II" initiatives precisely in order to generate such disunity.[139]

"Track two diplomacy" is a form of citizen diplomacy. It entails unofficial interactions between people from countries or groups in conflict for the purpose of promoting peaceful solutions to international disagreements. Coined in 1981 by Joseph Montville, the term suggests a complementary process to "track one" actions, which involve traditional diplomacy between official government representatives.[140] Track two diplomacy has been credited, for example, with helping to start the negotiating process that led to the 1993 Oslo peace agreement between Israel and the Palestinian Authority.[141] Conflict resolution scholars Mubarak Awad and Edy Kaufman explain that track two diplomacy is most appropriate in cases of "communal" struggle where there "is a deeply rooted conflict between peoples," such as in the South African and Israeli–Palestinian cases. In such circumstances it can help to start a political process and sustain it. "Both in Israel and in South Africa," they observe, "peace-making among official representatives needs to be constantly nourished by reconciliation, healing, and peace-building by people committed to working together across ethnic and national lines." It is less appropriate, they suggest, in "the few remaining Cold War struggles, such as North and South Korea, or Cuba and the United States."[142]

Yet Track II diplomacy has become a major strand in the U.S. approach to Cuba. This idea was first embodied in the 1992 Cuban Democracy Act (CDA) and then in the 1996 Helms-Burton Act.[143] Clinton's new regulations in 1998 and 1999 were premised on Track II, as were Bush's 2001 pledges to increase funding for nongovernmental groups inside Cuba, which he characterized as "the democratic opposition."[144] When U.S. officials refer to Track II, they suggest that their intentions are consistent with conflict resolution practitioners who follow in Montville's path. People-to-people initiatives, they say, are intended to help ordinary Cubans empower themselves. But the thrust of nearly all Track II initiatives, including those in the CDA, violate the spirit of track two diplomacy as a way to promote peace. First, they are government programs, not citizen initiatives. Second, their purpose is to enable one society to impose its will on another—the litmus test used to determine if a group deserves support is that it must oppose the Cuban government. In contrast, second track diplomacy is intended to build confidence between two peoples so that they can overcome hostilities and develop new relationships in mutually respectful ways. Coercion, which is the essence of the Cuban Track II initiatives, negates the very premises on which a meaningful second track diplomacy operates.[145]

While the Track II plans directed at Cuba over the last decade have been couched in the language of conflict resolution, they in fact more closely resemble the "Track Two" plan for Cuba advocated in 1962 by Edwin M. Martin, assistant secretary of state for inter-American affairs. Written two days before the United States discovered the missiles in Cuba, Martin's memo explained that

Track One would consist of a heightened effort to move along the present Mongoose lines. [As we discussed in chapter 1, Mongoose was the multifaceted CIA operation before the missile crisis intended to overthrow the Cuban government.] . . . Track Two would consist of an effort to engage Cubans more deeply, both within Cuba and abroad, in efforts of their liberation.[146]

In effect, Track Two would have served the same ends as Track One, but would have appeared more benign. The operation did not materialize because of the onset of the missile crisis.

In Latin America, the idea of Track II is associated more generally with Chile, where the United States did put its plans into effect. Initially designated as Track II, the operations over three years constituted a covert war against the Chilean government. In a September 2000 report to Congress, the CIA acknowledged that in 1970 it actively tried to prevent Salvador Allende Gossens from being elected democratically. The CIA did so, the report explains, with a two track operation: "This initiative considered both political action (Track I) and a military coup (Track II) to prevent an Allende presidency. Both Track I and Track II initiatives ran simultaneously."[147]

Cuban Track II programs today differ from those aimed at Chile three decades ago in two important respects. First, the Chile Track II operation was designed to encourage a coup against an elected leader in the event that Track I manipulations of the election failed. Without U.S.-style elections to manipulate in Cuba, today's Track II programs merge the efforts so that the kinds of activities associated with

Track I in Chile are aimed in Cuba at encouraging the overthrow of the government. Second, the Chile Track II plan was so secret that even the ambassador was not informed about it. The Cuban program is public and is articulated in U.S. laws.

Chile's Track I plan had three elements, and they were remarkably similar to the Track II schemes being used against Cuba today. The first element was *political action*, which involved giving money (including bribes) to political parties and groups that could be encouraged to oppose Allende. Some of those groups turned out to be neo-Nazi organizations which engaged in terror campaigns inside Chile, and some of whose members later engaged in international terrorism, such as the assassination of Orlando Letelier.[148] The second, a *propaganda campaign*, was a multi-faceted effort which included: using foreign journalists on the CIA payroll to produce distorted news about Chile; subsidizing Chile's largest circulation newspaper, which became "the most important channel for anti-Allende propaganda," as well as opposition party newspapers; financing a radio station, a newspaper that circulated nationally in Chile, and several magazines, all of which generated stories intended to frighten Chilean citizens about Allende's alleged "real" plans; distributing protest flyers that would seem to originate with disaffected Chilean groups; providing U.S. journalists with "scoops" based on "inside" sources, in order to distort their coverage of events.[149] The third, *economic pressures*, entailed such efforts as discouraging U.S. firms from investing in Chile. These were intended "to generate an economic crisis."[150] The Chile covert action program took longer to achieve its results than expected. It was only after three years—during which time the economy "screamed"; truckers hauling food were paid to strike; hundreds of false, negative stories about Allende appeared in the press; reputedly independent, outraged citizens marched scores of times; and the military received repeated nods by U.S. agents—that the Chilean generals staged a coup on September 11, 1973.

The Chilean example is still fresh in the minds of Cuba's leaders. Beyond the explicit threat that the current policy pretends to foist on Cuba, its haunting parallel to the Chile destabilization tells Cubans that the United States would exploit any democratic openings to sow seeds of disunity. They contend that their fear is not that Cubans will be able to vote in open elections or learn the "truth" about the revolutionary government, but that, as in Chile, the United States would intervene to distort democratic campaigns and would wage a propaganda war against the regime.

Such expectations are readily reinforced by the record thus far of what Track II appropriations have funded. The Clinton administration, for example, awarded large sums to rabid anti-Castro organizations such as the CANF and the Center for a Free Cuba, and the Bush administration has been careful to distribute money the same way—and especially to South Florida Cuban American organizations.[151] The quasi-public National Endowment for Democracy similarly has spent its Cuba resources exclusively on anti-Castro groups. These modest efforts seem to have had little impact in Cuba, except when an authoritarian bureaucrat reacts irrationally, by clamping down on an academic or a writer who may have become tainted by associating with one of the groups. Moderate Cuban officials say they recognize that the particular provocations really pose little threat to Cuba. But these Track II activities make them cautious about advocating more openness. They are not necessarily concerned about repercussions that might be taken against them. Rather, as sincere patriots who want to defend Cuba's sovereignty, criticism seems to serve the aims of U.S. policy and Track II by promoting disunity.[152]

It is difficult for a critic to propose reforms and to be patriotic, because there is no ambiguity about the ultimate goal of Track II programs. They are intended to achieve the objective of the embargo through other means. That objective, stated openly at the beginning of the CDA, is nothing less than the removal of Castro from power and the fundamental change in the regime "through the careful application of sanctions directed at the Castro government."[153] The 1996 Helms-Burton Act, which also contains Track II provisions, goes even further. It declares presumptuously that one criterion for determining whether a new regime in Cuba meets the U.S. standard of a "transition government" is that it "does not include Fidel Castro or Raul Castro."[154]

La Fruta Madura

Cubans say they have heard versions of the Helms-Burton rhetoric for almost two hundred years. The 1996 law, political scientist Carlos Alzugaray Treto observes, is merely the latest variant of the cavalier disregard for Cuban sovereignty that Secretary of State John Quincy Adams expressed in 1823. Cuba, Adams said, would one day "gravitate" into the "North American Union" by the same kind of natural law that governs an apple, which "cannot choose but fall to the ground." This attitude has been dubbed the "ripe fruit syndrome" or *la fruta madura*, and Cubans see it as the source of the U.S. impulse to intervene in Cuba's internal affairs.[155]

When the moment came for the fruit to drop in 1898, the United States believed it had to help the laws of nature. As Cuba was about to break loose from Spanish colonial ties, U.S. forces arrived to fight a "splendid little war," helping the Cubans to end Spanish rule. But, Alzugaray observes, "After thirty years of struggle the only thing gained [for Cuba] was a change of master." The United States ceded nominal independence to Cuba after three years of occupation on the condition that the new republic include in its constitution the "ignominious" Platt Amendment, which "gave Washington the authority to intervene in [Cuba's] internal affairs."[156]

U.S. officials provided seemingly noble rationalizations at the time to justify what they well recognized was a denial of Cuba's independence. Cubans, some said, were "like children" who would only harm themselves if given too much freedom. They had chosen "incompetents" in their municipal elections and needed the firm hand of the United States to guide them until they were fit for self-government.[157] Until "a better element has come to the front," U.S. Governor General Leonard Wood affirmed, full independence would mean "turning the island over to spoilation. It would be a terrific blow to civilization here."[158]

Beneath such expressions of concern for the Cuban people lay the real U.S. concern for geopolitical control of the region and for protection of significant U.S. investments. The "independents" threatened these because they equated sovereignty with the ability of Cubans to control the political and economic decisions on the island that would shape the extent to which there would be equity and social justice. The independents, historian Louis Pérez explains, were unwilling "to compromise national sovereignty to accommodate North American needs."[159] The United States had hoped that Cuban property owners, who thrived under colonial rule and who favored U.S. dominance, would be able to "rise" up and win political office. But the Cuban desire for independence proved too strong. With the United States unable to count on local elites to protect U.S. interests, it needed the right to intervene in order to assure U.S. hegemony.

It is understandable why Cubans assert that the Helms-Burton Act has all the earmarks of the 1901 Platt Amendment. The 1996 law arrogates to the United States, not to Cuba, the right to determine whether there has been an appropriate transition to democracy, that is, whether the Cubans have established a government that the United States can trust to rule the island in a "civilized" manner. It can earn that trust only after paying in full the claims of former property owners, in amounts determined by the United States. Cuba would have no right to negotiate those claims. It also would need to be "substantially moving toward a market-oriented economic system based on the right to own and enjoy property," regardless of how that undermined Cubans' desire to achieve social equity. Cuba would be required to hold U.S.-style elections and promote privately owned media, despite the likelihood the United States would try to undermine the integrity of both as it has in other countries. Political scientist Soraya Castro succinctly captures the Cuban point of view in describing how the law attempts to settle a century-old issue in exactly the same way as the Platt Amendment: "The spirit and the letter of this legislation demonstrated the essential conflict existing between Cuba and the United States: sovereignty versus domination."[160] Miami-based commentators may dismiss this conflict with facile sarcasm. David Rieff, for example, refers to "Castro's insistence on the sacred ideal of Cuban sovereignty" in describing Cuba's reaction to Helms-Burton. But he also acknowledges that both Cubans in the United States and on the island have long equated their own dignity with Cuban nationalism.[161]

Unlike the Platt Amendment, which relied on U.S. military power for enforcement, the Helms-Burton Act depends on U.S. economic power. The 1992 Cuban Democracy Act (CDA) had tightened the U.S. embargo by prohibiting subsidiaries of U.S. corporations in third countries from trading with Cuba. Backers expected that this would lead to the quick collapse of the regime, because Cuba would no longer be able to obtain essential products.[162] It had been able to circumvent the U.S. embargo for thirty years by trading with the socialist bloc on the basis of essentially barter arrangements, and by using limited hard currency reserves to buy goods from U.S. subsidiaries. In turn, it earned hard currency by selling to these companies. The demise of the socialist bloc meant Cuba had to pay for all imports with hard currency, and the CDA restrictions were intended to close the biggest loophole in the embargo and end Castro's rein.[163]

The strategy did not work. By 1995 Cuba had turned the corner and its economy was beginning to grow again. It had done so, in part, by encouraging foreign investment through a variety of structural changes. The Helms-Burton Act sought to close off this new line of sustenance for the regime by enabling former Cuban property owners to penalize companies that made these investments.[164] In Title III, they were given the right to sue the firms in a U.S. court for making any commercial use of their "expropriated" property, and the judgments could entail seizure of a company's assets in the United States. The law allowed the president to waive these provisions, and both Clinton and Bush have done so every six months in response to pressure from U.S. allies. But the threat that the provision might not be waived at some future point undermines Cuba's attractiveness for foreign investors. Without such a potentially harmful obstacle, Cuba's well-educated workforce, its lack of strong trade unions, its relatively well-developed infrastructure in comparison to other Third World countries, and its ability to use advanced technology might well have made it a popular site for global capital. Helms-Burton also codified the existing embargo regulations, making them that much more difficult to change.

Apart from the threat of Title III, the embargo itself has harmed the Cuban economy. Cuba recently asserted that the cumulative cost since 1959 had been $67 billion.[165] But during that time other countries also imposed trade sanctions on Cuba, and by the mid-1970s Cuba had chosen to integrate its economy with the CMEA countries, denying itself opportunities for trade with the West. Though a precise monetary amount of the damage that the U.S. embargo has caused over forty years is difficult to ascertain, the greatest impact certainly has occurred since the end of 1990, when the CMEA collapsed. With respect to the last decade, even the U.S. International Trade Commission has concluded that "U.S. economic sanctions—in particular, the extraterritorial restrictions added by the CDA and the Helms-Burton Act—appear to have had an adverse impact on Cuba's economy."[166]

The effects of the embargo are evident in many ways. Before the CDA cut off Cuba's trade with U.S. subsidiaries in third countries, 90 percent of what Cuba had purchased from these firms was food. It was then forced to buy from sources further away, using its scarce hard-currency resources on increased transportation costs.[167] This contributed to a rapid decline in caloric consumption, and for the first time since the 1960s, some Cubans fell below healthy nutritional levels. An analysis by the American Association for World Health (AAWH), the U.S. affiliate of the UN's World Health Organization, reported that "daily caloric intake dropped 33 percent between 1989 and 1993." The report asserted that the "ban on the sale of American foodstuffs has contributed to . . . an increase in low-birth-weight babies. In addition, food shortages were linked to a devastating outbreak of neuropathy . . . that temporarily blinded over 50,000 Cubans."[168] Cuba's health care system prior to 1989 had been widely praised for its broad coverage and ability to raise indicators to the level of advanced industrial countries. That system suffered significantly when access to major drugs was cut off, purchase of medical equipment was blocked, and delivery costs skyrocketed. On the basis of its year-long investigation, the 1997 AAWH study concluded "that the U.S. embargo of Cuba has dramatically harmed the health and nutrition of large numbers of ordinary Cuban citizens."[169]

Responding to the AAWH report, the State Department asserted in 1997 that Cuba would have been able to purchase drugs and medical supplies elsewhere, but chose to use its hard currency to develop health facilities only for tourists. But at the start of the 1990s U.S.-based pharmaceutical and medical-supply firms began to buy many of those other companies, and that closed off Cuban access to them. The CDA does permit U.S. firms to apply for licenses to sell medicine to Cuba, but the conditions had been so restrictive (a company had to be able to certify through "on-site" inspections that its products are not used by the Cuban military or in a way that violates human rights) as to render such permission meaningless.[170] Corporations were further discouraged from selling to Cuba by the red tape involved, because they must obtain a license for each separate shipment.[171]

In a report to the UN in 2001, Cuba went beyond food and medicine to detail how U.S. sanctions had impaired most sectors of the Cuban economy, by closing off the U.S. market to Cuban sugar, nickel, and tourism, and by denying Cuba access to advanced technology. The embargo, it said, was "cruel and merciless economic warfare."[172] Even if the hyperbole of such a charge is discounted, there is considerable evidence that the CDA and the Helms-Burton Act have impacted Cuba in more than symbolic ways. Cubans do believe that the United States is engaged in a serious economic war against it, determined this time to make the ripe fruit fall.

AN EXERCISE IN *REALISTIC EMPATHY*

For much of the twentieth century, U.S. presidents dominated the foreign policy process. But as the Cold War waned, analysts realized that this pattern was not immutable and was largely a function of the way the executive defined international problems as strategic threats, which enhanced the president's role as commander-in-chief. Even before the end of the cold war, Congress was quite important in shaping *intermestic* issues, those which had both international and domestic elements, such as trade. It should have come as no surprise, then, that when Cuba ceased to be perceived as a strategic threat, Congress would become more involved in determining U.S. policy toward the island.[173]

It was Congress that forged the 1992 Cuba Democracy Act, pressing it on a reluctant President George H. W. Bush who signed the CDA only after Governor Bill Clinton, his likely opponent in that year's presidential election, endorsed the bill.[174] When Republicans gained control of both chambers of Congress in 1995, they moved quickly to fashion legislation that tightened the embargo by focusing on foreign investors who seemed to have helped Cuba turn around the failing economy. The Clinton administration was out of the loop in drafting the initial bills, and the final version, which undercut the president's discretion, only got onto the White House radar at the last minute, at a politically inopportune moment for a veto.[175]

Now Congress is again challenging the president's Cuba policy. Since 1999, in a series of votes, it has attempted to relax the embargo by removing restraints on the sale of food and medicine and on travel to Cuba by U.S. citizens.[176] Congressional efforts have been backed by several corporate leaders, by prominent former U.S. officials, and by a coalition of church-related organizations. One notable crack in the embargo came after Hurricane Michelle devastated portions of Cuba in November 2001. The Bush administration relaxed licensing requirements on the sale of food and medicine, and by mid-2002, more than $90 million worth of goods had been sold since November 2001.[177]

In short, the picture Cuba paints of a monolithic United States pounding away relentlessly at a vulnerable Cuba does not quite capture the current reality. There certainly are U.S. groups and even officials who seek nothing less than the overthrow of Cuba's regime.[178] There also are some who advocate engagement with Cuba in ways that would serve common interests of both countries, for example, on matters of environmental protection or nuclear safety.[179] Others have proposed improved human rights conditions and political reforms in Cuba that would not necessarily undermine the regime.[180] Meaningful national elections, for example, could be held with restrictions on foreign funding, as they are in the United States. Some U.S. advocates of change in Cuba are quite supportive of Cuba's socialist aims and argue that changes are necessary in order to make it possible to realize those aims.[181] But their arguments are lost in Cuba amidst the cacophony of demands coming from the United States that are intended to overthrow the regime.

Similarly, the portrait of the United States painted by U.S. officials—of an altruistic superpower merely trying to help the Cuban people "pursue their hopes and dreams for a better life"—falsely depicts the real nature of U.S. policy.[182] Human rights advocates in Cuba—the very people the policy purportedly seeks to assist—have appealed to the United States to end the embargo, as have U.S. human rights critics of Cuba.[183] Pope John Paul II decried U.S. sanctions as "unjust and ethically unacceptable" during his 1998 trip to Cuba, when he also found common ground with Castro in denouncing the "blind market forces" of global capitalism.[184] At the same time, the black-and-white picture of Cuba many U.S. critics present—in which aging hard-liners control decisions and fear any openness that might challenge their power—distorts the internal dynamics in Cuba, where there are serious debates about reform. It also ignores the way Cuba has been open to cooperation with the United States when both countries have been able to benefit, such as on drug enforcement.[185]

Confronted by two opposing views of reality, there is often a temptation to resort to the cliché that the elusive truth lies somewhere in the middle. Instead, we propose that a perspective rooted in *realistic empathy* provides a way to appreciate the nature of the U.S.–Cuban relationship without ideological blinders. As applied to this case, an empathetic approach would begin with the assumption that neither the United States nor Cuba holds the balance of virtue, and that the aims of both countries deserve to be accorded respect. It requires careful listening to both sides, devoid of the temptation to rush to judgment. It then suggests an approach to reduce the hostility between them, and enable those who could find common ground to do so. The recommendation to empathize with both sides is not a proposal to sympathize or agree with both. Psychologist Ralph K. White offers a clear distinction between empathy and sympathy. Empathy, he explains,

> means simply understanding the thoughts and feelings of others. It is distinguished from sympathy, which is defined as feeling with others—as being in agreement with them. Empathy with opponents is therefore psychologically possible even when a conflict is so intense that sympathy is out of the question.[186]

An Asymmetrical Relationship

The first step in thinking empathetically is to place yourself in the other side's shoes. Imagine, for a moment, that you were a Cuban national security analyst. Could you fashion an argument for your colleagues to convince them that the United States does *not* pose a serious threat to Cuba's security? Would they find it credible that harsh rhetoric from U.S. officials, seemingly tacit support for terrorists who continue to plot attacks against Cuba, and enforcement of two restrictive embargo laws—the 1992 Cuban Democracy Act (CDA) and the 1996 Helms-Burton Act—are merely politicians' responses to domestic political pressure? Even if you believed that these measures were really much ado about nothing, could you recommend that your small country take a risk that such an assessment is wrong? No, it would verge on the irresponsible for a Cuban national security analyst to make that recommendation. If U.S. hostility in fact did reflect the true intentions of the United States, then complacence could lead to a U.S. attack. On the other hand, if Cuba acts inappropriately, responding to the United States as if it were an enemy when it really is not, then the resulting cost to Cuba would be continuation of the kind of hostility it has experienced for forty years. Such a state of affairs may be undesirable, but it is preferable to destruction. As a small country ninety miles from the United States, Cuba's rational cost–benefit calculation necessarily leads it to assume the worst about the United States. In fact, U.S. behavior provides them with abundant evidence for their case. Maj. Gen. Edward Atkeson (U.S. Army-Ret.) captured this calculation well in reflecting on his own military experience. He observed that there is

> a mindset in Cuba of the danger of U.S. aggression. It closely resembles our own perception of the threat posed by the Warsaw Pact at the height of the Cold War. We did not necessarily consider it likely, but the risks on the downside were so great that we had to devote substantial resources and effort to deterring it and to preparing a viable defense. Thus does the possibility of war with the United States appear to the Cubans.[187]

In contrast, the downside of miscalculation for the United States carries far fewer risks. Suppose the United States did treat Cuba's fears about a U.S. attack as if they were serious and not mere propaganda ploys, did end its efforts to transform Cuban society and respect Cuba's sovereignty, and did cancel the embargo unilaterally. If these actions did not reduce tension between the two countries, the only cost for the United States might be a domestic political one for a few people. Even if there were no gain vis-à-vis Cuba, the United States might benefit because this is the course U.S. allies have advocated, and it could help to remove a source of tension with them.

The United States and Cuba thus run different risks in approaching the relationship from an empathetic position, in believing that the other side is sincere. This fundamental asymmetry in the U.S.–Cuban relationship must be a starting point in any attempt at empathy. The United States clearly could be a threat to Cuba, but Cuba no longer poses a serious threat to the United States.[188] In circumstances of asymmetry, the initial burden of empathy generally falls on the more powerful actor because it has less to lose. In Cuba's case, there are two additional reasons for the United States to assume this burden.

First, there is the particular legacy of the more than one hundred years of U.S.–Cuban relations, during which time the larger power tended to treat with contempt the sovereignty and dignity of the smaller one. Second, there is Cuba's experience with the other superpower, the Soviet Union, in which the larger power also disregarded Cuba's assessments of threat, its fundamental needs, and its advice. The impact of that asymmetrical relationship on Cuba cannot be ignored in evaluating how Cuba reacts to U.S. proposals in the context of asymmetry today.

Were U.S. officials and U.S. advocacy groups to adopt an empathetic approach to Cuba, three changes would be necessary. They would need to: (1) no longer assume the worst about Cuba; (2) acknowledge the legitimacy of Cuban fears; and (3) renounce the Platt Amendment.

Stop Assuming the Worst about Cuba

The forty-year history of hostility between the two countries is replete with instances when U.S. officials and analysts have misconstrued Cuban intentions, refusing to accept benign explanations for Cuban behavior and interpreting it in the most threatening light. Consider the oft-repeated notion that Cuba was a Soviet surrogate.

Most scholars now conclude that Cuba's international activities throughout this period were animated primarily by Cuba's own ideology and interests, which combined revolutionary idealism, moralism, and pragmatism. The personal experiences of Cuban leaders convinced them they had a duty to support other countries engaged in struggles for independence, and that Cuba's ability to develop along the particular socialist path they envisioned required there to be similar socialist revolutions elsewhere so that cooperation among poor countries could be possible. Assistance to progressive countries also was one means of promoting Cuban national security, by making it politically more difficult for the Soviet Union to abandon Cuba and for the United States to attack it.[189] In Africa, for example, Cuba most often was pursuing its own particular goals—such as fighting against colonialism, supporting governments led by former anticolonial fighters with whom Cuba had had relations, and promoting its own leadership in the Non-Aligned Movement. There even were instances when Cuban actions might have been construed as serving U.S. interests.[190] Rather than acting as a puppet, Cuba related to the Soviet Union more like Israel did to the United States, somewhat like the tail wagging the dog.

Consider the following examples where the United States perceived Cuba was acting as a stalking horse for the Soviet Union:

- In the 1960s, after the missile crisis, Cuba actively supported insurgents in several countries in the hemisphere, including Venezuela and Bolivia. This subversion may have angered the United States, but it was not Soviet sponsored. As we examined in chapter 3, it was just the opposite, because the Soviet Union sharply opposed Cuba's support for armed struggle in Latin America. Their disagreements came close to ending the relationship between the two countries.
- In 1975 Cuba sent nearly 40,000 troops to Angola to support the newly independent government that was fighting a civil war against U.S.-backed forces. Such a large troop deployment would be a major commitment for any country and unprecedented for a small country such as Cuba. Yet Cuba did not even consult with the Soviet Union in advance of the decision to commit the troops, and informed the Soviets only after they were under way. The Soviet Union earlier had discouraged Cuba from considering such an operation, because it feared that Cuban involvement would undermine its détente efforts with the United States.[191]
- In the 1980s Cuba provided considerable support for the Nicaraguan government in its war with U.S.-backed insurgents (*contras*) and modest support for insurgents in the El Salvador civil war. This led the Reagan administration to denounce Cuba as a "Soviet surrogate" that posed a major threat to U.S. security.[192] However, Cuba and the Soviet Union had serious disagreements about Central America. The Soviets reportedly viewed the Sandinistas as too "indisciplined" to warrant a major commitment, which led Castro to demonstrate his displeasure with Soviet policy in 1985 by absenting himself from Soviet General Secretary Konstantin Chernenko's funeral.[193]

Cold War ideology may have blinded the United States to the reality of the Soviet–Cuban relationship, but it becomes important now for the United States to recognize it was mistaken. Such a recognition may enable Americans to see that Cuba has distinctive interests, and that its foreign policy in the Third World was one way a small country sought to overcome the asymmetry in power it experienced when dealing with the two superpowers.

Even a leader such as President Jimmy Carter, who came into office in 1977 disposed to improve relations with Cuba, succumbed to the ideological straightjacket. By October 1979 he had signed a presidential directive that ordered national security agencies to devise strategies for "isolating" Cuba.[194] His anti-Soviet National Security Adviser Zbigniew Brzezinski relentlessly had pressured the president to interpret every Cuban move as hostile. When Carter finally adopted this attitude, he began to paint himself into rhetorical corners, quickly responding to each new "challenge" with a tough stance, even when the reality turned out to contradict the allegations.[195] Wayne Smith, who was in charge of the State Department's Cuba desk at the time, recalls that in 1978 and 1979 Cuba made sincere efforts to be cooperative, but these were rebuffed. When Smith tried to provide the president with a "balanced assessment" of Cuba's role in Africa, noting that Cuba had "contributed to peaceful solutions and had been helpful to us," a National Security Council aide informed him that the NSC was interested only in emphasizing how "the Soviets and the Cubans are the aggressors." Smith wisely observes that "[t]rying to score such propaganda points against the other side has its dangers. It unnecessarily raises some tempers and encourages bellicose tendencies." In fact, he notes, such rhetoric did encourage some members of Congress to demand "that something be done" in the face of the Soviet–Cuban threat.[196]

What was Cuba to make of such shenanigans, where its actions seemed willfully misinterpreted and characterized as exactly the opposite of their reality? Cuban officials might have interpreted Brzezinski's mendacity as nothing more than a bureaucratic power play, which ultimately did lead to Secretary of State Cyrus Vance's resignation. But a small country cannot afford the luxury of such speculations. U.S. rhetoric had the potential to get out of hand, and Carter's seeming bad faith gave Cuba little reason to trust him.

Thus, Cuba readily interpreted signs of mounting discontent in early 1980 as evidence of a U.S. destabilization campaign, and reacted by permitting people to leave the island specifically if they departed on boats arriving from the United States.[197] The resulting Mariel exodus of 120,000 Cubans added to the U.S. public's sense that Carter's foreign policy was a failure, contributed to his defeat in the fall election, and brought U.S.–Cuban relations to their lowest point in at least a decade. What had started out in 1977 as significant movement toward détente between Cuba and the United States evolved into such hostility that the Reagan administration's harshness toward to island in 1981 seemed more like continuity than a sharp break. Certainly both sides contributed to the breakdown in trust, but it was the United States that repeatedly rejected benign explanations of Cuban behavior.

Acknowledge Legitimacy of Cuba's Threat Perception

International relations scholar Raymond Garthoff identifies the inability of U.S. and Soviet officials to see the world from each other's perspectives as the underlying disposition that ended détente between the two superpowers in the late 1970s and 1980s. Both sides believed they were merely reacting to the other, and both imagined the other to have aggressive intentions. This lack of empathy was especially dangerous in the way it led each superpower to misunderstand how the other defined its own security and threats to that security.[198] Incredibly, he notes, there were even some U.S. leaders who "have spoken and acted as if the Soviet Union has *no* legitimate security interests."[199]

Cuba today finds similar U.S. negations about its perception of threat to be incredible and insulting. As we examined earlier in the chapter, Cuba perceives it is under siege and has good reason to believe so. Unlike a superpower, though, it also feels enormously vulnerable, as any small country would in its circumstances. It pays extraordinarily close attention to every U.S. utterance, every small movement made by U.S. officials, while even U.S. analysts make broad generalizations about Cuban motives and interests, often discounting what officials in Cuba actually say. Cuban political scientist Soraya Castro highlights the asymmetry in awareness between the two countries in noting perceptively, "On the island, U.S. politics constitute a major determinant in the implementation of both foreign and domestic policy, whereas, in the United States, the Cuban case has little impact on foreign policy priorities."[200]

Cuban political scientist Carlos Alzugaray Treto helpfully explains that the United States and Cuba would naturally think about national security in different ways, because of their differences in size. The Cuban concept of security includes "economic, political, and even social aspects," he observes, "precisely because Cuba, as a small country, is more vulnerable than a big superpower like the United States to all kinds of pressures."[201] As we discussed in chapter 3, this difference in vulnerability between a small and great power was exactly what the Soviets could not comprehend about Cuba in 1962. As we noted there, a great power tends not even to think about whether it will be swallowed up by another power, whether its identity will be submerged by the interests of a larger state, or whether its internal life will be subject to the whims and dictates of outsiders. It tends to be concerned about military threats, because those are what could harm it. A small power, in contrast, must worry about much more because its vulnerabilities are so much greater.

Sincere acknowledgment that Cuba perceives itself to be threatened would be quite different than the sort of disparaging suggestion that the United States should curtail its hostile rhetoric, and even the embargo, in order to deprive the Cuban leadership of an excuse for its repression and the system's failings. The embargo has been a significant tactic in trying to destabilize the Cuban regime, but removing it merely so that other tactics might more successfully serve the same end would not make Cubans feel more secure.

Honest engagement is the only way in which Cuban leaders will begin to develop confidence that the United States has forsaken its goal of overthrowing the Cuban government. In instances when the United States has given Cuba such basic respect, by negotiating directly with Cuba to resolve bilateral problems, it has obtained accords that serve the interests of both countries. They have covered hijacking, fishing rights, boundary waters, immigration, and even nuclear safety. But the

United States also has a legacy of trying to manipulate Cuba indirectly—most often by way of the Soviet Union during the Cold War. Such behavior emphasizes the imbalance between the two countries, which in itself is threatening, and it disparages Cuba's legitimacy, which becomes a threat in the context of such unequal power. A sincere recognition of Cuba's circumstance, that it is a small country with the lone superpower hovering over it, would mean that if the United States had disagreements with Cuba's international behavior, it would take these up directly with Cuba or bring them to international bodies for resolution, as the United States does with other countries.

Instead, U.S. officials in the past have tried to exploit Cuba's sense of vulnerability. Even when Cuba has shown a willingness to accommodate what the United States perceived to be important security interests, U.S. policymakers have taken such offers as an indication of Cuban weakness and increased the intimidation. This legacy weighs on any effort to convince Cuban leaders that they should trust the United States. It should come as no surprise, then, that Cuba is wary about seeming to be weak and accommodating. Accommodations in the past seem to them only to have intensified U.S. determinations to wreak havoc on the island.

In August 1961, for example, Che Guevara approached Kennedy aide Richard Goodwin immediately after an OAS meeting in Uruguay. According to Goodwin, Guevara proposed that the United States and Cuba develop a modus vivendi, in which Cuba "could agree not to make any political alliance with the East" and "could also discuss the activities of the Cuban revolution in other countries." Cuba was thus offering to remove what came to be the two main U.S. concerns over the next thirty years, namely, Cuba's ties to the Soviet Union and its support for revolutionary movements. Yet when he returned to Washington, Goodwin assessed that this offer meant "that Cuba is undergoing severe economic stress, that the Soviet Union is not prepared to undertake the large effort necessary to get them on their feet." In turn he recommended that the United States use this opportunity to "intensify" economic and military pressure on Cuba and "step up covert activities."[202]

Similarly in 1981, as the United States increased its commitments in El Salvador in order to "draw the line" against "Soviet–Cuban aggression" in Central America, Cuba offered the United States a "compromise" involving a "political solution" for El Salvador. At a secret meeting between U.S. Secretary of State Haig and Cuban Vice President Rodríguez in Mexico, the Cuban leader then went even further, to propose a new framework for improved relations between the two countries. He said:

> You touched upon our difficulties and our vulnerability. This is true. We are vulnerable, and our people has suffered a great deal from the American blockade [embargo]. . . . If we could improve relations with the United States, then our conditions would be better.

But in order to obtain that, he emphasized, Cuba would not sacrifice its principles, which he delineated as:

> First: the sovereignty of Cuba—the inalienable right, being understood to include . . . the right to trade with the entire world, including the United States. Second: we have a right to solidarity with the countries of the "Third World," and in particular, with the countries of Latin America. Third: our friendship with the Soviet Union. . . . However, we do not believe that . . . is incompatible with the establishment of normalized relations between the United States and Cuba.[203]

Haig was cordial in response and agreed to follow-up meetings. But the Secretary of State "appears to have interpreted the meeting as evidence that U.S. pressure on Castro was working," as Cold War historian Peter Kornbluh astutely observes. "He returned to Washington to push, again, for a blockade."[204]

Renounce the Platt Amendment

Rodríguez's three principles embody the starting point for a serious engagement with Cuba. In stating them, he reminded Haig that mutual respect between sovereign countries neither required each one to approve of nor endorse the other's economic or political system. "We do not like the social system in the United States," he said. "But, naturally, that is the social system of the United States, and the American people are entitled to decide what they must do." Under this rubric, the United States could try to encourage Cuba to alter its system, that is, to embrace market and political reforms favored by the superpower, but it would do so in ways that respected Cuban sovereignty. It would, in effect, renounce the fundamental premise of the Platt Amendment, that the United States has the right to control Cuba's internal affairs.

It is only in the context of mutual respect for each other's sovereignty that exchanges about human rights are likely to generate any meaningful progress. There are some who argue that a Castro-led government will always repress political rights. They point to Cuba's trade with Canada, Europe, and Mexico to assert that these countries have not been able to parlay their trade into "a democratic transition on the island."[205] But this argument overlooks a fundamental difference between the United States and every other country with which Cuba now trades. The others have not and do not threaten Cuba's existence.

Were the United States to engage in normal trade with Cuba, it would be one important indicator that the war was over, which might permit Cuba to lower its guard. Any country under siege tends to tread on individual rights. Many Americans even demanded their government infringe on rights after September 11, 2001, in order to promote greater security, and Attorney General John Ashcroft seemed more than ready to restrict liberties at any whim.[206] Trade alone will not convince Cuba that it should lower its guard, especially if it is accompanied by Track II rhetoric about transforming the regime. But for these reasons, the embargo is not a meaningful bargaining chip or tool for pressure. Any reliance on it only exacerbates Cuban fears.

More generally, any time one country makes an effort to influence another country's internal affairs it must do so cautiously, whether this involves something fundamental, such as its political system, or merely symbolic, such as the kind of rice it eats. One of the hurdles advocates of global free trade have had to surmount is local resistance to the removal of nontariff barriers that seem to embody elements of national identity. When such efforts occur in the context of unequal power, even more caution and sensitivity is necessary. Yet in the case of Cuba, the United States not only has made demands in a cavalier fashion. It has used a double standard to condemn Cuba. At a minimum, empathy would require the United States to apply the same standards to its own behavior that it applies to Cuba.[207]

Such hypocrisy is evident in the State Department's annual human rights report. It is critical of excessive force used by Cuban police, for example, noting that "members of the security forces sometimes beat and otherwise abused human rights advocates, detainees, and prisoners. There continued to be numerous reports of disproportionate police harassment of black youths."[208] Yet such charges are made daily against the police in nearly every major U.S. city, and cruel treatment is common in many U.S. prisons.[209] The State Department's report also condemns Cuba because "Those who attempted to engage in unofficial union activities faced government harassment. Workers may lose, and many have lost, their jobs for their political beliefs, including their refusal to join the official union."[210] But if this standard were applied to the United States, "right-to-work" states such as Texas, which are notorious for the way they have facilitated the suppression of union organizing, would be judged much more harshly.[211] In fact, the suppression of unions in Mexico has been a major issue brought before the Commission for Labor Cooperation, the international adjudication unit established to enforce the North American Agreement on Labor Cooperation by the North American Free Trade Agreement (NAFTA).

Unquestionably, Cuba has suppressed its citizens' human rights. Yet even the State Department report acknowledges that there is no evidence of politically motivated killings or disappearances in Cuba, two of the worst human rights abuses that prevail in several Latin American countries that the United States does consider to be democratic. The seemingly unequal application of human rights standards to Cuba reinforces the belief that the criticisms are motivated by the same impulse to destroy the Cuban revolution that fueled U.S. propaganda campaigns throughout the last forty years. Cuba might be willing to discuss the charges, but only under circumstances in which the discussion is not perceived to be a trial conducted by a seemingly powerful aggressor.

EMPATHY OR DEATH

Without a Soviet Union, without an East–West Cold War—in the absence of, therefore, what were once thought by many to be compelling reasons for U.S.–Cuban enmity—a very real cold war between these two countries continues unabated. In the previous chapters, we have encountered a central reason as to why this might be the case: the inability of great powers and small countries to empathize with one another, to appreciate the fears, hopes, and motives of one so large (or so small). The Soviet Union and Cuba, allies of three decades, were abysmally unempathetic to one another, especially in the first decade of their relationship, as we have seen. So maybe it is not surprising that today relations between the world's lone superpower and a small country unwilling to bow before it are, in most respects, as glacial as ever.

We have endeavored in the preceding chapters to get inside the Cubans' perspective, as their relationship with the Russians evolved from, and was shadowed by, the traumatic events of the missile crisis. But can such an exercise as this contribute to bridging the gap, however modestly, between Cuba and the United States after the Cold War? The great British philosopher of empathy, Sir Isaiah Berlin, thought so. The kind of history represented in this book is a history straightforwardly directed at reducing misunderstanding and conflict. This kind of history, Berlin wrote, must have one overriding objective:

> To see the past through the eyes of those who lived through it, from the inside, as it were, and not merely as a succession of distant facts and events and figures in a procession to be described from some external vantage-point as so much material for narrative or statistical treatment. . . . [We can] achieve this kind of understanding, even though with considerable effort.[212]

So, via interviews, newly declassified documents, and whatever other "empathy facilitators" we could bring to bear, we have sought to make intelligible the Cuban response to the missile crisis, and the shadow of that crisis as it enshrouded them in their struggle with the Russians in the half dozen years thereafter.

What has this effort yielded? In sum, the portrait that emerges is of a leadership and a people almost completely at odds with both superpowers. In fact, the Cuban view of those events, and the way this view informed their relationship with their ostensibly friendly superpower of the 1960s, seems virtually incomprehensible to a North American readership if presented only in outline. The Cubans seem almost to be from some other planet. Their attitudes and behavior seem to make no sense, because as the superpowers tried desperately to defuse the crisis, the Cubans resented the very idea of a resolution to the crisis on the terms agreed to in Moscow and Washington. More, they did what they could to prolong the crisis and seemed unworried about increasing risk of a war that might have destroyed human civilization.

The same attitude, in fact, seems still to prevail in Cuba today. As he has for more than four decades, Castro often ends his speeches with the salutation, "*Patria o muerte*" ("Fatherland or Death"). Death may seem like an irrational option to people living in a great power, but for those in a weak country (or group), it becomes their last resort. Cuban leaders often ask people to remember "Baraguá." The *Granma* introduction to the Castro–Khrushchev letters was headlined "With the Historical Truth and Morale of *Baraguá*." It refers to an 1878 protest in Baraguá when the leader of the first Cuban war for independence, General Antonio Maceo, refused to give in to a superior Spanish force. It recalls the sense Israelis have about Masada. The true believers there may have seemed crazy, but they were willing to die rather than suffer domination by the attacking Romans. Buddhist monks who immolated themselves in 1963, protesting the tyranny of the U.S.-imposed ruler of South Vietnam, had only their lives as weapons. The idea is a very old one and has been repeated so many times that the wonder is that great powers have failed to understand it. This is how the Cubans see the world. *La patria* defines who they are; external control over that definition is the same as death.

In short, Cubans were and are willing to make the supreme sacrifice of themselves, their families, even their nation and conceivably other nations as well, in order to—in order to what? That is the question too seldom asked outside Cuba, because it seems not to have a rational answer. This, we now believe, is the answer: in order to retain their independence right up until the final hour. Yes, it meant that much to them—far more than what Castro often called "mere survival." It is safe to say that most North Americans reading this bare outline of the Cuban attitude will conclude that the Cubans have been crazy and suicidal, possessed by some mass psychosis perhaps. Or, at a minimum, they have been dangerously immature. Cubans, in other words, are beyond the pale, from that place a friend of ours has called "the planet of Cuba."

But that is not our conclusion, and it is not the conclusion legitimately to be drawn, we believe, from a study of the details—including (for the first time) many of the secret details presented in this book—of the Cuban reality at the time of the missile crisis and the half-dozen years thereafter. Were we to sum up our own view— our own conclusion—we could do no better than to cite Isaiah Berlin yet again.

What we believe emerges from the previous chapters is a portrait of a leadership and a people caught, as Berlin wrote in his classic study of nationalism, in "an all-too-human cry for independence . . . a cry for room in which men can seek to realise their natures, quirks and all, to live lives free from dictation or coercion."[213]

In chapters 1–4, we observed the origin, evolution, operation, and, finally, the resolution of the "cold war" between Cuba and the Soviet Union between October 1962 and August 1968. Through it all was the constant "all-too-human cry for independence." The documentary data and oral testimony we presented showed that this relationship was as cold as any cold war ever gets, overflowing with suspicion and hostility, with "negotiation" often being little more than issuing threats that left a good deal to the imagination of the threatened party. We saw, in addition, that a resolution of the Cuban–Soviet cold war became possible only when the shadow of the future overwhelmed the shadow of the missile crisis.

Something analogous, we believe, is now necessary to fundamentally alter the trajectory of U.S.–Cuban relations. From the Cuban standpoint, its relations with the United States are still held hostage to the missile crisis. Two of Cuba's "five points" are still on the table, after all these years: end the U.S. economic embargo of Cuba and return Guantanamo, site of a U.S. Naval base, to its rightful owner, Cuba. Were the United States to relent on these two points, a positive spiral of Cuban–U.S. cooperation could be initiated. The Cuban–U.S. cold war could end. The shadow of the missile crisis of four decades ago would give way to the shadow of a future that the United States and Cuba, neighbors barely ninety miles apart, will inevitably share.

Faure Chomón, Cuba's first ambassador to the Soviet Union, reflected in an interview on his experience as a Cuban official in dealing with big countries: the Soviet Union, the United States, and China. All three countries, he said, seemed incapable of treating Cuba with respect—the respect due an independent, sovereign nation, in exactly the same sense in which the big powers were independent sovereign nations. He quickly learned, he said, that "the big powers don't want us to have our own, independent ideas." He contrasted his impressions of dealing with these big powers with Cuba's experience with Vietnam. "It is interesting," he said, "that we never had problems with Vietnam. We understand each other because we are both independent, and we respect each other's independence. But the big powers don't want us to have our own independent ideas."[214]

It seems obvious why Cuba and Vietnam should "understand each other." Each is a socialist country that, in its way, defied both the Soviet Union and China, supposed allies. And of course, each refused to bend to the will of the United States no matter how much pressure the United States applied. A Vietnamese general once told us that he felt "at home" in Cuba because: "the weather is warm; the people are friendly; and everybody is united against a great hegemon directly to the north—China for the Vietnamese, the U.S. for Cuba."[215] The Vietnamese and the Cubans, especially in the 1960s, had a great deal in common. Empathy was, in a way, easy. It came naturally.

Yet empathy between big powers and small countries is another story. Indeed, the events of the 1960s highlight a moral that should be obvious, but obviously is not, about the absolute necessity that big powers learn to empathize with small countries. In October 1962 the United States and the Soviet Union (and the entire world) were brought to the brink of nuclear extinction because neither could comprehend Cuba, its revolution, and its newfound pride in being Cuban. It is one of the themes of this book, one borne out by the voluminous documentation and oral testimony now available, to which we have referred throughout the book. Yet this lesson—the necessity that big powers *should* empathize with small countries—was *not* learned by either the United States or the Soviet Union in the 1960s. As emphasized throughout this book, the Soviets relentlessly pressured the Cubans in ways the Cubans felt were not conducive to their own national security.

Regrettably the United States did not take from the missile crisis any lesson about the need for empathy, and that mistake proved very costly in Indochina. The American war in Vietnam, which escalated out of control from 1965 onward, was conducted by Washington as if the Cuban lesson from the missile crisis was irrelevant. The United States acted as if there were no threat at all to U.S. national security in engaging a small, backward nation militarily, pummelling it almost to bits. Surely "that little pissant country," as President Lyndon Johnson called Vietnam, would give in sooner or later. In fact, however, we now know that the North Vietnamese believed that the United States would eventually use nuclear weapons against them, causing deaths in the millions—mostly civilians, of course—and they had decided to make that level of sacrifice, if it came to that. They also expected the United States to invade across the 17th parallel, and that they would again become an occupied country. They had also resolved to endure that. The point is that in order to inflict even the hurt and damage the Vietnamese *expected*, the United States would have been forced to commit genocide—genocide by any reasonable definition of the term. And this, the United States (thankfully) would not do.[216]

The conduct and outcome of the American war in Vietnam demonstrated that a small, weak nation such as Vietnam, if organized, committed, and willing to sacrifice everything for what they take to be a noble objective, can bring a big power to its knees. But to appreciate this ahead of time and thus avoid similar disasters in the future, the great powers need to get inside the mindset, inside the heretofore unfathomable level of commitment of small but proud, organized and resistant nations and peoples, in order to appreciate just what the United States should expect when it attempts to push its weight around. And this, in the end, would keep all but the most irrational big powers from ever going down that road in the first place. In an ideal world, therefore, the big powers would have learned this lesson from the Vietnam War: not understanding one's adversary, even a poor, apparently weak and primitive adversary, can not only hurt you; it can bring your country to the brink of psychological collapse.

Alas, in this world, Cuba must be continuously on guard, virtually as if the Vietnam War had never occurred, as if the United States had not been humiliated by the Vietnamese communists. Cuba remains a potential "second Vietnam" for the United States, a fact that Fidel Castro does not hesitate to emphasize in his speeches. But other possibilities also include Somalia, Sudan, Syria, the Palestinian Territories, and, of course, the countries of the newly lumped and named "Axis of Evil"—Iraq, North Korea, and Iran. Approaching these countries with realistic empathy is not merely a nice "option"—an additional consideration as the United States plans its wars. It is a brutal necessity.

What would happen if the United States, the biggest of the big powers, were to develop a degree of empathy with Cuba? Michael Ignatieff has written that when both adversaries eventually begin to empathize with each other, a kind of mutual vantage point is reached from which both parties in a long-standing conflict are able to discern connections between their actions and the effects of those actions on others. In other words, I begin to see that to an extent, I am the cause of your effect. I am *responsible*, to an extent I never before realized. And you begin to see that you are the cause of my effect. You too are *responsible*. So both of us begin to see and feel that we are, in some measure, responsible for one another's suffering, and for our own suffering. According to Ignatieff, if the participants in this process of empathetic evolution—for example, nations with a history of animosity—find the courage to push it all the way to the end, reconciliation may occur. According to Ignatieff:

> Reconciliation means breaking the cycle of intergenerational vengeance. It means substituting the vicious downward spiral of violence with the virtuous spiral of mutually reinforcing respect. Reconciliation can stop the cycle of vengeance only if it can equal vengeance as a form of respect for the dead.[217]

Even if there were improved relations between Cuba and the United States, the two countries would likely find themselves in opposition on several international issues, and certainly on matters about their internal affairs. But discussions about their differences would be possible if they began from a position of empathy. Were U.S. officials to develop a degree of empathy for the Cubans, they would need to listen openly to what Cubans say rather than to presume they know best. They would hear that first the United States must deal with some of the "debris" of the missile crisis—the two big "leftovers" from October 1962. That is, they would need to end the embargo and to relinquish Guantánamo.

Calls for the return of Guantánamo and an end to the embargo reflect Cuba's fundamental interest in protecting its sovereignty and in ending the U.S. war against it; that is, in securing its very survival. At that point it would be reasonable to ask Cuba to empathize with the United States, to stop assuming the worst about U.S. intentions, to seize opportunities for improved relations, and to engage in serious discussions about the range of differences between the two countries. These would be based on mutual respect, not on asymmetrical power.[218]

Only under those circumstances might it be possible to imagine that a "virtuous spiral of mutually reinforcing respect" could begin. That is really all the Cubans (as well as the Vietnamese) have wanted from the United States. Or as Chomón put it, the United States and Cuba would then have achieved what Cuba and Vietnam had all along: "respect [for] each other's independence."

Appendix A

CHRONOLOGY OF EVENTS: 1963–1968

1963

January 2	On the fourth anniversary of the Cuban Revolution, Prime Minister Fidel Castro hints of a middle course for Cuba in ideological split between the Soviet Union and Peoples Republic of China, and stresses Cuba's right to determine its own individual course.
January 16	Castro urges the violent "overthrow" of imperialism by hemispheric revolutionaries.
January 22	France and West Germany sign treaty of cooperation ending four centuries of hostility that included three major wars within last 100 years: Franco-Prussian War (1870–71), First World War (1914–1918), and Second World War (1939–1945).
January 31	In a long letter promising Soviet support for Cuba, Premier Nikita Khrushchev invites Fidel Castro to visit the Soviet Union in April.
February 21	Venezuelan President Romulo Betancourt urges U.S. and Latin American allies to "restrict" access to Cuba and in order to check its attempts to export subversion.
March 19	President John F. Kennedy pledges to the Central American Presidents Conference that the United States will strengthen the Western Hemisphere's capacity to bar Cuban infiltration and propaganda.

April 12   Soviet Communist Party newspaper *Pravda* lists Cuba for the
                first time as a communist bloc member. Later in the month the
                Soviet Union issues postage stamps commemorating the Cuban
                Revolution.

April 27   Castro begins five-week visit across the Soviet Union, during
                which he is cheered at several mass rallies and he asserts that
                Soviet aid has prevented the overthrow of the Cuban govern-
                ment. In 1992 Castro recalled that during the trip Khrushchev
                inadvertently revealed to him Kennedy's secret promise to
                withdraw U.S. ballistic missiles from Turkey, which led to the
                Soviet removal of missiles from Cuba. At the end of the trip
                Castro receives a Soviet pledge to protect Cuba, increase aid,
                and a new trade agreement for sugar and oil.

May 25   The Organization of African Unity (OAU) is established at Ad-
                dis Ababa, Ethiopia, by 37 independent African nations.

June 3   Pope John XXIII dies. He had convened the Second Vatican
                Council which sought to reform the Catholic Church, but suc-
                cumbed to cancer after its first session.

June 10   In a commencement address at American University, Washing-
                ton, D.C., Kennedy calls for a reexamination of "our attitude to-
                ward the Soviet Union" by finding common ground with Rus-
                sians in "our mutual abhorrence of war." Asserting that "We are
                both caught up in a vicious and dangerous cycle in which sus-
                picion on one side breeds suspicion on the other, and new
                weapons beget counterweapons," Kennedy urges an end to the
                arms race, and he declares that the ultimate goal of current arms
                control negotiations is a "general and complete disarmament."

June 17   A Buddhist monk immolates himself in Saigon, South Vietnam;
                demonstrations against government repression of religion run
                from May to August.

June 19   Kennedy authorizes the CIA to renew support for Cuban exiles
                to engage in "hit-and-run attacks against appropriately selected
                targets" in Cuba. This program was extended in the fall of 1963
                to include operations in Cuba such as the sabotage of an elec-
                tric power plant, an oil refinery, and a sugar mill.

June 19   Castro warns Great Britain and France not to let their
                Caribbean islands be used as bases for rebel attacks on Cuba
                and threatens to attack the bases; he cites for first time the seri-
                ousness of counterrevolutionary guerrilla warfare in Matanzas
                province.

June 21   Cardinal Giovanni Montini succeeds Pope John XXIII, becoming Paul VI. He concludes Vatican II and is instrumental in implementing its reforms, including vernacularization and reform of the liturgy, devolution of considerable powers of dispensation from the Roman Curia onto the bishops, and relaxation of the rules on fasting and abstinence.

July 9   The United States bans virtually all financial transactions with Cuba in new move aimed at economic isolation. It also freezes $33 million in Cuban bank deposits in the United States, cuts Cuban overseas financial transactions, and bars Cuban use of the United States banking channels.

July 25   Cuba seizes the U.S. Embassy building and grounds in Havana, as a reprisal for the assets freeze.

August 5   The United States, Great Britain, and the Union of Soviet Socialist Republics sign the Limited Test Ban Treaty barring nuclear testing in the atmosphere, underwater, and in outer space.

August 28   A civil rights rally held by 300,000 people in Washington, D.C. hears the Rev. Martin Luther King, Jr. delivers his "I have a dream" speech at Lincoln Memorial.

August 30   The Washington–Moscow "hot line" communications link opens, designed to reduce risk of accidental war. It was proposed in the wake of experience the 1962 missile crisis.

September 15   Four young girls attending Sunday school in Birmingham, Alabama are killed when a bomb explodes at the Sixteenth Street Baptist Church, a popular location for civil rights meetings. Riots erupt in Birmingham, leading to the deaths of two more black youths.

November 1   Ngo Dinh Diem, president of South Vietnam, is deposed in a military coup backed by the United States; Diem and his brother, Ngo Dinh Nhu (head of the secret police), are then executed.

November 22   President Kennedy is shot and killed in Dallas, Texas; Vice President Lyndon B. Johnson is sworn in as President aboard Air Force One. Lee Harvey Oswald, the accused assassin, had been associated with a pro-Cuba organization, and earlier in the year had attempted to obtain a visa from the Cuban Embassy in Mexico to travel to Cuba.

December 2   Cuba announces the formation of the United Party of Socialist Revolution, a single party uniting representatives from various groups in Cuba, including the Popular Socialist Party (former communist party). It replaces the Integrated of Revolutionary Organizations (ORI).

December 31   At year's end there are 15,000 American military advisors in South Vietnam, up from 900 in 1960.

1964

January 8   British Leyland Motor Corporation defies U.S. requests to support economic sanctions against Cuba by selling 450 buses to Cuba with five-year option for 100 more.

January 22   Khrushchev reports that a new Soviet–Cuban trade pact will assure Cuban economic development. Castro emphasizes Cuba's strong ties with the Soviet Union and backs the policy of "peaceful coexistence."

March 31   Military officers stage a coup in Brazil against President João Goulart, reportedly with U.S. encouragement. The United States immediately recognizes the replacement government headed by Marshal Humberto Castelo Branco, army chief of staff. Two weeks later Castelo Branco pledges a tougher policy toward Cuba. Until then Brazil had opposed sanctions against Cuba and had maintained trade and diplomatic relations.

April 21   The United States warns Cuba not to interfere with reconnaissance flights over Cuban territory. Castro responds ten days later with a warning that Cuba will defend itself against the U.S. overflights and he announces the Soviet Union will turn over antiaircraft missile bases to Cuba.

May 2   Khrushchev warns that the U.S. actions against Cuba could lead to world war; he denies that the Soviet Union had agreed to the overflights in 1962. Two weeks later Soviet Deputy Premier Anastas Mikoyan says the Soviet Union would give Cuba military aid if the United States attacks.

June 11   A South African court sentences Nelson Mandela, leader of the African National Congress, to life imprisonment for plotting to overthrow the government.

June 21   Three Civil Rights workers helping blacks register to vote in Mississippi disappear after being arrested, jailed, and released on speeding charges. (It is later discovered that police handed them over to the Ku Klux Klan.) Their murdered remains are discovered after a search involving federal troops.

July 2   Johnson signs the 1964 Civil Rights Act into law; its provisions
                  give the federal government broad powers to fight discrimina-
                  tion.

July 6   Castro says Cuba will stop material aid to Latin American revo-
                  lutionaries if the United States stops supporting activities
                  against Cuba; he indicates that the Soviet Union had urged
                  Cuba to ease tensions with the United States. The United
                  States rejects Castro's overtures until Cuba ends its "depen-
                  dency" on the Soviet Union and ceases Latin American subver-
                  sion.

July 26   By a vote of 15–4 vote, the Organization of American States
                  (OAS) invokes sanctions against Cuba, including the severing
                  of diplomatic ties and the suspension of trade, for alleged ag-
                  gression against Venezuela. Castro responds by asserting
                  Cuba's right to aid revolutionary movements in any country
                  that acts against Cuba.

August 4   Johnson claims erroneously, as subsequent evidence indicates,
                  that North Vietnamese torpedo boats had attacked U.S. Navy
                  destroyers in the Gulf of Tonkin, off the coast of North Viet-
                  nam. He orders retaliatory air strikes and asks Congress for a
                  resolution of support. The resulting Gulf of Tonkin Resolution
                  authorizes the president to "take all necessary steps and mea-
                  sures to repel any armed attack against the forces of the United
                  States and to prevent further aggression." It provides the basis
                  for Johnson to send ground troops to Vietnam the next year and
                  to widen the scope of U.S. involvement in the war.

September 18   Castro announces cutbacks in planned purchased from non-
                  communist countries due to low world sugar prices; he says
                  that Cuba will not try to manufacture goods made more easily
                  in communist countries.

October 14   Soviet Communist Party leaders oust Khrushchev as First Sec-
                  retary and Premier, and fill the two positions, respectively, with
                  Leonid Brezhnev and Alexei Kosygin.

October 14   China explodes its first atomic weapon and becomes the fifth
                  nation (after the United States, the Soviet Union, Great Britain,
                  and France) to produce a nuclear bomb.

November 3   Johnson wins the presidential election in a landslide vote, de-
                  feating Republican Senator Barry Goldwater in forty-five of fifty
                  states. His victory is attributed in part to the Democrats' success
                  in depicting Goldwater as a prowar zealot.

November 10   Martin Luther King, Jr. accepts the Nobel Peace Prize in Oslo, Norway "on behalf of a civil rights movement which is moving with determination and a majestic scorn for risk and danger to establish a reign of freedom and a rule of justice."

December 12   Cuban exiles fire a bazooka at UN headquarters from across the East River during a speech by Ernesto "Che" Guevara, who heads Cuba's delegation to the General Assembly.

December 17   Guevara leaves New York for a three-month tour of Africa. On this first trip by a Cuban leader to sub-Saharan Africa, he meets with liberation and insurgent movements from several countries—including Angola, Guinea-Bisseau, Mozambique, the Congo, and Zaire—and promises Cuban support for their struggles.

Mid-December   A conference of Latin American communist parties, the first of its kind since 1929, meets in Havana. The conference, organized by the Soviet Union with Cuba's support, excludes pro-Chinese communist parties that had begun to form in Latin America. While China ignores the Havana conference in its media, Albania (a close ally of China) is openly critical, calling Castro a pseudo-communist who helps "revisionists." The conference develops a compromise position on the use of armed struggle to change existing capitalist regimes, which gives each party the license to determine whether armed struggle is appropriate in the context of its country's revolutionary development.

December 31   At year's end there are approximately 23,200 U.S. military advisors in South Vietnam.

1965

January 3   Cuba displays Soviet missiles and planes in a parade marking the sixth anniversary of the revolution. Castro asserts Cuba will be able keep political independence even without any economic aid. Three days later Cuba signs a trade pact with the Peoples Republic of China, noting publicly that it had been unable to reach economic agreement with the Soviet Union or to establish a reliable flow of aid.

February 4   Guevara deviates from his Africa trip for a one week visit to China. He meets with Communist Party chief Mao-tse Tung but fails to obtain Chinese agreement for increased aid or trade.

February 18   Cuba and the Soviet Union sign a five-year financial pact that reschedules the repayment of an estimated $500-million Cuban debt.

February 21   Black nationalist leader Malcolm X is shot to death at rally in New York City.

February 22   Guevara, in a speech delivered in Algiers, charges the Soviet Union and other socialist countries "are, to a certain extent, accomplices in the imperialist exploitation," because of "unequal" terms of trade with which they engage Third World countries. To underscore that Guevara's views reflected Cuba's official position, Castro has the speech reprinted and applauded in *Revolución*, the official party newspaper.

February 26   Johnson authorizes the deployment of the first regular U.S. armed forces to South Vietnam, to provide for defense of air-bases.

March 2   A sustained U.S. bombing campaign against North Vietnam, Operation Rolling Thunder, commences. It is a major escalation in the heretofore sporadic air campaign against North Vietnam.

March 7   "Bloody Sunday": Alabama state troopers use clubs and tear gas to attack an anti–voter discrimination march led by Martin Luther King, Jr.; nearly 100 are injured.

March 13   In a public address, Castro stresses the independence of Cuba's foreign policy, stating that "we are not anyone's satellite, and we never shall be!" He also calls upon the Soviet Union to stand by its ideals and render all the support it could to counter U.S. aggression, "taking whatever risks may be necessary for Vietnam."

April 1   Guevara gives up his Cuban citizenship and government positions, and leaves Cuba to wage a "struggle against imperialism" in Africa and Latin America. He leads a Cuban force that is waiting for him in Zaire. Cuba informs the Soviet Union about this operation three weeks after Guevara departs.

April 6   Johnson authorizes U.S. ground forces in South Vietnam to actively engage in offensive operations against enemy forces, beyond the defense of airfields. He then offers North Vietnam economic aid (including large-scale electric power development project) in exchange for peace. The offer is quickly rejected.

April 17   Students for a Democratic Society organize the first major anti–Vietnam War rally in Washington, D.C., which attracts at least 10,000 participants.

April 26   Cuba's largest cargo ship departs for Africa carrying arms and
                  supplies for anticolonial fighters in Mozambique and Guinea-
                  Bisseau. Also aboard are nine military instructors who will form
                  an advance group of a much larger force in Zaire.

April 28   The United States sends 23,000 Marines to the Dominican
                  Republic to suppress fighting against the military government
                  that had deposed a democratically elected regime in 1963.
                  Johnson acts on the basis of erroneous reports that there are
                  communists in the group fighting for the restoration of de-
                  mocracy, and fears the Dominican Republic could become
                  "another Cuba."

August 8   In a *Pravda* editorial, Soviet leaders renew their emphasis on
                  achieving peaceful coexistence—essentially rejecting a compro-
                  mise position about armed struggle forged at the prior Decem-
                  ber's Havana conference of Latin American communists.

August 11   Five days of riots break out in the Watts section of Los Angeles
                  causing 34 deaths and injuries to 1,000 people. Over 4,000 in-
                  dividuals are arrested.

October 3   The Communist Party of Cuba is established with Fidel Castro
                  as its head. Castro publicly releases Guevara's farewell letter in
                  which the champion of armed struggle recalls the "luminous
                  and sad days" of the missile crisis, and explains his departure by
                  writing that "other sierras of the world are calling for the con-
                  tribution of my humble efforts."

October 10   Hundreds of Cubans begin to depart from the small fishing port
                  of Camarioca as Castro opens the port to foreign boats so that
                  Cuban exiles can transport family members to the United
                  States. Within two months about 7,500 have arrived in the
                  United States through the Camarioca boatlift. Cuba and the
                  United States then agree to an airlift of Cuban refugees to the
                  United States. These so-called Freedom Flights bring more
                  than 200,000 exiles to the United States by 1973, when they
                  formally end, swelling the Cuban-American population in
                  Florida and New Jersey.

November 8   Soviet leaders accord Raul Castro, head of the Cuban Armed
                  Forces, a prominent place on the reviewing stand in Moscow for
                  the parade marking anniversary of Bolshevik Revolution. Three
                  weeks later he concludes a forty-five-day tour of Soviet bloc
                  countries during which he signs a new Cuban–Soviet coopera-
                  tion pact. At the same time, *Cuba Socialista*, the theoretical

journal of the new Cuban Communist Party, publishes an article by Fidel Castro that includes thinly veiled criticisms of Soviet international leadership. He asserts that Marxism is not a "religious doctrine, with its Rome, its Pope."

November 27   In the largest anti–Vietnam War gathering to date, more than 20,000 protestors rally at the Washington Monument over the Thanksgiving weekend.

December 31   At year's end there are approximately 200,000 U.S. troops in South Vietnam.

1966

January 2   India and Pakistan sign a Soviet-mediated peace pact on the Kashmir conflict. Castro discloses a sharp reduction in Cuba's trade with the Peoples Republic of China. The next month he charges that China has betrayed Cuba and is seeking to strangle the Cuban economy.

January 6   The Tricontinental Conference opens in Havana. This meeting of delegates representing communist parties and revolutionary organizations from every continent is cautiously endorsed by the Soviet Union, whose delegation is headed by Sharaf R. Rashidov, an alternate member of the Soviet Communist Party Politburo. The conference emphasizes the primacy of waging armed struggle against imperialism, which contrasts to the compromise agreed upon at the December 1964 meeting of Latin American communist parties. Many delegates urge greater Soviet support for North Vietnam. U.S. officials view the Tricontinental as an ominous indicator that there will be increased guerrilla activity in regions it seeks to stabilize, especially Latin America.

January 10   Castro pledges to provide doctors, vehicles, mechanics, and military instructors to Amílcar Cabral, leader of the independence movement in Guinea-Bissau who is participating the Tricontinental Conference.

February 13   Cuba announces a new trade pact with the Soviet Union, which includes $91 million in credits.

February 24   A military coup in Ghana deposes the government of President Kwame Nkrumah of Ghana while he is visiting North Vietnam on peace mission. Nkrumah had been Ghana's first head of state after independence. He had forged a new constitution and development plans for the nascent country and was a leading promoter of Pan-African unity.

March 11   General Suharto seizes power in Indonesia in a coup against President Sukarno. Sukarno was the first president after independence from Dutch colonial rule. In the 1950s he increasingly linked Indonesia to the People's Republic of China and he forged a national unity alliance with the Indonesia Communist Party. In 1965 the United States cut off economic assistance to Indonesia, but continued military assistance to the generals who organized the coup. The resulting Suharto dictatorship lasts for more than three decades.

March 14   Castro charges the Peoples Republic of China mounts a "fascist" drive against Cuba; he criticizes Mao and other "senile" leaders of China whom he blames for the Cuban–Chinese tension.

March 29   At the twenty-third Congress of the Communist Party of the Soviet Union, Cuba's chief delegate, Armando Hart, criticizes Soviet caution: "For victory over imperialism in Vietnam it is necessary to put an end, using all the available means and taking the necessary risk, to that criminal aggression which is the bombing of Democratic Republic of Vietnam."

June 1   Soviet Communist Party General Secretary Leonid Brezhnev scores U.S. "provocative actions" around the Guantanamo Naval Base and reaffirms Soviet–Cuban ties. The following day Soviet President Nikolai Podgorny pledges aid against U.S. aggression.

June 30   The National Organization of Women (NOW) is founded in Washington, D.C.

November 2 Johnson signs the Cuban Adjustment Act (P.L. 89-732), which permits a Cuban citizen to become a U.S. "permanent resident" after one year in the United States. During that year Cubans were automatically eligible to apply for "parole" status, which effectively meant that Cubans arriving on any U.S. territory could gain citizenship four years sooner than immigrants from other countries.

December 31 At year's end there are approximately 380,000 U.S. troops in South Vietnam.

1967

February 14 A majority of OAS members sign the Regional Treaty for the Prohibition of Nuclear Weapons in Latin America (Treaty of

Tlatelolco) in Mexico City. An outgrowth of the Cuban Missile Crisis, it requires signatories not to possess, produce, or test nuclear weapons, or to allow their deployment by another country within the territory or possessions of these countries. It is the first major arms control agreement in which countries agree to renounce the presence of nuclear weapons on their own land. Cuba refuses to sign the treaty.

March 13   Castro publicly criticizes the pro-Soviet communist parties of Latin America, stating that "those who are not revolutionary fighters cannot be called communists." He pointedly declares that the Cuban Revolution "will never ask anybody's permission to maintain its own position either in matters of ideology, or on domestic or foreign affairs."

April 15   100,000 antiwar protesters rally in New York; 20,000 rally in San Francisco.

April 16   Presna Latina publishes a letter from Che Guevara to the Organization of the Solidarity of the Peoples of Africa, Asia, and Latin America (the Tricontinental), which declares that through "liberation struggles" in Latin America, "the Cuban Revolution will today have a task of much greater revelence: creating a Second or a Third Vietnam. . . ."

April 21   A "Colonel's Coup" deposes the democratic government of Greece; all moderate and leftist politicians arrested; King Constantine is exiled for opposing coup.

May 30   Following months of nationwide violence in Nigeria, Odumegwu Ojukwu, the military governor of the eastern region, declares it to be the independent Republic of Biafra. This sets the stage for the prolonged civil war that follows.

June 5   The Six-Day War begins in the Middle East as Israeli forces cross the borders of Egypt, Jordan, and Syria in surprise attacks. Israel seizes control of all of the land on the west bank of the Jordan River, previously ruled by Jordan, including the old (eastern) portion of Jerusalem; the Sinai Peninsula, which had been part of Egypt; and the Golan Heights, which had been Syrian territory.

June 17   China announces it has exploded its first hydrogen bomb.

June 23   President Johnson and Soviet Premier Kosygin meet in Glassboro, N.J. Their summit includes discussions about the Vietnam War, disarmament, and the Middle East. Kosygin is nonresponsive to Johnson's requests for the Soviet leader to pressure Cuba on ending the support for revolutionary movements in Latin America.

June 27 · In the first visit to Cuba by a Soviet head of state, Kosygin arrives at Havana on his way back to Moscow from the Glassboro summit and a UN session called in response to the Six-Day War. His meetings with Cuban officials occur without public fanfare. Castro reportedly criticizes Soviet foreign policy, comparing the Soviet position on the Middle East conflict to Khrushchev's withdrawal of missiles from Cuba in 1962. The Cuban and Soviet leaders also disagree over Cuba's support for Latin American revolutionary movements.

August 1 · The first meeting of the Latin American Solidarity Organization (LASO) opens in Havana. Created by the 1966 Tricontinental Conference, nearly all of the delegations are dominated by noncommunist party organizations committed to armed struggle. Cuban President Osvaldo Dorticos pledges Cuba will provide aid to these groups. The eleven-day convention ends by approving a manifesto that declares armed revolt is the "fundamental line of revolution in Latin America," and by locating LASO's permanent secretariat in Havana.

September 25 · OAS foreign ministers approve a seventeen-point draft resolution against subversion in response to U.S., Venezuelan, and Bolivian allegations of Cuban support for guerrillas.

October 9 · U.S.-trained Bolivian rangers kill Che Guevara in the village of Vallegrande after capturing him in a surprise attack.

October 21 · More than 200,000 anti–Vietnam War demonstrators gather in Washington, D.C., for a rally that culminates in a "March on the Pentagon." Holding hands to form a circle around the building, protestors fail to achieve their proclaimed goal of "levitating" it. U.S. public opinion on the war shifts, as polls for the first time find more Americans oppose than support U.S. policy in Vietnam.

November 3 · World press reports suggest that the absence of Castro and Dorticos at celebrations in Moscow, marking the fiftieth anniversary of the Bolshevik revolution, is a rebuke to the Soviet Union. The Cuban delegation is headed by José R. Machado Ventura, at the time a relatively minor official in the Cuban Communist Party. He is the only representative from a socialist state who does not deliver a public congratulatory message to the Soviet Union.

December 31 · At year's end there are approximately 430,000 U.S. troops in South Vietnam.

1968

January 2

Castro announces that reduced oil shipments from the Soviet Union will require Cubans to "sacrifice," but he asserts that austerity will be short-lived as a program for economic self-sufficiency develops, especially if Cuba achieves its planned ten-ton sugar harvest in 1970. He calls on the Cuban people to "emulate Che [Guevara]" and he designates 1968 to be named in his honor as "The Year of the Heroic Guerrilla," which also highlights Cuba's differences with the Soviet Union. A ten-story-high mural of Guevara, facing Revolution Plaza, is unveiled. (It is on the facade of a building that had housed the Ministry of Industry, which Guevara headed, and now houses the Ministry of the Interior.)

January 23

North Korea seizes the U.S. Navy spy ship *Pueblo*; eighty-two surviving crew members are captured and held in prison for eleven months.

January 23

The first plenary meeting of the Cuban Communist Party's Central Committee convenes, during which Fidel Castro delivers a secret twelve-hour speech. Raul Castro chairs the meeting in which nine members of the pro-Soviet "microfaction" are charged with conspiring against the Cuban leadership and working with foreign diplomats to weaken Cuba. The Central Committee ousts the microfaction members from the Communist Party and supports their prosecution as "traitors to the revolution." They receive prison sentences that vary from three to fifteen years.

January 30

South Vietnamese insurgents (Vietcong) launch a surprise nationwide attack at the start of the lunar new year holiday (Tet). The Tet Offensive against U.S. and South Vietnamese government installations, including the U.S. embassy, causes massive damage, but the Vietcong sustain heavy casualties. Though the Vietcong "lose" every battle during the offensive, the attacks galvanize U.S. public opinion against continued involvement in the conflict, in part because the Johnson administration confidently had asserted U.S. forces had killed and imprisoned so many guerrillas that such a coordinated and widespread assault would not be possible.

March 13

Castro announces a "revolutionary offensive" against "the lazy, the parasites, and the privileged" who live off the work of others. The campaign closes or nationalizes 55,000 small private enterprises, including bars, auto repair shops, food stands, restaurants, and groceries. Nightclubs are shut down. "We did not make a revolution here to establish the right to do business," he asserts. Contrasting Cuban communism to that advocated by the pro-Soviet microfaction and practiced in other socialist countries, he argues that "We do not want a communist man to be molded by stimulating his greed, his individualism, his individual appetites!" He then emphasizes Cuba's desire to follow its own path: "We have known the bitterness of having to depend to a considerable degree on things that come from outside and how that can become a weapon and at least creates a temptation to use it against our country. Let us struggle to achieve maximum independence regardless of the cost."

March 23   The Cuban–Soviet economic agreement for 1968 is announced, revealing a 13 percent decrease below the previous year.

March 31   Johnson announces that he will not run for reelection in order to devote his efforts to ending the war in Vietnam.

April 4   The Rev. Martin Luther King, Jr. is assassinated by a sniper while in Memphis, Tennessee, to support a strike by sanitation workers. His death sparks several days of rioting in major U.S. cities, including New York and Washington.

May 12   Peace talks between the United States and North Vietnam begin in Paris.

May 30   The Soviet Communist Party newspaper *Pravda* excoriates "reactionaries who follow the writings of men who call for revolutionary change of the entire social system." In praising the French Communist Party approach of developing a united front to promote peaceful change, *Pravda* indicates the Kremlin's irritation with Cuba's foreign policy.

June 5   Senator Robert F. Kennedy is shot (and dies the next day) in Los Angeles at a celebration for his victory in the California presidential primary. He had announced his candidacy on March 16 and subsequently won four of five primaries in his quest for the Democratic nomination.

July 1   The United States, the Soviet Union, and sixty other nations sign the Nuclear Non-Proliferation Treaty. It obliges states without nuclear weapons at the time not to make or acquire such weapons and designates the International Atomic Energy Commission to develop, promote, and monitor safeguards for the peaceful uses of nuclear energy.

August 20

Thousands of Soviet and Warsaw Pact armed forces invade Czechoslovakia and depose the regime of Alexander Dubcek. The economic and political reforms of "Prague Spring" are overturned, and Soviet troops remain as an occupation army to enforce renewed controls over the economy and Czech politics and culture. Communist parties in West Europe, Romania, China, Albania, and many Third World nations condemn the invasion.

August 23

Castro endorses the Soviet invasion of Czechoslovakia. While acknowledging that the sovereignty of the Czeckoslovak state had been violated, he justifies the action as necessary because "the Czechoslovak regime was heading toward capitalism and was inexorably heading toward imperialism." Arguing that "the community of socialist nations" could not permit this to happen, he emphasizes that the "communist ideal cannot, for a single moment, exist without internationalism," that is, without supporting those who struggle against "imperialism."

August 28

Confrontations between the police and antiwar protestors at the Democratic Party's national convention in Chicago results in riots, curfews, and near martial law in the city. The convention nominates Vice President Hubert Humphrey as the party's presidential candidate.

September 16

Orlando Bosch and other Cuban exiles fire a bazooka at a Polish freighter docked in the port of Miami. Bosch is jailed for the terrorist act and then paroled in 1972. In 1976 he allegedly is involved in a terrorist bombing of a Cuban civilian airliner which kills all seventy-three people aboard the plane. Arrested in Venezuela, he is subsequently released at the urging of Otto Reich (then U.S. ambassador to Venezuela and currently assistant secretary of state for Western Hemispheric Affairs), and he returns to the United States illegally. President George H. W. Bush pardons him in 1990 for the violation of his 1972 parole, and he is permitted to live in the United States.

October 6

The democratically elected government in Peru of President Fernando Belaunde Terry is overthrown in a bloodless coup. General Juan Velasco Alvardo, the head of the military junta, institutes a series of major reforms intended to reduce economic inequality. These include land redistribution and the nationalization of entities owned by multinational corporations. Castro wryly observes that this unorthodox revolution occurred "as if a fire had started in the fire house." Velasco begins the process of restoring diplomatic and trade relations with Cuba.

October 12   Mexican police kill more than thirty students and injure hundreds in an attempt to quell demonstrations ten days before the opening of the Olympic Games in Mexico City.

October 16   Cuba and the Soviet Union sign a scientific cooperation pact.

October 31   Johnson orders a halt to U.S. bombing of North Vietnam.

November 5   Richard Nixon is elected president of the United States.

Appendix B

TEXT OF LETTER DATED 15 NOVEMBER FROM PRIME MINISTER FIDEL CASTRO OF CUBA TO ACTING SECRETARY GENERAL U THANT

U N I T E D   N A T I O N S

Press Services
Office of Public Information
United Nations, N.Y.

(For use of information media -- not an official record)

Press Release SG/1378
16 November 1962

TEXT OF LETTER DATED 15 NOVEMBER FROM PRIME MINISTER
FIDEL CASTRO OF CUBA TO ACTING SECRETARY-GENERAL U THANT

Following is the text of a communication from Prime Minister Castro to Acting Secretary-General U Thant, transmitted by Ambassador Carlos M. Lechuga, Permanent Representative of Cuba to the United Nations:

(Unofficial translation from Spanish)

15 November 1962

"His Excellency, U Thant, Acting Secretary-General of the United Nations
"Your Excellency,
"The conciliatory action which you are conducting as Acting Secretary-General of this world organization is very closely linked with the latest world events concerning the crisis in the Caribbean.
"There is no need, therefore, to dwell upon each and every one of the events, circumstances and incidents which have occurred in these weeks of extreme tension.
"I should like to refer solely to the following matter: we have given you -- and we have also given it publicly and repeatedly—our refusal to allow unilateral inspection by any body, national or international, on Cuban territory. In doing so, we have exercised the inalienable right of every sovereign nation to settle all problems within its own territory in accordance with the will of its Government and its people.
"The Soviet Government, carrying out its promise to Mr. Kennedy, has withdrawn its strategic missiles, an action which was verified by United States officials on the high seas.

(more)

"We should like to repeat once more that the installation of these weapons was nothing other than an act of legitimate self-defense on the part of the Republic of Cuba against the aggressive policy which the United States has been pursuing against our country since the very triumph of the Revolution. This did not confer any right upon the Government of the United States with respect to Cuba, since all our actions have been effected within the framework of international law and in exercise of the sovereign prerogatives of our state. It was, however, the pretext used to perpetrate acts of force which brought the world to the edge of war. The pretext has now disappeared. Nevertheless officials of the United States Government declare that they do not consider themselves bound by any promise, among other reasons because Cuba has not permitted the inspection of its territory.

"The United States, resorting to the law of force, is constantly violating our territory through the use of air forces based in various parts of the Caribbean and on aircraft carriers which it is employing against us.

"We have given proof that we are ready for a worthy peace. We have put forward five points as guarantees, the minimum which any sovereign nation can ask for. We have handed over the body of Major Anderson who died while carrying out an illegal flight over Cuban soil. We have warned the Government of the United States that it must stop these acts of violation of our sovereignty and at the same time we have done everything possible to prevent the occurrence of any incidents in connection with these acts.

"What have we obtained in exchange? The violations have increased in number; every day the incursions of war planes over our territory become more alarming; military aircraft harass our air bases, make low-level flights over our military defenses and photograph not only the dismantled strategic missile installations but in fact our entire territory, foot by foot and inch by inch.

"The capture of the leader of a group of spies trained by the CIA and directed by it, here in Cuba, has shown us how the photographs taken by the spying planes serve for guidance in sabotage and in their operations and has also revealed, among other things, a design to cause chaos by provoking the deaths of 400 workers in one of our industries.

"This impairs in its essence the security of our nation and outrages the dignity of our people. The object has been not only to secure advantages for military and sub versive purposes through information and detailed knowledge of our industrial instal- lations and defense arrangements, but also in addition to humiliate and demoralize th Cuban people.

(more)

"These are typically Hitlerite methods for softening the resistance of peoples.

"Mr. Acting Secretary-General, no sovereign state can allow its air space to be violated in this manner without feeling an impairment of its dignity. If in addition this violation is perpetrated by the reconnaissance aircraft of an enemy which openly threatens our country, tolerating it means, more than a lack of dignity, a shameful submission to the enemy. We cannot be asked to accept this by virtue of the discussions which are taking place with regard to the crisis, for the integrity of our physical space and the sovereignty of Cuba will never be negotiable.

"We for our part have not failed to give constant warnings to the aggressors.

"On 27 October, in the midst of the crisis, the Cuban Government declared that it would never acknowledge the vandalic and piratical privilege of any war plane to violate our air space since this was essentially a threat to our security and facilitated the conditions for a surprise attach. Cuba's right to resist such violations can never be renounced.

"Today again through this communication which we are sending you as Secretary-Gnneral of the United Nations, we wish to give warning that to the extent of the fire power of our anti-aircraft weapons, any war plane which violates the sovereignty of Cuba, by invading our air space, can only do so at the risk of being destroyed.

"If the United States sincerely desires -- as we ourselves desire -- to take steps toward the solution of the present problems, it should begin by respecting these elementary rights of our country.

"In the history of our Republic, the United States has more than once intervened in our domestic affairs, with the use of force. It secured this right in the first constitution of our Republic, by virtue of a law adopted by the United States Congress, and supported by an army of occupation. The present action of the United States is designed to reinstate, in fact, these militaristic and imperialist privileges.

"The long history of struggle of our country, culminating in full sovereignty and national dignity after a century-long fight written in blood and heroism, cannot be reversed. A powerful military force could annihilate us but it could never make us yield and we should first demand a very high price of the pirates who dared to invade the soil of the Cuban fatherland. And even if we should die our banner would fly victoriously because we are defending something even more sacred than our right as a sovereign nation in the concert of free nations of the earth.

(more)

"We are sounding the necessary alarm for the defense of world peace, we are
defending the right of the small countries to be considered on a footing of equality,
we are telling all the peoples of the earth that before the imperialist enemy there
can be no weakening. The path of calm and stern vigilance, strong in the security
of a response commensurate with the magnitude of the aggression, is the only way to
the salvation of peace.

"Our right to live is something which cannot be discussed by anyone.

"But if our right to live is made conditional upon an obligation to fall to our
knees, our reply once again is that we will not accept it.

"We believe in the right to defend the liberty, the sovereignty and the
dignity of this country, and we shall continue to exercise that right to the last
man, woman or child capable of holding a weapon in this territory.

"May I reiterate to you the expression of my highest consideration.

                              Fidel Castro
                              Prime Minister of the
                                  Revolutionary Government."

                    * *** *

Appendix C

SPEECH GIVEN BY MAJOR FIDEL CASTRO RUZ, PRIME MINISTER OF THE REVOLUTIONARY GOVERNMENT AND FIRST SECRETARY OF THE CENTRAL COMMITTEE OF THE COMMUNIST PARTY OF CUBA, ANALYZING EVENTS IN CZECHOSLOVAKIA, FRIDAY, AUGUST 23, 1968— YEAR OF THE HEROIC GUERRILLA

(Translation of the transcript made by the Revolutionary Government's Department of Stenographic Transcriptions.)

As was announced today, we are appearing here tonight to analyze the situation in Czechoslovakia. We are going to make this analysis in the light of the revolutionary positions and international maintained by our Revolution and our Party.

Some of the things that we are going to state here will be, in some cases, in contradiction with the emotions of many; in other cases, in contradiction with our own interests; and, in others, they will constitute serious risks for our country.

However, this is a moment of great importance for the revolutionary movement throughout the world. And it is our duty to analyze the facts objectively and express the opinion of our political leadership, the opinion that represents the judgment of the members of our Central Committee, of the leaders of our mass organizations, of the members of our Government, and that we are sure is profoundly compatible with the tradition and sentiments of our people.

It seems to us necessary, in the first place, to make a brief analysis of our position in relation to events that have been taking place in Czechoslovakia.

Our people have a good deal of information about these events, and, although no, as we may say, official exposition of the position of our Party regarding those events has ever been presented—among other reasons because the events were still in progress, and we are not obliged to analyze each thing going on in the world every day—we were observing developments in the political process in that country.

A whole series of changes began taking place in Czechoslovakia at approximately the beginning of this year. It began with talk of, or rather the actual resignation of Mr. Novotny as Secretary of the Party, although he continued on as President of the Republic. This was followed by the desertion of an important military figure to the United States. Then a series of demands arose that he (Novotny) also abandon his post as President of the Republic. And a series of events and phenomena followed.

A process of what was termed democratization began. The imperialist press invented another word, the word "liberalization," and began to differentiate between progressives and conservatives—calling progressives those who supported a whole series of political reforms, and conservatives the supporters of the former leadership. It was evident—and we must give our opinion about both: the conservatives and the liberals.... It rather reminds us of the past history of Cuba, that division between conservatives and liberals, a situation which, of course, was not expected in the political processes of socialist revolutions.

This had a series of repercussions throughout the world. Some began to sympathize with the so-called liberals or proponents of democratization. And we watched events unfold.

And, for example, on April 24, 1968, the paper *Rude Pravo*, organ of the Communist Party of Czechoslovakia, published an article entitled "The Favorable Reaction of the U.S. Press toward Events in Czechoslovakia."

"*Rude Pravo*, organ of the Communist Party of Czechoslovakia, today pointed out that the United States expects a more intelligent foreign policy to result from the new orientation adopted by Prague."

IN OUR OPINION, ANYTHING THAT BEGINS TO RECEIVE THE PRAISE, SUPPORT OR ENTHUSIASTIC APPLAUSE OF THE IMPERIALIST PRESS NATURALLY BEGINS TO AROUSE OUR SUSPICIONS.

It seems that the continuation of this is missing, but this news dispatch reported the reaction of the U.S. press to the changes in Czechoslovakia with considerable delight, and without doubt, the U.S. press, the capitalist press, the imperialist press, reacted most favorably to the changes in Czechoslovakia. Of course, in our opinion, anything that begins to receive the praise, support, or enthusiastic applause of the imperialist press naturally begins to arouse our suspicions.

Later, on May 2, 1968, the following appeared: "Czechoslovakia reiterates its request that the United States return Czechoslovak gold.

"The Prague Government repeated its demand that Washington rapidly return Czechoslovak gold being held by the U.S. Government.

"In a note delivered today to the U.S. Embassy, the Czechoslovak Government described the U.S. attitude as lacking in seriousness and urged that Washington promptly remit an advance of 18,433 kilos of gold that it holds and that rightfully belongs to Czechoslovakia. The gold was stolen by the Nazis from Czechoslovakia and confiscated by the United States as a guarantee of the settling of accounts between the two countries."

Later, on June 11, 1968: "Possible U.S. Loan to Czechoslovakia." And the article said:

> "The possibility of a U.S. loan to Czechoslovakia was proposed today, according to competent sources, by the Vice-President of the National Bank of New York during a conversation with Czechoslovak banking leaders.
>
> "The Vice-President of the American banking firm, Miroslava Kriz, stated that Poland and Yugoslavia have also received large loans from U.S. banks without having thereby to alter the socialist principles of their societies."

So here, to defend the idea of the loan, we find the argument being offered that another country—Poland, in this instance, one of the countries that sent troops to Czechoslovakia—had received large loans from U.S. banks. A detail in itself noteworthy, is it not?

And on June 18, 1968: "German Magazine Affirms that Czechoslovakia Solicited Credits from the GFR."

"The weekly *Spiegel* revealed today that Prague, fearing economic reprisals from Moscow, turned recently to Bonn for a credit.

"The Federal Government, however," according to the weekly, "preferred to avoid increased tensions with the USSR, and the Council of Ministers therefore approved the ideas put forth by Minister of the Economy Schiller to provide guarantees for a loan to Prague through the World Bank.

"*Spiegel* says that, in exchange, Czechoslovakia has promised to grant a wider range of action to the GFR commercial mission in Prague and has alluded, as well, to the possibility of a normalization of diplomatic relations between the two countries at the beginning of next year."

"Economic Conference between Representatives of Czechoslovakia and West Germany, June 27."

It says: "A two-day conference between Czechoslovakia and West Germany on present economic problems got under way today.

"The conference was organized by the Bonn Foreign Policy Society and the International Political and Economic Institute of Prague.

"The Czechoslovak group is headed by the Director of the aforementioned Institute, Dr. Antonin Anejdarek, while the German representation is headed by the President of the Foreign Policy Society of Bonn, Ambassador Von Walther, who was GFR Ambassador to Moscow until the end of last year.

"Von Walther stressed that the German participants wished to know Czechoslovakia's economic needs and possibilities. He intimated that West Germany is prepared to expand its economic relations with Czechoslovakia substantially.

"Dr. Anejdarek stated that the conference will serve to clarify possibilities and concretely aid the future development of economic relations between the two countries," etc., etc.

You all recall that, following our recognition of the German Democratic Republic, the German Federal Republic promptly broke relations with us, and that situation has continued up to the present day.

WE KNOW HOW ALL THOSE GOVERNMENTS BEHAVE AND, ABOVE ALL HOW THE GERMAN FEDERAL REPUBLIC BEHAVES, BEING, AS IT IS, THE PRINCIPAL PAWN OF YANKEE IMPERIALISM.

Here you see a whole series of things—the beginning of a "honeymoon" in the relations between the liberals and imperialism. I have simply referred to certain incidents of an economic nature occurring on different dates because throughout that entire process a whole series of events of a political nature took place. A real liberal fury was unleashed; a whole series of political slogans in favor of the formation of opposition parties began to develop, in favor of openly anti-Marxist and anti-Leninist theses, such as the thesis that the Party should cease to play the role which the Party plays within socialist society and begin to play the role there of a guide, supervising some things but, above all, exerting a sort of spiritual leadership—in short, that the reins of power should cease to be in the hands of the Communist Party; the revision of certain fundamental postulates to the effect that a socialist regime is a regime of transition from socialism to communism, a governmental form known as the dictatorship of the proletariat. This means a government where power is wielded in behalf of one class and against the former exploiting classes, by virtue of which in a revolutionary process political rights, the right to carry on political activities, cannot be granted to the former exploiters, whose objective would be precisely to struggle against the essence and the raison d'etre of socialism. A series of slogans began to be put forward, and in fact certain measures were taken such as the establishment of a bourgeois form of "freedom" of the press. This means that the counterrevolution and the exploiters, the very enemies of socialism, were granted the right to speak and write freely against socialism. As a matter of fact, a process of seizure of the principal information media by the reactionary elements began to develop. As regards foreign policy, a whole series of slogans of open rapprochement toward capitalist concepts and theses and of rapprochement towards the West appeared. Of course, all of this was linked to a series of unquestionably correct slogans. It was some of these slogans which won a certain amount of sympathy for the liberalization or democratization movement. Even some European Communist Parties, facing their own problems and contradictions, began to express their sympathy for the liberalization movement. It was a situation which everyone was trying to use to his advantage, to resolve related problems stemming from incorrect methods of government, bureaucratic policy, separation from the masses and, in short, a whole series of problems for which the former leadership was held responsible. There was also talk about the need to create their own forms for the development of the socialist revolution and the socialist system in Czechoslovakia.

Thus these tendencies were developing simultaneously, some of which justified the change and others of which turned that change toward an openly reactionary policy. And this divided opinion.

THE CZECHOSLOVAK REGIME WAS HEADING TOWARD CAPITALISM AND WAS INEXORABLY HEADING TOWARD IMPERIALISM.

We, on the other hand, were convinced—and this is very important—that the Czechoslovak regime was dangerously inclined toward a substantial change in the system. In short, we were convinced that the Czechoslovak regime was heading toward capitalism and was inexorably heading toward imperialism. Of this we did not have the slightest doubt.

We must begin by saying this because we also want to say certain things about other matters related to the situation there. As to this matter, there are some people in the world who do not share these opinions. Many considered that this danger did not exist. Many tendencies favored certain freedom of artistic expression and some of those things. Because, naturally, there are many people in the world who are sensitive to these problems. Many mistakes, many blunders, have been made in this area. And, naturally, certain concepts exist in relation to how to approach this problem. The intellectuals are also concerned over the problem of Vietnam and all those questions, although it must also be said that part of the progressive thought of the world, facing its own problems, the problems of Europe in general, the problems of the developed world, the problems of the developed societies, is more concerned with all these questions which are of less concern to the greater part of the world than it is with the problems of the world which lives under imperialist oppression, under neocolonialism and under the exploitation of capitalism in the underdeveloped regions of the world. And for the thousands of millions of human beings who, for all intents and purposes, are living without hope under conditions of starvation and extreme want there are questions in which they are more interested than the problem of whether or not to let their hair grow. This might be a very controversial issue, but these are not the things that are worrying people who are faced with the problem of whether or not they will have the possibility or hope of eating.

Thus some welcomed the positive aspects of that change, and others were concerned over its negative aspects; some were in favor of the new form arising from that situation and had a certain faith in it, and others had none.

Provisionally, we reached this conclusion: we had no doubt that the political situation in Czechoslovakia was deteriorating and going downhill on its way back to capitalism and that it was inexorably going to fall into the arms of imperialism.

This is very important. I believe that this opinion which we honestly held and still hold is very important in determining our position in relation to these events.

Naturally, the imperialist world enthusiastically welcomed this situation. The imperialist world encouraged it in every way, and, without a doubt, the imperialists rubbed their hands with glee in thinking about the disaster which, in one way or another, that would constitute for the socialist world.

On many occasions the imperialists have publicly stated what their policy is in relation to the socialist countries of Eastern Europe. And in Congress, in the press, they always talk about encouraging the liberal tendencies and even about promoting, of making available, some selective economic aid and of using every means of contributing to creating an opposition to socialism there. The imperialists are carrying out a campaign, not only in Czechoslovakia but in all the countries of Eastern Europe, even in the Soviet Union. They are trying in every way to conduct a publicity campaign in favor of the way of life of developed industrial society, in favor of the tastes and the consumer habits of the developed bourgeois societies. They promote it over the radio, through what they call cultural exchange, and very subtly they try to awaken among the masses the admiration and desire for those tastes and for those consumer habits, understanding full well that these feelings will develop in inverse ratio to the revolutionary sentiments of the masses and the spirit of sacrifice of the masses.

The imperialists make a lot of use of the bourgeois facade, all the luxury of a class society which has greatly developed the art of refinement in consumption and luxury, but under no circumstances can these be the aspirations of the socialist societies or of the peoples who are striving toward communism. And they exploit—they do it everywhere—their kitchen equipment and appliances, their cars, their refrigerators, their laces and their luxury of all kinds. This is a weapon which they constantly use in their magazines, their propaganda.

They have a policy, which they call their policy for Eastern Europe, by virtue of which they manipulate their resources, their trade and things of that nature. They do not do this with Cuba. Cuba is the victim of constant persecution in all markets to prevent us from buying, to prevent us from selling, to prevent us from getting a single seed, to prevent us from buying anything. And they implacably carry out this policy against Cuba. Why? The question must be raised as to why. They know they do not have the slightest chance of infiltrating our country with these maneuvers. This is known by the imperialists; they are well aware of it. They don't have the slightest chance of using these maneuvers here to break or weaken the revolutionary spirit of the Cuban people. That is why they wage a constant and implacable war against us, always trying to push us into the worst position, which has been their policy at all times.

On the contrary, it is well known that no type of trade between Cuba and the United States is going on, because, although in their measures they always left in the stipulation about medicine and all that, it only serves as a fig leaf because not even medicine can be bought. In fact, they have prohibited the sale of medicine to our country.

WE CONSIDERED THAT CZECHOSLOVAKIA WAS MOVING TO-WARD A COUNTERREVOLUTIONARY SITUATION, TOWARD CAPI-TALISM AND INTO THE ARMS OF IMPERIALISM.

The imperialists have obliged us to spend much more money for all the things we have needed. The blockade has made it difficult for us to acquire many of the most essential things which are priced very high and created all those problems we have spoken of on other occasions.

And right here I wish to make the first important affirmation: we considered that Czechoslovakia was moving toward a counterrevolutionary situation, toward capitalism and into the arms of imperialism.

So, this defines our first position in relation to the specific fact of the action taken by a group of socialist countries. That is, we consider that it was absolutely necessary, at all costs, in one way or another, to prevent this eventuality from taking place.

Bear with me, because I plan to analyze this in the light of our ideas.

Discussion of the form is not, in the final analysis, the most fundamental factor. The essential point to be accepted, or not accepted, is whether or not the socialist camp could allow a political situation to develop which would lead to the breaking away of a socialist country, to its falling into the arms of imperialism. And our point of view is that it is not permissible and that the socialist camp has a right to prevent this in one way or another. I would like to begin by making it clear that we look upon this fact as an essential one.

Nevertheless, it is not enough to simply accept the fact—and nothing more—that Czechoslovakia was headed toward a counterrevolutionary situation and that it was necessary to prevent it. It is not enough to simply come to the conclusion that there was no alternative there but to prevent this, and nothing more.

We must analyze the causes and ask what factors made this possible and created the necessity for such a dramatic, drastic and painful measure. What are the factors that created the necessity for a step which unquestionably entailed a violation of legal principles and international norms that, having often served as a shield for the peoples against injustice, are highly esteemed by the world?

Because what cannot be denied here is that the sovereignty of the Czechoslovak State was violated. This would be a fiction, an untruth. And that violation was, in fact, of a flagrant nature.

And I am going to refer to this point, to our concept of sovereignty, to legal principles and political principles. From a legal point of view, this cannot be justified. This is very clear. In our opinion, the decision made concerning Czechoslovakia can only be explained from a political point of view, not from a legal point of view. Not the slightest trace of legality exists. Frankly, none whatever.

What are the circumstances which have permitted a remedy of this kind, a remedy which places the revolutionary movement the world over in a most difficult situation, a remedy which constitutes a truly traumatic situation for an entire people—which is the present situation in Czechoslovakia? For this measure means that an entire people must endure the highly disagreeable circumstance of seeing its country occupied by armies of other countries, even though they are armies of socialist countries, a situation in which millions of citizens of a country must today face the tragedy of making a decision between remaining passive before these circumstances and this fact—which is so reminiscent of episodes of the past—and choosing to struggle in camaraderie with pro-Yankee spies and agents, in camaraderie with the enemies of socialism, in camaraderie with the agents of West Germany and all that fascist and reactionary rabble, with all those who, under the cloak of the situation, will try to pass themselves off as defenders of sovereignty, of patriotism and of the liberty of Czechoslovakia.

Quite logically, this experience and this action constitute a bitter and tragic situations for the people of Czechoslovakia. That is why it is not enough to simply come to the conclusion that it was an inexorable necessity—or even an unquestionable obligation, if you like—of the socialist countries to prevent such eventualities from occurring, but we must analyze the causes, the factors and the circumstances that made possible a situation in which, after 20 years of communism in Czechoslovakia, a group of personalities—whose names, incidentally, do not appear anywhere—found it necessary to appeal to other countries of the socialist camp to send their armies to prevent the triumph of the counterrevolution in Czechoslovakia and the triumph of the intrigues and conspiracies of the imperialist countries interested in tearing Czechoslovakia away from the community of socialist nations.

Gentlemen, is it conceivable that a situation could occur, under any circumstance, after 20 years of communism in our country, of communist revolution, of socialist revolution, in which a group of honest revolutionaries, in this country, horrified by the prospect of an advance—or rather a retrogression—to counterrevolutionary positions and toward imperialism could find themselves obliged to request the aid of friendly armies to prevent such a retrogression from occurring? What would have happened to the communist conscience of this people? What would have happened to the revolutionary awareness of this people? To the dignity of this people? To the revolutionary morale of this people? If such a situation could arise some day, what would have happened to all those things which, for us, are the essentials of the Revolution?

WE BELIEVE THAT IT IS A FUNDAMENTAL DUTY AND RESPONSIBILITY OF THE LEADERS OF A REVOLUTION TO AVERT THE DEVELOPMENT OF DEFORMATIONS CAPABLE OF PRODUCING SUCH CIRCUMSTANCES.

Needless to say, no circumstance of this kind will ever present itself in our country. First of all, because we believe that it is a fundamental duty and responsibility of the leaders of a revolution to avert the development of deformations capable of producing such circumstances.

And secondly, gentlemen, for an unquestionably practical reason. Not only for a basic moral reason—because we could ask ourselves what is to be thought of a revolution that, after 20 years, had to resort to such procedures in order to survive—but also for this very simple practical reason: from whom would the top leaders of this country request the sending of armies? Because the only armies in our vicinity are the Yankee army and the armies of the puppets allied with the Yankee imperialists, and we are too isolated in this part of the world for there ever to exist even the remotest possibility of asking for help from allied armies in order to save this Revolution. And it must be said that I know of no one capable of submitting himself to such humiliation even should he have the need and the possibility of doing so.

What kind of Communists would we be, and what kind of communist revolution would this be, if, at the end of 20 years, we were to find ourselves forced to do such a thing in order to save it?

Whenever we have thought of outside help the only idea that has ever come into our minds was that of outside help to fight against imperialist troops and against imperialist armies.

I am now analyzing these circumstances simply because I know that, logically, our people must be concerned over the clarification of this problem.

We cannot conceive of such things within the Revolution.

I do not believe that justification can be found in the appeal from top personalities, since the sole justification can only be the simple political fact that Czechoslovakia was moving toward a counterrevolutionary situation and that this seriously affected the entire socialist community.

And, beyond this, no "fig leaves" of any kind are necessary. It is the straightforward political fact in itself, with all its consequences and all its far-reaching implications.

But we were asking if it is enough to simply recognize this fact and nothing more or it is an elemental obligation to seek out all of the political consequences of this extremely bitter experience.

And, we repeat, how have these circumstances been made possible? An analysis of the factors involved must be undertaken. And it behooves the communist movement as an unavoidable duty to undertake a profound study of the causes that have given rise to such a situation, which is inconceivable to us, the Cuban revolutionaries; a situation which is impossible for us, the Cuban revolutionaries, who, obliged to carry out our Revolution here, 90 miles from the imperialists, know that we cannot permit ourselves to fall into such a situation, because it would mean the end, pure and simple, of the

Revolution and our finding ourselves in the worst condition of slavery at the hands of our implacable enemies. Obviously, this is not the time to make or pretend to make that profound analysis, but we can cite some facts and ideas: bureaucratic methods in the leadership of the country, lack of contact with the masses—contact which is essential in every true revolutionary movement—neglect of communist ideals.

And what do we mean by neglect of communist ideals? We mean forgetting that men in a class society, the exploited in a class society, the enslaved, struggle for a whole series of ideals, and when they speak of socialism and communism they are not only speaking of a society where exploitation does actually disappear and the poverty resulting from that exploitation disappears, and the underdevelopment resulting from that exploitation disappears, but they are speaking also of all those beautiful aspirations that constitute the communist ideal of a classless society, a society free from selfishness, a society in which man is no longer a miserable slave to money, in which society no longer works for personal gain, and all of society begins to work for the satisfaction of all needs and for the establishment among men of the rule of justice, fraternity, equality and all those ideals of human society and of the peoples who have always aspired to achieving those objectives. And these objectives are possible, as we have explained on other occasions, as we explained amply last July 26.

In future stages it will be necessary for our revolutionary people to go deeply into the concepts of what they understand by a communist society. The ideal of the communist society cannot be the ideal of the industrialized bourgeois society; it cannot, under any circumstances, be the ideal of a bourgeois-capitalist consumers' society.

THOSE WHO STRUGGLE FOR COMMUNISM IN ANY COUNTRY IN THE WORLD CAN NEVER FORGET THE REST OF THE WORLD.

The communist ideal cannot, for a single moment, exist without internationalism. Those who struggle for communism in any country in the world can never forget the suffering, underdevelopment, poverty, ignorance and exploitation that exist in a part of the world or how much poverty and destitution have accumulated there. They can never forget, for a single moment, the needs of that part of the world, and we believe that it is impossible to instill in the masses a truly internationalist outlook, a truly communist outlook, if they are allowed to forget the realities of the world, the dangers of confrontation with imperialism that those realities entail and the dangers of growing soft when the people are made to forget those real problems and when the attempt is made to move the masses through material incentives and the promises of more consumer goods alone.

We can say—and today it is necessary to speak clearly and frankly—that we have seen to what extent those ideals and those internationalist sentiments, that state of alertness and that awareness of the world's problems have disappeared or are very weakly expressed in certain socialist countries of Europe. We would not say in all those countries, but in more than one socialist country in Europe. Those who have visited those countries, including the Cuban scholarship students, have often come back completely dissatisfied and displeased and have said to us: "Over there the youth are not being educated in the ideals of communism and in the principles of internationalism; the youth there are highly influenced by all the ideas and tastes prevalent in the countries of Western Europe. In many places the main topic of conversation is money and incentives of this or that type, material incentives of all kinds, material gains and salaries." As a matter of fact, an internationalist and communist conscience is not being developed in those places.

Some have told us in amazement: "There is no such thing as volunteer work; volunteer work is paid for. Pay for this kind of work is a general thing. It is considered there that true volunteer work is almost an anti-Marxist heresy." All sorts of things are done, even to such a point where the degree of skill in landing an airplane or making a parachute jump determines the granting of one kind of incentive or another. The sensibilities of many of our men have been injured more than once by such vulgar use of material incentives or such vulgar commercialization of the conscience of men.

And, together with this, the preaching of peace. There has been incessant, widespread preaching of peach within socialist countries. And we ask ourselves, why all these campaigns? Do we say this because we are in favor of war? Do we say this because we are the enemies of peace? We are not the enemies of peace; we are not in favor of wars; we do not advocate universal holocaust. I feel obliged to say this because when we analyze these questions there is always the immediate cliché, the schemata, the accusations of warmongering, of promoting war, of being irresponsible and so on and so forth.

Our position on this matter is clear. No one can question the danger posed to the world by the existence of imperialism and the aggressiveness of imperialism.

No one can question the danger posed to the world by the tremendous contradiction which the existence of a great part of the world under imperialist domination and the earnest desire, the need of peoples to free themselves from the imperialist yoke represents.

The real promoters of war, the real adventurers, are the imperialists. Now then, these dangers are real; they are a reality! And those realities cannot be changed by simply preaching, in one's own house, an excessive desire for peace. In any case, the preaching should be done in the enemy's camp and not in one's own camp, because this would only contribute to stifling the combat spirit, to weakening the people's readiness to face the risks, sacrifices, and all the consequences imposed by the international situation. That international situation demands all kinds of sacrifices, not only the possible ultimate sacrifice of one's life but also material sacrifices.

And when the peoples know that the realities of the world, the independence of the country, and internationalist duties demand investments and sacrifices in the strengthening of the defense of the country, the masses are much better prepared to work with enthusiasm to achieve this, to make sacrifices, understanding this need, being conscious of the dangers which arise when the people have been stirred up and softened by a constant, foolish and inexplicable campaign in favor of peace. It is a very strange way of defending peace. That is why we, who at the beginning did so many foolish things out of ignorance or naiveté, for a long time now have not painted any signs around saying: "Long Live Peace," "Long Live This," "Long Live That." Because at the beginning, out of mimicry, by imitation, we repeated things as they arrived here, until we reached a point—well, what is the meaning of "Long Live Peace"? Let's place that sign in New York: "Long Live Peace" in New York, "Long Live Peace" in Washington. Let's preach peace over there, among the only people responsible for there not being any guarantee of peace, among those who are the only real warmongers, the only ones responsible for war, among the only people among whom the preaching if peace could help at least in weakening the huge taxes which are imposed on the people to finance their adventurous, aggressive, colonialist, imperialist and exploiting wars, not here in our camp.

WHEN WE GIVE SOME TECHNICAL AID, WE DO NOT THINK OF SENDING A BILL TO ANYONE.

A series of opinions, a series of ideas, a series of practices incomprehensible to us, which have really contributed to slackening and softening the revolutionary spirit of the socialist countries: ignorance of the problems of the underdeveloped world, ignorance of the shocking misery which exists, tendencies toward maintaining practices of trade with the underdeveloped world which are the same practices of trade which the developed bourgeois capitalist world maintains. I'm not talking about all the socialist countries, but several of them.

Technical aid. Gentlemen, our country is a country—as you know—which is in great need of technicians, great need of technicians! However, when we give some technical aid, we do not think of sending a bill to anyone, because we think that the least a developed country, a socialist country, a revolutionary country, can do to help the underdeveloped world is to send technicians.

We cannot imagine sending a bill to anyone for arms which we give him or sending a bill to anyone for technical aid, or even reminding him of it. Because if we are going to give aid and then bring up the fact every day, what we will be doing is constantly humiliating those whom we are aiding. I don't thing there is any need to go around preaching about it too much.

And that is the way we act. Moreover, it is not a virtue; it cannot be considered a virtue. It is something elementary. And the day that we have thousands or tens of thousands of technicians, truly, gentlemen, the most elementary of our duties will be to contribute at least with technical aid for the countries which liberate themselves after us and which need our aid.

None of these ideas has ever been put forward before. All these problems which have a lot to do with communist conscientiousness, with internationalist conscientiousness, and which do not play the role they should in the education of the masses within the socialist camp have a lot to do with the explanation of these horrible instances of weakening which constitute the explanation of the reasons for these situations.

All of us know that the leadership which Czechoslovakia had, generally, for 20 years was a leadership plagued with many vices: dogmatism, bureaucracy and, in short, many things which cannot be presented as examples of truly revolutionary leadership.

When we speak here, when we present our thesis about the liberal nature of this group so warmly greeted by imperialism, it does not mean in any way that we are expressing our solidarity with that leadership. We must bear in mind that that leadership, with which we have had relations from the very beginning, even sold this country, at a high price, many weapons which were the spoils of war seized from the Nazis, weapons for which we have been paying, and still today are paying for, which belonged to Hitler's troops which occupied Czechoslovakia. I am not referring, of course, to the weapons which, as an industrial product, a country has to produce, especially if it is a country with a limited economy. We do not intend to say: give the weapons which you manufacture in your industry, as part of the social production of the people and of exchange, to a country of relatively few resources. But they sold us many weapons which belonged to the Nazi armies, and we have had to pay for them, and we are still paying for them.

And that is a fact. It is as if we were to hold back the rifles we took from Batista from a country which had just freed itself from imperialism and needed them, and then, to make matters even worse, we were to charge the impoverished, destitute and underdeveloped country for them. It is as if one day we were to send the San Cristóbal carbines, the Springfields and other weapons which the Batista army had to any country that liberates itself and asks us to send them, and then charged the country in question for them as if it were a big business deal.

Is there any doubt that this is outside the framework of the most elementary concept of the duty of a revolutionary country toward another country? On many occasions they sold us very outdated factories. We have seen the results of many of the economic concepts on which they base their business transactions, on which they base their eagerness to sell any old junk, and it must be stated that these practices led to their selling old, outdated junk to a country which is making a revolution and has to develop, I won't say it always happened that way. But all the concepts of self-financing, profits, gains and material incentives put into practice by foreign trade agencies lead to an eagerness to sell any old junk to an underdeveloped country. And this of course, leads to conflicts, discontent, misunderstandings and a deterioration of relations with the underdeveloped world.

And these are facts. If today we must state bitter truths, must admit some bitter truths, let's take advantage of the occasion—not as an opportunity, but as a necessity—to explain some things that would otherwise remain unexplained.

We would be very unjust if we didn't point out that we have known, and our country has known, many technicians from different countries. And they include many Czechoslovak technicians, many good men who have worked loyally and enthusiastically in this country. But I am not referring to men, I am referring to institutions—and, above all, institutions that deform men. And, despite the existence of institutions that deform men, we have often seen men who have resisted deformation by institutions.

Prior to this experience that we are analyzing today, we have had other experiences—that is, all these experiences that explain how one phenomenon leads to another, to another and to another. And there comes the time within a society when—far from having revolutionary conscience, communist conscience, developed—one finds that what has developed is individualism, selfishness, tastes of another type, indifference on the part of the masses and a decrease rather than an increase in enthusiasm.

TO THE EXTENT THAT WE DEVELOP ALONG THE PATH OF REVOLUTION, ENTHUSIASM WILL BECOME EVER MORE POLITICALLY AWARE, AND THIS POLITICALLY AWARE ENTHUSIASM WILL INCREASE, NOT DECREASE.

For that reason, there are some who ask whether enthusiasm is decreasing or increasing in Cuba and whether, if we have it now, we will still have it later, or, if it comes later, is it absent now? This is something that has never concerned us, because experience has taught us that, to the extent that we develop along the path of revolution, enthusiasm will become ever more politically aware, and this politically aware enthusiasm will increase, not decrease; the people's spirit of sacrifice, discipline, capacity for work and dedication will all grow.

That is what our own revolutionary experience has taught us. And we cannot conceive of that diminishing. We believe that to the extent that we advance it will be even greater, and that when our country reaches a higher phase, achieves a communist society, this enthusiasm, this conscientiousness, will reach incomparably higher levels that those ever before known.

We have seen the workers' attitude develop, the workers' willingness to do difficult work, their willingness to do volunteer work, to renounce overtime pay and a whole series of things like that develop. It is no longer the attitude of 10 or of 50 or 1000, but of hundreds of thousands of people throughout this country: tens of thousands of young people who go where they are sent—the Isle of Pines, Pinar del Rio, Camaguey, any place—live under difficult conditions, under very difficult living conditions.

And we have seen how this spirit has spread throughout our country year after year as that political awareness grows.

There are thousands of young people ever ready to go anywhere as technicians specializing in different fields, thousands of young people stating their willingness to go fight wherever they are needed. Our constant problem here is that everyone dreams of some day being permitted to leave the country to help the revolutionary movement wherever he may be needed.

In other words, the internationalist conscience of our people has developed, the communist conscience of our country has developed by the day.

And that, unquestionably, is a real achievement of this Revolution, because this Revolution is in touch with the realities of the world around us. Perhaps the circumstance of having the enemy so close is to our advantage. It is to our advantage not to have large armies close by to protect us. It is better to know that here we must depend on our own ability to resist; on our people's willingness to fight, to sacrifice; on our people's readiness to give their lives. And not only because this Revolution was made through the efforts of this people, not only because this Revolution was not imported in any way, but because ours is a very autochthonous revolution which has had to defend itself in difficult situations against an ever-present, very powerful enemy.

Our people have developed their traditional spirit of struggle, of combat, their willingness to face any danger. And naturally all these factors have contributed to the development of our revolutionary conscientiousness.

From the point of view of socialist ideas, from the point of view of revolutionary ideas, what is called for is not a justification, but rather an explanation, an analysis of how such circumstances could arise in a country such as Czechoslovakia.

And such circumstances did arise, the need did develop. That the need arose is unquestionable. It is clear that there was only one alternative, that of preventing it. But, in order to prevent it, of course, the price that must be paid is high indeed.

For a people such as ours, that, throughout the history of its revolutionary development, had to face the problem of interventions, that had to struggle against the policy of Yankee imperialism, it is logical that many would react emotionally in the face of the fact that armies from outside the nation's borders had to come in to prevent a catastrophe.

And since, logically, for various reasons, our conscience has been shaped by the concept of repudiating such deeds, only the development of the political awareness of our people will make it possible for them to determine when such an action becomes necessary and when it is necessary to accept it, even in spite of the fact that it violates rights such as the right of sovereignty which—in this case, in our opinion—must give way before the most important interests of the world revolutionary movement and the struggle of the people against the imperialists, which, as we see it, is the basic question. And, undoubtedly, the breaking away of Czechoslovakia and its falling into the arms of imperialism would have been a rude blow, an even harder blow to the interests of the worldwide revolutionary movement.

We must learn to analyze these truths and to determine when one interest must give way before other interests in order not to fall into romantic or idealistic positions that are out of touch with reality.

We are against all those with bourgeois liberal reforms within Czechoslovakia. But we are also against the liberal economic reforms that were taking place in Czechoslovakia and that have been taking place in other countries of the socialist camp, as well.

WE MAINTAIN THE POSITION THAT WE SHOULD NOT TELL THEM HOW TO CARRY OUT THE CONSTRUCTION OF SOCIALISM, BUT WE CAN ANALYZE WHAT THEY HAVE DONE.

Naturally, we maintain the position that we should not tell them how to carry out the construction of socialism, but we can analyze what they have done—a series of reforms that increasingly tended to accentuate mercantile relations within a socialist society: personal gain, profit, all those things.

An article published in the newspaper *Pravda* pointed out the following fact in regard to Czechoslovakia. It reads as follows: "The CPSU is constantly perfecting the style, the forms and the methods of the construction of the Party and the State. This same work is being carried out in other socialist countries in a tranquil process based on the fundamentals of the socialist system."

But this statement is very interesting. It says: "Unfortunately, discussions concerning economic reform in Czechoslovakia developed on another basis. That discussion centered on the one hand, around a global criticism of all development proceeding from the socialist economy and, on the other, around the proposal to replace the principles of planning with spontaneous mercantile relations, granting a broad field of action to private capital."

Does this, by chance, mean that the Soviet Union is also going to curb certain currents in the field of economy that are in favor of putting increasingly greater emphasis on mercantile relations and on the effects of spontaneity in those relations, and those which have even been defending the desirability of the market and the beneficial effect of prices based on that market? Does it mean that the Soviet Union is becoming aware of the need to halt those currents? More than one article in the imperialist press has referred jubilantly to those currents that also exist within the Soviet Union.

And when we read these declarations we ask ourselves if this means that they have become aware of this problem.

In any event, we consider it very interesting that this has been pointed out in this *Pravda* editorial.

There is more than one question that disturbs us. It disturbs us that, so far, there has been no direct imputation against Yankee imperialism in any of the statements made by the countries that sent their divisions to Czechoslovakia, or in the explanation of the events. We have been informed exhaustively concerning all the preceding events, all the facts, all the deviations, all about that rightist group, all about that liberal group; we have been informed of their activities.

The activities of the imperialists and the intrigues of the imperialists are known, and we are disturbed to see that neither the Communist Party nor the Government of the Soviet Union, nor the governments of the others countries that sent their troops to Czechoslovakia, have made any direct accusation against Yankee imperialism for its responsibility in the events in Czechoslovakia.

Certain vague references to world imperialism, to world imperialist circles, and some more concrete statements concerning the imperialist circles of West Germany have been made. But who doesn't know that West Germany is simply a pawn of Yankee imperialism in Europe, the most aggressive, the most obvious pawn—that it is a pawn of the CIA, a pawn of the Pentagon and a pawn of the imperialist Government of the United States? And, certainly, we wish to express our concern over the fact that in none of the statements is a direct imputation made against Yankee imperialism, which is the principal culprit in the world plot and conspiracy against the socialist camp. And it is necessary that we express this preoccupation.

The events in Czechoslovakia only confirm the correctness of the positions and the theses that our Revolution and our Party have maintained: our positions in the Tricontinental Conference, our positions in the OLAS and our positions on all international problems. A series of facts confirms this point of view.

It is well known, for example, that one of the problems that explains. . . that has been a constant source of irritation in our relations with many countries in the socialist camp and with many Communist Parties is the problem of Yugoslavia. Some may have wondered at the reasons for Cuba's attitude of constantly pointing to the role that the League of Yugoslav Communists plays in the world, the role of instrument of imperialism that this party plays in the world.

THE PRINCIPAL PROMOTER OF ALL OF THAT POLICY OF BOURGEOIS LIBERALISM, ITS PRINCIPAL DEFENDER, WAS THE ORGANIZATION OF THE SO-CALLED YUGOSLAV COMMUNISTS.

At this very moment, in relation to the events in Czechoslovakia, the principal promoter of all of that policy of bourgeois liberalism, its principal defender, was the organization of the so-called Yugoslav Communists. They enthusiastically applauded all the liberal reforms, the concept of the Party ceasing to be the instrument of revolutionary power—that the exercise of power cease to be a function of the

Party—because this is very closely allied to the concept of the League of Yugoslav Communists. All of those ideas of a political nature that completely depart from Marxism, all of those economic concepts, are closely tied to the ideology of the League of Yugoslav Communists. And our country has been a constant accuser of that organization.

Nevertheless, as you know, in recent times, many Communist Parties, and among them the Communist Parties of the Warsaw Pact, began to forget the role and the nature of the League of Yugoslav Communists.

Yugoslavia began to be called a communist country; the League of Yugoslav Communists began to be called a communist party and be invited to meetings of socialist countries, to meetings of mass organizations and of the Communist Parties. And this is what gave rise to our constant opposition, our constant disagreement, our constant discrepancies—expressed on a number of occasions. And these are facts.

This organization—as the agent of imperialism—was one of the principal promoters of the deformations of Czechoslovakia's political process. Some will say I am exaggerating, but I am going to prove this with facts.

Tito was received as a hero in Prague just a few weeks ago. And why was this? Because of ideological softening, of a political weakening in the awareness of the masses.

And we asked ourselves, how could this be? How far can things go when this well-known revisionist element historically denounced by the revolutionary movement—a man who has served as an agent of imperialism—could be received by a people practically as a hero?

Now, of course, Tito is one of the noisiest in attacking the action taken by the Warsaw Pact countries in Czechoslovakia.

I was saying that some people may wonder why we have been so persistent in our statements against the League of Yugoslav Communists.

I want to relate a very important incident that took place at the beginning of the Revolution, concerning our relations with Yugoslavia. It was in 1959, at a time when the first laws in our country had already been drawn up, when our nation had already made laws such as the Agrarian Reform Law, which brought us to a face-to-face confrontation with imperialism, when the United States had already begun to hatch its first conspiracies against us.

At that time we did not have any diplomatic relations with the USSR or with any other countries of the socialist camp. We were forced to buy our weapons from certain capitalist countries. We bought our first arms in Belgium and in Italy.

Because of imperialist pressure—in fact at first not pressure but CIA conspiracies—one of the ships which arrived from Belgium was blown up at the cost of some 80 lives. Later, the Belgian Government, under pressure from the U.S. Government, stopped selling us weapons. While the United States trained the mercenaries that would be sent against us, it also pursued a policy of blocking our arms purchases.

At that time the United States also pressured Italy. At the time we were purchasing 16 howitzers—16 howitzers—in Italy. We had received just four and the ammunition for the other twelve. As a result of the Yankee imperialist pressure, they didn't sell us the other twelve howitzers. That left us with just the four howitzers and ammunition for more, but without the other twelve pieces.

In the face of this situation, we went to the Government of Yugoslavia in an attempt to buy weapons. We even attempted to see whether it might sell us the twelve howitzers, some 120-mm. mortars and certain other arms. And here is the report from the comrade who was assigned this mission, Major José R. Fernández Alvarez.

Here we have the question in a nutshell. That is why I am going to read this report. It states: "In 1959, due to the defeat of the Batista tyranny, there was a need to acquire military equipment. This equipment was urgently needed so as to defend the Revolution, which, because of the laws and measures that were being drawn up, would have to face the hatred of its logical enemies, those who would attempt to destroy the Revolution.

"Following orders, we approached the Ambassador of the Republic of Yugoslavia at the end of 1959 or the beginning of 1960 in a very informal way. Later, Major Raúl Castro and I paid a visit to the Yugoslav Embassy, located at 42nd Street and Third Avenue in Miramar.

"During that visit the Minister of the Revolutionary Armed Forces informed the Yugoslav Ambassador of Cuba's interest in acquiring arms and equipment—especially light infantry weapons, rifles, machine guns, rocket launchers, mortars and ammunition for these arms.

"The Ambassador was quite evasive, and, when the Minister raised the question of payments, he stated that in regard to weapons special attention was given to payment, without going into detail. The Minister told the Ambassador that I would keep in touch with him in order to be informed as to prices and the arms available, and to carry out negotiations in this matter.

"This mission was extremely difficult to carry out, since the lists were delayed, evasive excuses were constantly made and it was claimed that the weapons were not available, that they had to be manufactured and that information on prices had not arrived. And when I finally did get the price lists—for special, small-caliber weapons—the prices were exorbitant even when compared with those on the world market.

"Both before and after this time other comrades traveled to Yugoslavia, where other requests were made concerning the purchase of weapons, and the results were similar, since additional obstacles were raised.

"I can state that no transaction whatsoever could be closed, despite our requests and great need, because the representation of Yugoslavia there and here in Cuba did not make it feasible."

"THE YUGOSLAVS STATED THAT THE AMOUNT OF THE TRANS-ACTION DID NOT JUSTIFY THE DIFFICULTIES THEY WOULD RUN INTO WITH THE UNITED STATES FOR HAVING SOLD WEAPONS TO US.

"The conclusion we must draw from all this is that the attitude of Yugoslavia was definitely opportunistic, since they insisted on payment in cash—in dollars—and at a black market price for the few items offered.

"They stated that the amount of the transaction did not justify the difficulties they would run into with the United States for having sold weapons to us. They stalled in providing both lists and price quotations and proposed that transactions be carried on through a private business enterprise in Yugoslavia so that it would not appear as a business transaction with that country.

"In general they appeared, on the one hand, not only unwilling to cooperate but even anxious not to close the transaction, and, on the other hand, opportunistic, or at least inclined toward dissuading us through the terms they set for the transaction."

This was the attitude of that socialist country, that communist, revolutionary country, when our country, faced with the first threats of imperialist aggression, wished to purchase arms. And that is why there are no Yugoslav bullets here.

And imagine our surprise a few months later—one day while looking through the files of the Batista government—when we found this document which I am going to read. It states:

"From the Military Attaché of the Cuban Embassy, Mexico City, D.F., December 13, 1958. General in Chief Francisco Tabernilla Dolz, M. M. N. P. J. E. M. G., Ciudad Militar, Marianao.

"My dear Friend: Enclosed find a number of photographs which were turned over to me by the Ambassador of Yugoslavia in this country, a great friend of mine.

"On one occasion I spoke to him after I was instructed to obtain information from him personally on the possibility of purchasing weapons. He informed me that they could supply us with several types of the arms we might need, such as 30.00 rifles, ammunition, etc. He also spoke of the type of PT boats which appear in the photographs, which could be very useful to us.

"He said that they could supply us with ample quantities of these boats and that we would find them economical, since they (the Yugoslavs) employ cheap labor and have the best shipyards in the world nowadays, next to those of Great Britain.

"These torpedo boats can do better than 40 kilometers per hour and are equipped with two antiaircraft machine guns and one antiaircraft cannon as well as torpedo tubes. They have plenty of torpedoes, which are low priced.

"I explained to him that all orders for the purchase of any type of armament had been suspended for the moment, since a sufficient supply had been acquired from other sources, but he told me that, in any event, he would furnish me with the exact specifications, selling price, delivery data and freight charges to our ports.

"As soon as I receive this information, I will forward it to you immediately." He then continued writing about other matters. "Signed: Lt. Col. (G. T.) A. P. Chaumont, Military Attaché."

Those who have read the story of the Moncada attack know that this Chaumont was precisely the army officer who perpetrated dozens of murders at the Moncada Garrison after the attack. He was the most criminal of all the army officers there. He murdered dozens of prisoners, and later was sent to Mexico. He was a great friend of the Yugoslav Ambassador, a man who—only 18 days before the triumph of the Revolution, in December 1958, after thousands upon thousands of Cubans had been murdered in the course of the two years that we had been fighting—on behalf of the Yugoslav Government and following consultation, offered all types of weapons—including torpedo boats, etc.—on advantageous terms.

You may imagine our indignation and surprise when we came across this document and saw the signature it bears. And our indignation was all the greater because when we needed weapons to defend ourselves from the imperialists the Yugoslav Government raised every kind of obstacle and did not sell us a single weapon. Yet it had offered weapons to Batista when our war was nearing its end.

How could we have any but the worst opinion of the role played by that Party, considering that when Batista could no longer get weapons even from the imperialists—by then even the Yankees would not sell him weapons!—these gentlemen were offering him weapons on good terms?

The communist movement ostracized that party—and justly so—for many years. Countless newspaper articles have been published by every Party against that organization, denouncing and criticizing it. Later, of course, some Parties forgot all about that, and its friends, followers and apologists also began to forget in the warmth of the upsurge of policies of ideological softening in the revolutionary movement that have led to the present painful situation.

And we ask ourselves if this bitter experience in Czechoslovakia may not lead to the correcting of those mistakes and to the rejection of the League of Yugoslav Communists as a communist party, as a revolutionary party, and to its exclusion from the meetings of the mass organizations and political organizations of the socialist camp.

We are witnessing many interesting things that have arisen from these events.
WE HAVE DISAGREED WITH, BEEN DISPLEASED AT, AND PROTESTED AGAINST THE FACT THAT THESE SAME COUNTRIES

HAVE BEEN DRAWING CLOSER ECONOMICALLY, CULTURALLY AND POLITICALLY TO THE OLIGARCHIC GOVERNMENTS OF LATIN AMERICA.

It is understandable that the countries of the Warsaw Pact sent their armies to destroy the imperialist conspiracy and the progress of counterrevolution in Czechoslovakia. However, we have disagreed with, been displeased at, and protested against the fact that these same countries have been drawing closer economically, culturally and politically to the oligarchic governments of Latin America, which are not merely reactionary governments and exploiters of their peoples, but also shameless accomplices in the imperialist aggressions against Cuba and shameless accomplices in the economic blockade of Cuba. And these countries have been encouraged and emboldened by the fact that our friends, our natural allies, have ignored the vile and treacherous role enacted by those governments against a socialist country, the policy of blockade practiced by those countries against a socialist country.

And at the same time that we understand the need for the spirit of internationalism, and the need to go to the aid—even with troops—of a fraternal country to confront the schemes of the imperialists, we ask ourselves if that policy of economic, political and cultural rapprochement toward those oligarchic governments that are accomplices in the imperialist blockade against Cuba will come to an end.

In the face of this situation, it is well to see now how these countries react.

It says: "The whole Latin American bloc in the forum of the nations of the world expressed its unanimous repudiation of this Russian intervention in Czechoslovakia. A spokesman for the group said 'We all received the news of this intervention with sorrow, and we express our solidarity with the Czechoslovaks.

"'The political consequences which this Soviet intrusion in the internal affairs of Czechoslovakia will have will be the strengthening of the anti-Soviet tendency in Latin America,' the spokesman said," etc.

And then it said: "The source said this Soviet attitude, the theory of spheres of influence which they themselves have so often criticized, would make it possible for the United States to assume the right to invade Cuba, since it is within its security area."

These puppet governments have already begun to prepare the theory that Cuba must be invaded, because it is within their security area. And it is these countries—with the single exception of Mexico, whose government is the only one which has not participated in the blockade aggressions and imperialist actions against Cuba—it is all these oligarchic governments, toward which they have shown great consideration and tact, which are the ringleaders in the United Nations of the clamor and the attacks on the socialist camp over the events in Czechoslovakia. Things have even gone so far as for these same countries of the Latin American bloc to propose a meeting of the General Assembly; they are the most rabid critics of the Soviet Union and the other countries of the socialist camp as a result of these events. And these are the countries which have been accomplices in the aggressions against Cuba; countries which have no moral right to talk about sovereignty or the like; countries which have no moral right to talk about interventions because they have been accomplices in all the crimes committed by imperialism against the peoples, such as the brutal counterrevolutionary action perpetrated in the Dominican Republic, the aggressions against Cuba and many other countries and the aggressions against other peoples in Latin America. The oligarchic governments themselves, such as those of Brazil, Paraguay and other countries, sent troops to the Dominican Republic and are now leading the attack on and the condemnation of the socialist camp for the events in Czechoslovakia.

What magnificent reasoning, and how this reveals the correctness of the positions taken by the Cuban Revolution in relation to these events!

WE ALSO WONDER WHETHER THAT POLICY WILL BE RECTIFIED OR WHETHER IT WILL BE CONTINUED ALONG THE PATH OF POLITICAL, ECONOMIC AND CULTURAL RAPPROCHEMENT WITH THOSE COUNTRIES.

And we also wonder whether that policy will be rectified or whether it will be continued along the path of political, economic and cultural rapprochement with those countries.

One of them, Argentina, even shelled a Soviet fishing vessel—shelled it! I believe they even wounded one of the members of the vessel's crew. Afterwards they were like beasts over there, lying in wait for another boat. They commit flagrant, indecent actions against everybody, yet that soft line has been followed in regard to them—a line which, in our opinion, only encourages their position as accomplices in the aggressions against Cuba.

There is a most interesting news dispatch here which says: "Caracas, August 21—Venezuela has decided to suspend its talks with the Soviet Union and the communist bloc in relation to the resumption of diplomatic relations in protest against the invasion of Czechoslovakia.

"The announcement was made by Foreign Minister Ignacio Iribarren Borges at a press conference. The statement reads textually:

"'In view of the news of the invasion of Czechoslovakia by troops of the Soviet Union and other Eastern European countries, the Government of Venezuela maintains that this action against the sovereignty and territorial integrity of that country constitutes an open violation of the principles of nonaggression and self-determination of the peoples contained in the United Nations Charter and the principles of nonintervention formulated in Resolution 2131 of the General Assembly and invariably defended by Venezuela.

"'The events which have taken place are a source of grave concern to the Venezuelan Government, since they constitute a violation of the legal international order, a brazen use of superior force and a serious setback for the aspirations for peaceful coexistence among the peoples.

"'The Venezuelan Government considers that the invading troops should immediately and unconditionally withdraw.

"'The Government of Venezuela voices the feeling of the Venezuelan people in expressing its profound solidarity and sympathy with the Czechoslovak people.'"

None of these statements were made, none of these attitudes were voiced, none of these issues were brought up by the Venezuelan Government during the landing of Yankee forces in the Dominican Republic.

No relations were broken, no business was shelved, no economic relations were disturbed—nothing at all like this happened. And now they permit themselves the luxury of throwing in the face of the countries of the socialist camp this type of relations which the latter have actually been begging them for, this type of relations which they have been begging that government, which is one of the most reactionary and dyed-in-the-wool of the accomplices of Yankee imperialism. And now they throw it in the faces of the socialist countries.

These are the results of such a policy when the chips are down, at the moment of truth.

Something similar is happening to the Communist Parties of Europe, today trapped in their own indecision. And we wonder whether possibly in the future the relations with Communist Parties will be based on principled positions or whether they will continue to be guided by their degree of willingness to maintain a spineless attitude, to be satellites, lackeys—a situation in which only those that maintain a spineless attitude, say "yes" to everything and never assume an independent position on anything would be considered friendly.

So there you have those who criticized us on innumerable occasions, today overwhelmed by the worst kind of confusion.

Our Party did not hesitate to help the Venezuelan guerrillas when a rightist and treacherous leadership, betraying the revolutionary line, abandoned the guerrillas and entered into shameless collusion with the regime. At that time we presented our analysis as to which side was right—that scheming, politicking group that betrayed the combatants, that betrayed those who had given their lives, or those who kept the flag of rebellion flying. We did not take into consideration the number of the rightist group; we took into consideration where right lay. We did not take into consideration how many members of the Central Committee or the Political Bureau were involved, because right does not necessarily equate with numbers.

And at that time the revolutionaries who remained holding aloft the banner of guerrilla struggle were in the minority. And we maintained the same position we hold today when we supported the guerrillas over and above the rightist leadership of Venezuela, when, for the same reason, we supported the Guatemalan guerrillas against the treachery and scheming of the rightist leadership in Guatemala, when we backed the Bolivian guerrillas against the schemes and betrayal of the rightist leadership in Bolivia. Yet we were accused of being adventurers, of interfering in the affairs of other countries, of interfering in the affairs of other Parties.

I ask myself, in the light of the facts and in the light of the bitter reality that persuaded the nations of the Warsaw Pact to send their forces to crush the counterrevolution in Czechoslovakia, and—according to their statement—to back a minority in the face of a majority with rightist positions, if they will also cease to support these rightist, reformist, sold-out, submissive leaderships in Latin America that are enemies of the armed revolutionary struggle, that oppose the peoples' liberation struggle.

And, with the example of this bitter experience before them, I wonder whether or not the Parties of those countries, in line with the decision, made in Czechoslovakia, will cease to support those rightist groups that betray the revolutionary movement in Latin America.

WE DO NOT AND CANNOT BELIEVE IN THE POSSIBILITY OF AN IMPROVEMENT IN RELATIONS BETWEEN THE SOCIALIST CAMP AND THE U.S. IMPERIALIST GOVERNMENT AS LONG AS THAT COUNTRY PERFORMS THE ROLE OF INTERNATIONAL GENDARME AND ENEMY OF REVOLUTIONS EVERYWHERE IN THE WORLD

Certainly, we do not believe in the possibility of an improvement in relations between the socialist camp and imperialism under the present conditions, or under any conditions as long as that imperialism exists. We do not and cannot believe in the possibility of an improvement in relations between the socialist camp and the U.S. Imperialist Government as long as that country performs the role of international gendarme, aggressor against the peoples and enemy and systematic opponent of revolutions everywhere in the world. Much less can we believe in any such improvement in the midst of an aggression as criminal and cowardly as that being waged against Vietnam.

Our position on this is very clear: one is consistent with world realities and is truly internationalist and genuinely and decidedly supports the revolutionary movement throughout the world, in which case relations with the imperialist Government of the United States cannot be improved; or relations with the imperialist U.S. Government will improve, but only at the cost of withholding consistent support from the worldwide revolutionary movement.

This is our thesis; this is our position.

I have here a dispatch datelined Washington, August 22: "Soviet intervention in Czechoslovakia compromises any improvement in relations between East and West, U.S. Secretary of State Dean Rusk stated today.

"The situation created could block ratification of the Non-Proliferation Treaty by the U.S. Senate, he added.

"The U.S. chief diplomat made this statement to the press on leaving a White House Cabinet meeting in which the problem of Czechoslovakia and the Vietnam situation were discussed."

This can hardly fail to delight us. Our people know the position of the Cuban delegation regarding this famous Non-Proliferation Treaty, which virtually gives a permanent concession to the large powers for the monopoly of nuclear weapons and the monopoly of technology in a field of energy that is going to be indispensable to the future of mankind. We were concerned, above all, by the fact that many countries of the world, including our own, would be obliged to accept the U.S. imperialist Government's monopoly on those weapons, which could be used at any moment against any people, particularly in view of the fact that the proposed treaty was also accompanied by an astonishing declaration concerning the defense of the signatory nations that might be threatened with nuclear weapons. Such countries as Vietnam, countries such as Cuba, that did not choose to accept that type of treaty, and much less sign it in a situation in which the aggression against Vietnam is being constantly intensified, are left outside the realm of any protection, and thus fall into the category in which the imperialists would theoretically have the right to attack us with nuclear arms. And, of course, everyone knows our position.

In view of the facts, in the face of an imperialism that is always plotting, always conspiring against the socialist camp, we ask ourselves whether or not the idyllic hopes of an improvement in relations with the imperialist Government of the United States will continue to be maintained. We ask ourselves if, consistent with events in Czechoslovakia, a position may be adopted that will imply a renunciation of such idyllic hopes in relation to Yankee imperialism. And the dispatch states that an improvement in relations will be compromised and that there is the danger of nonratification of the treaty. In our opinion, that would be the best thing that could happen.

Now then, these are, in our opinion, the two most important questions. The TASS statement explaining the decision of the Warsaw Pact governments states in its concluding paragraph: "The fraternal countries firmly and resolutely offer their unbreakable solidarity against any outside threat. They will never permit anyone to tear away even one link of the community of socialist States." And we ask ourselves: "Does that declaration include Vietnam? Does that statement include Korea? Does that statement include Cuba? Do they or do they not consider Vietnam, Korea and Cuba links of the socialist camp to be safeguarded against the imperialists?"

In accordance with that declaration, Warsaw Pact divisions were sent into Czechoslovakia. And we ask ourselves: "Will Warsaw Pact divisions also be sent to Vietnam if the Yankee imperialists step up their aggression against that country and the people of Vietnam request that aid? Will they send the divisions of the Warsaw

Pact to the Democratic People's Republic of Korea if the Yankee imperialists attack that country? Will the send the divisions of the Warsaw Pact to Cuba if the Yankee imperialists attack our country, or even in the case of the threat of a Yankee imperialist attack on our country, if our country requests it?" (PROLONGED APPLAUSE)

WE ACKNOWLEDGE THE BITTER NECESSITY THAT CALLED FOR THE SENDING OF THOSE FORCES INTO CZECHOSLOVAKIA; WE DO NOT CONDEMN THE SOCIALIST COUNTRIES THAT MADE THAT DECISION

We acknowledge the bitter necessity that called for the sending of those forces into Czechoslovakia; we do not condemn the socialist countries that made that decision. But we, as revolutionaries, and proceeding from positions of principle, do have the right to demand that they adopt a consistent position with regard to all the other questions that affect the world revolutionary movement.

There is no reason to hide the fact that great danger confronts our country. The advocates of an armed aggression against Cuba are all out rubbing their hands with glee. Only today a news dispatch came in calling for just that.

We must state how we see these questions. Is it perhaps a matter of the principle of sovereignty? Has it by chance been a law that has protected and protects our country from a Yankee invasion? Nobody believes that. If it were a matter of law, if it were the principle of sovereignty that had to protect our country, the Revolution would have disappeared from the face of the earth long ago. What has protected this Revolution, what has made it possible, has been the blood shed by the sons of this people, the blood shed fighting against Batista's thugs and armies, the blood shed fighting against the mercenaries, the determination that exists here to die to the last man in defense of the Revolution that was demonstrated in the October Crisis, the imperialists' knowledge that they could never stage a maneuverlike military pushover here. What defends this Revolution is not an abstract, internationally recognized legal principle.

This Revolution is defended by the unity of our people, their revolutionary awareness, their readiness for combat, their decision to die to the last man in defense of the Revolution and our country!

I don't believe that even our enemies have any doubts as to this people's courage and spirit. What defends the sovereignty of a country, what defends a just cause, is a people capable of feeling that cause as its own, of cherishing a deep conviction as to the justice of that cause and the decision to defend it at any price. That is precisely what protects our Revolution and what protects the sovereignty of our country in the face of the imperialist threat that has always existed here.

The imperialists have not given up for one instant their dream of destroying our country. Those dangers will naturally increase now. Therefore, now, precisely now—because things must be spoken of at the right time—we are once more going to explain what our position is, the position of our Revolutionary Government, regarding the United States. And we state it now, precisely when speaking out has very real significance and is not simply declamatory or theoretical, and we state it with all the more reason because of certain speculations that have been circulated concerning a possible bettering of relations between Cuba and the United States.

The Revolutionary Government has at no time shown the slightest interest in bettering its relations with the imperialist Government of the United States; it has not shown it and it will not show it, nor will it give it the slightest attention or express directly or indirectly, tacitly or openly, any kind of willingness to hold conversations with that government as long as that government remains the international gendarme, bulwark of world reaction, enemy of the revolutionary movements, aggressor in Vietnam, aggressor in the Dominican Republic and intervener in revolutionary movements. This has been, is, and will unquestionably continue to be the position of the Revolutionary Government of Cuba.

NEVER, UNDER ANY CIRCUMSTANCE, EVEN IN THE MOST DIFFICULT CIRCUMSTANCES, WILL THIS COUNTRY APPROACH THE IMPERIALIST GOVERNMENT OF THE UNITED STATES

Never, under any circumstance—and the comrades of our Central Committee know this; they know that this is the line adopted by our Committee—never, under any circumstance, even in the most difficult circumstances, will this country approach the imperialist Government of the United States—not even should it one day place us in the situation of having to choose between the continued existence of the Revolution or such a step. Because, gentlemen, that would be the moment at which the Revolution would have ceased to exist.

And if the day should ever come when this Revolution had to buy its security and its survival at the price of some concession to the Yankee imperialists, we would prefer—as our Central Committee unanimously would prefer and as our people would prefer—this people to disappear with the Revolution rather than survive at such a price! (PROLONGED APPLAUSE)

In the United States there are honest people, progressive people who oppose the blockades, the aggressions, all these things. Naturally, we have always had a friendly attitude toward those who honestly maintain those positions; people who oppose the war in Vietnam, people who oppose the imperialist policy of the United States.

But, regarding the Government of that country, our position is absolutely and unmistakably clear: we are not interested in economic relations, and we are even less interested in diplomatic relations of any kind.

They have been carrying out their criminal blockade for ten years. They taught us to find the way to defend ourselves against this; they taught us how to forge a revolutionary awareness. They know by now that it will not be easy to crush us, that we are not going to shrink from their threats or yield to them and that it will not be easy to starve us to death under any circumstance.

We have struggled forward in these ten years by making enormous efforts. The time is not far off when we will begin to receive the fruits of these efforts. Very well: we are prepared to go on for twenty years, or a lifetime, without any relations whatsoever with them. And we repeat: under whatever circumstances! That is, we shall wait until Yankee imperialism ceases to be Yankee imperialism. And we shall have enough patience and sufficient tenacity to persevere as long as may be necessary. That is our position. And we believe that this alone can be the true revolutionary position.

We know they will attempt to intimidate us. They will not succeed. They will find it very difficult to instill fear here, to frighten this country, because this country has learned in the last ten years how to live face to face with this enemy, confronting this enemy's threats.

And we are sincere when we say that we prefer plain speaking. We even prefer a position which involves risks to those indefinite situations which could encourage a slackening in our combat preparedness.

We have not had a combat alert for some time. There has not been a really tense situation for some time. Now, since these recent developments, some news agencies have reported that our forces had been placed in a state of partial alert. Yes, immediately! Our forces can never be taken by surprise.

Our philosophy of struggle includes a series of fundamental concepts: they will never catch us off guard! We prefer to have too many alerts to being taken by surprise. And we have always—under all circumstances—been prepared, all our forces in a state of alert, to avoid the possibility of surprise.

Our philosophy is well known: here the order to open fire will never need to be given, for this order is always in effect. Always! There is no need to give the order; it is unnecessary. No one will ever enter this country against our will. And the circumstances will never arise in which anyone could enter here without encountering fierce and implacable combat from the first moment. There is no need to give the order to open fire!

Nor will the order to "cease fire" ever be given in case of an aggression! We will never accept any form of surrender!

These are three fundamental concepts of our philosophy, right here under the very nose of Yankee imperialism. And all our people are imbued with this philosophy and are calmly determined to lay down their lives to the last man. That is also part of our philosophy.

MEN HAVE TO DIE, ONE WAY OR ANOTHER. THE SAD WAY TO DIE IS TO DIE IN SHAME, WITH ONE'S BACK TO THE ENEMY.

Men have to die, one way or another. The one sad way to die is to die in shame, with one's back to the enemy. We are not in favor of war, but revolutionaries would rather die in battle than as the result of natural causes. Naturally, we are not going to provoke wars just to avoid death by natural causes. Revolutionaries cannot always do what they want to do or whatever pleases them the most, for their duty will always come first and foremost.

As a matter of fact, all of our people are well aware of this—no one has the slightest doubt about it—and that is what really defends our sovereignty.

The imperialists will begin by threatening us. The future will be much more entertaining than the past. We will never halt our work or our development plans. The enemy will not succeed even in this. Our present level of organization will help us carry out our plans. We will carry these plans ahead, strengthen our defenses and step up our combat training.

Well, here comes the first one: a news dispatch from Brazil, quoting a newspaper which is a spokesman for the oligarchy.

The dispatch reads: "The Soviet intromission in an internal affair of Czechoslovakia reopens the Cuban question which seemed to have been closed and forgotten." This is the opening statement in a long editorial published yesterday by *Jornal do Brasil*.

"The newspaper, in a commentary entitled 'There and Here,' says textually:

"'After the entry of Russian troops into Czechoslovak territory, several issues concerning the world's balance of power should be automatically reevaluated.

"'One cannot help but recognize that now the presence of Cuba takes on another meaning in the light of the cold and brutal reality that caused the Soviet Union to feel insecure simply because a country in the communist orbit considered it necessary to indulge in a debate over freedom. Moscow's intolerance did not hesitate in brushing aside order in favor of brute force.

"'If the USSR can besmirch the principle of the peoples' self-determination, considering Czechoslovakia a common territory under her ideological jurisdiction, the same doctrine cannot be invoked to prevent the Cuban case from being considered in the light of specific interests of continental unity.

"'There are well-known differences between these two cases. In the first place, Czechoslovakia did not break with the principles of socialism, nor did she politically oppose the bloc to which she belongs. Only internally did she abolish the rigidity of the stifling dictatorship and drift toward a debate in which the word "freedom" came to be considered as a dimension without which socialism is a hoax.

"'The situation of Cuba is quite different: the Havana government is not in harmony with the group of continental countries, whose commitments are to democracy and freedom. The communist regime of Havana, in addition to being an exception, arrogates to itself the mission of exporting subversion to the point of financing groups which disturb the democratic order in Latin America.

"'As long as the Soviet Union was capable of allowing the winds of freedom to sweep through Czechoslovakia, the world was under impression that finally the major powers, the leaders of blocs, were taking a more tolerant attitude rather than resorting automatically to military intervention. But the scene was unexpectedly and brutally altered. The weight of Soviet violence fell on the Czechoslovak attempt to try out freedom.

"'The situation changes automatically in respect to Cuba, not as a result of any compensation, but by the mere fact that it is necessary to reevaluate the balance of forces on the world scene. The Cuban problem will be reopened, and Brazil, which aligned itself in the defense of the principle of nonintervention, will have to bear in mind that the Rio de Janeiro Treaty is the document on which to base the reexamination of the problem.

"'As of yesterday morning, the Cuban question, therefore, has become a current issue and calls for reconsideration without the mistaken connotations which caused it to be viewed unrealistically. The Soviet aggression against Europe exposes its flank in Latin America to an inevitable examination,' concludes the editorial contained in yesterday's issue of *Jornal do Brasil* (August 22)."

And then they try to say this is a realistic examination!

There is a slight difference, gentlemen of *Jornal do Brasil* and the rest of the oligarchs, and that is that in a few hours we Cuban revolutionaries would throw the best divisions of Brazil out of Cuba with a swift kick in the pants. (APPLAUSE)

And against the best divisions of the imperialist Government of the United States we are willing, like the Vietnamese, to fight for one hundred years, if necessary. (APPLAUSE)

That is the only slight difference, imperialists and oligarchs. We gladly uphold our positions, and we will uphold them always without being frightened by any kind of threats.

PATRIA O MUERTE! VENCEREMOS! (OVATION)

NOTES

PROLOGUE

1. Guevara referred to the missile crisis as "the Caribbean crisis" in the original version of his letter ("los días luminosos y tristes de la crisis del Caribe"). The appellation "Caribbean" for the crisis was the Soviet formulation. Cubans refer to the events as the October Crisis. Even in 1965, when Guevara wrote his farewell letter, Cuba had described the episode as the "October Crisis." Still, most contemporary Cuban references to Guevara's letter faithfully reproduce the original language. We were struck, then, by a memento James Blight and janet Lang received from one Cuban colleague on which Guevara's letter is excerpted but altered, referring to the "October Crisis" instead of the "Caribbean crisis." Why had the words been changed? Blight and Lang asked. They were told that many people "assumed that Guevara made an honest mistake" in hastily writing his letter. No Cuban and certainly not Che Guevara, it was explained, would *ever* use the official *Soviet* terms for the crisis of October 1962, and so his words have been "corrected." This information was inaccurate. Guevara's letter is widely reproduced in Cuba as it was written originally, with the reference to the "Caribbean crisis." But the memento's "correction," and the explanation for the alteration, interestingly embody two themes of the entire book.

First, Cuba experienced the crisis in October 1962 differently than either the Soviet Union or the United States, and the differing interpretations of the crisis profoundly influenced Cuba's relations with both superpowers. Cuban historian Oscar Zanetti explained to us that "in those days 'monthly crises' and mobilizations were frequent—the January crisis, the July crisis." Similarly, Cuban political scientist Carlos Alzugaray noted that "what defined each crisis was the moment in which it happened." Thus Cubans highlight their repeated experience of facing destruction by designating the missile crisis as one among many. It is distinguished merely by *when* it occurred, in October, not by its nature. The Soviets saw the crisis as a superpower confrontation that occurred in the Caribbean, that is, on the high seas where the U.S. quarantine blocked Soviet ships. This view devalued both Cuba's role in the crisis and the way in which U.S. threats to Cuba may have caused it. The Soviet phrasing also countered the U.S. charge that the crisis was created by the Soviet Union placing ballistic missiles in Cuba. Americans embody that interpretation in the commonly used name of the confrontation, the Cuban missile crisis. Second, for Cubans to apply their own name to the crisis is a matter of national dignity—and even sovereignty and survival—because by doing so they emphasize their distinctive understanding of the crisis, which concerns the threat and vulnerability Cuba experienced at the hands of both superpowers.

We have been unable to determine why Guevara happened to use the phrase "Caribbean crisis," and we suggest it is a question worthy of subsequent research.

2. Armstrong, a former investigative reporter for the *Washington Post*, had pioneered journalistic efforts to use the 1974 Freedom of Information Act (FOIA). Though journalists and scholars increasingly were using the FOIA, they had no way to compare their documents with those received by others, or even to know what others already had obtained. Armstrong founded the National Security Archive in 1985 with a group of journalists and scholars hoping to create a centralized repository for these materials. Since then the Archive has become the world's largest nongovernmental library of declassified documents. It also is a research institute on international affairs, a public interest law firm that seeks to defend and expand public access to government information, and an indexer and publisher of government documents. Today its efforts have extended to several countries throughout the world. Information about the organization is available at its website: www.gwu.edu/~nsarchiv/nsa/the_archive.html.

3. The meeting took place on Hawk's Cay, Florida. See J. Anthony Lukas, "Class Reunion; Kennedy's Men Relive the Cuban Missile Crisis," *New York Times Magazine*, August 30, 1987, pp. 22–27, 51, 58, 61.

4. The three were: Fyodor Burlatsky, head of the Philosophy Department, Social Sciences Institute, Moscow, who had written speeches for Khrushchev and traveled with the Soviet leader to Bulgaria in May 1962; Sergo Mikoyan, editor of the scholarly journal *Latinskaya amerika*, had been personal secretary to his father, Soviet First Deputy Premier Anastas I. Mikoyan, and had traveled with him to Cuba in early November 1962; Georgy Shakhnazarov, a senior staff member of the Central Committee of the Communist Party of the Soviet Union and a personal aide to Gorbachev, was also a historian of the Cold War.

5. The transcripts of the March and October 1987 meetings, as well as the interviews with Kennedy Administration officials, are reproduced in James G. Blight and David A. Welch, *On the Brink: Americans and Soviets Reexamine the Cuban Missile Crisis*, 2nd ed. (New York: Farrar, Straus and Giroux, 1990).

6. The transcript of the 1989 Moscow meeting is reproduced in Bruce J. Allyn, James G. Blight, and David A. Welch, eds., *Back to the Brink: Proceedings of the Moscow Conference on the Cuban Missile Crisis, January 27–28, 1989*, CSIA Occasional Paper No. 9 (Lanham, Md.: University Press of America, 1992).

7. Lee Hockstader, "Preparing for Harder Times, Cuba Tries to Become More Self-Sufficient," *Washington Post*, July 29, 1990; Andrew Zimbalist, "Dateline Cuba: Hanging on in Havana," *Foreign Policy*, no. 92, fall 1993.

8. Cuba had had cordial relations with Panama and had created several "front" corporations that enabled it to purchase goods from the United States, bypassing the U.S. embargo. Noriega's removal closed down this operation. Ominously, U.S. prosecutors also attempted to link Cuba to alleged illegal drug trafficking that was at the heart of their case against Noriega (Frederick Kempe and Paul M. Barrett, "Prosecutors Concentrate on the Cuban Connection in Government's Drug Case against Noriega," *Wall Street Journal*, March 5, 1990, p. A16; "Noriega's Surrender: Indictments; Drug Importing Charged," *New York Times*, January 4, 1990, p. A12).

9. Ann Devroy, "U.S. Employs 'Verbal Policy' in Attempt to Isolate Castro," *Washington Post*, April 3, 1990, p. A15; David Hoffman, "Bush and Gorbachev Hail New Cooperation: Disagreement Continues on Nicaragua," *Washington Post*, December 4, 1989, p. A1; Philip Brenner and Saul Landau, "Passive-Aggressive," *NACLA Report on the Americas*, vol. 24, no. 3 (November 1990), pp. 14–17.

10. Mimi Whitefield, "Soviet Paper Urges an End to 'Philanthropy' for Cuba," *Miami Herald*, October 3, 1990, p. 21A; "Soviets to Review Foreign Aid: Gorbachev Cautions Funds May Be Cut," *Washington Post*, July 25, 1990, p. A16.

11. Thomas L. Friedman, "Soviet Turmoil; Gorbachev Says He's Ready to Pull Troops Out of Cuba and End Castro's Subsidies," *New York Times*, September 12, 1991, p. A1.

12. The complete text of that remarkable conference may be found in James G. Blight, Bruce J. Allyn, and David A. Welch, *Cuba on the Brink: Castro, the Missile Crisis, and the Soviet Collapse* (New York: Pantheon, 1993).

13. Blight et al., *Cuba on the Brink*, p. 211.

14. Castro remarked at one point in the conference, "I think that all these things should be brought to light—I mean the papers, the documents—once and for all" (Blight et al., *Cuba on the Brink*, p. 225).

15. Jacques Lévesque, *The USSR and the Cuban Revolution: Soviet Ideological and Strategical Perspectives, 1959–77*, trans. Deanna Drendel Leboeuf (New York: Praeger, 1978), pp. 102–4; D. Bruce Jackson, *Castro, the Kremlin and Communism in Latin America* (Baltimore: Johns Hopkins Press, 1969), pp. 28–29.

16. Ernesto Che Guevara, "Message to the Tricontinental: 'Create Two, Three . . . Many Vietnams,'" in *Venceremos! The Speeches and Writings of Ernesto Che Guevara*, ed. John Gerassi (New York: Simon and Schuster, 1968), p. 420.

17. U.S. Congress, Senate, Committee on the Judiciary, "The Tricontinental Conference of African, Asian and Latin American Peoples," A Staff Study, 89th Cong., 2nd Sess., June 7, 1966, p. 93. Also see Lévesque, *The USSR and the Cuban Revolution*, pp. 119–21.

18. For exemplary speeches, see Martin Kenner and James Petras, eds., *Fidel Castro Speaks* (New York: Grove Press, 1969), pp. 171–213. On Castro's support for the Bolivian expedition see Jon Lee Anderson, *Che Guevara: A Revolutionary Life* (New York: Grove Press, 1997), pp. 678–82. On Guevara's problems with the Bolivian Communist Party, see Ernesto Che Guevara, *Bolivian Diary*, ed. Mary-Alice Waters, trans. Michael Taber (New York: Pathfinder, 1994), pp. 96–97, 101–2.

19. Fidel Castro, "A Necessary Introduction," and Inti Peredo, "My Campaign with Che," in Guevara, *Bolivian Diary*, pp. 58–61, 101–2, 334–41, 344–45. Manuel Piñeiro, a high Cuban intelligence official who coordinated Cuba's support to revolutionary organizations in Africa and Asia, laid the failure of Guevara's mission directly at the feet of Mario Monje, general secretary of the Bolivian Communist Party: "First of all . . . Monje didn't do what he had promised the leaders of the Cuban Revolution. Second, the guerrilla base was detected prematurely" (Manuel Piñeiro, *Che Guevara and the Latin American Revolutionary Movements*, ed. Luis Suárez Salazar, trans. Mary Todd [Melbourne, Australia: Ocean Press, 2001], p. 66). Also see Anderson, *Che Guevara*, pp. 704–5.

20. Lévesque, *The USSR and the Cuban Revolution*, pp. 130–31.

21. Jorge I. Domínguez, *To Make the World Safe for Revolution: Cuba's Foreign Policy* (Cambridge, Mass.: Harvard University Press, 1989), pp. 72–73.

22. "Fidel Castro's 2 January Speech on Anniversary," trans. from Havana Domestic Radio and Television Services in Spanish 1616 GMT, 2 Jan 68, by the U.S. Foreign Broadcast Information Service, January 3, 1968; available at: http://lanic.utexas.edu/la/cb/cuba/castro.html.

23. The proceedings of the Central Committee's meeting, other than Castro's speech, were reported prominently in Cuba's major newspaper, *Granma*. See *Granma*, Weekly Review (English), February 4 and 11, 1968.

24. Castro asserted that "Comrade Aníbal Escalante is responsible for having promoted the sectarian spirit to its highest possible level, of having promoted an organization which he controlled. . . . He simply allowed himself to be blinded by personal ambition" ("Fidel Castro Denounces Sectarianism" [speech of March 26, 1962], Ministry of Foreign Relations, Republic of Cuba, Political Documents: 2, pp. 21, 23). Also see Jorge I. Domínguez, *Cuba: Order and Revolution* (Cambridge, Mass.: Harvard University Press, 1978), pp. 210–11; Tad Szulc, *Fidel: A Critical Portrait* (New York: William Morrow, 1986), pp. 570–71; Sheldon B. Liss, *Fidel! Castro's Political and Social Thought* (Boulder, Colo.: Westview, 1994), pp. 23–24.

25. *Granma*, Weekly Review (English), February 11, 1968, p. 2. Rodriguez himself had been a leader of the PSP, but he had supported Castro's July 26th Movement in 1958 while much of the PSP leadership was cool or hostile to the revolutionaries. His numerous theoretical works on Marxism-Leninism, which conformed closely to Soviet positions, and his decades-long support for the Soviet Union, made his charges all the more powerful.

26. After the Central Committee meeting, Escalante was formally tried as a "traitor to the Revolution" and sentenced to fifteen years in prison. Other members of the microfaction received prison sentences of three to twelve years. See *Granma*, Weekly Review (English), February 11, 1968, p. 7; Juan de Onis, "Cuba to Try 9 in Faction That Backed Soviet Line," *New York Times*, January 29, 1968, p. 1; Ruben Salazar, "Cuba to Put 40 Pro-Soviet Reds on Trial in Purge," *Los Angeles Times*, January 29, 1968, p. 1.

27. Jorge Pollo, interview with the authors and with Janet M. Lang, May 25, 1993, Havana, Cuba. David Lewis was the interpreter.

28. *Granma*, Weekly Review (English), February 4, 1968, p. 1.

29. The August 23, 1968, speech is reprinted in appendix C. It is the official translation of the transcript made by the Cuban government's Department of Stenographic Transcription, as printed in *Granma*, Weekly Review (English), August 25, 1968.

CHAPTER 1

1. Bruce J. Allyn, James G. Blight, and David A. Welch, eds., *Back to the Brink: Proceedings of the Moscow Conference on the Cuban Missile Crisis, January 27–28, 1989*, CSIA Occasional Paper No. 9 (Lanham, Md.: University Press of America, 1992), p. 7.

2. This framework is repeated in the revised edition: Graham Allison and Philip Zelikow, *Essence of Decision: Explaining the Cuban Missile Crisis*, 2nd ed. (New York: Longman, 1999), p. 77. Dean Rusk originally used the metaphor "eyeball to eyeball" during the crisis. See Dean Rusk, as told to Richard Rusk, *As I Saw It* (New York: Penguin, 1991), p. 237.

3. Major Rudolph Anderson, Jr. was killed on October 27, 1962, when his U-2 surveillance plane was shot down over Cuba by a Soviet surface-to-air missile (SAM).

4. This frame of reference was encouraged by early memoirs of the Kennedy administration, such as Arthur M. Schlesinger, Jr., *A Thousand Days: John F. Kennedy in the White House* (Boston: Houghton Mifflin, 1965), chaps. 30–31, and Robert F. Kennedy, *Thirteen Days: A Memoir of the Cuban Missile Crisis* (New York: New American Library, 1969).

5. CIA Intelligence Memorandum, "Recent Soviet Military Aid to Cuba," August 20, 1962, in Laurence Chang and Peter Kornbluh, *The Cuban Missile Crisis, 1962: A National Security*

Archive Documents Reader (New York: New Press, 1992), Document No. 11, pp. 57–60; "Memorandum on Cuba," August 20, 1962, in *CIA Documents on the Cuban Missile Crisis, 1962*, ed. Mary S. McAuliffe, HRP: 92-9 (Washington, D.C.: Central Intelligence Agency, 1992), Document No. 5, pp. 19–20. Also see Allison and Zelikow, *Essence of Decision*, pp. 78–81.

6. "President Kennedy's Statement on Soviet Military Shipments to Cuba," September 4, 1962, in Laurence Chang, *The Cuban Missile Crisis, 1962*, A National Security Archive Document Set (Alexandria, Va.: Chadwyck-Healey, 1990) [Hereafter referred to as *CMC Document Set*], Document No. 00340. Also see Ernest R. May and Philip D. Zelikow, eds., *The Kennedy Tapes: Inside the White House during the Cuban Missile Crisis* (Cambridge, Mass.: Harvard University Press, 1997), pp. 36–38; Arthur M. Schlesinger, Jr., *Robert Kennedy and His Times* (New York: Ballantine, 1978), p. 545; Raymond L. Garthoff, *Reflections on the Cuban Missile Crisis*, rev. ed. (Washington, D.C.: Brookings Institution, 1989), p. 31; Carlos Lechuga, *In the Eye of the Storm: Castro, Khrushchev, Kennedy and the Missile Crisis*, trans. Mary Todd (Melbourne, Australia: Ocean Press, 1995), pp. 38–41.

7. S.J. Res. 230 (Public Law 87-733), October 3, 1962.

8. James G. Blight and David A. Welch, *On the Brink: Americans and Soviets Reexamine the Cuban Missile Crisis*, 2nd ed. (New York: Farrar, Straus and Giroux, 1990), pp. 247–48.

9. Blight and Welch, *On the Brink*, pp. 43, 248.

10. Allyn et al., *Back to the Brink*, pp. 121, 141.

11. May and Zelikow, *The Kennedy Tapes*, pp. 47–117; "Transcript of the first Executive Committee Meeting, October 16, 1962" and "Transcript of the second Executive Committee Meeting, October 16, 1962," in Chang and Kornbluh, *The Cuban Missile Crisis*, Documents No. 15 and 16, pp. 85–115.

12. Kennedy, *Thirteen Days*, pp. 25–26; May and Zelikow, *The Kennedy Tapes*, p. 100. In 1989, former National Security Adviser McGeorge Bundy observed that "if [the Soviets] had raised the question [of deploying ballistic missiles to Cuba] in the relatively straightforward way that previous deployments had occurred . . . it would have been certainly different and more difficult for us in terms of any forceful action to undo that deployment" (Allyn et al., *Back to the Brink*, p. 20). Also see Blight and Welch, *On the Brink*, pp. 28, 240–48).

13. Schlesinger, *A Thousand Days*, pp. 796–797. Also see May and Zelikow, *The Kennedy Tapes*, pp. 91–92.

14. Scott D. Sagan, *Moving Targets: Nuclear Strategy and National Security* (Princeton, N.J.: Princeton University Press, 1989); Robert Jervis, *The Meaning of the Nuclear Revolution: Statecraft and the Prospect of Armageddon* (Ithaca, N.Y.: Cornell University Press, 1989).

15. Apart from fear of a nuclear war, the concern about maintaining U.S. credibility in general influenced why policymakers viewed the Cuban revolution as a threat even before it established ties to the Soviet Union. See our discussion of this problem in the epilogue, pp. 153–54.

16. Michael R. Beschloss, *The Crisis Years: Kennedy and Khrushchev, 1960–1963* (New York: HarperCollins, 1991), p. 225; Aleksandr Fursenko and Timothy Naftali, *One Hell of a Gamble: Khrushchev, Castro, and Kennedy, 1958–1964* (New York: W. W. Norton, 1997), p. 227.

17. Nikita S. Khrushchev, *Khrushchev Remembers*, trans. and ed. Strobe Talbott (Boston: Little, Brown, 1970), p. 458.

18. Allison and Zelikow, *Essence of Decision*, pp. 92–93; Garthoff, *Reflections on the Cuban Missile Crisis*, pp. 206–8; Blight and Welch, *On the Brink*, pp. 30–31. During the crisis, the United States estimated the Soviets had 44 ICBMs.

19. Garthoff, *Reflections on the Cuban Missile Crisis*, pp. 45–46. Also see Arnold L. Horelick, "The Cuban Missile Crisis: An Analysis of Soviet Calculations and Behavior," *World Politics*, vol. 16, April 1964.

20. May and Zelikow, *The Kennedy Tapes*, p. 100.

21. Quoted in Blight and Welch, *On the Brink*, p. 23. During the crisis itself, McNamara said that "speaking strictly in military terms, really in terms of weapons, it [the introduction of ballistic missiles in Cuba] doesn't change it [the US–Soviet strategic balance] at all, in my personal opinion. My views are not shared by the [Joint] Chiefs [of Staff]" (May and Zelikow, *The Kennedy Tapes*, p. 133). Also see McGeorge Bundy, *Danger and Survival: Choices About the Bomb in the First Fifty Years* (New York: Random House, 1988), pp. 451–52.

22. Blight and Welch, *On the Brink*, pp. 30–31. Also see discussion on pp. 202–4.

23. Schlesinger, *A Thousand Days*, p. 840. Also see Allison and Zelikow, *Essence of Decision*, pp. 121–22.

24. Alexander L. George, *Forceful Persuasion: Coercive Diplomacy as an Alternative to War* (Washington, D.C.: United States Institute of Peace Press, 1991), p. 36.

25. *CINCLANT Historical Account of Cuban Crisis—1963*, Serial: 000119/J09H, 29 April 1963 [Hereafter referred to as *CINCLANT Historical Account*], in *CMC Document Set*, Document No. 003087, pp. 164–67.

26. This view was expressed cogently by McGeorge Bundy and Theodore Sorensen in 1989 at the Moscow Conference on the missile crisis. See Allyn et al., *Back to the Brink*, pp. 103–5.

27. "National Security Action Memorandum No. 181," August 23, 1962, in *CMC Document Set*, Document No. 00295; *CINCLANT Historical Account*, pp. 39–40; James G. Hershberg, "Before the 'Missiles of October': Did Kennedy Plan a Military Strike Against Cuba?" in *The Cuban Missile Crisis Revisited*, ed. James A. Nathan (New York: St. Martin's, 1992), pp. 252–54.

28. *Problems of Communism*, Special Edition, vol. 41, spring 1992, pp. 75–96.

29. Robert S. McNamara, *In Retrospect: The Tragedy and Lessons of Vietnam* (New York: Times Books, 1995), p. 21.

30. Anatoli I. Gribkov and William Y. Smith, *Operation ANADYR: U.S. and Soviet Generals Recount the Cuban Missile Crisis* (Chicago: edition q, 1994), pp. 10–11; James G. Richter, *Khrushchev's Double Bind: International Pressures and Domestic Coalition Politics* (Baltimore: Johns Hopkins University Press, 1994), pp. 104–8, 144–48; Richard Ned Lebow and Janice Gross Stein, *We All Lost the Cold War* (Princeton, N.J.: Princeton University Press, 1994), pp. 58–61. Also see Fursenko and Naftali, *One Hell of a Gamble*, pp. 154–156, 170–171; Allison and Zelikow, *Essence of Decision*, pp. 94–97.

31. "Address by Roswell Gilpatric, Deputy Secretary of Defense, before the Business Council at the Homestead, Hot Springs, Virginia," October 21, 1961, Unclassified Speech No. 1173-61, in *CMC Document Set*, Document No. 00115.

32. Beschloss, *The Crisis Years*, pp. 329–32.

33. Beschloss, *The Crisis Years*, p. 332; Fursenko and Naftali, *One Hell of a Gamble*, p. 139; Allison and Zelikow, *Essence of Decision*, p. 95.

34. Blight and Welch, *On the Brink*, p. 29. Also see Allison and Zelikow, *Essence of Decision*, pp. 93–94.

35. "Minutes of the First OPERATION MONGOOSE meeting," December 1, 1961, and "The Cuba Project," February 20, 1962, in Chang and Kornbluh, *The Cuban Missile Crisis*, Documents No. 4 and 5, pp. 20–37. Also see Select Committee to Study Governmental Operations with Respect to Intelligence Activities, *Alleged Assassinations Plots Involving Foreign Leaders*, An Interim Report, no. 94-465, U.S. Senate, 94th Cong., 1st Sess., November 20, 1975, pp. 139–41; Garthoff, *Reflections on the Cuban Missile Crisis*, pp. 7–9.

36. "Eighth Meeting of Consultation of Ministers of Foreign Affairs of the American Republics; Punta del Este, January 22–31, 1962: Final Act, Signed January 31, 1962," in U.S. Department of State, Historical Office, *American Foreign Policy, Current Documents, 1962*, Washington, D.C., 1966, Document No. III-12, pp. 326–27. The United States also had sought approval for an OAS-approved hemispheric trade embargo against Cuba, but the member states agreed only to suspend "trade with Cuba in arms and implements of war." See Dean Rusk, "United States Proposal of Four Major Actions against the Government of Cuba," January 25, 1962, in *American Foreign Policy, Current Documents, 1962*, Document No. III-10, pp. 318–19; Sergo Mikoyan, "La Crisis del Caribe, en retrospectiva," *America Latina* (Moscow), no. 4 (April 1988), p. 45; Blight and Welch, *On the Brink*, p. 238.

37. Fursenko and Naftali, *One Hell of a Gamble*, pp. 152–54. Also see James G. Blight, Bruce J. Allyn, and David Welch, *Cuba on the Brink: Castro, the Missile Crisis, and the Soviet Collapse*, enlarged paperback ed. (Lanham, Md.: Rowman & Littlefield, 2002), p. 196; Herbert L. Matthews, *Revolution in Cuba* (New York: Scribner's, 1975), p. 208.

38. Khrushchev, *Khrushchev Remembers*, p. 494.

39. Allyn et al., *Back to the Brink*, pp. 7, 10; Blight et al., *Cuba on the Brink*, pp. 141–61; Gribkov and Smith, *Operation ANADYR*, pp. 12–13. Also see Vladislav Zubok and Constantine Pleshakov, *Inside the Kremlin's Cold War: From Stalin to Khrushchev* (Cambridge, Mass.: Harvard University Press, 1996), p. 260; Garthoff, *Reflections on the Cuban Missile Crisis*, pp. 6–9; Allison and Zelikow, *Essence of Decision*, pp. 82–86. Fursenko and Naftali (*One Hell of a Gamble*, pp. 156–60) report that the Soviet intelligence community had concluded by April 1962 that there was a decreasing likelihood of a U.S. invasion, but its evidence for this conclusion also indicated there had been increased U.S. support for counterrevolutionary activity within Cuba. With such an ambiguous analysis, they argue, "The KGB was hedging its bets about a U.S. invasion" (p. 159).

40. Kiva L. Maidanik, interview done for the authors by Svetlana Savranskaya, June 6, 1993, Moscow, Russian Federation. The transcript of the interview was also translated by Dr. Savranskaya. Both versions are in the authors' possession. Also see Richter, *Khrushchev's Double Bind*, pp. 137–38, 149–50.

41. Khrushchev, *Khrushchev Remembers*, p. 493. Also see Fursenko and Naftali, *One Hell of a Gamble*, pp. 167–70; Herbert S. Dinerstein, *The Making of a Missile Crisis: October 1962* (Baltimore: Johns Hopkins University Press, 1976), p. 187; Jacques Lévesque, *The USSR and the Cuban Revolution: Soviet Ideological and Strategical Perspectives, 1959–77*, trans. Deanna Drendel Leboeuf (New York: Praeger, 1978), pp. 34–35, 39; Adam Ulam, *Expansion and Coexistence: The History of Soviet Foreign Policy, 1917–1967* (New York: Praeger, 1968), pp. 543–44, 688–89. Georgy Kornienko, deputy Soviet ambassador to the United States during the missile crisis, recalled in 1991 "how inspired he [Khrushchev] was by the victory at Playa Girón. . . . This was a crucial moment, since Khrushchev became more assured that the prospect of future socialist countries in the Western Hemisphere was realistic." James G. Blight, David Lewis, and David A. Welch, eds., *Cuba between the Superpowers, Antigua, 3–7 January, 1991: Transcript of the Meetings* (Providence, R.I.: Center for Foreign Policy Development of the Thomas J. Watson Jr. Institute for International Studies, Brown University, 1991), p. 29.

There appear to have been several other Soviet motives as well. Lebow and Stein cogently argue that Khrushchev believed that placing missiles in Cuba simultaneously served all of his objectives even though to an observer the goals were incompatible: protecting Cuba from a U.S. invasion, redressing the strategic imbalance, "achieving 'pyschological equality' to compel a fundamental shift in American foreign policy," promoting detente, and salvaging his "domestic reforms" (Lebow and Stein, *We All Lost the Cold War*, pp. 60–61). For a discussion of these objectives see Lebow and Stein, *We All Lost the Cold War*, Chapter 2; Blight and Welch, *On the Brink*, pp. 116–17; Allison and Zelikow, *Essence of Decision*, pp. 88–91, 99–109.

42. Blight et al., *Cuba on the Brink*, pp. 358–62.

43. "Khrushchev Message of October 23, 1962," in *Problems of Communism*, Special Edition, vol. 41, spring 1992, pp. 31–32.

44. Fursenko and Naftali, *One Hell of a Gamble*, pp. 259–60; Blight et al., *Cuba between the Superpowers*, pp. 66, 117–18. The letters are reprinted in *Problems of Communism*, spring 1992, pp. 37–50.

45. Blight et al., *Cuba between the Superpowers*, pp. 66–68. Kornienko noted (p. 68) that the original draft of the second letter sent to Kennedy demanded missiles be withdrawn from Turkey and Italy. But in the final draft, Italy was omitted because Khrushchev had remarked on the 26th, in deciding to send a less demanding message, that he would "come back" to the Turkish missiles at another time, and therefore the person who wrote the final draft of the "second" letter excluded Italy. For a more elaborate though slightly different version of the events that led to the dispatch of the two letters, see Fursenko and Naftali, *One Hell of a Gamble*, pp. 257–63, 273–77.

46. The full text of the letter is reprinted in Chang and Kornbluh, *The Cuban Missile Crisis*, Document 45, p. 189 and in Blight et al., *Cuba on the Brink*, pp. 481–82. For a discussion of the motivations behind Castro's release of it in 1990, see Blight et al., *Cuba on the Brink*, pp. 474–81.

47. Blight et al., *Cuba on the Brink*, p. 116; Blight et al., *Cuba between the Superpowers*, pp. 92–93, 99–100, 118. Also see Nikita S. Khrushchev, *Khrushchev Remembers: The Glasnost Tapes*, trans. and ed. Jerrold L. Schecter, with Vyacheslav V. Luchkov (Boston: Little, Brown, 1990), p. 177.

48. Reprinted in Chang and Kornbluh, *The Cuban Missile Crisis*, Document 54, p. 239.

49. Blight et al., *Cuba on the Brink*, pp. 482–83, 486.

50. Blight and Welch, *On the Brink*, p. 343; Blight et al., *Cuba between the Superpowers*, pp. 92–93, 99–100; Fursenko and Naftali, *One Hell of a Gamble*, pp. 272–73, 283–86.

51. "Cable from Soviet Foreign Minister Gromyko to USSR Ambassador to Cuba Alekseev, 27 October 1962," in *Cold War International History Project Bulletin*, Woodrow Wilson International Center for Scholars, Nos. 8–9 (winter 1996/1997), p. 291.

52. Gribkov and Smith, *Operation ANADYR*. p. 72.

53. Allyn et al., *Back to the Brink*, p. 148.

54. Quoted in Allison and Zelikow, *Essence of Decision*, p. 355. Also see George, *Forceful Persuasion*, pp. 36–37.

55. Dino A. Brugioni, *Eyeball to Eyeball: The Inside Story of the Cuban Missile Crisis* (New York: Random House, 1991), p. 461.

56. Gribkov and Smith, *Operation ANADYR*, p. 65.

57. Gribkov and Smith, *Operation ANADYR*, pp. 66–67. The actual firing appears to have been done by Major General Georgy A. Voronkov. See Blight and Welch, *On the Brink*, p. 339; Adela Estrada Juaréz, "The General Who Gave the Order to Fire," *Granma Weekly Review*, April 23, 1989, p. 8.

58. Gribkov and Smith, *Operation ANADYR*, pp. 62–63.

59. "Dobrynin's Cable to the Soviet Foreign Ministry, 27 October 1962," in *Cold War International History Project Bulletin*, Woodrow Wilson International Center for Scholars, Washington, D.C., no. 5 (spring 1995), pp. 79–80. Also see Zubok and Pleshakov, *Inside the Kremlin's Cold War*, pp. 266–67; Kennedy, *Thirteen Days*, pp. 108–9; Garthoff, *Reflections on the Cuban Missile Crisis*, p. 86.

60. James G. Blight, *The Shattered Crystal Ball: Fear and Learning in the Cuban Missile Crisis* (Savage, Md.: Rowman & Littlefield, 1990), p. 134. For a discussion about the role fear played in resolving the crisis, see chapters 7 and 8. Also see Fursenko and Naftali, *One Hell of a Gamble*, pp. 284–87.

61. Gribkov and Smith, *Operation ANADYR*, p. 69.

62. Khrushchev, *Khrushchev Remembers: The Glasnost Tapes*, pp. 177–78, 183.

63. In 1993, remarking on the Kennedy–Khrushchev agreement, Castro said in an NBC interview that "just a phrase would have been enough. . . . The United States provides guarantees that are satisfactory to Cuba. Cuba should have been able to take part in that discussion, and say which guarantees would be satisfactory to our country." Quoted in Lechuga, *In the Eye of the Storm*, p. 106.

64. Fursenko and Naftali, *One Hell of a Gamble*, chap. 15; Blight et al., *Cuba on the Brink*, pp. 74–75; Lechuga, *In the Eye of the Storm*, pp. 157–62. Sergo Mikoyan, a leading Soviet scholar on Latin America and for many years the editor of the official Soviet journal on Latin American politics, *Latinskaya Amerika*, accompanied his father to Cuba. When his mother died, his father sent him to Moscow for the funeral but stayed himself because of the urgency of the crisis (authors' interview with Sergo Mikoyan, Moscow, January 30, 1989).

65. "Notes of Conversation between A. I. Mikoyan and Fidel Castro," November 3, 1962, *Cold War International History Project Bulletin*, no. 5 (spring 1995), p. 93. [Hereafter cited as "Mikoyan MemCon, November 3, 1962."] Sergo Mikoyan made the comment about "Fidel's agent" in an interview with the authors in Arlington, Virginia on June 29, 1995. Also see Vladislav M. Zubok, "'Dismayed by the Actions of the Soviet Union': Mikoyan's Talks with Fidel Castro and the Cuban Leadership, November 1962," *Cold War International History Project Bulletin*, no. 5 (spring 1995), p. 90.

66. Blight et al., *Cuba on the Brink*, pp. 94–100. The Ilyushin (IL-28) light bombers were outdated Soviet aircraft. Some versions were capable of carrying nuclear payloads, and six out of the forty-two planes sent to Cuba were nuclear-capable. Of the forty-two planes, only six were completely assembled but they had not been tested for flight (Gribkov and Smith, *Operation ANADYR*, p. 27; *CINCLANT Historical Account*, p. 15). There was some confusion at the time about whether the planes belonged to Cuba or whether they were still the property of the Soviet Union. U.S. officials believed they were Cuban ("Summary Record of the 16th Meeting of the Executive Committee of the National Security Council," U.S. State Department, *Foreign Relations of the United States, 1961–1963* [hereafter cited as *FRUS, 1961–1963*], vol. XI, Document No. 130, November 1, 1962 (Washington, D.C.: Government Printing Office, 1996), p. 340. In 1992, Castro explained that the Soviets had not turned over any of the planes to the Cuban government (Blight et al., *Cuba on the Brink*, p. 91). The United States listed the IL-28s among the "offensive" weapons to be removed from Cuba, because, as Raymond Garthoff explained in 1992, "the airplane was officially listed as being nuclear-capable" and it had a presumed range of 600 nautical miles (Blight et al., *Cuba on the Brink*, pp. 95–96). The Soviet Union insisted they were defensive, intended to help Cuba defend its coast against terrorist intervention. For a comprehensive account of the IL-28 issue, see Garthoff, *Reflections on the Cuban Missile Crisis*, pp. 104–18.

67. However Kennedy had included "bomber aircraft" in his October 23 quarantine proclamation, as Garthoff observes (*Reflections on the Cuban Missile Crisis*, p. 104).

68. "Khrushchev Message of October 28, 1962," *Problems of Communism*, spring 1992, p. 52. Khrushchev's effort to save face by denying the offensive nature of the missiles was helpfully pointed out to us in an interview with Sergo Mikoyan, July 5, 1995. Also see Sergo Mikoyan, "La Crisis del Caribe, en retrospectiva," *America Latina* (Moscow), no. 4 (April 1988).

69. "Mikoyan's Mission to Havana: Cuban-Soviet Negotiations, November 1962," *Cold War International History Project Bulletin*, no. 5 (spring 1995), p. 103.

70. "Khrushchev Oral Message of November 11, 1962," *Cold War International History Project Bulletin*, no. 5 (spring 1995), pp. 85, 87.

71. "Transcription of Conversation between A. I. Mikoyan and Fidel Castro, November 12, 1962," in Gribkov and Smith, *Operation ANADYR*, appendix 1, Document 7 [hereafter cited as "Mikoyan MemCon, November 12, 1962"], pp. 192, 195.

72. "Khrushchev Message of Nov. 13, 1962," *Problems of Communism*, spring 1992, p. 89. Also see Philip Brenner, "Kennedy and Khrushchev on Cuba: Two Stages, Three Parties," *Problems of Communism*, spring 1992, p. 25; Lechuga, *In the Eye of the Storm*, p. 149; Tomás Diez Acosta, *La Operación Anadir* (Havana, Cuba: Military History Study Center, 1991), p. 152.

73. Fursenko and Naftali, *One Hell of a Gamble*, pp. 306-10; Lechuga, *In the Eye of the Storm*, p. 153.

74. "Khrushchev Oral Message of November 19, 1962," *Problems of Communism*, spring 1992, p. 100.

75. For a discussion of this point, see Blight, *The Shattered Crystal Ball*, pp. 134-46. Also see Garthoff, *Reflections on the Cuban Missile Crisis*, pp. 131-35; Khrushchev, *Khrushchev Remembers: The Glasnost Tapes*, p. 180.

76. McNamara articulated this view in 1992, concluding that "in this age of high-technology weapons, crisis management is dangerous, difficult and uncertain. . . . Therefore, we must direct our attention to crisis avoidance." Blight et al., *Cuba on the Brink*, p. 41. Also see Garthoff, *Reflections on the Cuban Missile Crisis*, pp. 154-55, 191-92.

77. Garthoff, *Reflections on the Cuban Missile Crisis*, p. 132. Also see James M. Goldgeier, *Leadership Style and Soviet Foreign Policy* (Baltimore: Johns Hopkins University Press, 1994), p. 72.

78. Khrushchev, *Khrushchev Remembers*, p. 504.

79. Ulam, *Expansion and Coexistence*, p. 630. One Central Committee critic charged, during the meeting at which the chairman was ousted, that Khrushchev "carried the world to the brink of nuclear war, and . . . damaged the international prestige of our government, our party, our armed forces" (quoted in Fursenko and Naftali, *One Hell of a Gamble*, p. 354).

80. Lechuga, *In the Eye of the Storm*, pp. 176-81.

81. We appreciate the March 1, 2002 communication from Cuban political scientist Carlos Alzugaray Treto, who explained the origin of the Cuban terminology as follows: "at the beginning, [Caribbean Crisis and October Crisis were] used interchangeably but with time, Cubans began to settle for 'crisis de octubre,' because there were so many crises with the United States that what defined each crisis was the moment in which it happened and not the place." Of course, another reason for the Cuban designation might have been that it was a short-hand way to distinguish the Cuban interpretation of the crisis from that of the Soviets, which would be consistent with our analysis of Cuban-Soviet tensions in chapter 3.

82. In addition to Castro's secret speech about the crisis, reprinted in chapter 2, see his extensive remarks, and those of other Cuban veterans, in Blight et al., *Cuba on the Brink*, pp. 53-317. Two other useful accounts that provide the Cuban perspective on the crisis are: Lechuga, *In the Eye of the Storm*, and Sergio del Valle Jiménez, ed., *Peligros y Principios: La Crisis de Octubre desde Cuba* (Havana, Cuba: Editora Verde Olivo, 1992). For analyses of Cuba's perspective on the crisis, see Philip Brenner, "Thirteen Months: Cuba's Perspective on the Missile Crisis," in Nathan, *The Cuban Missile Crisis Revisited*, pp. 187-217; Blight et al., *Cuba on the Brink*, chap. 1; Thomas G. Paterson, "Fixation with Cuba: The Bay of Pigs, Missile Crisis, and

Covert War against Castro," in *Kennedy's Quest for Victory*, ed. Thomas G. Paterson (New York: [publisher], 1989), pp. 136–41; Tad Szulc, *Fidel: A Critical Portrait* (New York: William Morrow, 1986), pp. 562–92; Jorge I. Domínguez, "The @#$%& Missile Crisis (Or, What Was 'Cuban' about U.S. Decisions during the Cuban Missile Crisis?" *Diplomatic History*, vol. 24, no. 2 (spring 2000).

83. We discuss U.S. reasons for considering Cuba to be a threat in the Epilogue. For a sample of representative analyses by others, see Morris H. Morley, *Imperial State and Revolution: The United States and Cuba, 1952–1986* (Cambridge, England: Cambridge University Press, 1987); Richard E. Welch, Jr., *Response to Revolution: The United States and the Cuban Revolution, 1959–1961* (Chapel Hill: University of North Carolina Press, 1985); Jorge I. Domínguez, *To Make a World Safe for Revolution: Cuba's Foreign Policy* (Cambridge, Mass.: Harvard University Press, 1989); Thomas G. Paterson, *Contesting Castro: The United States and the Triumph of the Cuban Revolution* (New York: Oxford University Press, 1994); Wayne S. Smith, *The Closest of Enemies: A Personal and Diplomatic Account of U.S.–Cuban Relations since 1957* (New York: W. W. Norton, 1987); Philip W. Bonsal, *Cuba, Castro, and the United States* (Pittsburgh: University of Pittsburgh Press, 1972); Maurice Halperin, *The Rise and Decline of Fidel Castro: An Essay in Contemporary History* (Berkeley: University of California Press, 1972); Louis A. Pérez, Jr., *Cuba and the United States: Ties of Singular Intimacy* (Athens: University of Georgia Press, 1990).

84. del Valle Jiménez, *Peligros y Principios*, p. 48.

85. Agreements on August 4 and September 30, 1961, called for the Soviets to supply IL-28 bombers, MIG-15 fighter planes, MI-4 helicopters, torpedo boats, advanced communication equipment and military specialists (Lechuga, *In the Eye of the Storm*, p. 18). But by December 1961 the Soviets had not shipped any of the promised items (Fursenko and Naftali, *One Hell of a Gamble*, pp. 139–40, 146). In a 1991 interview with the authors, Sergei Khrushchev asserted that before the Bay of Pigs his father believed the United States would crush the Cuban revolution, and that the Cuban victory convinced him the revolution had staying power. Also see his comments in Blight et al., *Cuba Between the Superpowers*, pp. 16–17.

86. Khrushchev, *Khrushchev Remembers*, p. 492.

87. Blight et al., *Cuba on the Brink*, p. 196.

88. "Action at N.S.C. Meeting, Friday, May 5 (Recommended Decisions for NSC Meeting on Cuba)," May 5, 1961, and "Record of Actions by the N.S.C. at Its 483rd Meeting," May 5, 1961, *CMC Document Set*, Document Nos. 00074 and 00075.

89. See note 35.

90. Arthur Schlesinger characterized Operation Mongoose in 1992 as "a marginal operation . . . they didn't do very much and at no point was a [U.S.] military invasion contemplated" (Blight et al., *Cuba on the Brink*, p. 159). Also see Fursenko and Naftali, *One Hell of a Gamble*, pp. 156–58; comments in Blight and Kornbluh, *Politics of Illusion*, pp. 113–18, 124, 127–28, 254–55.

91. Michael T. Klare and Peter Kornbluh, eds., *Low Intensity Warfare: Counterinsurgency, Proinsurgency, and Antiterrorism in the Eighties* (New York: Pantheon, 1988); Stephen Sloan "Introduction," in *Low-Intensity Conflict: Old Threats in a New World*, eds. Edwin G. Corr and Stephen Sloan (Boulder, Colo.: Westview, 1992), pp. 6–7; Ivan Molloy, *Rolling Back Revolution: The Emergence of Low Intensity Conflict* (London: Pluto Press, 2001), chap. 1.

92. *Alleged Assassinations Plots Involving Foreign Leaders*, pp. 139–49; Chang and Kornbluh, *The Cuban Missile Crisis*, Documents 5 (pp. 23–37), 7 (pp. 40–47), 9 (pp. 52–53); Schlesinger, *Robert Kennedy and His Times*, pp. 513–27; James G. Blight and Peter Kornbluh, *Politics of Illusion: The Bay of Pigs Reexamined* (Boulder, Colo.: Lynne Rienner, 1998), chap. 5.

93. Brig. Gen. Edward Lansdale, "Review of Operation Mongoose," July 25, 1962, in Chang and Kornbluh, *The Cuban Missile Crisis*, Document 7, pp. 40–47; Select Committee to Study Governmental Operations with Respect to Intelligence Activities, *Alleged Assassination Plots Involving Foreign Leaders, An Interim Report*, No. 94-465, U.S. Senate, 94th Cong., 1st Sess., Nov. 20, 1975, pp. 71–169; José Pérez Fernández, "Report on the U.S. Government's Plans for Using the CIA and the Terrorist Organizations to Assassinate Leaders of the Cuban Revolution, Especially Commander in Chief Fidel Castro, in *U.S. War on Cuba*, eds. José Ramón Fernández and José Pérez Fernández (Melbourne, Australia: Ocean Press, 2001), pp. 77–81, 83–86.

94. Halpern's remarks were made on May 31, 1996, at a conference on the Bay of Pigs at Musgrove Plantation, Georgia, sponsored by Brown University. Also see Schlesinger, *Robert Kennedy and His Times*, p. 514.

95. Blight et al., *Cuba between the Superpowers*, p. 11; Fabian Escalante Font, *CUBA: la guerra secreta de la CIA* (Havana, Cuba: Editorial Capitán San Luis, 1993), chap. 7; Richard Helms, "Memorandum for the Record, 'MONGOOSE Meeting with the Attorney General,' 16 October 1962," in McAuliffe, *CIA Documents on the Cuban Missile Crisis*, Document 49, pp. 153–54; "Covert Activities," A Memorandum from "William K. Harvey, CIA Representative for Operation Mongoose," August 7, 1962, p. 5 (available from the National Security Archive, Washington, D.C.); Fursenko and Naftali, *One Hell of a Gamble*, p. 159.

96. Allyn et al., *Back to the Brink*, p. 7.

97. Donna Rich Kaplowitz, *Anatomy of a Failed Embargo: U.S. Sanctions against Cuba* (Boulder, Colo.: Lynne Rienner, 1998); Michael Krinsky and David Golove, *United States Economic Measures against Cuba* (Northampton, Mass.: Aletheia Press, 1993), pp. 92–93; "Proclamation 3447: Embargo on All Trade with Cuba," February 3, 1962, *CMC Document Set*, Document No. 00162.

98. Hershberg, "Before the 'Missiles of October,'" p. 250; "Big Maneuver Opens," *New York Times*, April 10, 1962; "President Joins Fleet Manuevers," *New York Times*, April 14, 1962. In the *CMC Document Set*, see "Outline of Significant Exercise: Lantphiblex 1–62," April 9, 1962, Document No. 00200; "Major Exercise Report, Quick Kick," Serial 03A24862, September 20, 1962, Document No. 00431; "Report of the Commander in Chief U.S. Atlantic Fleet Upon Being Relieved," Serial 00308/J101A, April 30, 1963, Document No. 03088. Also see Garthoff, *Reflections on the Cuban Missile Crisis*, p. 6. Radio Havana denounced "Quick Kick" as a "rehearsal" for a U.S. invasion of Cuba ("Caribbean Maneuver Called War Rehearsal," April 8, 1962, *CMC Document Set*, Document No. 00199).

99. "Memorandum of Discussion at the 411th Meeting of the National Security Council," June 25, 1959, in *FRUS, 1958–1960*, Volume VI, Document No. 325, pp. 541–43. Robbins (*The Cuban Threat*, pp. 9–12) identifies the three countries against which Cuba was involved as the Dominican Republic, Panama, and Haiti, citing sources that indicate the attack against Nicaragua was launched from Costa Rica and was not carried out by Cubans. Also see Domínguez, *To Make a World Safe for Revolution*, pp. 26, 117–18; Blight et al., *Cuba between the Superpowers*, pp. 25–26. In 1992 Castro explained with some detail the origins of Cuba's support for subversive efforts against the Dominican Republic's dictatorship. He contended that "a number of political leaders all over Latin America"—he mentioned Venezuelan President Rómulo Betancourt and Costa Rican President José Figueres—"were working to aid revolutionary movements in Latin America when I was a student in the university." In 1947 he participated in a failed expedition against Dominican dictator Rafael Trujillo. Later Dominican revolutionaries assisted the July 26th Movement's struggle against Cuban dictator Fulgencio Batista, "and we were committed to helping them," he added. Blight et al., *Cuba on the Brink*, pp. 230–32.

100. Blight et al., *Cuba between the Superpowers*, p. 37. Also see Schlesinger, *A Thousand Days*, pp. 779–80.

101. Blight et al., *Cuba on the Brink*, pp. 232–33. After 1963, splits between the Venezuelan Communist Party and groups supported by Cuba became a source of tension between Cuba and the Soviet Union. Castro alluded to this in his 1968 speech on the Soviet invasion of Czechoslovakia. He said then: "Our party did not hesitate to help the Venezuelan guerrillas when a rightist and traitorous leadership [i.e., the Venezuelan Communist Party], deviating from the revolutionary line, abandoned the guerrillas and entered into shameful connivance with the regime." *Granma*, August 24, 1968, p. 4. Also see Lévesque, *The USSR and the Cuban Revolution*, p. 123; Inti Peredo, "My Campaign with Che," in Ernesto Che Guevara, *The Bolivian Diary of Ernesto Che Guevara*, ed. Mary-Alice Waters (New York: Pathfinder, 1994), p. 341; W. Raymond Duncan, *The Soviet Union and Cuba: Interests and Influence* (New York: Praeger, 1985), p. 70. For a helpful discussion of the criteria Cuba used in deciding to support for revolutionary groups, see Domínguez, *To Make a World Safe for Revolution*, pp. 115–19. For the CIA's assessment of Cuban support of Venezuelan guerrillas in 1962, see "Cuban Training of Latin American Subversives," Central Intelligence Agency Memorandum, March 27, 1963, p. 38; available from the National Security Archive, Washington, D.C.

102. The OAS formally excluded "the present government of Cuba" because its "Marxist-Leninist ideology" was "incompatible with the principles and standards" of the inter-American system. See U.S. Congress, 100th Cong., 2nd Sess., Senate and House, "Inter-American Relations," Report Prepared for the Use of the Committee on Foreign Relations and Committee on Foreign Affairs, December, 1988, S. Prt. 100-168, pp. 278–79; Schlesinger, *A Thousand Days*, pp. 781–83; Edwin McCammon Martin, *Kennedy and Latin America* (Lanham, Md.: University Press of America, 1994), pp. 199–200.

103. Fidel Castro, "The Duty of a Revolutionary Is to Make the Revolution: The Second Declaration of Havana," in *Fidel Castro Speaks*, eds. Martin Kenner and James Petras (New York: Grove Press, 1969), p. 104. The first "Declaration of Havana," on September 2, 1960, was a strong denunciation of an August OAS resolution, approved at a foreign ministers meeting in San José, Costa Rica. The meeting rebuffed a U.S. effort to condemn Cuba and passed a watered down resolution that opposed—without mentioning specific countries—all intervention by non-American states in the affairs of the hemisphere. In the "Declaration of Havana," Castro proclaimed it "The duty of peasants, workers, intellectuals, Negroes, Indians, young and old, and women, to fight for their economic, political and social claims; the duty of oppressed and exploited nations to fight for their liberation; the duty of each nation to make common cause with all the oppressed, colonized, exploited or attacked peoples, regardless of their location in the world or the geographical distance that may separate them." See Fidel Castro, "Havana Declaration," FBIS Report Date 19680902, available through the University of Texas-LANIC, Castro Speeches Database. Also see Hugh Thomas, *The Cuban Revolution* (New York: Harper and Row, 1977), pp. 515, 517; Welch, *Response to Revolution*, pp. 55–56.

104. Domínguez, *To Make a World Safe for Revolution*, p. 28; Schlesinger, *Robert Kennedy and His Times*, pp. 580, 585; "Implications of Cuba's Renewed Campaign of Incitation to Violent Revolution in Latin America," November 12, 1963, *CMC Document Set*, Document No. 03170.

105. For a sustained and well documented thesis on why the United States, as an imperial power, could not accept the Cuban revolution, see Morley, *Imperial State and Revolution*, especially chapter 7.

106. Lévesque, *The USSR and the Cuban Revolution*, pp. 32–33, 40–41.

107. Khrushchev remarks in his memoirs that "from a tactical standpoint, it [Castro's declaration] didn't make much sense." Khrushchev, *Khrushchev Remembers*, p. 492. But Wayne Smith's analysis of Castro's reasoning, that it would have placed the Soviets in the awkward position of allowing a socialist country to be invaded by the United States, seems quite sensible. Smith, *The Closest of Enemies*, pp. 53–54. Also see Lévesque, *The USSR and the Cuban Revolution*, p. 32. In a 1985 interview Castro observed that in preparation for the Bay of Pigs invasion "I gave not only a military but a political response: I proclaimed the socialist nature of the Revolution. . . . Therefore, our people were fighting against the invasion organized by the United States and for socialism" (Frei Betto, *Fidel and Religion* [Havana: Publications Office of the Council of State, 1987], p. 229). Tad Szulc offers an alternative explanation in arguing that Castro had planned to announce in a May 1 speech that the Cuban revolution was a "socialist revolution," but that the circumstances of the impending invasion made an early announcement "logical." It aroused "patriotic passion" that would "make the new official ideology fully acceptable" (Szulc, *Fidel*, p. 548). Indeed, in the May Day speech Castro once again asserted the socialist nature of the revolution.

108. Jacques Lévesque argues that a significant indicator of the Soviet attitude is "that until April 11, 1962, *Pravda*'s basic articles and editorials on Cuba . . . carefully avoided using the word 'socialist' to describe the Cuban reality (*The USSR and the Cuban Revolution*, pp. 32–35; the quotation appears on p. 35). Also see Fursenko and Naftali, *One Hell of a Gamble*, pp. 160–61.

109. Quoted in Lévesque, *The USSR and the Cuban Revolution*, p. 36.

110. "Los Grandes Méritos de Lenin y Los Éxitos de la URSS," in Fidel Castro, *La Revolucion de Octubre y La Revolucion Cubana* (Havana, Cuba: Ediciones del Departamento de Orientación Revolucionaria del Comité Central del Partido Comunista de Cuba, 1977), p. 49.

111. Jorge I. Domínguez, *Cuba: Order and Revolution* (Cambridge, Mass.: Harvard University Press, 1978), pp. 210–11; Szulc, *Fidel*, p. 570.

112. "Fidel Castro Denounces Sectarianism" (Speech of March 26, 1962), Ministry of Foreign Relations, Republic of Cuba, Political Documents: 2, pp. 12, 16, 21, 23. Also see Sheldon B. Liss, *Fidel! Castro's Political and Social Thought* (Boulder, Colo.: Westview, 1994), pp. 23–24.

113. Blight et al., *Cuba on the Brink*, p. 206.

114. Blight et al., *Cuba on the Brink*, p. 198. Castro offered a similar explanation four months after the crisis ended in an interview with Claude Julien. He said that "because we were receiving important aid from the socialist camp we estimated that we could not slink away [from the offer of missiles]." He added then, "It was not to assure our own defense, but first to reinforce socialism at an international scale." Claude Julien, "Sept Heures avec M. Fidel Castro," *Le Monde*, March 22, 1963, p. 6 [translation by the authors].

115. Szulc, *Fidel*, p. 582.

116. Castro said in 1992 that, in terms *"primarily* of Latin America . . . becoming a military base would imply a very high political cost [emphasis his]." He added, "if the issue had been the defense of Cuba, we would have preferred not to have the missiles," but the Cuban leadership interpreted the Soviet request as "imperative to strengthen the socialist camp." Blight et al., *Cuba on the Brink*, p. 242.

117. "Fidel Castro's 23 October Interview," broadcast on Havana radio and television, *Foreign Broadcast Information Service*, Report Date, October 24, 1962; available at: http://lanic.utexas.edu/la/cb/cuba/castro/1962/19621024.

118. Guevara and Aragonés traveled to Moscow from August 27 to September 2, 1962, with the revised document. In 1989, in an interview and at a January 1989 conference in Moscow on the missile crisis sponsored by Harvard University's Center for Science and International Affairs,

Aragonés explained that the purpose of the trip was to obtain Soviet acquiescence to Fidel's changes in the agreement, and to urge the Soviets to make it public immediately. According to Aragonés, Khrushchev rejected their plea, and then promised that if the United States reacted aggressively to the missile emplacement, the Soviets would "send the Baltic fleet." Blight and Welch, *On the Brink*, pp. 333–34, 401. In 1992, Castro recalled that it was his brother, Raul, who brought back Khrushchev's promise to send the Baltic fleet in July 1962. See Blight et al., *Cuba on the Brink*, pp. 83–84. Khrushchev's promise was a hollow one, because the Baltic fleet at the time was ice-bound part of the year and would have been little threat to invading U.S. forces. But the Cuban leadership apparently understood the promise to be a metaphor for a Soviet military response.

119. Khrushchev, *Khrushchev Remembers*, pp. 493–94. Also see comments by Andrei Gromyko in 1989, in Allyn et al., *Back to the Brink*, p. 20, and analysis in Blight et al., *Cuba on Brink*, pp. 349–51.

120. Blight et al., *Cuba on the Brink*, p. 85. Also see Castro's secret speech, chapter 2, pp. 41–42. Notably in 1989 Castro's political acumen was endorsed implicitly by former National Security Adviser McGeorge Bundy who observed that "if [the Soviets] had raised the question [of deploying ballistic missiles to Cuba] in the relatively straightforward way that previous deployments had occurred . . . it would have been certainly different and more difficult for us in terms of any forceful action to undo that deployment" (Bruce J. Allyn, James G. Blight, and David A. Welch, eds., *Back to the Brink: Proceedings of the Moscow Conference on the Cuban Missile Crisis, January 27–28, 1989*, CSIA Occasional Paper No. 9 [Lanham, Md.: University Press of America, 1992], p. 20; also see Blight and Welch, *On the Brink*, pp. 28, 40, 240–48).

121. See text of 1968 speech in chapter 2, p.42. In 1984 Castro told Tad Szulc that "we really trusted that they [the Soviets], for their part, were acting with the knowledge of the entire situation. We did not have all the information to be able to make a complete evaluation of the situation." Szulc, *Fidel*, p. 583.

122. Blight et al., *Cuba on the Brink*, pp. 205–6. The Cuban version of the agreement is in chapter 2, pp. 36–39. The Soviet version is reprinted in Gribkov and Smith, *Operation ANADYR*, pp. 185–88. Also see Lechuga, *In the Eye of the Storm*, pp. 36–37.

123. "Dortícos en la ONU: En Defensa de Cuba," *Bohemia*, October 12, 1962, pp. 48ff; "Excerpts from Cuban President's Speech in the UN," *New York Times*, October 9, 1962, p. 14.

124. Theodore C. Sorensen, interview with the authors, April 13, 1992, New York City. Sorensen was Counselor to President John F. Kennedy, a position that thereafter would be called presidential chief of staff.

125. William D. Rogers, personal communication to the authors.

126. In 1989 Sergio del Valle reported that 270,000 people had been mobilized to fight (Allyn et al., *Back to the Brink*, p. 106). He later reported the precise number of military personnel as 269,203, and a total mobilization including the militia (Mass Defense or DP in the Spanish acronym) of 400,000 combatants (*Peligros y Principios*, p. 141). Also see Blight et al., *Cuba on the Brink*, p. 211.

127. Nikita S. Khrushchev, letter to Fidel Castro, October 23, 1962. Quoted (by Fidel Castro) in Blight et al., *Cuba on the Brink*, p. 213.

128. Fidel Castro, intervention at the January 1992 conference in Havana on the Cuban missile crisis. Quoted in Blight et al., *Cuba on the Brink*, p. 213.

129. "Fidel Castro's 23 October Interview," broadcast on Havana radio and television, *Foreign Broadcast Information Service*, Report Date, October 24, 1962.

130. This has been confirmed during many interviews done by the authors since 1989. See also Blight et al., *Cuba on the Brink*, p. 21, for an anecdote told by Ricardo Alarcon, now President of the Cuban National Assembly, about one of his humanities professors at the University of Havana, who despite his age, infirmity, and hostility to Fidel Castro marched down into the trenches "to be with his people at the moment of truth." In addition, see Edmundo Desnoes, *Memories of Underdevelopment*, trans. by the author (New York: New American Library, 1967). In this, one of Cuba's most famous novels of the early revolutionary period (made into an even more famous film with the same title), one can see in detail how Cubans coped with what they believed was their fate—oblivion, in October 1962. Near the end of the novel (p. 151), the protagonist and narrator says:

> The island seems to be covered with missiles all over. They'll brush us away, put us out, they're going to sink this alligator island into the bottom of the Caribbean. then the battleships will sail over us and say: "This is where Cuba used to be." And the waves, the tides, will sweep over the island that had sunk into the bottom of the sea.

131. Authors' interview with Juan Antonio Blanco in Havana in March 1990, when Blanco was a senior staff member of the Americas Department of the Central Committee of the Cuban Communist Party. It has been confirmed since then by many Cubans with similar memories.

132. Khrushchev, *Khrushchev Remembers: The Glasnost Tapes*, p. 177. Also see Blight et al., *Cuba on the Brink*, pp. 474–75. In a cable on October 28, 1962, Khrushchev advised Castro "not to be carried away by sentiment . . . to show patience, firmness and even more firmness. But we mustn't allow ourselves to be carried away by provocations, because the Pentagon's unbridled militarists . . . are trying to frustrate the agreement and provoke you into actions that could be used against you." Blight et al., *Cuba on the Brink*, pp. 482–83.

133. Castro read from the letter in his 1968 speech. See chapter 2, p. 55. The whole letter is reprinted in Blight et al., *Cuba on the Brink*, pp. 489–91, but the English translation there varies slightly from the text in chapter 2. The version in chapter 2 was translated from the original Spanish by the Office of the Cuban President. The version in *Cuba on the Brink* was taken from the English edition of *Granma International*, December 2, 1990. Cuba published the complete Spanish version in the daily *Granma* on November 23, 1990. Jorge Risquet, then a member of the Cuban Politburo, provided a detailed analysis of Castro's letters in 1991 that emphasized the tactical orientation of Castro's cables to Khrushchev. See Blight et al., *Cuba between the Superpowers*, pp. 85–88. In a 1991 interview Risquet added that Castro had been mindful of the way in which Stalin refused to believe the Germans were attacking in 1941, and so did not place his forces then on full alert. Castro, Risquet said, did not want Khrushchev to make the same sort of mistake. Also see Lechuga, *In the Eye of the Storm*, pp. 87–88.

134. "Cable from Soviet Foreign Minister Gromyko to USSR Ambassador to Cuba Alekseev, 27 October 1962," p. 291.

135. "Memorandum of Conversation: A. I. Mikoyan with Fidel Castro, Osvaldo Dorticós Torrado, Raul Castro, Ernesto Guevara, Emilio Aragones, and Carlos Rafael Rodriguez, 4 November 1962," *Cold War International History Project Bulletin*, no. 5 (spring 1995), p. 98. [Hereafter cited as "Mikoyan MemCon, November 4, 1962."] In 1992 Castro similarly remarked, "They could have informed us of the messages of the 26th and the 27th. There was time to do that." Blight et al., *Cuba on the Brink*, p. 214.

136. Fidel Castro, intervention at the January 1992 Havana conference on the Cuban missile crisis, in Blight, et al, *Cuba on the Brink;* p. 214 (emphasis in the original).

137. Jon Lee Anderson, *Che Guevara: A Revolutionary Life* (New York: Grove Press, 1997), p. 544; Thomas, *The Cuban Revolution*, p. 636; Matthews, *Revolution in Cuba*, p. 213. Immediately after the crisis, Castro even refused to see Soviet Ambassador Alekseev, with whom he had had a warm relationship. Khrushchev, *Khrushchev Remembers*, p. 500; Fursenko and Naftali, *One Hell of a Gamble*, pp. 288-89.

138. Castro declared that the only effective guarantee "that there will be no aggression against Cuba" would be: (1) a cessation of the U.S. economic embargo and U.S. pressure on other countries to cut commercial links to Cuba; (2) an end to U.S. subversive activities against Cuba, including the "organization of invasions by mercenaries" and "the infiltration of spies and saboteurs"; (3) "cessation of the piratical attacks" from bases in the United States and Puerto Rico; (4) an end to violations of Cuban airspace; (5) U.S. withdrawal from Guantanamo Naval Base. The Five Points were asserted in a letter from Cuba's permanent representative to the UN to UN Acting Secretary General U Thant, October 28, 1962. It is reprinted in Laurence Chang and Peter Kornbluh, eds., *The Cuban Missile Crisis, 1962* (New York: New Press, 1992), pp. 241-42. They were published the next day in Havana: "Fija Fidel Las Cinco Garantias Contra La Agresion a Cuba," *Revolucion*, October 29, 1962.

139. The transcript of their meeting is reprinted in "Nuestra Derecho a la Paz se Está Abriendo Paso en El Mundo," *Verde Olivo*, November 11, 1962, pp. 14-15. Also see "Summary of [U Thant's] Meeting with President Dorticós, Premier Castro and Foreign Minister Roa of Cuba," October 31, 1962, UN Archives Call Number: Dag 1/5.2.2.6.2:1, in *CMC Document Set*, Document No. 01747. Also see Lechuga, *In the Eye of the Storm*, pp. 122-32; del Valle Jiménez, *Peligros y Principios*, pp. 174-76; Brenner, "Thirteen Months: Cuba's Perspective on the Missile Crisis," pp. 201-2.

140. "Mikoyan MemCon, November 4, 1962," p. 95. For an elaboration of the Cuban position on inspections, see Lechuga, *In the Eye of the Storm*, chap. 8.

141. Carlos Rafael Rodriguez, who had been a leader of the PSP and in 1962 was head of the National Institute of Agrarian Reform, then returned to the issue of verification, and argued that if the Cubans allowed inspection of the ports, the United States would demand more, such as inspections of the interior of the country. Mikoyan responded: "The imperialists are not the point. Such a verification is necessary for us. If the imperialists protest we can send them to hell" ("Memorandum of Conversation: A. I. Mikoyan with Fidel Castro, Osvaldo Dorticós, Raul Castro, Ernesto Guevara and Carlos Rafael Rodriguez, 5 November 1962," *Cold War International History Project Bulletin*, no. 5 (spring 1995), pp. 103-4. The Cuban notes on this meeting are available as "Document II: Mikoyan and Cuban Leadership, Havana, 5 November 1962," *Cold War International History Project Bulletin*, no. 6 (winter 1996/1997), pp. 342-43. Also see "Mikoyan MemCon, November 12, 1962," p. 191.

142. "The President's News Conference of November 20, 1962," in *CMC Document Set*, Document No. 02493. On December 14 the president wrote to Khrushchev that "we have never wanted to be driven by the acts of others into war in Cuba. The other side of the coin, however, is that we do need to have adequate assurances that all offensive weapons are removed from Cuba and are not reintroduced." See *Problems of Communism*, spring 1992, p. 118. In 1970 the Nixon administration offered a new U.S. promise to the Soviets not to invade Cuba, in the form of a restatement of the 1962 pledge with fewer conditions. See Brenner, "Kennedy and Khrushchev on Cuba," p. 25.

143. Lechuga, *In the Eye of the Storm*, pp. 139-44.

144. "A. I. Mikoyan to CC CPSU re. 1 November 1962 Meeting with Stevenson, 2 November 1962," *Cold War International History Project Bulletin*, no. 6 (winter 1996/1997), pp. 314–15.

145. Blight et al., *Cuba on the Brink*, p. 297. Notably in January 1963 Kennedy approved the creation of special office in the State Department ("Coordinator of Cuban Affairs") to orchestrate policy decisions and recommend "new courses of action" with respect to Cuba. At about the same time the Defense Department recommended increasing political, economic, psychological, and military pressure against Cuba (Schlesinger, *Robert Kennedy and His Times*, p. 580). The State Department Coordinator reported in mid-April that the "present covert policy in Cuba" included: support for "the efforts of certain Cuban exiles . . . who believe the Castro regime can be overthrown from within"; "placing of incendiary devices and/or explosives with suitable time delay within the hull or cargo to disable or sink Cuban vessels"; "introducing abrasives or other damaging materials into the propulsion, communication and other systems of the ship" ("Memorandum From the Coordinator of Cuban Affairs [Cottrell] to the Special Group,"*FRUS*, *1961–1963*, vol. XI, Document No. 318, April 18, 1963, pp. 769–70). In May the Joint Chiefs of Staff recommended to the president that support for the counterrevolutionaries should include U.S. air attacks on Cuban air defense systems ("Course of Action Related to Cuba," Internal Paper JCSM-360-63, May 10, 1963, in *CMC Document Set*, Document No. 03103).

On June 19 the president authorized the CIA to support a limited program of "hit-and-run attacks against appropriately selected targets" in Cuba, and this was extended in the fall of 1963 to include operations in Cuba such as the sabotage of an electric power plant, an oil refinery and a sugar mill ("Alleged Assassination Plots Involving Foreign Leaders," p. 173; Desmond Fitzgerald, "Memorandum for the Record," *FRUS, 1961–1963*, vol. XI, Document No. 348, June 19, 1963, pp. 837–38; "Paper Prepared by the Central Intelligence Agency for the Standing Group of the National Security Agency: Proposed Covert Policy and Integrated Program of Action towards Cuba,"*FRUS, 1961–1963*, vol. XI, Document No. 346, June 8, 1963, pp. 828–34). Also see "Memorandum from the Chief, Special Affairs Staff, Central Intelligence Agency (FitzGerald) to the President's Special Assistant for National Security Affairs (Bundy), *FRUS, 1961–1963*, vol. XI, Document No. 357, August 9, 1963; Blight and Kornbluh, *Politics of Illusion*, pp. 121–23; Felix I. Rodriguez and John Weisman, *Shadow Warrior* (New York: Simon and Schuster, 1989), pp. 119–25; Morley, *Imperial State and Revolution*, pp. 152–53, Fursenko and Naftali, *One Hell of a Gamble*, pp. 327–28; del Valle Jiménez, *Peligros y Principios*, pp. 204–7.

146. Reprinted in Garthoff, *Reflections on the Cuban Missile Crisis*, p. 216. In a similar vein, a November 14, 1962 Defense Department review of the lessons from the crisis asserted that the Soviets withdrew the missiles because they "saw they were going to face conflict in Cuba and lose" (Chang and Kornbluh, *The Cuban Missile Crisis*, Document 81, p. 310).

147. James A. Nathan, "The Heyday of the New Strategy: The Cuban Missile Crisis and the Confirmation of Coercive Diplomacy," in Nathan, *The Cuban Missile Crisis Revisited*, p. 26.

148. Richard Ned Lebow, "The Traditional and Revisionist Interpretations Reevaluated: Why Was Cuba a Crisis?" in Nathan, *The Cuban Missile Crisis Revisited*, p. 178. Also see Schlesinger, *A Thousand Days*, p. 797; Allison, *Essence of Decision*, p. 231; Richard Ned Lebow, *Nuclear Crisis Management, A Dangerous Illusion* (Ithaca, N.Y.: Cornell University Press, 1987), p. 138.

149. James A. Nathan, "The Missile Crisis: His Finest Hour Now," *World Politics*, vol. 27, no. 2 (January 1975), p. 269.

150. May and Zelikow, *The Kennedy Tapes*, pp. 393–409; "Department of Defense Operations during the Cuban Missile Crisis," February 12, 1963, in *CMC Document Set*, Document No. 02925, p. 4.

151. Kennedy, *Thirteen Days*, pp. 127–28.

152. "Dobrynin's Cable to the Soviet Foreign Ministry, 27 October 1962," pp. 79–80; James Hershberg, "Anatomy of a Controversy: Anatoly F. Dobrynin's Meeting with Robert F. Kennedy, Saturday, 27 October 1962," in *Cold War International History Project Bulletin*, no. 5 (spring 1995), pp. 75, 77–78; Lebow and Stein, *We All Lost the Cold War*, pp. 120–25.

In a letter to James Blight in 1987, former secretary of state Dean Rusk revealed that on October 27 Kennedy

> instructed me to telephone the late Andrew Cordier, then at Columbia University [Cordier was Dean of Columbia's School of Business and had been UN parliamentarian], and dictate to him a statement which would be made by U Thant . . . proposing the removal of both the Jupiters and the missiles in Cuba. Mr. Cordier was to put that statement in the hands of U Thant only after further signal from us (reprinted in Blight and Welch, *On the Brink*, pp. 83–84).

In effect, Kennedy was giving himself an option to avoid an attack on Cuba, a way of satisfying the Soviet demand for a missile trade without seeming to bow to a Soviet ultimatum. Also see Blight and Welch, *On the Brink*, pp. 113–15; David A. Welch and James G. Blight, "The Eleventh Hour of the Cuban Missile Crisis: An Introduction to the ExComm Transcripts," *International Security*, vol. 12, no. 3 (winter 1987/1988), pp. 5–29; Lebow and Stein, *We All Lost the Cold War*, pp. 127–29; Rusk, *As I Saw It*, pp. 240–41; Mark J. White, "Dean Rusk's Revelation: New British Evidence on the Cordier Ploy," *Newsletter*, Society for Historians of American Foreign Relations, September 1994.

153. James A. Nathan, *Anatomy of the Cuban Missile Crisis* (Westport, Conn.: Greenwood Press, 2001), pp. 95–100, 118–19; Lebow and Stein, *We All Lost the Cold War*, pp. 14, 120–30, 320–22; Nathan, "The Missile Crisis," p. 280.

154. Schlesinger, *A Thousand Days*, p. 841.

155. Vladislav Zubok and Constantine Pleshakov (*Inside the Kremlin's Cold War*, pp. 260–61) provide an example of how Khrushchev resisted pressure to expand Soviet objectives during the crisis when the Soviet Deputy Foreign Minister proposed using Berlin as a lever to end the confrontation. They quote the Soviet leader as responding: "We are here trying to get ourselves out of this *avantyura* [reckless gamble] and now you are pulling us into another one."

156. Robert S. McNamara and James G. Blight, *Wilson's Ghost: Reducing the Risk of Conflict, Killing, and Catastrophe in the 21st Century* (New York: Public Affairs, 2001), p. 191. For other critiques, see Lebow, *Nuclear Crisis Management*; Scott Sagan, *The Limits of Safety: Organizations, Accidents and Nuclear Safety* (Princeton, N.J.: Princeton University Press, 1993). In 1987 Dean Rusk similarly commented:

> A major lesson both for us and for the Russians is that we have to do what we can to prevent such crises from arising, because they're just too damn dangerous. That impression is not automatically passed along from one generation [of policymakers] to the next (Blight and Welch, *On the Brink*, p. 180).

157. Nathan, "The Missile Crisis," p. 273; Lebow and Stein, *We All Lost the Cold War*, p. 359; Ulam, *Expansion and Coexistence*, p. 630; Garthoff, *Reflections on the Cuban Missile Crisis*, pp. 182–83.

158. Blight, *The Shattered Crystal Ball*, pp. 6–9.

159. Kennedy seems to have drawn the lesson from this experience that it was imperative for the two superpowers to work out their differences peacefully, rather than to confront each other. His call for arms control negotiations and a new approach to superpower relations in a 1963

commencement address at American University is evidence of the impact the crisis had on him. Blight, *The Shattered Crystal Ball*, p. 144; Garthoff, *Reflections on the Cuban Missile Crisis*, pp. 132, 161; Beschloss, *The Crisis Years*, pp. 597-600.

160. Mark Kramer, "The 'Lessons' of the Cuban Missile Crisis for Warsaw Pact Nuclear Operations," in *Cold War International History Project Bulletin*, no. 5 (spring 1995), p. 110. Also see Garthoff, *Reflections on the Cuban Missile Crisis*, p. 184.

161. Garthoff, *Reflections on the Cuban Missile Crisis*, p. 181. Also see Richter, *Khrushchev's Double Bind*, p. 194.

162. Lechuga, *In the Eye of the Storm*, pp. 186-90.

163. "Mikoyan MemCon, November 12, 1962," pp. 194-95.

164. The Soviets called the troops that it left behind a "motorized rifle unit." It was "something between a regiment and division," former General Anatoli I. Gribkov said in 1994. "We didn't call it a brigade because we didn't want it to be provocative. We left it in Cuba for symbolic purposes, to show a Soviet presence in Cuba" (authors' interview with Gribkov, April 5, 1994, in Washington, D.C.). But according to notes from a conversation between Castro and Khrushchev in 1963, Khrushchev was reluctant to maintain Soviet troops on the island. It was the Cuban leader who asserted that the brigade would serve as a kind of trip-wire to deter U.S. aggression, "like the celebrated missiles. So long as they are there," Castro remarked, "American military circles are convinced that an attack on Cuba would inevitably lead to war with the Soviet Union" (quoted in Fursenko and Naftali, *One Hell of a Gamble*, p. 332).

165. Blight et al., *Cuba on the Brink*, pp. 224-25.

CHAPTER 2

1. The Cuban Missile Crisis is known in Cuba as the "October Crisis." In the former Soviet Union it was called the "Caribbean Crisis."

2. Castro asked for weapons in a letter to Nikita Khrushchev in September 1961 and the Soviets agreed to provide a long list of armaments, including surface-to-air missiles. But by December 1961 the Soviets had not shipped any of the promised items (Aleksandr Fursenko and Timothy Naftali, *One Hell of a Gamble: Khrushchev, Castro, and Kennedy, 1958-1964* [New York: W. W. Norton, 1997], pp. 139-40, 146).

The Cuban sense of a U.S. threat derived from two sources. First, the Cuban leadership believed that the United States would not accept the April 1961 defeat at the Bay of Pigs without trying to overthrow the Cuban government again. Second, it had evidence that the United States was trying to overthrow the Cuban government through a plan called Operation Mongoose. Operation Mongoose was a multifaceted program to destabilize the Cuban government. It was authorized by President Kennedy on November 30, 1961. The first face was political isolation, and the United States pursued this in part by pressuring Latin American countries to suspend Cuba's membership in the Organization of American States in January 1962. The second was economic, and, in February 1962, the United States formalized its unilateral economic embargo against Cuba, and encouraged U.S. allies to cut trade with Cuba. Finally, there was a so-called low intensity war against Cuba that envisioned a U.S. military invasion as the final blow. The low intensity war was intended to include the sabotage of tractors, factories and machinery; the burning of fields; the contamination of sugar awaiting export; and the resupply of anti-Castro guerrillas who engaged in terror tactics throughout the island. There was also an associated though independent operation to assassinate Fidel Castro. The CIA station in Miami out of which Operation Mongoose was run cost $50 million to $60 million a year, according to Sam Halpern, deputy to CIA Deputy Director for Operations and the principal CIA official overseeing the operation. This figure, however, did not account for any funds spent by the more than 30 other agencies involved. (Halpern's remarks were made on May 31, 1996 at a conference on the Bay of Pigs at Musgrove Plantation, Georgia, sponsored by Brown University.) Mongoose was the largest CIA covert operation undertaken until that time. See Laurence Chang and Peter Kornbluh, *The Cuban Missile Crisis, 1962: A National Security Archive Documents Reader* (New York: New Press, 1992), Documents 5 (pp. 23–37), 7 (pp. 40–47), 9 (pp. 52–53); Select Committee to Study Governmental Operations with Respect to Intelligence Activities, *Alleged Assassination Plots Involving Foreign Leaders*, An Interim Report, no. 94-465, U.S. Senate, 94th Cong., 1st Sess., 20 November 1975, pp. 139–149; Arthur M. Schlesinger, Jr., *Robert Kennedy and His Times* (New York: Ballantine Books, 1978), pp. 513–527; James G. Blight and Peter Kornbluh, *Politics of Illusion: The Bay of Pigs Reexamined* (Boulder, CO: Lynne Rienner, 1998), chapter 5.

While there is evidence that considerable terrorist activity did occur in 1962—in 1991, Gen. Fabian Escalante Font cited "5,700 acts of terrorism, sabotage, and murder"—it is not clear if the activities of the guerrillas were actually Mongoose directed. Cuban officials, nonetheless, perceived them as part of the same plan. See James G. Blight, David Lewis and David A. Welch, eds., *Cuba Between the Superpowers, Antigua, 3–7 January, 1991: Transcript of the Meetings* (Providence, RI: Center for Foreign Policy Development of the Thomas J. Watson Jr. Institute for International Studies, Brown University, 1991), p. 11; Fabian Escalante Font, *CUBA: la guerra secreta de la CIA* (Havana: Editorial Capitán San Luis, 1993), chapter 7; Richard Helms, "Memorandum for the Record, 'MONGOOSE Meeting with the Attorney General'," 16 October 1962," *CIA Documents on the Cuban Missile Crisis, 1962*, ed., Mary S. McAuliffe, HRP: 92-9 (Washington, D.C.: Central Intelligence Agency, 1992), Document 49, pp. 153–154; "Covert Activities," A Memorandum from "William K. Harvey, CIA Representative for Operation Mongoose," August 7, 1962, p. 5 (available from the National Security Archive, Washington, D.C.); Fursenko and Naftali, *One Hell of a Gamble*, p. 159.

A contrasting assessment of the importance of Mongoose is offered by Domingo Amuchastegui, a former Cuban intelligence analyst now living in the United States. He argues that the Cuban intelligence community discounted the possibility of a U.S. invasion, despite the terrorist activities, because of the lack of international support for such an action and the likely casualty toll. But, he asserts, the Cuban leadership dismissed such assessments because it believed "the United States would not be satisfied until it had exacted its revenge [for the Bay of Pigs] and destroyed the Cuban Revolution" (Domingo Amuchastegui, "Cuban Intelligence and the October Crisis," in *Intelligence and the Cuban Missile Crisis*, eds. James G. Blight and David A. Welch [London: Frank Cass, 1998], p. 97).

3. Marshal Sergei S. Biryuzov, Soviet deputy defense minister and commander of the Soviet strategic rocket forces, headed the delegation.

4. Notably, on October 23, 1962—the day after President Kennedy announced the presence of Soviet missiles in Cuba—the Organization of American States, at the private urging of the United States, approved a resolution calling for the immediate withdrawal of the missiles. It recommended individual and collective measures, including the use of force to stop military shipments to Cuba.

5. Castro acknowledged in later interviews that defense of the island also was a motivation for accepting the missile proposal. See Tad Szulc, *Fidel: A Critical Portrait* (New York: William Morrow, 1986), p. 580; Frank Mankiewicz and Kirby Jones, *With Fidel: A Portrait of Castro and Cuba* (New York: Ballantine, 1975), p. 152.

6. The six members of the Secretariat of the Integrated Revolutionary Organizations (ORI) were Prime Minister Fidel Castro Ruz, Minister of Defense Raul Castro Ruz, Minister of Industry Ernesto ("Che") Guevara de la Serna, Secretary of the Central Committee Emilio Aragonés Navarro, Cuban President Osvaldo Dorticós Torrado, and Chair of the ORI Blas Roca.

7. Guevara and Aragonés traveled to Moscow from August 27 to September 2, 1962, with the revised document.

8. Rodion Y. Malinovsky, Soviet Defense Minister. Raul Castro had drafted the original version with Malinovsky during a two-week trip to the Soviet Union in the first half of July 1962 (Raymond L. Garthoff, *Reflections on the Cuban Missile Crisis*, rev. ed. [Washington, D.C.: Brookings Institution, 1989], p. 17; Carlos Lechuga, *In the Eye of the Storm: Castro, Khrushchev, Kennedy and the Missile Crisis*, trans. Mary Todd [Melbourne, Australia: Ocean Press, 1995], pp. 36–37).

9. The missile crisis intervened to cancel plans for Khrushchev's visit. He never did travel to Cuba. At the urging of the Soviet leader, Castro traveled to the Soviet Union in April and May 1963.

10. Article 51 of the United Nations Charter states: "Nothing in the present Charter shall impair the inherent right of individual or collective self-defense if an armed attack occurs against a Member of the United Nations, until the Security Council has taken measures necessary to maintain international peace and security. Measures taken by Members in the exercise of this right of self-defense shall be immediately reported to the Security Council and shall not in any way affect the authority and responsibility of the Security Council under the present Charter to take at any time such action as it deems necessary in order to maintain or restore international peace and security."

11. The dates were never filled in. For the Soviet version, see Anatoli I. Gribkov and William Y. Smith, *Operation ANADYR: U.S. and Soviet Generals Recount the Cuban Missile Crisis* (Chicago: edition q, 1994), pp. 185–88.

12. The ministers were Raul Castro Ruz and Rodion Y. Malinovksy.

13. The club was located on the outskirts of Havana.

14. Soviet military experts had calculated that the missiles could be camouflaged by the "dense palm tree forests" in Cuba. In fact, palm trees do not grow in dense forests, and Cuban palm trees bear little resemblance to Soviet missiles. See Gribkov and Smith, *Operation ANADYR*, pp. 39–40; Blight et al., *Cuba between the Superpowers*, pp. 77, 153.

15. After a high flying U.S. reconnaissance plane, a U-2, was shot down over the Soviet Union in 1960, President Eisenhower curtailed the U-2 surveillance program. President Kennedy, at the recommendation of Secretary of State Dean Rusk, was reluctant to make much use of the U-2 over the territory of other countries because of the possible political repercussions were another U-2 to be hit by a surface-to-air missile (SAM). But he authorized a U-2 flight over Cuba on August 29, 1962, to determine the nature of the Soviet military buildup on the island. A second flight was made on September 5. Both missions, however, were unable to gain clear photos of the Cuban interior, and the CIA urged the president to permit more missions. But only flights made on the periphery of Cuban airspace—actually twenty-five miles from shore—were approved. It was not until October 14, 1962, that the CIA sent up another flight directly over Cuba, and that one photographed the medium range ballistic missile sites. The pilot of that plane, Major Rudolph Anderson, Jr. was killed on October 27, 1962, when his U-2 was shot down over Cuba by a Soviet SAM. See Dino A. Brugioni, *Eyeball to Eyeball: The Inside Story of the Cuban Missile Crisis* (New York: Random House, 1991), pp. 103–4, 116–17, 135–45, 163–64; James G. Blight, Bruce J. Allyn, and

David A. Welch, *Cuba on the Brink: Castro, the Missile Crisis, and the Soviet Collapse*, enlarged paperback ed. (Lanham, Md: Rowman & Littlefield, 2002), pp. 101–14; Garthoff, *Reflections on the Cuban Missile Crisis*, pp. 42, 82–85; Graham Allison and Philip Zelikow, *Essence of Decision: Explaining the Cuban Missile Crisis*, 2nd ed. (New York: Longman, 1999), pp. 335–37.

16. Presumably this is a reference to General Issa Alexandrovich Pliyev, the commander of Soviet forces on the island.

17. The Soviet plan called for three sites for launching medium range ballistic missiles (MRBMs) and two sites for intermediate range ballistic missiles (IRBMs), with twelve missiles (eight launchers) at each site. In addition, the Soviets intended to deploy twelve decoy missiles, for a total of seventy-two ballistic (ground-to-ground) missiles in all. There also were twenty-four SAM complexes with six missiles each, and two cruise missile regiments with eighty missiles at each. None of the IRBMs were delivered to Cuba. By October 28, eighteen of the MRBMs were operational (Gribkov and Smith, *Operation ANADYR*, pp. 26–27, 169). The CIA estimated on October 22 that twenty-three of the twenty-four SAM sites were operational ("Supplement 3 to Joint Evaluation of Soviet Missile Threat in Cuba," October 22, 1962, in McAuliffe, *CIA Documents on the Cuban Missile Crisis*, Document No. 81, p. 281).

18. Castro had ordered a state of full alert early in the afternoon of October 22 upon learning that Kennedy would be making a major address at 7:00 P.M. that evening (Sergio del Valle Jiménez, ed., *Peligros y Principios: La Crisis de Octubre desde Cuba* [Havana, Cuba: Editora Verde Olivo, 1992], p. 140).

19. In addition to Operation Mongoose, the United States had begun military exercises in the Caribbean in the spring of 1962. Most prominent were "Lantphibex 1-62" and "Quick Kick," each of which involved approximately 40,000 troops. Lantphibex 1-62 included a practice invasion of Vieques, an island off the coast of Puerto Rico, with a force of 10,000 troops. See Garthoff, *Reflections on the Cuban Missile Crisis*, p. 6; James G. Hershberg, "Before the 'Missiles of October': Did Kennedy Plan a Military Strike against Cuba?" in *The Cuban Missile Crisis Revisited*, ed. James A. Nathan (New York: St. Martin's, 1992), p. 250; "Report of the Commander in Chief U.S. Atlantic Fleet upon Being Relieved," Serial 00308/J101A, April 30, 1963, Document No. 03088; and "Major Exercise Report, Quick Kick," Serial 03A24862, September 20, 1962, Document No. 00431, both in Laurence Chang, ed., *The Cuban Missile Crisis, 1962*, A National Security Archive Document Set (Alexandria, Va.: Chadwyck-Healey, 1990) [hereafter referred to as *CMC Document Set*].

There also was a political hysteria about Cuba developing in the U.S. Congress to which Castro may have been alluding. In speeches and hearings, several Republican senators and representatives held hearings and made speeches about the growing military presence in Cuba. Most important were the charges by Senators Kenneth Keating (R-NY) and Homer Capehart (R-IN), which asserted there were Soviet ballistic missiles in Cuba. In mid-September, Keating along with several other leading Senate Republicans called for a blockade of Cuba. See Schlesinger, *Robert Kennedy and His Times*, p. 545; Garthoff, *Reflections on the Cuban Missile Crisis*, p. 31, Lechuga, *In the Eye of the Storm*, pp. 38–41.

20. For example, Khrushchev asserted in his October 23 response to Kennedy's public address about the missiles that "We confirm that armaments now on Cuba, regardless of classification to which they belong, are destined exclusively for defensive purposes, in order to secure Cuban Republic [sic] from attack of aggressor." In a letter to Kennedy on October 26, 1962, he stated: "All the means located there, and I assure you of this, have a defensive character, are on Cuba solely for the purposes of defense." *Problems of Communism*, Special Edition, vol. 41, spring 1992, pp. 32, 39.

21. At the 1992 Havana Conference, Castro remarked that "Not only was it a mistake to deploy the missiles secretly, . . . but it was a mistake to give Kennedy false information, having gotten into the game of the character of the weapons: whether they were offensive or defensive. . . . We refused to play that game, and in the public statements of the government, and then at the UN, we always said that Cuba considered that it had the sovereign right to have the kind of weapons it considered convenient." Blight et al., *Cuba on the Brink*, p. 350. Notably in 1989, former National Security Adviser McGeorge Bundy observed that "if [the Soviets] had raised the question [of deploying ballistic missiles to Cuba] in the relatively straightforward way that previous deployments had occurred . . . it would have been certainly different and more difficult for us in terms of any forceful action to undo that deployment" (Bruce J. Allyn, James G. Blight, and David A. Welch, eds., *Back to the Brink: Proceedings of the Moscow Conference on the Cuban Missile Crisis, January 27-28, 1989*, CSIA Occasional Paper No. 9 [Lanham, Md.: University Press of America, 1992], p. 20; also see Blight and Welch, *On the Brink*, pp. 28, 40, 240-48).

22. See note 7. In 1989, in an interview, and at a January 1989 conference in Moscow on the missile crisis, sponsored by Harvard University's Center for Science and International Affairs, Aragonés explained that the purpose of the trip was to obtain Soviet acquiescence to Fidel's changes in the agreement, and to urge the Soviets to make the agreement public immediately. According to Aragonés, Khrushchev rejected their plea, and then promised that if the United States reacted aggressively to the missile emplacement, the Soviets would "send the Baltic fleet." James G. Blight and David A. Welch, *On the Brink: Americans and Soviets Reexamine the Cuban Missile Crisis*, 2nd ed. (New York: Farrar, Straus and Giroux, 1990), pp. 334, 401; Allyn et al., *Back to the Brink*, pp. 123-124.

In 1992 Fidel Castro recalled that it was his brother, Raul, who brought back in July 1962 Khrushchev's promise to send the Baltic fleet (Blight et al., *Cuba on the Brink*, pp. 83-84). Khrushchev's promise was a hollow one, because the Baltic fleet at the time was ice-bound part of the year and would have been little threat to invading U.S. forces. But the Cuban leadership apparently understood the promise to be a metaphor for a Soviet military response.

23. On October 3, 1962 President Kennedy signed S.J. Res. 230 (Public Law 87-733). It stated that the United States "is determined to prevent by whatever means may be necessary, including the use of arms, the Marxist-Leninist regime in Cuba from extending, by force or the threat of force, its aggressive or subversive activities to any part of this hemisphere."

24. The Soviet spelling is Biryuzov. See note 3.

25. Sharaf R. Rashidov was an alternate member of the Presidium of the Central Committee of the Communist Party of Uzbekistan. He also was a candidate to the Presidium of the Communist Party of the Soviet Union. He was selected to head the delegation presumably to give credibility to the cover story that this was an agricultural mission (Fursenko and Naftali, *One Hell of a Gamble*, p. 181).

26. Dr. Osvaldo Dorticós Torrado was president of Cuba in 1962 and 1968.

27. This is the how the Cuban leadership referred to Soviet ambassador to Cuba Aleksandr Alekseev, who arrived in Cuba as ambassador on June 11, 1962. The Cuban ambassador to the Soviet Union, who arrived there on May 17, 1962, was Dr. Carlos Olivares Sanchez.

28. *Gusanos* is the term that the Cuban leadership used in referring to Cubans who exiled themselves or who sought to leave Cuba. It means *worms*.

29. Raymond L. Garthoff explains that the intelligence community discounted these kinds of reports because "there were literally thousands of reports of missiles in Cuba in the period *before* [emphasis in original] any missiles were actually brought there" ("U.S. Intelligence in the Cuban Missile Crisis," in Blight and Welch, *Intelligence and the Cuban Missile Crisis*, p. 22).

30. In Khrushchev's memoirs, he claims that he first thought about deploying missiles to Cuba on a visit to Bulgaria in 1962. See Nikita S. Khrushchev, *Khrushchev Remembers*, ed. Strobe Talbott (Boston: Little, Brown, 1970), pp. 493–94. Also see Blight and Welch, *On the Brink*, pp. 235-36, 238, 295.

31. The reference here is obscure. It may have been Carlos Rafael Rodríguez, who in 1962 was president of the National Institute of Agrarian Reform. Rodriguez was one of the few leaders of the Popular Socialist Party (which had been the communist party of Cuba before 1959) who became an official in the Revolutionary government, and he served at times as a trusted emissary to the Soviet Union. He traveled to the Soviet Union in December 1962 and met with Khrushchev. The reference also might be to the Cuban ambassador to the Soviet Union, Carlos Olivares.

32. See note 17.

33. Mariel is a port near Havana. The matter of a creating a Soviet submarine base in Cuba became an issue in 1970, when it appeared that the Soviets were beginning to construct such a base at Cienfuegos. Relying on the so-called Kennedy–Khrushchev agreement that ended the missile crisis, Henry Kissinger, who was then national security adviser, pressured the Soviets to abandon construction of the base. See Henry Kissinger, *White House Years* (Boston: Little, Brown, 1979), pp. 632-52. Also Raymond L. Garthoff, *Détente and Confrontation: American-Soviet Relations from Nixon to Reagan*, rev. ed. (Washington, D.C.: Brookings Institution, 1994), pp. 87-95.

34. Dorticós made his speech on October 8, 1962. In it he asserted

the guiding motive of the foreign policy of the United States regarding Cuba is clearly and obviously that of overthrowing the Revolutionary Government of Cuba.... This is taking place in the middle of, and surrounded by, a press, radio and television campaign that fills the political stage of the United States with a warlike hysteria. Together with this, there are the reiterated and insolent and insulting statements made by Senators and Representatives.... Because of this joint resolution [S.J. Res. 230— see note 23]... the United States Government is calling up reservists and intends to train Cuban contingents, within the regular United States army, to be used against the Cuban government.... What can we say about this? We can say that Cuba has armed itself. We have a right to arm ourselves, to defend ourselves.... We have armed ourselves against our will, against our better nature, because we were forced to.... Otherwise we should be jeopardizing and undermining the sovereignty of our country... ..We have armed because the Cuban people has the legitimate right, given to it by history itself, to defend its sovereign decisions.... Furthermore, we are not obliged by anyone or anything to explain to the Congress of the United Nations [sic] what we do to defend our territorial integrity.... [If] we are attacked, we will defend ourselves. I repeat, we have sufficient means with which to defend ourselves; we have indeed our inevitable weapons, the weapons which we would have preferred not to acquire and which we do not wish to employ.

("Address by His Excellency Dr. Osvaldo Dorticós," UN General Assembly, Provisional Verbatim Record of the 1145th Plenary Meeting, October 8, 1962 [A/PV.1145], *CMC Document Set*, Document No. 00542, pp. 20, 31, 36, 47. Translated by the United Nations. The Spanish text is reprinted in *Bohemia* [Havana, Cuba], October 12, 1962, pp. 48-71, 74.)

35. In 1989 Sergio del Valle reported that 270,000 people had been mobilized to fight (Allyn et al., *Back to the Brink*, p. 106); he later reported the precise number of military personnel as 269,203, and a total mobilization including the militia (Mass Defense or DP in the Spanish acronym) of 400,000 combatants (del Valle Jiménez, *Peligros y Principios*, p. 141).

36. On October 22, 1962, Kennedy sent a letter to Khrushchev, accompanied by the text of his television address in which he revealed the discovery of the missiles and announced the

quarantine. In the letter, the U.S. president recalled that "I publicly stated that if certain developments in Cuba took place, the United States would do whatever must be done to protect its own security and that of its allies. . . . Despite this, the rapid development of long-range missile bases and other offensive weapon systems in Cuba has proceeded. I must tell you that the United States is determined that this threat to the security of this hemisphere be removed" (*Problems of Communism*, Special Edition, vol. 41, spring 1992, pp. 30–31).

37. The Soviet ambassador, Valerian A. Zorin, was president of the Security Council for the month of October 1962. Notably, though Cuba was not a member of the Security Council, Cuba's ambassador to the United Nations, Mario García Incháustegui, was invited to attend the emergency session of the Security Council from October 23 to October 25.

38. *New York Times*, October 24, 1962, p. 25 provides excerpts of the statements by Zorin, García Incháustegui, and U.S. Ambassador Adlai E. Stevenson. Also see del Valle Jiménez, *Peligros y Principios*, pp. 157–58. The Council did not act on any of the proposed resolutions, and following the emergency session, Acting Secretary General U Thant called on the United States, the Soviet Union, and Cuba to resolve the crisis peacefully by suspending simultaneously for two to three weeks arms shipments to Cuba and the naval quarantine, in order to facilitate negotiations. Thomas J. Hamilton, "UN Sends Notes: Talks Proposed while Both Shipments and Blockade Cease," *New York Times*, October 25, 1962, p. 1.

39. For details of the mobilization, see del Valle Jiménez, *Peligros y Principios*, pp. 140–46.

40. The chief of staff of the Cuban army was Sergio del Valle Jiménez.

41. At the 1992 Havana conference, Gen. Anatoli Gribkov revealed publicly for the first time that the Soviets had brought tactical nuclear missiles ("Lunas") to Cuba during the crisis. There were twelve Lunas on the island, each of which was capable of traveling twenty-five to thirty-one miles with a nuclear warhead that was the equivalent of 2,000 pounds of TNT. Blight et al., *Cuba on the Brink*, pp. 58–61. Also see Gribkov and Smith, *Operation ANADYR*, pp. 4–7; Fursenko and Naftali, *One Hell of a Gamble*, pp. 211–12. The U.S. military designated the Lunas as FROG (Free Rocket Over Ground) missiles, and the Navy was aware of the Lunas during the crisis, though it did not know that they were configured to carry a nuclear warhead. See "Current Intelligence Weekly Review: Soviet Military Forces in Cuba," *CMC Document Set*, Document No. 02359, November 16, 1962; "Secretary of Defense's Report for the Congress," Document No. 02795, December 29, 1962; and *CINCLANT Historical Account of Cuban Crisis—1963*, Serial: 000119/J09H, April 29, 1963 [Hereafter referred to as *CINCLANT Historical Account*], Document No. 003087, pp. 12–13. Also see "Supplement 7 to Joint Evaluation of Soviet Missile Threat in Cuba," October 27, 1962, in McAuliffe, *CIA Documents on the Cuban Missile Crisis*, no. 98, p. 325.

42. Low altitude reconnaissance, in contrast to the U-2s that flew at 70,000 feet, was necessary for the detailed surveillance that an invasion would require. The low level reconnaissance was conducted by F8-U Crusader photographic aircraft. Between October 23 and November 15, 1962 "more than 80 sorties composed of from 2 to 10 aircraft totaled more than 100 hours of photographic surveillance," according to a Department of Defense News Release. See *CMC Document Set*, Document No. 02628 ("Actions of Military Services in Cuban Crisis Outlined," Press Release No. 1942–62, November 29, 1962).

43. General Gribkov reports that in July 1962 Khrushchev had mandated that the nuclear weapons in Cuba could be fired only on a direct order from Moscow. However, he explains, "Khrushchev saw tactical atomic weapons, meant for the battlefield, in a different light. With their short ranges and low yields, such arms apparently did not carry, in his mind, much risk of drawing an overwhelming retaliation." In effect, the Soviet generals in Cuba believed they had author-

ity to use the tactical nuclear weapons until October 22. A few hours before Kennedy's speech on October 22, Soviet Defense Minister Malinovsky "withdrew the authority Khrushchev had delegated in July" by ordering Soviet forces to "take immediate steps to raise combat readiness and to repulse the enemy together with the Cuban army and with all the power of the Soviet forces, except [ballistic missiles and tactical nuclear missiles]." Gribkov and Smith, *Operation ANADYR*, pp. 7, 62–63, 183. Also see Fursenko and Naftali, *One Hell of a Gamble*, pp. 241–43.

44. Candelaria is a town in the western province of Pinar del Rio.

45. The U-2 was downed on October 27, 1962, over the eastern part of the island by a Soviet surface-to-air missile (SAM). Lt. Gen. Stepan Grechko, commander of all Soviet air defenses on the island, and his deputy, Lt. Gen. Leonid S. Garbuz, were responsible for the order to fire. The actual firing appears to have been done by Major General Georgy A. Voronkov. See Blight and Welch, *On the Brink*, p. 339; Gribkov and Smith, *Operation ANADYR*, pp. 66–67; Adela Estrada Juaréz, "The General Who Gave the Order to Fire," *Granma Weekly Review*, April 23, 1989, p. 8.

46. The full text of the letter is reprinted in Chang and Kornbluh, *The Cuban Missile Crisis*, Document 45, p. 189. There is still uncertainty about whether the letter had an impact on Khrushchev's decision to withdraw the missiles from Cuba. Though dated October 26, the letter was finished early in the morning of October 27 and the translated and encrypted version arrived at the Soviet Foreign Ministry only at 1:10 A.M. on October 28. Oleg Troyanovsky reported in 1992 that "the letter was read to Khrushchev over the phone and was circulated to the Politburo" prior to their meeting on the morning of October 28, during which they drafted Khrushchev's statement about withdrawing missiles (Blight et al., *Cuba on the Brink*, p. 116; also see Blight et al., *Cuba between the Superpowers*, pp. 92–93, 99–100). The Soviet leader's son, Sergei Khrushchev, recalled in 1991 that the letter did influence his father. "As a matter of fact," he said, "this letter worried Khrushchev . . . it confirmed his point of view . . . that the missiles should be withdrawn" (Blight et al., *Cuba between the Superpowers*, p. 118; also see Nikita S. Khrushchev, *Khrushchev Remembers: The Glasnost Tapes*, trans. and ed. Jerrold L. Schecter, with Vyacheslav V. Luchkov (Boston: Little, Brown, 1990, p. 177). Indeed, Khrushchev advised Castro in a cable on October 28 "not to be carried away by sentiment and to show firmness. . . . But we mustn't allow ourselves to be carried away by provocations, because the Pentagon's unbridled militarists . . . are trying to frustrate the agreement and provoke you into actions that could be used against you" (Chang and Kornbluh, *The Cuban Missile Crisis*, Document 54, p. 239). Khrushchev also may have been influenced by the cable from Soviet Ambassador Alekseev, which summarized Castro's letter and arrived late on October 27 (Blight and Welch, *On the Brink*, p. 343; Blight et al., *Cuba between the Superpowers*, pp. 92–93, 99–100; Fursenko and Naftali, *One Hell of a Gamble*, pp. 272–73, 283–86).

47. Ironically the idea that Castro had urged Khrushchev to launch a first strike nuclear attack on the United States has become a popular notion—even though his position as he explains here was much more complex and nuanced—in part because of the news stories that characterized his letter this way when it was first made public in 1989. See, for example, Michael Dobbs, "Soviet Missiles Aimed at U.S. in '62 Crisis: Castro Urged Strike, Conferees Are Told," *Washington Post*, January 28, 1989, p. A1; Dan Fisher, "Soviets Disclose They Had Warheads in Cuba; Seminar on '62 Missile Crisis Reveals That U.S. Cities Were Targeted; Castro Plea for Attack Told," *Los Angeles Times*, January 29, 1989, p. 1. In an effort to counter this interpretation, in 1990 the Cuban Communist Party newspaper *Granma* published the exchange of letters between Castro and Khrushchev that the Cuban leader excerpts in this speech. The letters are available in Chang and Kornbluh, *Cuban Missile Crisis*, Documents 54, 55, 57, and 58, pp. 239–40, 243–44. For a

discussion of the motivations behind Castro's release of it in 1990, and a copy of the editorial in *Granma* that accompanied the letters and was probably written by Castro, see Blight et al., *Cuba on the Brink*, pp. 474–81.

48. Alberto Korda (1928–2001) was a prominent Cuban photographer who is most famous for his 1960 photograph of Che Guevara (wearing a beret and gazing into the distance), which has been reproduced endlessly on posters and T-shirts.

49. The five points were demands whose fulfillment Castro insisted could be the only effective guarantee "that there will be no aggression against Cuba": (1) a cessation of the U.S. economic embargo and U.S. pressure on other countries to cut commercial links to Cuba; (2) an end to U.S. subversive activities against Cuba, including the "organization of invasions by mercenaries" and "the infiltration of spies and saboteurs"; (3) "cessation of the piratical attacks" from bases in the United States and Puerto Rico; (4) an end to violations of Cuban airspace; (5) U.S. withdrawal from Guantanamo Naval Base. See "Letter dated 28 October 1962 from the Permanent Representative of Cuba to the United Nations," UN General Assembly, October 29, 1962, No. A/5271, in Chang and Kornbluh, *The Cuban Missile Crisis*, Document 56, pp. 241–42. Also see "Fija Fidel Las Cinco Garantias Contra La Agresion a Cuba," *Revolucion*, October 29, 1962. For Castro's summary of them in 1992, see Blight et al., *Cuba on the Brink*, pp. 214–15.

50. For a discussion of whether Khrushchev actually believed the Cubans shot down the U-2, see Blight and Welch, *On the Brink*, pp. 339–40; Blight et al., *Cuba on the Brink*, pp. 116–17, 119.

51. The United States had asserted the Kennedy–Khrushchev agreement ending the crisis required on-site inspection in Cuba to assure that the missile bases were being fully dismantled and that the missiles, IL-28 bombers, and Komar patrol boats were being returned to the Soviet Union. On November 15 Kennedy sternly told Khrushchev that the Soviets had not "fulfilled your commitments" under the terms of the agreement. "There has been no United Nations verification that other missiles were not left behind," he said, "and, in fact, there have been many reports of their being concealed in caves and elsewhere, and we have no way of satisfying those who are concerned about these reports." *Problems of Communism*, Special Edition, vol. 41, spring 1992, p. 93. Also see note 62.

52. Castro is referring to Nazi Germany's surprise attack against the Soviet Union on June 22, 1941, ending the 1939 nonaggression pact between the two countries. With 4,000,000 soldiers and more than 3,000 tanks and 5,000 aircraft, the Nazis killed half of the Soviet army and destroyed 95 percent of the Soviet Union's tanks in the first three months, and subsequently occupied the western quarter of the country.

53. The letter was written on January 31, 1963. Part of it is quoted later in Castro's speech. The full text is reprinted in Chang and Kornbluh, *The Cuban Missile Crisis*, Document 82, pp. 319–29.

54. Anastas Mikoyan, First Deputy Premier of the Soviet Union, arrived in Havana on November 2 and remained there until November 26, 1962 (Fursenko and Naftali, *One Hell of a Gamble*, chap. 15).

55. In fact, there are Soviet and Cuban versions of memoranda of conversations between Mikoyan and the Cuban leadership. The Soviet version is reprinted as "Mikoyan's Mission to Havana: Cuban–Soviet Negotiations, November 1962," *Bulletin*, Cold War International History Project, Woodrow Wilson International Center for Scholars, spring 1995, pp. 93–109, 159. The Cuban version is reprinted as "Document I: Cuban Record of Conversation, Mikoyan and Cuban Leadership, Havana, 4 November 1962," and "Document II: Mikoyan and Cuban Leadership, Havana, 5 November 1962," *Bulletin*, Cold War International History Project, Woodrow Wilson

International Center for Scholars, winter 1996/1997, pp. 339–43. Also, "Transcription of Conversation between A. I. Mikoyan and Fidel Castro, November 12, 1962," in Gribkov and Smith, *Operation ANADYR*, appendix 1, Document 7.

56. U Thant, Acting Secretary General of the United Nations, was in Cuba on October 30–31. See Philip Brenner, "Thirteen Months: Cuba's Perspective on the Missile Crisis," in Nathan, *The Cuban Missile Crisis Revisited*, pp. 201–2. The transcript of their meeting is reprinted in "Nuestra Derecho a la Paz se Está Abriendo Paso en El Mundo," *Verde Olivo*, November 11, 1962, pp. 14–15.

57. The Ilyushin (IL-28) light bombers were outdated Soviet aircraft. Some versions were capable of carrying nuclear payloads, and six out of the forty-two planes sent to Cuba were nuclear-capable. Of the forty-two planes, only six were completely assembled but they had not been tested for flight (Gribkov and Smith, *Operation ANADYR*, p. 27; *CINCLANT Historical Account*, p. 15). There was some confusion at the time about whether the planes belonged to Cuba or whether they were still the property of the Soviet Union. U.S. officials believed they were Cuban, and this belief was reinforced when Carlos Lechuga, Cuba's ambassador to the United Nations, made a public claim to that effect on November 8 ("Summary Record of the 16th Meeting of the Executive Committee of the National Security Council," U.S. State Department, *Foreign Relations of the United, 1961–1963* [hereafter cited as *FRUS, 1961–1963*], vol. XI, Document No. 130, November 1, 1962 (Washington, D.C.: Government Printing Office, 1996), p. 340; "Telegram from the Mission to the United Nations to the Department of State," *FRUS, 1961–1963*, vol. XI, Document No. 163, November 8, 1962, p. 414; Jorge I. Domínguez, "The @#$%&: Missile Crisis (Or, What Was 'Cuban' about U.S. Decisions during the Cuban Missile Crisis?)" *Diplomatic History*, vol. 24, no. 2 (spring 2000), p. 314. In 1992 Castro explained that the Soviets had not turned over any of the planes to the Cuban government (Blight et al., *Cuba on the Brink*, p. 91).

58. "Document II: Mikoyan and Cuban Leadership, Havana, 5 November 1962," p. 343.

59. The matter of the IL-28 bombers had become an important source of tension between the United States and the Soviet Union in the days immediately after the crisis. The United States listed them among the "offensive" weapons to be removed from Cuba. The Soviet Union insisted they were defensive, and Cuba saw them as a means of defending the coast against terrorist intervention. However, by November 13 the Soviet leadership had decided to accede to U.S. demands. Khrushchev wrote to Kennedy that "I can assure the President that those planes will be removed from Cuba . . . in 2–3 months." See "Khrushchev Message of Nov. 13, 1962," *Problems of Communism*, Special Edition, vol. 41, spring 1992, p. 89. Also see Philip Brenner, "Kennedy and Khrushchev on Cuba: Two Stages, Three Parties," *Problems of Communism*, Special Edition, vol. 41, spring 1992, p. 25; Lechuga, *In the Eye of the Storm*, p. 149; Tomás Diez Acosta, *La Operación Anadir* (Havana, Cuba: Military History Study Center, 1991), p. 152. Fursenko and Naftali report that Khrushchev's anger over Castro's intransigence led the Soviet leader and the Presidium to decide on November 16 to bow to Kennedy's insistence that the bombers be removed immediately (*One Hell of a Gamble*, p. 306).

60. In 1963 the CIA provided assistance for Cuban exiles to set up bases in the Caribbean and Central America from which they launched terrorist attacks against Cuba. In January 1963 Kennedy approved the creation of special office in the State Department ("Coordinator of Cuban Affairs") to orchestrate policy decisions and recommend "new courses of action" with respect to Cuba. The State Department coordinator reported in mid-April that the "present covert policy in Cuba" included: support for "the efforts of certain Cuban exiles . . . who believe the Castro regime can be overthrown from within"; "placing of incendiary devices and/or explosives with suitable

time delay within the hull or cargo to disable or sink Cuban vessels"; "introducing abrasives or other damaging materials into the propulsion, communication and other systems of the ship" ("Memorandum from the Coordinator of Cuban Affairs [Cottrell] to the Special Group,"*FRUS, 1961–1963*, vol. XI, Document No. 318, April 18, 1963, pp. 769–70). Still, throughout the first half of 1963 senior U.S. officials debated about which groups to support, what actions the U.S. would encourage, and whether the groups could be controlled. On June 19 the president authorized the CIA to support a limited program of "hit-and-run attacks against appropriately selected targets" in Cuba, and this was extended in the fall of 1963 to include operations in Cuba such as the sabotage of an electric power plant, an oil refinery, and a sugar mill ("Alleged Assassination Plots Involving Foreign Leaders," p. 173; Desmond Fitzgerald, "Memorandum for the Record," *FRUS, 1961–1963*, vol. XI, Document No. 348, June 19, 1963, pp. 837–38; "Paper Prepared by the Central Intelligence Agency for the Standing Group of the National Security Agency: Proposed Covert Policy and Integrated Program of Action towards Cuba,"*FRUS, 1961–1963*, vol. XI, Document No. 346, June 8, 1963, pp. 828–34). Also see John McCone, "Memorandum for the Record," *FRUS, 1961–1963*, vol. XI, Document No. 304, March 29, 1963; Thomas A. Parrott, "Memorandum for the Record,"*FRUS, 1961–1963*, vol. XI, Document No. 323, April 25, 1963; "Memorandum From the Chief, Special Affairs Staff, Central Intelligence Agency (FitzGerald) to the President's Special Assistant for National Security Affairs (Bundy), *FRUS, 1961–1963*, vol. XI, Document No. 357, August 9, 1963; Blight and Kornbluh, *Politics of Illusion*, pp. 121–23; Felix I. Rodriguez and John Weisman, *Shadow Warrior* (New York: Simon and Schuster, 1989), pp. 119–25; Morris H. Morley, *Imperial State and Revolution: The United States and Cuba, 1952–1986* (New York: Cambridge University Press, 1987), pp. 152–53, Fursenko and Naftali, *One Hell of a Gamble*, pp. 327–28, del Valle Jiménez, *Peligros y Principios*, pp. 204–7).

61. In fact, in November 1962 the United States had estimated there were only 16,000 Soviet military personnel in Cuba, though the estimate was revised in 1963 to 22,000 *(CINCLANT Historical Account,* p. 6; Garthoff, *Reflections on the Cuban Missile Crisis,* p. 35). Garthoff notes that Castro publicly stated in 1979 that there were 40,000 Soviet troops in Cuba, "but little attention was paid to the revelation" *(Reflections on the Cuban Missile Crisis,* p. 36). When a Soviet general stated at the 1989 Moscow conference on the missile crisis that the actual number was 42,000, former secretary of defense Robert McNamara acknowledged that U.S. planning for an invasion was based on an estimate of only 10,000 to 12,000 Soviet troops on the island. "[W]e were misinformed," he remarked, noting that in light of the new information an invasion would have resulted in a "bloody battle" (Allyn et al., *Back to the Brink*, pp. 28, 99). Gribkov and Smith report that there were 41,902 Soviet troops in Cuba on October 24, 1962 (*Operation ANADYR*, p. 28).

62. The United States and the Soviet Union had agreed to use the International Committee of the Red Cross (ICRC) to inspect Soviet ships. It is not clear which country first proposed using the ICRC (Lechuga, *In the Eye of the Storm*, pp. 124, 128; "Telegram from the Department of State to the Mission to the United Nations," *FRUS, 1961–1963*, vol. XI, Document No. 132, November 1, 1962, p. 343; "The Secretary General's Meeting with Mr. Paul Ruegger, Representative of the International Committee of the Red Cross," *CMC Document Set*, Document No. 02004, November 6, 1962).

63. This was on November 15, 1962. The planes were on low-level reconnaissance missions that began on November 1 to observe the dismantling of the missiles, and also to prepare for a U.S. invasion, which remained as an active possibility during this period. See Fursenko and Naftali, *One Hell of a Gamble*, p. 304; Szulc, *Fidel*, p. 585; *CINCLANT Historical Account*, p. 14; "Summary of Record of the 16th Meeting of the Executive Committee of the National Security Council," *FRUS, 1961–1963*, vol. XI, Document No. 130, November 1, 1963.

64. It appears that the U.S. suspension of low level flights was prompted largely by the desire to show some moderation in order to "bring [the Soviets] along on agreement on the ILs," as U.S. Ambassador Adlai E. Stevenson had remarked to Under Secretary of State George Ball ("Memorandum of Telephone Conversation between the Permanent Representative to the Mission to the United Nations [Stevenson] and the Under Secretary of State [Ball]," *FRUS, 1961–1963*, vol. XI, Document No. 175, November 13, 1962, p. 451). However, a few days later the ExComm did recommend to the president the continued suspension of low-level reconnaissance flights in order to avoid the complications that would arise if Cuban anti-aircraft did shoot down a U.S. plane. But the ExComm warned that the suspension should not last "many more days" so that the Cubans did not conclude that "the threat to shoot down our reconnaissance planes has scared us away" ("Summary Record of the 26th—A Meeting of the Executive Committee of the National Security Council," *FRUS, 1961–1963*, vol. XI, Document No. 190, November 17, 1962, p. 481). Kennedy authorized the resumption of low-level flights on December 6, but the guidelines specified that "low-level missions" should be used only when there were "specific indications of a target of special interest" ("National Security Action Memorandum No. 208," *FRUS, 1961–1963*, vol. XI, Document No. 232, December 4, 1962, p. 591).

65. Ultimately 3,000 Soviet troops remained in Cuba. This brigade became a source of tension between Cuba and the United States in 1979, when Sen. Frank Church (D-ID) claimed it was a "combat" brigade and President Jimmy Carter demanded the Soviets withdraw the brigade. See David D. Newsom, *The Soviet Brigade in Cuba* (Bloomington: Indiana University Press, 1987). In a personal interview with the authors on April 5, 1994, Gen. Anatoli Gribkov said the brigade was "named a 'motorized rifle brigade'—something between a division and a regiment—because we wanted it to sound less formidable." The Soviets left it in Cuba "for symbolic purposes, to show there was a Soviet presence in Cuba," he said. But according to notes from a conversation between Castro and Khrushchev in 1963, Khrushchev was reluctant to maintain Soviet troops on the island. It was the Cuban leader who asserted that the brigade would serve as a kind of trip-wire to deter U.S. aggression, "like the celebrated missiles. So long as they are there," Castro remarked, "American military circles are convinced that an attack on Cuba would inevitably lead to war with the Soviet Union" (quoted in Fursenko and Naftali, *One Hell of a Gamble*, p. 332).

66. See note 53.

67. The two leaders met in New York during the 15th session of UN General Assembly. Castro was in New York September 18–28 and Khrushchev was there from September 19 to October 13, 1960.

68. Brenner, "Thirteen Months," p. 202.

69. Castro arrived in the Soviet Union on April 27, 1963, and stayed there forty days. See Fursenko and Naftali, *One Hell of a Gamble*, pp. 329–34; Jacques Lévesque, *The USSR and the Cuban Revolution* (New York: Praeger, 1978), pp. 92–95; del Valle Jiménez, *Peligros y Principios*, p. 196.

70. Castro gave a major speech in Red Square on April 23. For the text see, "Castro Speech at Red Square," April 23, 1963; available at: http://lanic.utexas.edu/la/cb/cuba/castro.html.

71. Llewelyn Thompson was an ambassador-at-large in 1962 and had been U.S. ambassador to the Soviet Union. He was the principal Soviet specialist on the Executive Committee (ExComm) of the National Security Council during the crisis.

72. Anatoly F. Dobrynin.

73. Khrushchev may have been reading from his November 4, 1962 message to Kennedy, in which he criticized the United States for including the IL-28 bombers and Komar patrol boats

on a list of offensive weapons to be removed from Cuba. "If," he concluded, "additional demands are made, then that means only one thing—the danger that the difficulties on the way to eliminating tension created around Cuba will not be removed. But that may raise then new consequences" (*Problems of Communism*, Special Edition, vol. 41, spring 1992, pp. 75–76).

74. The U.S. Jupiter (IRBM) missiles in Turkey became a pressing issue in the missile crisis on October 27, when Khrushchev publicly proposed they be removed in exchange for the removal of missiles from Cuba. Kennedy, in a message conveyed by Attorney General Robert Kennedy to Soviet Ambassador Anatoly Dobrynin on October 27, secretly informed the Soviets that the United States would remove the Jupiter missiles, but he emphasized that this decision was not in "exchange" for the removal of the Soviet missiles in Cuba ("Dobrynin's Cable to the Soviet Foreign Ministry, 27 October 1962," *Bulletin*, Cold War International History Project, Woodrow Wilson International Center for Scholars, spring 1995, pp. 79–80; "Memorandum from Attorney General Kennedy to Secretary of State Rusk," *FRUS, 1961–1963*, vol. XI, Document No. 96, October 30, 1962, p. 271). Khrushchev alluded to this agreement in a private cable to Kennedy on October 28:

> You may have noticed that in my message to you on October 28, which was to be published immediately, I did not raise this question [of the Jupiters]—precisely because I was mindful of your wish conveyed through Robert Kennedy. But all the proposals . . . took into account the fact that you had agreed to resolve, [sic] the matter of your missile bases in Turkey consistent with what I had said in my message of October 27 and what you stated through Robert Kennedy in his meeting with Ambassador Dobrynin on that same day." ("Khrushchev Confidential Message of October 28, 1962," *Problems of Communism*, Special Edition, vol. 41, spring 1992, p. 61)

Also see Jim Hershberg, "Anatomy of a Controversy: Anatoly F. Dobrynin's Meeting with Robert F. Kennedy, Saturday, 27 October 1962," *Bulletin*, Cold War International History Project, Woodrow Wilson International Center for Scholars, spring 1995, pp. 75, 77–78. For analyses of the missiles in Turkey, see Philip Nash, *The Other Missiles of October: Eisenhower, Kennedy, and the Jupiters, 1957–1963* (Chapel Hill: University of North Carolina Press, 1997); Barton J. Bernstein, "Reconsidering the Missile Crisis: Dealing with the Problems of the American Jupiters in Turkey," in Nathan, *The Cuban Missile Crisis Revisited.*

75. This is a reference to the Cuban charges in January 1968 that agents in the Soviet embassy in Havana had conspired with Aníbal Escalante to interfere in Cuba's internal affairs. See chapter 4 of this book for an analysis of the Escalante and "microfaction" trial.

76. See note 60.

77. Ricardo Bofill was a professor of the history of the philosophy at the University of Havana in the 1960s, where he taught Marxism. On January 25, 1968, the Central Committee formally charged him with being a member of the microfaction in the Communist Party that was critical of the Cuban government leadership for its supposed deviations from orthodox Marxist doctrine. Bofill's manuscript, "Points for a Critical History of the Cuban Revolution," provided the basis for his imprisonment on the charge of distributing "enemy propaganda."

78. In a speech on June 13, 1964, Cuban Defense Minister Raul Castro "charged that '470 provocations' by personnel of the United States Naval Base at Guantanamo had taken place since April 20." *New York Times*, June 15, 1964. On June 25, 1964, the Cuban government "reported that a sentry at the Guantanamo Naval Base shot and seriously wounded a Cuban soldier late last night. Tonight, Premier Fidel Castro said that a denial of the incident, issued by the State Department in Washington during the day, was 'ridiculous.'" *New York Times*,

June 26, 1964. Also see *CMC Document Set*, Document No. 03153 ("Declaration of the Cuban Government"); Norberto Fuentes, *Nos Impusieron La Violencia* (Havana, Cuba: Editorial Letras Cubanas, 1986).

79. The systematic bombing of North Vietnam began in 1965.

80. Khrushchev recalls that Malinovsky had estimated that the United States would "crush" Cuba's forces in "'something on the order of two days.'" Khrushchev, *Khrushchev Remembers: The Glasnost Tapes*, pp. 181–82. This was confirmed by Sergo Mikoyan in 1987 (Blight and Welch, *On the Brink*, p. 241).

81. During the 1961 Bay of Pigs invasion, the Cuban air force consisted of a few T-33 training planes, World War II vintage B-26 bombers, and British-built Sea Furies. The Sea Furies sank two vital exile supply ships, the *Houston* and *Río Escondo*. (However, a focus on this action, and Kennedy's refusal to launch a "second" air strike which might have destroyed more of the Cuban planes, tends to obscure even more significant problems with the Bay of Pigs invasion. See Peter Kornbluh, "Introduction: *History Held Hostage*," in *Bay of Pigs Declassified: The Secret Report on the Invasion of Cuba*, ed., Peter Kornbluh (New York: New Press, 1998); Lyman B. Kirkpatrick, "Inspector General's Survey of the Cuban Operation, October 1961," in Kornbluh, *Bay of Pigs Declassified*; *CMC Document Set*, Document No. 00090 ("The Taylor Report on Limited War Programs," 13 June 1961, Memorandum No. 2, p. 1); Piero Gleijeses, "Ships in the Night: The CIA, the White House and the Bay of Pigs," *Journal of Latin American Studies*, vol. 27, no. 1 (1995); Juan Carlos Rodríguez, *The Bay of Pigs and the CIA* (New York: Ocean Press, 1999), pp. 137–42.

82. The Katyusha is a Soviet multiple rocket launcher. A truck-mounted 122-mm version with forty tubes, while relatively inaccurate, can generate considerable destruction in a given area. See Harriet Fast Scott and William F. Scott, *The Armed Forces of the USSR*, 3rd ed. (Boulder, Colo.: Westview, 1984), p. 156.

83. During the crisis, U.S. intelligence estimated that it would require ten days to secure the island after an invasion, with U.S. forces suffering 18,483 casualties. This estimate was qualified, though, with the caution that "the spectrum of resistance might range from absolute submission by the Cubans to all out resistance." *See CINCLANT Historical Account*, p. 56. An August 8, 1962 Joint Chiefs of Staff projection estimated that "The duration of a U.S. military presence in Cuba is contingent upon such factors as the will of Castro-Cuban forces to resist invasion, the degree of popular support a defeated Castro might receive for the conduct of residual guerrilla operations. . . . Following the establishment of essential military control of the island, a substantial U.S. military commitment may be required in Cuba for a significant period of time." See Chang and Kornbluh, *Cuban Missile Crisis*, Doc. 8, p. 51.

CHAPTER 3

1. Quoted in Carla Anne Robbins, *The Cuban Threat* (New York: McGraw-Hill, 1983), p. 47, from the original, *Verde Olivo*, October 10, 1968.

2. Gianni Minà, *An Encounter with Fidel*, trans. Mary Todd (Melbourne, Australia: Ocean Press, 1991), p. 92.

3. "Summary of [U Thant's] Meeting with President Dorticós, Premier Castro and Foreign Minister Roa of Cuba," October 31, 1962, UN Archives Call Number: Dag 1/5.2.2.6.2:1, in *CMC Document Set*, Document No. 01747. Also see Carlos Lechuga, *In the Eye of the Storm: Castro,*

Khrushchev, Kennedy and the Missile Crisis, trans. Mary Todd (Melbourne, Australia: Ocean Press, 1995), pp. 122-32; Sergio del Valle Jiménez, ed., *Peligros y Principios: La Crisis de Octubre desde Cuba* (Havana, Cuba: Editora Verde Olivo, 1992), pp. 174-76.

4. "4th Anniversary of the Cuban Revolution," January 2, 1963, as reported by *Foreign Broadcast Information Service*, January 3, 1963; available in the University of Texas-LANIC "Castro Speech Database," at http://lanic.utexas.edu/la/cb/cuba/castro.html. Dramatically Castro said:

> When Mr. Kennedy threatened to turn us into a nuclear target in efforts to intimidate us, what happened then? The people shouted: fatherland or death! . . . This explains the attitude of our people, the wherefores of the measures we took in the face of imperialist aggression. . . . That is why we took measures to arm ourselves, and that is why we agreed with the Soviet Union on the weapons that were set up here, because we understood that we were fulfilling two obligations: one toward the country, fortifying its defenses in view of imperialist threats, and one obligation toward the peoples of the socialist camp; that is, an international proletarian duty.

5. Minà, *An Encounter with Fidel*, p. 92.

6. "Fidel Castro's 23 October Interview," broadcast on Havana radio and television, *Foreign Broadcast Information Service*, Report Date, October 24, 1962; available at: http://lanic.utexas.edu/la/cb/cuba/castro/1962/19621024.

7. Cat Stevens, "The First Cut Is the Deepest," released January 1968 on the album *New Masters*. Born Steven Demetre Georgiou, the singer-songwriter was known as Cat Stevens until 1978, when he converted to Islam and changed his name again, to Yusef Islam. "The First Cut Is the Deepest" became an international hit in the 1970s, sung by British rock star Rod Stewart.

8. The metaphor of the "two scars" for the Cubans is from an interview with Kiva L. Maidanik, done for the authors by Svetlana Savranskaya, June 6, 1993, Moscow, Russian Federation. Maidanik spent three decades in several Soviet institutes working on Latin America in various capacities analyzing Cuba. The transcript of the interview was also translated by Dr. Savranskaya. Both versions are in the authors' possession.

9. "Notes of Conversation between A. I. Mikoyan and Fidel Castro, 3 November 1962," *Cold War International History Project Bulletin*, no. 5 (spring 1995), p. 93. [Hereafter cited as "Mikoyan MemCon, November 3, 1962."]

10. "Memorandum of Conversation: A. I. Mikoyan with Fidel Castro, Osvaldo Dorticos Torrado, Raul Castro, Ernesto Guevara, Emilio Aragones, and Carlos Rafael Rodríguez, 4 November 1962," *Cold War International History Project Bulletin*, no. 5 (spring 1995), p. 95. [Hereafter cited as "Mikoyan MemCon, November 4, 1962."] The Amendment historically has been linked to the U.S.-Spanish refusal to include Cuban delegates in the peace treaty negotiations, and by implication Castro also was pointing to Cuba's exclusion from the agreement that ended the missile crisis. On the Platt Amendment, see Louis A. Pérez, Jr., *Cuba: Between Reform and Revolution* (New York: Oxford University Press, 1988), pp. 185-88; Lars Schoultz, *Beneath the United States: A History of U.S. Policy toward Latin America* (Cambridge, Mass.: Harvard University Press, 1998), pp. 147-48.

11. The five points were listed in a letter from Cuba's permanent representative to the UN to UN Acting Secretary General U Thant, October 28, 1962. It is reprinted in Laurence Chang and Peter Kornbluh, eds., *The Cuban Missile Crisis, 1962* (New York: New Press, 1992), pp. 241-42. They were published the next day in Havana: "Fija Fidel Las Cinco Garantias Contra La Agresion a Cuba," *Revolucion*, October 29, 1962. For Castro's retrospective analysis of the five points in 1992, see James G. Blight, Bruce J. Allyn, and David A. Welch, *Cuba on the Brink: Castro, the*

Missile Crisis and the Soviet Collapse, enlarged paperback ed. (Lanham, Md.: Rowman & Little-field, 2002), pp. 214-15. Lechuga (*In the Eye of the Storm*, pp. 104-5) provides an informative discussion of their meaning.

12. Fidel Castro, letter to UN Acting Secretary General U Thant, November 15, 1962, p. 4 of the UN Press Services version of November 16. The letter is reprinted in full in appendix B.

13. "Mikoyan MemCon, November 3, 1962," pp. 93-94. The record of these conversations is likely very accurate because the transcriber was Aleksandr Alekseev, a central figure in Cuban–Soviet relations between 1962 and 1968, when he was the Soviet ambassador in Havana. He was so deeply pro-Cuban that he often would refuse to deliver messages to Cuban leaders if he felt they would find them offensive—which was fairly often. He remarked to us in 1990 that "I am actually more Cuban than Russian, except for two things. First, I can't stand cigars, though I smoke cigarettes. And second, although I have tried, I cannot understand baseball. Except for those two deficiencies, I may as well be Cuban" (interview with the authors in Moscow, March 20, 1990).

14. "Mikoyan MemCon, November 3, 1962," p. 93.

15. Authors' interview with Sergo Mikoyan, January 30, 1989.

16. "Memorandum of Conversation, A. I. Mikoyan with Oswaldo Dorticós, Ernesto Guevara, and Carlos Rafael Rodriquez, Evening, 5 November 1962," *Cold War International History Project Bulletin*, no. 5 (spring 1995), p. 109. [Hereafter cited as "Mikoyan MemCon, 5 November 1962."]

17. Anastas Mikoyan's cable to Khrushchev was sent on November 17, 1962, from Havana, and is quoted in Aleksandr Fursenko and Timothy Naftali, *One Hell of a Gamble: Khrushchev, Castro & Kennedy, 1958-1964* (New York: Norton, 1997), pp. 305-6. Mikoyan's tone is remarkably similar to that of Secretary of State John Quincy Adams (who wrote the 1823 Monroe Doctrine), when he remarked disparagingly in 1821 that his experience with Latin Americans had led him to believe that "Civil dissension was infused into all their seminal principles. War and mutual destruction was in every member of their organization, moral, political, and physical" (quoted in Schoultz, *Beneath the United States*, p. 4).

18. Nikita Khrushchev, *Khrushchev Remembers: The Glasnost Tapes*, trans. and ed. Jerrold L. Schecter (Boston: Little, Brown, 1990), p. 178.

19. Nikita Khrushchev to Anastas Mikoyan, November 16, 1962. Quoted in Fursenko and Naftali, *One Hell of a Gamble*, p. 306.

20. "Mikoyan MemCon, 5 November 1962," p. 108.

21. Discussions between Mikoyan and Castro, 19 November 1962, signed by Mikoyan, drafted and sent by Alekseev; Archive of the Soviet Ministry of Foreign Affairs; provided to the authors in 1991 by Felix Kovaliev, then chief of the archival division. The translation was produced in May 1991, at the authors' request, by Dr. Stephen D. Shenfield, a British Sovietologist and international relations scholar formerly at Brown University's Watson Institute for International Studies.

22. "Mikoyan MemCon, 5 November 1962," p. 108, 159.

23. Discussions between Mikoyan and Castro, November 19, 1962.

24. Fursenko and Naftali, *One Hell of a Gamble*, pp. 309-10; "Statement Read by the President [Kennedy] at a News Conference, November 20, 1962," in U.S. Department of State, Historical Office, *American Foreign Policy, Current Documents, 1962*, Washington, D.C., 1966, Document No. III-106, pp. 461-62.

25. "Mikoyan MemCon, 5 November 1962," p. 109.

26. Ernesto (Che) Guevara, comment to Anastacio Cruz Mancilla, from "Memorandum of Conversation, November 6, 1964, E. Pronsky with Anastacio Cruz Mancilla, November 13, 1964" (classification: secret); Russian National Archive, File No. 5, List No. 49, Document No. 759.

27. This is how Tad Szulc (*Fidel: A Critical Portrait* [New York: William Morrow, 1986], p. 602), for example, distinguishes Guevara and Castro.

28. Ernesto (Che) Guevara, "Vietnam and the World Struggle for Freedom," in *Che Guevara Speaks*, ed. George Lavan (New York: Pathfinder, 1967), p. 159.

29. Ernesto (Che) Guevara, "Man and Socialism in Cuba," in *Venceremos!: The Speeches and Writings of Che Guevara*, ed. John Gerassi (New York: Simon and Schuster, 1968), p. 398.

30. Saul Landau, "Poster Boy of the Revolution," *Washington Post Book World*, October 19, 1997, p. X1.

31. Fidel Castro, "Second Declaration of Havana," in *Fidel Castro Speaks*, eds. Martin Kenner and James Petras (New York: Grove Press, 1969), pp. 104–6.

32. On Guevara's contribution to Castro's thinking, and on the closeness of the two men, see Sheldon B. Liss, *FIDEL! Castro's Political and Social Thought* (Boulder, Colo.: Westview, 1994), pp. 36–38. This book more generally provides an insightful examination of how Castro's rhetoric and ideas related to his political behavior.

33. Castro told us in an interview in Havana on April 10, 2001, that while he had read some of Karl Marx's work as a youth, socialism was an idea that had come to him from experience. "My father owned a large farm," he explained, "and the workers whom he employed would purchase their food and necessities from the farm's store. [In 1985 Castro remarked in an interview with Frei Betto that his father owned 800 hectares (about 2,000 acres) of land, and leased another 10,000 hectares or about 25,000 acres, though "most of it was hilly" (Frei Betto, *Fidel and Religion* [Havana, Cuba: Publications Office of the Council of State, 1987], pp. 93–94).] The store kept an account and deducted what they bought from their wages. I worked in the store when I was very young, maybe even at five years old. When a worker would ask for a pound of sugar, I would charge him for a pound and give him two pounds. So you see, the first expropriations I carried out were against my own family's farm."

34. Saul Landau, "Introduction: Asking the Right Questions about Cuba," in Philip Brenner, William LeoGrande, Donna Rich, and Daniel Siegel, *The Cuba Reader: The Making of a Revolutionary Society* (New York: Grove Press, 1989), pp. xviii–xix.

35. Fidel Castro, "Radio and Television Speech to the Cuban People," October 23, 1962.

36. Liss, *FIDEL! Castro's Political and Social Thought*, pp. 33–35.

37. José Martí, "Our America," in *José Martí Reader: Writings on the Americas*, eds. Deborah Shnookal and Mirta Muñiz (New York: Ocean Press, 1999), p. 119.

38. This is the way the passage was translated in the December 3, 1990, introduction to the publication in *Granma*, the Cuban communist-party daily, of the Castro–Khrushchev letters during the missile crisis. The introduction and letters are reprinted in full in Blight et al., *Cuba on the Brink*, pp. 474–91. The passage from Guevara's "Farewell Letter" is on page 475. The author of the introduction also translated it this way in the conclusion to the introductory material: "the sad and luminous days of October 1962" (p. 480). The full text is in Lavan, ed., *Che Guevara Speaks*, pp. 139–41. There, the translator uses the order Guevara had in the original Spanish, but changes the nuance slightly to "brilliant yet sad days of the Caribbean crisis" (p. 140). "Sad and luminous" is more in keeping with the elegiac tone throughout the letter, however.

39. On the "strategy of the strong" versus the "strategy of the weak," see Townsend Hoopes, *The Limits of Intervention*, updated ed. (New York: Longman, 1973), pp. 126–30. Hoopes uses this notion, which he attributes to William Pfaff, to explain how North Vietnam could withstand U.S. bombing and the seemingly insuperable difficulties of the so-called Ho Chi Minh Trail to get supplies to their allies in the south, the National Liberation Front. See also Robert S. McNamara,

James G. Blight, and Robert K. Brigham, with Thomas J. Biersteker and Col. Herbert Y. Schandler, *Argument without End: In Search of Answers to the Vietnam Tragedy* (New York: Public Affairs, 1999), pp. 252-53. The strategy of the weak available to Third World countries was markedly different from that used by European states. Austria, for example, successfully managed to avoid Soviet domination by obtaining Western protection without incurring the obligations and risks of NATO membership (Günter Bischof, *Austria in the First Cold War, 1945-55: The Leverage of the Weak* [New York: St. Martin's, 1999], pp. 142-49). But Cuba was precluded from using such a strategy, because the United States would not negotiate with it as the Soviet Union was willing to negotiate with Austria, and the Soviet Union was unwilling to offer itself to Cuba as a deterrent in the same way that the Western powers guaranteed Austria's neutrality.

40. See Jorge I. Domínguez, "Pipsqueak Power: The Centrality and Anomaly of Cuba," in *The Suffering Grass: Superpowers and Regional Conflict in Southern Africa and the Caribbean,* eds. Thomas G. Weiss and James G. Blight (Boulder, Colo.: Lynne Rienner, 1992), pp. 57-78, esp. pp. 65-72.

41. See McNamara et al., *Argument without End,* pp. 250-53.

42. Lechuga, *In the Eye of the Storm,* pp. 195-211; Peter Kornbluh, "Kennedy and Castro: The Secret Quest for Accommodation," National Security Archive Electronic Briefing Book No. 17, August 16, 1999; available at: www.gwu.edu/~nsarchiv/NSAEBB/NSAEBB18/index.html.

43. Jean Daniel, "Unofficial Envoy," *The New Republic,* December 14, 1963.

44. "*Playboy* Interview: Fidel Castro," *Playboy,* January 1967, p. 70.

45. Jorge I. Domínguez, *To Make a World Safe for Revolution: Cuba's Foreign Policy* (Cambridge, Mass.: Harvard University Press, 1989); Lee Lockwood, *Castro's Cuba, Cuba's Fidel,* expanded ed. (Boulder, Colo.: Westview, 1990). Fidel Castro provided the handwritten epigraph to Lockwood's remarkable series of interviews with the Cuban leader in the mid-1960s: "*El deter de todo revolucionario es hacer le revolucion!*" (The duty of a revolutionary is to make the revolution!)

46. Szulc, *Fidel: A Critical Portrait,* p. 602.

47. William M. LeoGrande, "Evolution of the Nonaligned Movement," *Problems of Communism,* vol. 29, January/February 1980, pp. 35-52; David Deutschmann and Deborah Shnookal, eds., *The Right to Dignity: Fidel Castro and the Nonaligned Movement* (Melbourne, Australia: Ocean Press, 1989).

48. The notion of "political space" is from Michael Erisman and John Kirk, who argue that Cuban foreign policy "can be seen as a tumultuous and at times even tragic quest for political space." The explain: "Inevitably, smaller states find themselves operating to some degree within the shadows that larger actors cast across the global stage. One obvious move to counteract the potential liabilities inherent in this situation would be to try to nurture a multifaceted network of international ties, the ultimate aim of the LDC [less developed country] being to push back as far as possible the constraining socioeconomic-political boundaries within which it must function. To the extent that this diversification strategy is successful, its practitioners will in effect have enlarged their political space" (H. Michael Erisman and John M. Kirk, "Introduction: Cuba and the Struggle for Political Space in the 1990s," in *Cuban Foreign Policy Confronts a New International Order,* eds. H. Michael Erisman and John M. Kirk (Boulder, Colo.: Lynne Rienner, 1991), p. 2. Erisman elaborates this idea in H. Michael Erisman, *Cuba's Foreign Relations in a Post-Soviet World* (Gainesville: University Press of Florida, 2000), pp. 42-47. He then demonstrates how it might explain Cuban foreign policy since the end of the Cold War (pp. 146-205).

49. Julia E. Sweig, *Inside the Cuban Revolution: Fidel Castro and the Urban Underground* (Cambridge, Mass.: Harvard University Press, 2002), pp. 2-9.

50. Fidel Castro, speech of February 22, 1963, quoted in Piero Gleijeses, *Conflicting Missions: Havana, Washington, and Africa, 1959–1976* (Chapel Hill: University of North Carolina Press, 2002), p. 22.

51. Gleijeses, *Conflicting Missions,* pp. 28–29.

52. On the anti-Khrushchev brief by Dmitry Polyanski of October 1964, see Fursenko and Naftali, *One Hell of a Gamble,* pp. 353–55.

53. Dmitry Polyanski, anti-Khrushchev brief of October 1964. Quoted in Fursenko and Naftali, *One Hell of a Gamble,* p. 354.

54. Dmitry Polyanski, quoted in Fursenko and Naftali, *One Hell of a Gamble,* p. 352.

55. Dmitry Polyanski, quoted in Fursenko and Naftali, *One Hell of a Gamble,* p. 354.

56. Jorge I. Domínguez, *Cuba: Order and Revolution* (Cambridge, Mass.: Harvard University Press, 1978), pp. 210–11; Szulc, *Fidel,* p. 570.

57. Fabio Grobart, interview with Tad Szulc, in Szulc, *Fidel,* p. 612. See pages 611–13 on Grobart's views, when he was chairman of the Historical Institute of the Marxist-Leninist Movement in Cuba, of Escalante and the microfaction. Jorge Domínguez notes that one of Raul Castro's charges against the microfaction was that they criticized Cuban policy in the missile crisis and praised Soviet policy. See Domínguez, *To Make a World Safe for Revolution,* p. 74.

58. The phrase "essential tension" is that of the late historian of science, Thomas S. Kuhn. See especially his "The Essential Tension: Tradition and Innovation in Scientific Research," in Thomas S. Kuhn, *The Essential Tension: Selected Studies in Scientific Tradition and Change* (Chicago: University of Chicago Press, 1977), pp. 225–39. See also, in the same volume by Kuhn, "A Function for Thought Experiments," pp. 240–65. According to Kuhn, creative thought and action is most likely when a situation is composed in part of traditional frameworks, and in part of novel data or findings. This may be a fruitful way to understand Cuba's views toward the Soviet Union following the death of Guevara in October 1967, and the Cuban conditional endorsement of the Soviet intervention in Czechoslovakia in August 1968. We elaborate this idea in the following chapter.

59. Domínguez, "Pipsqueak Power," especially p. 57.

60. The "David and Goliath" image was one of Martí's favorites. Castro used a passage from Martí to this effect in the *Second Declaration of Havana* of February 4, 1962: "I have lived inside the monster and know his guts; and my sling is the sling of David" (Kenner and Petras, *Fidel Castro Speaks,* p. 85).

61. Jorge Pollo, interview with the authors and with janet M. Lang, May 25, 1993, Havana, Cuba; David Lewis was the interpreter.

62. Jorge Pollo, interview, May 25, 1993.

63. Jorge Pollo, interview, May 25, 1993.

64. The announcement that the Cuban revolution would follow a Marxist-Leninist path was made in a December 1, 1961, speech. It is reprinted as "Los Grandes Méritos de Lenin y Los Éxitos de la URSS," in Fidel Castro, *La Revolucion de Octubre y La Revolucion Cubana* (Havana, Cuba: Ediciones del Departamento de Orientación Revolucionaria del Comité Central del Partido Comunista de Cuba, 1977), p. 49.

65. J. William Fulbright, quoted in Randall Bennett Woods, *Fulbright: A Biography* (New York: Cambridge University Press, 1995), p. 335. Fulbright's remark, which he repeated publicly on many occasions, was first made during and after the abortive CIA-backed invasion of Cuban exiles at the Bay of Pigs in April 1961.

66. On Cuban–Soviet relations in the period after the Cuban missile crisis emphasizing the Cuban perspective, see Domínguez, *To Make a World Safe for Revolution,* pp. 61–78; Szulc, *Fi-*

del: A Critical Portrait, pp. 562-618; H. Michael Erisman, *Cuba's International Relations: The Anatomy of a Nationalistic Foreign Policy* (Boulder, Colo.: Westview, 1985), pp. 25-33. On the Soviet side of the relationship, see Jacques Lévesque, *The USSR and the Cuban Revolution: Soviet Ideological and Strategical Perspectives, 1959-77*, trans. Deanna Drendel Leboeuf (New York: Praeger, 1978); Cole Blasier, *The Giant's Rival: The USSR and Latin America* (Pittsburgh: University of Pittsburgh Press, 1983), pp. 103-7; Yuri Pavlov, *Soviet-Cuban Alliance: 1959-1961* (New Brunswick, N.J.: Transaction, 1994), pp. 69-80; W. Raymond Duncan, *The Soviet Union and Cuba: Interests and Influence* (New York: Praeger, 1985), chap. 3.

67. Karen Brutents, interview with the authors, March 25, 1995, Fort Lauderdale, Florida. Brutents was a Third World specialist in the International Department of the Communist Party of the Soviet Union, with a particular specialization in Africa. He was thus most closely involved with the Cubans after 1975, when the Cubans became heavily involved in Angola, although he also had contact with them much earlier, due to Che Guevara's travels throughout Africa in the early- and mid-1960s.

68. Sergo Mikoyan, interview with the authors, June 29 and July 5, 1995, Washington, D.C.

69. Mikhail Heller and Aleksandr Nekrich, *Utopia in Power: The History of the Soviet Union from 1917 to the Present*, trans. Phyllis B. Carlos (New York: Summit, 1986), p. 607.

70. On Khrushchev's January 1963 letter to Castro, see Fidel Castro, "Secret Speech" (chapter 2 of this book), and his discussion of it in Blight et al., *Cuba on the Brink*, pp. 222-25; the letter is reproduced on pages 489-91 of *Cuba on the Brink*; on Castro's visit to the Soviet Union, see Blight et al., *Cuba on the Brink*, pp. 210-11.

71. Fidel Castro, quoted in Domínguez, *To Make a world Safe for Revolution*, p. 68.

72. On the treaty, see John R. Redick, "The Tlatelolco Regime and Nonproliferation in Latin America," *International Organization*, vol. 35, no. 1, (winter 1981), pp. 103-34.

73. Cuba signed the treaty in 1995. See: Fidel Castro interview with *El Sol de Mexico*, January 31, 1995, available at: lanic.utexas.edu/la/cb/cuba/castro/1995/19950131; Carlos Rafael Rodriguez, "Why We Have Points of Concurrence with the Soviet Union," in Brenner et al., *The Cuba Reader*, pp. 295-96.

74. "Paper Prepared by the Central Intelligence Agency for the Standing Group of the National Security Council: Proposed Covert Policy and Integrated Program of Action towards Cuba," June 8, 1963, in United States Department of State, *Foreign Relations of the United, 1961-1963*, vol. XI: Cuban Missile Crisis and Aftermath (Washington, D.C.: Government Printing Office, 1997), Document No. 346, p. 828 [hereafter cited as: *FRUS 1961-1963*, vol. XI]; Desmond Fitzgerald, "Memorandum for the Record," June 19, 1963, *FRUS, 1961-1963*, vol. XI, Document No. 348, pp. 837-38; "Memorandum of Meeting with President Johnson, December 19, 1963," in *FRUS 1961-1963*, vol. XI, Document No. 388, pp. 904-9; James G. Blight and Peter Kornbluh, eds., *Politics of Illusion: The Bay of Pigs Invasion Reexamined* (Boulder, Colo.: Lynne Rienner, 1998), pp. 122-28; Felix I. Rodriguez and John Weisman, *Shadow Warrior* (New York: Simon and Schuster, 1989), pp. 119-23.

75. U.S. Congress, Senate, Select Committee to Study Governmental Operations with Respect to Intelligence Activities, *Alleged Assassinations Plots Involving Foreign Leaders*, An Interim Report, No. 94-465, 94th Cong., 1st Sess., November 20, 1975, pp. 71-190. A 1994 study, based on Cuban files, alleges several hundred attempts: Claudia Furiati, trans. Maxine Shaw, *ZR Rifle: The Plot to Kill Kennedy & Castro* (Melbourne, Australia: Ocean Press, 1994). Also see Fabian Escalante, *CIA Targets Fidel: Secret 1967 CIA Inspector General's Report on Plots to Assassinate Fidel Castro* (Melbourne, Australia: Ocean Press, 1996).

76. Tad Szulc, "Cuba on Our Mind," *Esquire*, February 1974, pp. 90-91.

77. Fidel Castro, speech in Havana, January 2, 1965; quoted in Maurice Halperin, *The Taming of Fidel Castro* (Berkeley: University of California Press, 1981), pp. 156–58.

78. Ernesto (Che) Guevara, speech in Algiers to the Second Seminar of the Organization of Afro-Asian Solidarity, February 25, 1965, in Lavan, *Che Guevara Speaks*, pp. 107–8.

79. Quoted in Gleijeses, *Conflicting Missions*, p. 104. Also see Jon Lee Anderson, *Che Guevara: A Revolutionary Life* (New York: Grove Press, 1997), pp. 626–27.

80. See McNamara et al., *Argument without End,* especially chapter 5, "Escalation: 1961–1965," pp. 151–218.

81. Fidel Castro, speech in Havana, May 1, 1965. Quoted in Halperin, *Taming of Fidel Castro*, p. 163.

82. Fidel Castro, speech at the University of Havana, March 13, 1965, in Kenner and Petras, *Fidel Castro Speaks*, p. 110.

83. Ernesto Che Guevara, "Farewell Letter" to Fidel Castro, April 1, 1965. Quoted in Blight, et al., *Cuba on the Brink*, p. 475. The quotation comes from the introduction to the Castro–Khrushchev correspondence during the missile crisis, first published in November 1990 and reprinted in full in *Cuba on the Brink.*

84. Ernesto (Che) Guevara, "Farewell Letter" to Fidel Castro, April 1, 1965, in Lavan, *Che Guevara Speaks*, p. 140. This volume contains the complete English text of the letter.

85. Fidel Castro, "PURSC Central Committee Presentation, Speech at Havana's Chaplin Theater," October 4, 1965; *Foreign Broadcast Information Service*, Report Date October 4, 1965; available at: http://lanic.utexas.edu/la/cb/cuba/castro.html.

86. D. Bruce Jackson, *Castro, the Kremlin and Communism in Latin America* (Baltimore: Johns Hopkins Press, 1969), pp. 28–29; Lévesque, *The USSR and the Cuban Revolution*, pp. 102–4.

87. Lévesque, *The USSR and the Cuban Revolution*, pp. 119–21.

88. U.S. Congress, Senate, Committee on the Judiciary, "The Tricontinental Conference of African, Asian and Latin American Peoples," A Staff Study, 89th Cong., 2nd Sess., June 7, 1966, p. 93.

89. Leo Huberman and Paul M. Sweezy, "The Tricontinental and After," *Monthly Review*, April 1966, p. 6.

90. Fidel Castro, Speech at the University of Havana, March 13, 1967, in Kenner and Petras, *Fidel Castro Speaks*, p. 131.

91. Fidel Castro, Speech at the University of Havana, March 13, 1967, in Kenner and Petras, *Fidel Castro Speaks,* p. 134.

92. The November 4 date is in Fidel Castro, *Che: A Memoir*, ed. by David Deutschmann (Melbourne, Australia: Ocean Press, 1994), p. 5. Anderson (*Che Guevara*, p. 701) cites the date as November 3, 1966.

93. Anderson, *Che Guevara*, p. 720.

94. Ernesto (Che) Guevara, Message "From Somewhere in the World," published in *Prensa Latina*, April 16, 1967, in Lavan, *Che Guevara Speaks*, pp. 144–59.

95. Guevara, "From Somewhere in the World," p. 158.

96. Kiva Maidanik, interview for the authors with Svetlana Savranskaya, June 6, 1993, Moscow, Russian Federation. The transcript of the interview was also translated by Dr. Savranskaya. Both are in the authors' possession.

97. Kiva Maidanik interview.

98. Kiva Maidanik interview.

99. Kiva Maidanik interview.

100. Kiva Maidanik interview.

101. Kiva Maidanik interview.

102. Sergo Mikoyan, interview with the authors, June 25 and July 5, 1995.

103. Sergo Mikoyan, interview with the authors, June 25 and July 5, 1995.

104. Aleksandr Alekseev, interview with Svetlana Savranskaya, May 25, 1993, Moscow, Russian Federation.

105. Aleksandr Alekseev, interview with Svetlana Savranskaya, May 25, 1993, Moscow, Russian Federation.

106. Jon Lee Anderson quotes Guevara's widow, Aleida March, as saying that she thought Darusenkov was not sympathetic to her husband, that he was a "provocateur," in part (apparently) because when Darusenkov came to her house after Guevara's death to offer condolences, he asked her: "Why did Che go to Bolivia, when he was a foreigner?" (Anderson, *Che Guevara*, p. 761; see also p. 580). Aleida March believed Darusenkov was a Soviet spy who was monitoring her husband. However that may have been, we believe, on the basis of many interviews and a good deal of informal interaction besides, that few Soviet officials from the period were more pro-Cuban than Oleg Darusenkov. By all accounts, he was Guevara's best friend among the Soviets as well. Of course, by late 1967, after Guevara's death, Darusenkov had become head of Cuban affairs at the Central Committee of the Communist Party of the Soviet Union. And no one, not even Castro himself, made Darusenkov's life as difficult as Guevara, whose commitment to armed struggle ran completely counter to the views of the Soviet leadership under Brezhnev and Kosygin. In addition to having been in the center of decision with regard to Soviet policy on Cuba, we have also found Darusenkov to be a careful interviewee, who does his homework with declassified documents, before speaking about events from decades past.

107. Oleg Darusenkov, interview with the authors, June 1, 1996, St. Simons Island, Georgia.

108. Oleg Darusenkov, interview with the authors, June 1, 1996, St. Simons Island, Georgia.

109. Chapter 2, p. 67.

110. Chapter 2, p. 67.

111. Faure Chomón, interview with the authors, April 29, 1995, Havana, Cuba. We are grateful to the eminent Cuban poet Pablo Armando Fernandez, for facilitating this interview and also acting as interpreter.

112. Faure Chomón, interview with the authors, April 29, 1995, Havana, Cuba.

113. On the career of Manuel Piñeiro, see Manuel Piñeiro, *Che Guevara and the Latin American Revolutionary Movements*, ed. Luis Suarez, trans. Mary Todd (Melbourne, Australia, Ocean Press, 2001).

114. See Domingo Amuchastegui, "Cuban Intelligence and the October Crisis," in James G. Blight and David A. Welch, eds., *Intelligence and the Cuban Missile Crisis* (London: Frank Cass, 1998), pp. 88–119, especially pp. 89–91. This chapter is the only scholarly piece of its kind on the subject. While the author did not have access to classified Cuban documents in the preparation of the chapter, it is nonetheless copiously documented and cross referenced. In addition, the author, who was a young Cuban intelligence officer working for Piñeiro at the time of the missile crisis, drew extensively on his memory and also the memories for former colleagues.

115. Manuel Piñeiro, interview with the authors, April 29, 1995, Havana, Cuba.

116. Amuchastegui, "Cuban Intelligence and the October Crisis," p. 105. This was also confirmed to us by a former high-ranking Cuban intelligence official, who spoke to us on a "not-for-attribution" basis in an interview in Havana, January 6, 1995.

117. Manuel Piñeiro, interview with the authors, April 29, 1995.

118. Isaiah Berlin, "Herder and the Enlightenment," in Isaiah Berlin, *The Proper Study of Mankind: An Anthology of Essays*, ed. Henry Hardy and Roger Hausheer (New York: Farrar, Straus and Giroux, 1997), pp. 357–435.

119. Berlin, "Herder and the Enlightenment," p. 429.

120. Isaiah Berlin, "The Bent Twig: On the Rise of Nationalism," in Isaiah Berlin, *The Crooked Timber of Humanity*, ed. Henry Hardy (New York: Knopf, 1991), pp. 238–61.

121. Thomas C. Schelling, *The Strategy of Conflict* (Cambridge, Mass.: Harvard University Press, 1960).

122. Thomas C. Schelling, *Arms and Influence* (New Haven, Conn.: Yale University Press, 1966), pp. 109, 121–22.

123. See Domínguez, "Pipsqueak Power," especially pp. 65–69, for an application of considerable virtuosity of Schelling's ideas to Cuban deterrence.

124. Schelling, *Strategy of Conflict*, p. 20.

125. Schelling, *Strategy of Conflict*, p. 11.

126. Schelling, *Strategy of Conflict*, p. 11.

CHAPTER 4

1. Felix Pita, interview with the authors, April 29, 1995, Havana, Cuba.

2. Our reconstruction of events in this period has benefitted from several interviews with Oleg Darusenkov. Classified Cuban and Russian documents from this period remain unavailable. We are grateful to Oleg Darusenkov for sharing his informed recollections of the Castro–Kosygin discussions with us. We were fortunate enough to discuss those meetings with Darusenkov on many occasions, having first met him in Moscow in January 1989. Furthermore, he was able to consult his notes from the conversations prior to our interviews with him. The full story of this episode remains to be told, when the relevant documents are released in Havana and Moscow. But Oleg Darusenkov's recollections, which are rich and informative on their own, also seem to us to coincide with other views of what happened in Havana between Castro and Kosygin, both Cuban and Russian, which were given to us on a "not-for-attribution" basis. Darusenkov was the interpreter of the Castro–Kosygin meeting.

3. Malcolm Gladwell, *The Tipping Point* (New York: Knopf, 2001).

4. Domingo Amuchastegui, who was a young Cuban intelligence officer at the time, working for Manuel Piñeiro, emphasizes this point. See his "Cuban Intelligence and the October Crisis," in James G. Blight and David A Welch, eds., *Intelligence and the Cuban Missile Crisis* (London: Frank Cass, 1998), pp. 88–119. He believes, along with many present and former Cuban officials, that threat-exaggeration—and the KGB's absolutely essential role in providing such information—was one way the KGB tried to establish and maintain control over their Cuban counterparts.

5. Fidel Castro, speech at the University of Havana, March 13, 1967, in Martin Kenner and James Petras, eds., *Fidel Castro Speaks* (New York: Grove Press, 1969), pp. 115–35.

6. See Robert E. Quirk, *Fidel Castro* (New York: Norton, 1993), p. 558.

7. Shlomo Levav, interview with Maurice Halperin in 1975. In Maurice Halperin, *The Taming of Fidel Castro* (Berkeley: University of California Press, 1981), p. 245. For an examination of similarities between Cuba and Israel, see Philip Brenner and Edy Kaufman, "The Tail without a Dog," *Davar* (Tel Aviv), June 10, 1992.

8. Halperin, *Taming of Fidel Castro*, p. 247. Yoram Shapira and Edy Kaufman ("Cuba's Israel Policy: The Shift to the Soviet Line," *Cuban Studies*, vol. 8, no. 9, January 1978) provide a su-

perb overview of Cuban–Israeli relations. Their discussion of Cuba's decision not to break relations with Israel in 1967 is on pages 24–25.

9. *Foreign Relations of the United States, 1964–1968*, vol. XIV, Soviet Union, The Glassboro Summit, June 1967, Document 235, June 25, 1967.

10. *Foreign Relations of the United States, 1964–1968*, vol. XIV, Document 235.

11. *Foreign Relations of the United States, 1964–1968*, vol. XIV, Document 237, June 25, 1967.

12. Oleg Darusenkov, interview with the authors, June 1, 1996, St. Simons Island, Georgia.

13. Arnold Kalinin, interview with the authors, April 29, 1995, Havana, Cuba.

14. Oleg Darusenkov, interview with the authors, September 5–6, 1997, Washington, D.C.

15. Oleg Darusenkov, interview with the authors, June 1, 1996.

16. Oleg Darusenkov, interview with the authors, June 1, 1996.

17. See Blight et al., *Cuba on the Brink*, pp. 91–93.

18. K. S. Karol, *Guerrillas in Power: The Course of the Cuban Revolution*, trans. Arnold Pomerans (New York: Hill and Wang, 1970), pp. 306–7.

19. This point was emphasized to us by Carlos Franqui, a former member of Castro's July 26th Movement and, after the triumph of the Revolution, editor of the newspaper *Revolucion*. Franqui, interview with the authors, January 26, 1995, Washington, D.C. We are grateful to Enrique Pumar for serving as interpreter and transcriber for the interview.

20. See Jorge I. Domínguez, "Pipsqueak Power: the Centrality and Anomaly of Cuba," in Thomas G. Weiss and James G. Blight, eds., *The Suffering Grass: Superpowers and Regional Conflict in Southern Africa and the Caribbean* (Boulder, Colo.: Lynne Rienner, 1992), pp. 65–69 for an insightful analysis of the way Castro has used his *reputation* for obstinacy and irrationality to help him achieve his objectives.

21. See Jacques Lévesque, *The USSR and the Cuban Revolution: Soviet Ideological and Strategical Perspectives, 1959–1977*, trans. Deanna Drendel Leboeuf (New York: Praeger, 1978), pp. 130–31; see also Philip Brenner and James G. Blight, "The [Missile] Crisis and Cuban–Soviet Relations: Fidel Castro's Secret 1968 Speech," *Bulletin of the Cold War International History Project*, issue 5 (spring, 1995), pp. 1, 81–87.

22. Fidel Castro, "Speech at the Close of the Conference of the Organization of Latin American Solidarity," University of Havana, August 10, 1967. In Kenner and Petras, *Fidel Castro Speaks*, pp. 145–63. [Hereafter cited as Castro Speech, August 10, 1967.]

23. Castro Speech, August 10, 1967, p. 154.

24. Castro Speech, August 10, 1967, p. 158.

25. Castro Speech, August 10, 1967, p. 160. The designation of the Escalante group has been called several things. We use the term *microfaction*, rather than *microfraction* or *minifaction*. Microfaction seems to be the most common usage, and so we stick with it.

26. Castro Speech, August 10, 1967, p. 161.

27. Castro Speech, August 10, 1967, p. 163.

28. Regis Debray, *Le Critique des Armes* (Paris: Seuil, 1974), p. 245.

29. Tad Szulc, *Fidel: A Critical Portrait* (New York: William Morrow, 1986), p. 595.

30. Fidel Castro, eulogy for Che Guevara, delivered in Havana at the Plaza of the Revolution, October 18, 1967, in Kenner and Petras, *Fidel Castro Speaks*, pp. 164–68.

31. Fidel Castro, a eulogy for Ernesto (Che) Guevara, a speech delivered at the Plaza de la Revolucion, October 18, 1967, in Kenner and Petras, *Fidel Castro Speaks*, pp. 164–68.

32. See Jon Lee Anderson, *Che Guevara: A Revolutionary Life* (New York: Grove Press, 1997), p. xii.

33. Lévesque, *The USSR and the Cuban Revolution*, p. 131.

34. See Szulc, *Fidel*, p. 610; and Halperin, *The Taming of Fidel Castro*, pp. 269–70.

35. Domínguez, *To Make a World Safe for Revolution*, p. 73.

36. Karol, *Guerrillas in Power*, pp. 467–68.

37. Jorge Enrique Mendoza, column in *Granma*, February 4, 1968, p. 1. (This is the English edition. The original Spanish edition appeared the day before, on February 3.)

38. Mendoza, *Granma*, February 4, 1968, p. 1.

39. This was the (incorrect) surmise of Maurice Halperin, who was living in Havana at the time. See *The Taming of Fidel Castro*, p. 273.

40. Maurice Halperin, then a resident of Havana, heard speculation to this effect. See *The Taming of Fidel Castro*, p. 275. Likewise, K. S. Karol, who had just arrived in Havana, was told by his sources that the Soviets might wish to replace Fidel Castro with Raul Castro. See *Guerrillas in Power*, pp. 467–68.

41. *Granma*, February 3, 1968.

42. Oleg Darusenkov, interview with the authors, September 5–6, 1997, Washington, D.C.

43. This point was strongly emphasized by Oleg Darusenkov in an interview with the authors, September 5–6, 1997; and by Kiva Maidanik, interview with Svetlana Savranskaya, June 6, 1993, in Moscow, Russian Federation.

44. Fidel Castro, "Speech at the University of Havana," March 13, 1968, in Kenner and Petras, *Fidel Castro Speaks*, pp. 225–83. [Hereafter cited as Castro Speech, March 13, 1968.]

45. Castro Speech, March 13, 1966, p. 276.

46. Castro Speech, March 13, 1966, p. 278.

47. Castro Speech, March 13, 1966, p. 248.

48. This was confirmed in their interviews by both Oleg Darusenkov and Kiva Maidanik. See notes 43 and 44 of this chapter.

49. "Castro Anniversary Speech In Santa Clara," July 26, 1968; Foreign Broadcast Information Service Report Date 19680729; available at: http://lanic.utexas.edu/la/cb/cuba/castro.html.

50. Carlos Rafael Rodríguez, the old-line communist who had embraced the July 26th Movement before the Revolution and who was both a well-read theoretician and skillful government planner, emerged as the member of the Cuban leadership who would consistently frame policies so that they straddled the thin line between serving Soviet interests and being subservient to them. For a concise statement of how he viewed Cuban foreign policy in relation to the Soviets, see Carlos Rafael Rodríguez, "Why We Have Points of Concurrence with the Soviet Union," in Philip Brenner, William LeoGrande, Donna Rich, and Daniel Siegel, *The Cuba Reader: The Making of a Revolutionary Society* (New York: Grove Press, 1989), pp. 294–96.

51. Recent documentary evidence suggests that Soviet agents, acting as provocateurs, actually may have been responsible for posters that appeared in Prague calling for Czechoslovakia to withdraw from the Warsaw Pact. The Cubans would not have known this at the time. See Mark Kramer, "The Prague Spring and the Soviet Invasion of Czechoslovakia: New Interpretations (second of two parts)," *Bulletin of the Cold War International History Project*, issue 3 (fall 1993). Also see Jaromir Navratil, comp. and ed., *The Prague Spring, 1968* (Budapest: Central European Press, 1998), especially chap. 3.

52. Karol, *Guerrillas in Power*, p. 505.

53. Felix Pita, interview with the authors, April 29, 1995, Havana Cuba.

54. Felix Pita, interview with the authors, April 29, 1995.

55. Fidel Castro, "Radio and Television Address to the Cuban People," August 23, 1968. Quoted in *Granma*, August 25, 1968, p. 1. This official translation of the speech is reprinted in appendix C of this volume. All quotations from this speech are taken from the *Granma* English edition of August 25. [Hereafter cited as Castro Speech, August 23, 1968.]

56. Castro Speech, August 23, 1968, p. 2.

57. Castro Speech, August 23, 1968, p. 4.

58. Castro Speech, August 23, 1968, p. 2.

59. Castro Speech, August 23, 1968, p. 4.

60. Castro Speech, August 23, 1968, p. 2.

61. Saul Landau, interview with the authors, July 9, 1996, Washington, D.C.

62. Thomas Nagel, *Mortal Questions* (New York: Cambridge University Press, 1979), pp. 54–55.

63. Nagel, *Mortal Questions*, p. 74.

64. Reinhold Niebuhr, *The Irony of American History* (New York: Scribner's, 1952), p. 37.

65. Robert Axelrod, *The Evolution of Cooperation* (New York: Basic Books, 1984), p. 124.

EPILOGUE

1. "Fidel Castro's 23 October Interview," broadcast on Havana radio and television, *Foreign Broadcast Information Service*, Report Date, October 24, 1962; available at: http://lanic.utexas.edu/la/cb/cuba/castro/1962/19621024.

2. Speech by Fidel Castro, Havana, September 22, 2001; official English translation distributed the Ministry of Foreign Relations; available at: www.cuba.cu/gobierno/discursos/2001/ing/f220901i.html.

3. Fidel Castro remarks at a conference on the October Crisis, January 9–12, 1992, Havana, Cuba; transcribed in James G. Blight, Bruce J. Allyn, and David Welch, *Cuba on the Brink: Castro, the Missile Crisis, and the Soviet Collapse*, enlarged paperback ed. (Lanham, Md.: Rowman & Littlefield, 2002), p. 298.

4. Initially, for example, the gasoline ration for private cars was cut in half, and regular blackouts (i.e., short periods of no electricity) were instituted. In 1991 the government enacted further restrictions, for example, by reducing the bread ration to two rolls per day and by disconnecting the electricity of homes that had not cut power use by 10 percent. See Gillian Gunn, "Cuba's Search for Alternatives," *Current History*, February 1992.

5. The complete introduction and the correspondence in full, from *Granma Weekly* (English Edition), December 3, 1990, is reprinted in Blight et al., *Cuba on the Brink*, pp. 474–91. The Spanish version was published in the daily *Granma* on November 23, 1990.

6. Khrushchev wrote in his updated memoir, published in September 1990, that "Castro suggested . . . we should launch a preemptive strike against the United States" (Khrushchev, *Khrushchev Remembers: The Glasnost Tapes*, trans. and ed. Jerrold L. Schecter [Boston: Little, Brown, 1990], p. 177).

7. The editorial introduction, widely attributed to Castro himself, points out that "more than half of the current Cuban population hadn't been born in those crucial days of October 22–28, 1962. . . . But even most of those who lived through the events in the Soviet Union, the United States, and Cuba, are unfamiliar with the messages exchanged between October 26, 1962, and October 31, 1962 [between Castro and Khrushchev]" (Blight et al., *Cuba on the Brink*, p. 475).

8. Notably the editorial begins with a quotation from Che Guevara's 1965 "Farewell Letter" in which he wrote, "I felt at your side the pride of belonging to our people in the sad and luminous days of the Caribbean crisis" ("With the Historical Truth and Morale of Baraguá," in Blight et al., *Cuba on the Brink*, p. 475).

9. Blight et al., *Cuba on the Brink*, pp. 480–81.

10. "Fija Fidel Las Cinco Garantias Contra La Agresion a Cuba," *Revolucion*, October 29, 1962. Castro declared that the only effective guarantee "that there will be no aggression against Cuba" would be: (1) a cessation of the U.S. economic embargo and U.S. pressure on other countries to cut commercial links to Cuba; (2) an end to U.S. subversive activities against Cuba, including the "organization of invasions by mercenaries" and "the infiltration of spies and saboteurs"; (3) "cessation of the piratical attacks" from bases in the United States and Puerto Rico; (4) an end to violations of Cuban airspace; and (5) U.S. withdrawal from Guantanamo Naval Base. Castro repeated the five points to U Thant, Acting Secretary General of the United Nations, who traveled to Cuba on October 30 to seek permission for international verification that the missiles were being removed. The transcript of their meeting is reprinted in "Nuestra Derecho a la Paz se Está Abriendo Paso en El Mundo," *Verde Olivo*, November 11, 1962, pp. 14–15. Also see "Summary of [U Thant's] Meeting with President Dorticós, Premier Castro and Foreign Minister Roa of Cuba," October 31, 1962, UN Archives Call Number: Dag 1/5.2.2.6.2:1; in Laurence Chang, ed., *The Cuban Missile Crisis, 1962*, A National Security Archive Document Set (Alexandria, Va.: Chadwyck-Healey, 1990) [hereafter referred to as *CMC Document Set*], Document No. 01747.

11. The United States extracted the lease for the Guantanamo Naval Base from Cuba in 1903, in exchange for the withdrawal of U.S. occupation forces, and it acknowledges Cuban ownership of the land by depositing a $3,000 check each year as a lease payment (Cuba has declined to cash the checks). Rights to the base were included in the Platt Amendment, which the United States insisted Cuba include in its first constitution, and in a 1903 treaty ending U.S. occupation. (See "The Platt Amendment," in Philip Brenner, William LeoGrande, Donna Rich, and Daniel Siegel, *The Cuba Reader: The Making of a Revolutionary Society* [New York: Grove Press, 1989], pp. 30–31.) When Cuba abrogated the Platt Amendment in 1934, the United States negotiated a new agreement that permitted it to remain at Guantanamo Bay "in perpetuity." For a trenchant analysis of the role the Guantanamo Naval Base has played in the history of U.S.–Cuban relations, see Olga Miranda Bravo, *Vecinos Indeseables: La Base Yanqui de Guantánamo* (Havana, Cuba: Editorial de Ciencias Sociales, 1998), especially pp. 111–19 on the legitimacy of the 1934 agreement as a basis for continuing U.S. control of the territory. Also see Rafael Hernández Rodriguez, "Cuba's National Security and the Question of the Guantánamo Naval Base," in *Subject to Solution: Problems in Cuban–U.S. Relations*, eds. Wayne S. Smith and Esteban Morales Dominguez (Boulder, Colo.: Lynne Rienner, 1988), pp. 106–11.

12. U.S. Congress, House, "Cuban Liberty and Democratic Solidarity (*Libertad*) Act of 1996," Conference Report No. 104-468, March 1, 1996, 10th Cong., 2nd Sess., p. 43.

13. "26 July Speech," July 21, 1963, as reported by *Foreign Broadcast Information Service*, August 1, 1963; available in the University of Texas-LANIC "Castro Speech Database" http://lanic.utexas.edu/la/cb/cuba/castro.html.

14. Mary Pat Flaherty, David B. Ottaway, and James V. Grimaldi, "How Afghanistan Went Unlisted as Terrorist Sponsor," *Washington Post*, November 5, 2001. For an overview of Afghanistan's support for international terrorism before September 11, 2001, see Judith Miller, "Holy Warriors: Killing for the Glory of God, in a Land Far from Home," *New York Times*, January 16, 2001. The U.S. State Department's rationale for including Cuba on the list of terrorist states can be found in "Patterns of Global Terrorism—2001," released by the Office of the Coordinator for Counterterrorism, May 21, 2002, and available at: http://www.state.gov/s/ct/rls/

pgtrpt/2001/html/10249.htm. For a critique of the rationale used to place Cuba on the terrorism list, see Anya K. Landau and Wayne S. Smith, "Keeping Things in Perspective: Cuba and the Question of International Terrorism" (Washington, D.C.: Center for International Policy, 2001); available at: www.ciponline.org/cuba/ipr/keepingthingsinperspective.pdf.

15. Otto J. Reich, "U.S. Foreign Policy in the Western Hemisphere," remarks to the Center for Strategic and International Studies, Washington, D.C., March 12, 2002; U.S. Department of State, Bureau of Public Affairs, released March 13, 2002; available at: www.state.gov/p/wha/rls/rm/8751.htm. This was Reich's first speech after being sworn in as assistant secretary of state for Western Hemisphere affairs.

16. David Halberstam, *The Best and the Brightest* (Greenwich, Conn.: Fawcett, 1973), p. 85.

17. Jorge I. Domínguez, *To Make the World Safe for Revolution: Cuba's Foreign Policy* (Cambridge, Mass.: Harvard University Press, 1989), p. 7.

18. Domínguez, *To Make the World Safe for Revolution*, pp. 79–80; Phyllis Greene Walker, "The Cuban Military," in Brenner et al., *The Cuba Reader*, pp. 280–83; Carla Anne Robbins, *The Cuban Threat* (New York: McGraw-Hill, 1983), pp. 186–89.

19. H. Michael Erisman, *Cuba's Foreign Relations in a Post-Soviet World* (Gainesville: University Press of Florida, 2000), pp. 98–104; Jorge I. Domínguez, "Pipsqueak Power: The Centrality and Anomaly of Cuba," in *The Suffering Grass: Superpowers and Regional Conflict in Southern Africa and the Caribbean*, eds. Thomas G. Weiss and James G. Blight (Boulder, Colo.: Lynne Rienner, 1992), p. 65–66; Domínguez, *To Make the World Safe for Revolution*, pp. 148–52; Paula Pettavino and Philip Brenner, "More than Just a Game," *Peace Review*, vol. 11, no. 4 (Winter 1999).

20. Richard M. Nixon, "Rough Draft of Summary of Conversation between the Vice President and Fidel Castro," 25 April 1959, reprinted in Jeffrey J. Safford, "The Nixon–Castro Meeting of 19 April 1959," *Diplomatic History*, vol. 4, no. 4 (fall 1980), p. 431.

21. Thomas G. Paterson, *Contesting Castro: The United States and the Triumph of the Cuban Revolution* (New York: Oxford University Press, 1994), pp. 242, 258. These plans were consistent with goals outlined by the State Department in October 1959. See "Memorandum from the Assistant Secretary of State for Inter-American Affairs (Rubottom) to the Under Secretary of State for Political Affairs (Murphy): Current Basic United States Policy toward Cuba," October 23, 1959, in United States Department of State, *Foreign Relations of the United, 1958–1960*, vol. VI: Cuba [hereafter cited as *FRUS, 1958–1960*, vol. VI] (Washington, D.C.: Government Printing Office, 1991), Document No. 376, pp. 635–37.

22. "Memorandum of Discussion at the 411th Meeting of the National Security Council," June 25, 1959, in *FRUS, 1958–1960*, vol. VI, Document No. 325, pp. 541–43. Robbins (*The Cuban Threat*, pp. 9–12) identifies the three countries as the Dominican Republic, Panama, and Haiti, citing sources that indicate the attack against Nicaragua was launched from Costa Rica and was not carried out by Cubans. All of the raids failed, and Cuba has acknowledged its active support only for the one against Trujillo. Many governments in the hemisphere had long condemned these tyrannies. A U.S. Senate committee observed years later that the Dominican Republic's Rafael Trujillo "was a brutal dictator, and both the Eisenhower and Kennedy Administrations encouraged the overthrow of his regime by Dominican dissidents" (U.S. Congress, Senate, Select Committee to Study Governmental Operations with Respect to Intelligence Activities, *Alleged Assassinations Plots Involving Foreign Leaders*, An Interim Report, no. 94-465, 94th Cong., 1st Sess., November 20, 1975, p. 191). The Dominican dissidents ultimately assassinated Trujillo, apparently with U.S. acquiescence.

23. "Memorandum from the Secretary of State to the President: Current Basic United States Policy toward Cuba," *FRUS, 1958–1960*, vol. VI, Document No. 387, p. 657. Morley (*Imperial*

State and Revolution, p. 85) notes that by the end of November 1959 even "the supposedly accommodating [U.S.] Ambassador [Philip] Bonsal decried Cuba's 'independent position in world affairs' and its refusal to echo U.S. positions in global regional forums." Wayne S. Smith (*The Closest of Enemies: A Personal and Diplomatic Account of U.S.-Cuban Relations since 1957* [New York: Norton, 1987], p. 52) recalls that "by October 1959 most of us in Havana" had decided Castro was turning toward the Soviet Union. Richard E. Welch, Jr. (*Response to Revolution: The United States and the Cuban Revolution, 1959-1961* [Chapel Hill: University of North Carolina Press, 1985], p. 48) point outs that by midsummer 1959, Nixon "was convinced that Castro was a danger as well as a nuisance," and began urging President Dwight D. Eisenhower to destabilize the Cuban government.

24. "First Declaration of Havana," September 2, 1960, in Julio García Luis, ed., *Cuban Revolution Reader: A Documentary History of 40 Key Moments of the Cuban Revolution* (Melbourne, Australia: Ocean Press, 2001), pp. 45-51. The declaration came four days after the OAS approved the Declaration of San Jose (28 August 1960), in which the foreign ministers implicitly condemned Cuba for permitting the "extracontinental intervention" by the Soviet Union and China that "endangers American solidarity and security" and reaffirmed "the principle of nonintervention by any American state in the internal or external affairs of the other American states." In the Second Declaration of Havana, on February 4, 1962, Castro declared—in response to Cuba's expulsion from the OAS—that it is "The duty of every revolutionary to make the revolution" (Martin Kenner and James Petras, eds., *Fidel Castro Speaks* [New York: Grove Press, 1969], p. 104).

25. John Lewis Gaddis, *Strategies of Containment: A Critical Appraisal of Postwar American National Security Policy* (New York: Oxford University Press, 1982), p. 92; Melvyn P. Leffler, "National Security," in *Explaining the History of American Foreign Relations*, eds. Michael J. Hogan and Thomas G. Paterson (New York: Cambridge University Press, 1991), pp. 203-5.

26. These assumptions were embodied in a 1950 policy paper prepared for and adopted by the National Security Council, "NSC-68: United States Objectives and Programs for National Security (April 14, 1950)." NSC-68 provided a framework and justification for responses to perceived communist challenges throughout the Cold War. It is reprinted in Ernest R. May, *American Cold War Strategy: Interpreting NSC 68* (Boston: Bedford Books, 1993), pp. 23-81. In 1999 Paul Nitze, the principal author of NSC-68, explained that in

the three years preceding NSC-68, President Truman had already made crucial political decisions regarding the direction of foreign policy. Most far-reaching of these was his determination to pick up an exhausted Britain's mantle as a global, balancing power. Thus those who drafted NSC-68 mapped out an approach toward goals already set. These goals reflected a courageous and, even at the time, controversial decision on the part of Truman to commit the United States to a leading, interventionist role in peacetime world affairs for the first time in its history ("NSC-68 and U.S. Foreign Policy Today," *SAIS Review*, vol. 19, no. 1 (1999), pp. 1-2).

Kennedy's Secretary of State, Dean Rusk, recalled in his memoirs how these assumptions guided his own thinking:

In the events of the postwar period the Communist world posed our primary challenge with its return to a doctrine of world revolution, supported by acts of aggression on the ground to bring it about. . . . It looked as though this mud slide of communism would continue unless stopped" (as told to Richard Rusk, *As I Saw It* [New York: Penguin, 1991], pp. 128-29).

27. Gaddis, *Strategies of Containment*, pp. 201–2; Thomas G. Paterson, "Introduction: John F. Kennedy's Quest for Victory and Global Crisis," in *Kennedy's Quest for Victory: American Foreign Policy, 1961–1963*, ed. Thomas G. Paterson (New York: Oxford University Press, 1989), pp. 10–11; Peter H. Smith, *Talons of the Eagle: Dynamics of U.S.–Latin American Relations*, 2nd ed. (New York: Oxford University Press, 2000), chap. 7. Smith (p. 164) succinctly summarizes the U.S. outlook: "In the eyes of Cold Warriors, the consolidation of any left-wing regime in the Western Hemisphere would have dire and dangerous implications for U.S. national security and for the global distribution of power."

28. As we discuss in chapter 1, the credibility of the U.S. nuclear deterrent was a central concern for policymakers with regard to the Soviet Union, but that worry focused on preserving the perception that the United States both maintained and would use a nuclear arsenal. They believed that such a perception would deter any rational opponent from using nuclear weapons against the United States, in the fear that the United States would inflict unacceptable levels of destruction in return.

29. Gaddis, *Strategies of Containment*, pp. 96–103.

30. Stephen G. Rabe, *The Most Dangerous Area in the World: John F. Kennedy Confronts Communist Revolution in Latin America* (Chapel Hill: University of North Carolina Press, 1999), pp. 20–26. Thomas G. Paterson, "Fixation with Cuba: The Bay of Pigs, Missile Crisis, and Covert War against Castro," in Paterson, *Kennedy's Quest for Victory*, pp. 124–25. He notes (p. 123) that "President Kennedy spent as much or more time on Cuba as on any other foreign policy problem."

31. A May 1961 interagency task force report emphasized that the Cuban threat was related to the damage Cuba could inflict on U.S. prestige, and hence power, rather than to the harm it might impose on particular U.S. interests:

Continuing bloc arms shipments to Cuba . . . will probably not be an important threat to U.S. interests. There is no danger of effective direct attack against the U.S. It is highly unlikely that Castro will overtly attack other nations in the Americas. . . . As an exporter of physical aids to revolution—there is no doubt that Cuba is being used as a base for export of the communist-fidelista revolution. . . . At the present time, there is no hard evidence of an actual supply of arms or armed men going from Cuba to other countries to assist indigenous revolutionary movements. There have been allegations of such support being given in Colombia and other countries. There has been some movement of individual armed agents into other countries and some Cuban effort to train the revolutionaries of other countries. The export of physical aid to revolutionary movements, while important, is much less significant than the threat posed by Castro's example and general stimulus to these movements. . . . He has provided a rallying point and a source of ideological support for communist movements everywhere; and often for left-wing nationalist movements. One of his principal objectives is to identify and unify the nationalist left and the communists. He has provided a working example of a communist state in the Americas, successfully defying the United States. Thus he has appealed to widespread anti-American feeling, a feeling often shared by noncommunists. His survival, in the face of persistent U.S. efforts to unseat him, has unquestionably lowered the prestige of the United States and the presence of Castroist extremist elements are often an important obstacle to orderly social and economic reform. . . . There is no doubt that Castro's regime adds significant support to communist efforts to take over the hemisphere, and is a source of strength to communist efforts in every country. However, Castro could not hope to succeed without the conditions of social unrest, widespread poverty and general economic discontent on which the Communist Revolution prospers. If the island of Cuba should sink beneath the waves tomorrow, we still would have to face a significant and steadily growing communist threat in the hemisphere. The fall of Castro would be a severe defeat for the Sino-Soviet bloc, but it would not be, by any means, the end of the battle ("Paper Prepared for the National Security Council by an Interagency Task Force on

Cuba, Washington, May 4, 1961," U.S. State Department, *Foreign Relations of the United, 1961–1963*, vol. X: Cuba, 1961–1962 [hereafter cited as *FRUS, 1961–1963*, vol. X] [Washington, D.C.: Government Printing Office, 1997], Document No. 202).

32. Jorge I. Domínguez ("U.S.–Latin American Relations during the Cold War and Its Aftermath," in *The United States and Latin America: The New Agenda*, eds. Victor Bulmer-Thomas and James Dunkerley [London: Institute of Latin American Studies, 1999], pp. 38–39) argues that "Cuba and its foreign policy shaped (and misshaped) much of U.S. policy towards the region" during the Cold War, because this was the only time when "a country in this region became a military and political ally of the chief adversary of the United States." As a result, U.S. policy toward Latin America during this epoch deviated from other periods in that "ideology was repeatedly more important than balance-of-power or economic considerations."

33. "Long Term Outlook for Cuba: Attachment, Memorandum Prepared by Director of Central Intelligence [John] McCone," November 13, 1962, in United States Department of State, *Foreign Relations of the United, 1961–1963*, vol. XI: Cuban Missile Crisis and Aftermath [hereafter cited as *FRUS, 1961–1963*, vol. XI] (Washington, D.C.: Government Printing Office, 1997), Document No. 174, pp. 445–46; "Situation and Prospects in Cuba," National Intelligence Estimate 85-63, June 14, 1963, in *FRUS, 1961–1963*, vol. XI, Document No. 347, p. 836. Kennedy's assistant secretary of state for inter-American affairs, Edwin McCammon Martin (*Kennedy and Latin America* [Lanham, Md.: University Press of America, 1994], p. 24), recalled in his memoirs that he considered Cuba to be a "communist satellite" as early as 1960.

34. Jean Daniel, "Unofficial Envoy," *The New Republic*, December 14, 1963, p. 16.

35. "Memorandum for the Record," November 12, 1963, in *FRUS, 1961–1963*, vol. XI, Document No. 377, p. 889. Also see Arthur M. Schlesinger, Jr., *Robert F. Kennedy and His Times* (New York: Ballantine, 1978), pp. 580–81, 592–93.

36. Gregory F. Treverton, "Cuba in U.S. Security Perspective," in *U.S.–Cuban Relations in the 1990s*, eds. Jorge I. Domínguez and Rafael Hernández (Boulder, Colo.: Westview, 1989), p. 71.

37. Philip Brenner, "The Thirty Year War," *NACLA: Report on the Americas*, November 1990.

38. Zbigniew Brzezinksi, *Power and Principle: Memoirs of the National Security Adviser, 1977–1981*, rev. ed. (New York: Farrar, Straus, and Giroux, 1985), pp. 180–81.

39. U.S. Department of State, Bureau of Public Affairs, "Cuba's Renewed Support for Violence in Latin America," Special Report No. 90, December 14, 1981; reprinted in U.S. Congress, Senate Committee on the Judiciary, "The Role of Cuba in International Terrorism and Subversion," Hearings before the Subcommittee on Security and Terrorism, 97th Cong., 2nd Sess., February 26, March 4, 11, and 12, 1982, Serial No. J-97-97, appendix, pp. 213–20. Also see Domínguez, *To Make the World Safe for Revolution*, chap. 5; Erisman, *Cuba's Foreign Relations in a Post-Soviet World*, pp. 85–100.

40. For thoughtful analyses about the way the United States could have served its interests in the 1980s vis-à-vis Cuba by overcoming its ideological rigidity, see Wayne S. Smith, "The Cuban–Soviet Alliance," in Smith and Morales, *Subject to Solution*, pp. 9–13; Richard J. Payne, *Opportunities and Dangers of Soviet–Cuban Expansion: Toward a Pragmatic U.S. Policy* (Albany: State University of New York Press, 1988), pp. 18–24 and the proposals in chaps. 2–6.

41. "Cuba's Renewed Support for Violence in Latin America," p. 213. The 1984 Kissinger Commission Report on Central America pointed to these schools in recommending increasing exchange programs in the United States for democratic leaders, which could counter the Cuban training (Henry A. Kissinger, *Report of the National Bipartisan Commission on Central America* [Washington, D.C.: Goverment Printing Office, 1984]).

42. Philip Brenner, *From Confrontation to Negotiation: U.S. Relations with Cuba* (Boulder, Colo.: Westview, 1988), pp. 17–44. This policy is evident as early as June 1963, in a CIA plan for a covert operations against Cuba submitted to the National Security Council for approval ("Paper Prepared by the Central Intelligence Agency for the Standing Group of the National Security Council: Proposed Covert Policy and Integrated Program of Action towards Cuba," June 8, 1963, in *FRUS 1961–1963*, vol. XI, Document No. 346, p. 828). The proposal plainly asserts:

> This program is based on the assumption that current U.S. policy does not contemplate outright military intervention in Cuba or a provocation which can be used as a pretext for an invasion of Cuba by United States military forces. It is further assumed that U.S. policy calls for the exertion of maximum pressure by all means available to the U.S. Government, short of military intervention, to prevent the pacification of the population and the consolidation of the Castro/Communist regime. The ultimate objective of this policy would be to encourage dissident elements in the military and other power centers of the regime to bring about the eventual liquidation of the Castro/Communist entourage and the elimination of the Soviet presence from Cuba.

43. That moniker comes from Theodore Draper (*Castro's Revolution: Myths and Realities* [New York: Praeger, 1962], p. 59), who wrote that the invasion "was one of those rare politico-military events—a perfect failure." For recent studies on the failure, see James G. Blight and Peter Kornbluh, eds., *Politics of Illusion: The Bay of Pigs Invasion Reexamined* (Boulder, Colo.: Lynne Rienner, 1998); Peter Kornbluh, ed., *Bay of Pigs Declassified: The Secret CIA Report on the Invasion of Cuba* (New York: New Press, 1998); Piero Gleijeses, "Ships in the Night: The CIA, the White House and the Bay of Pigs," *Journal of Latin American Studies*, vol. 27, no. 1 (February 1995).

44. *Alleged Assassinations Plots Involving Foreign Leaders*, pp. 74–82, 117–18; Blight and Kornbluh, *Politics of Illusion*, pp. 83–86; Peter Kornbluh, "Introduction: History Held Hostage," in Kornbluh, *Bay of Pigs Declassified*, pp. 8–10.

45. Edward G. Lansdale, "The Cuba Project," Memorandum to the National Security Council, Special Group (Augmented), January 18, 1962, in *CMC Document Set*, Document No. 00141; *Alleged Assassinations Plots Involving Foreign Leaders*, pp. 135–63; Blight and Kornbluh, *Politics of Illusion*, pp. 112–18; Schlesinger, *Robert F. Kennedy*, pp. 513–17.

46. Blight and Kornbluh, *Politics of Illusion*, pp. 113–18, 124, 127–28, 254–55. Also *Alleged Assassinations Plots Involving Foreign Leaders*, pp. 146–47; Schlesinger, *Robert F. Kennedy*, p. 585.

47. "Memorandum from Gordon Chase of the National Security Council Staff to the President's Special Assistant for National Security Affairs (Bundy)," February 14, 1963, in *FRUS, 1961–1963*, vol. XI, Document No. 282. Chase wrote (pp. 699–700): "There seems to be very little doubt that Cuba has been substantially isolated from the Free World. . . . This isolation has not come about accidentally. We have actively encouraged this isolation unilaterally (shipping restrictions), bilaterally (representations to certain countries trading with Cuba), and multilaterally (OAS)." Also see Welch, *Response to Revolution*, pp. 94–97.

48. "Eighth Meeting of Consultation of Ministers of Foreign Affairs of the American Republics; Punta del Este, January 22–31, 1962: Final Act, Signed January 31, 1962," in U.S. Department of State, Historical Office, *American Foreign Policy, Current Documents, 1962*, Washington, D.C., 1966, Document No. III-12, pp. 326–27. The United States also had sought approval for an OAS-approved hemispheric trade embargo against Cuba, but the member states agreed only to suspend "trade with Cuba in arms and implements of war." See Dean Rusk,

"United States Proposal of Four Major Actions against the Government of Cuba," January 25, 1962, in *American Foreign Policy, Current Documents, 1962*, Document No. III-10, pp. 318–19.

49. James G. Blight, David Lewis, and David A. Welch, "Cuba between the Superpowers, Antigua, 3–7 January 1991: Transcript of the Meetings"; typescript (available from Brown University's Watson Institute for International Studies, Providence, R.I.), p. 38. Also see Schlesinger's comments in Blight and Kornbluh, *Politics of Illusion*, pp. 124–25; comments by Robert McNamara and Theodore Sorensen in Bruce J. Allyn, James G. Blight, and David A. Welch, eds., *Back to the Brink: Proceedings of the Moscow Conference on the Cuban Missile Crisis, January 27–28, 1989*, CSIA Occasional Paper No. 9 (Lanham, Md.: University Press of America, 1992), pp. 9, 105, 188–89; comments by McGeorge Bundy and McNamara in James G. Blight and David A. Welch, *On the Brink: Americans and Soviets Reexamine the Cuban Missile Crisis*, 2nd ed. (New York: Farrar, Straus and Giroux, 1990), pp. 249–50.

50. Robert McNamara candidly remarked in 1989 that "if I had been a Cuban leader, I think I might have expected a U.S. invasion" (Allyn et al., *Back to the Brink*, p. 7). Schlesinger (*Robert F. Kennedy*, p. 541) observed in 1978 that "Castro had the best grounds for feeling under siege . . . the Mongoose campaign left little doubt that the American government was trying to overthrow him."

51. Aleksandr Fursenko and Timothy Naftali, *One Hell of a Gamble: Khrushchev, Castro and Kennedy, 1958–1964* (New York: Norton, 1997), pp. 151–54; Sergo Mikoyan, "La Crisis del Caribe, en retrospectiva," *America Latina* (Moscow), no. 4 (April 1988), p. 45; Blight and Welch, *On the Brink*, p. 238.

52. For a thoughtful overview of how documents have enabled us to appreciate the missile crisis, see Thomas Blanton, "Annals of Blinksmanship," *Wilson Quarterly*, summer 1997. For an examination of the role fear played in the evolving decisions during the crisis, see James G. Blight, *The Shattered Crystal Ball: Fear and Learning in the Cuban Missile Crisis* (Lanham, Md.: Rowman & Littlefield, 1990). Also see Richard Ned Lebow and Janice Gross Stein, *We All Lost the Cold War* (Princeton, N.J.: Princeton University Press, 1994), pp. 143–45. The transcripts of the ExComm meetings are reprinted in Ernest R. May and Philip D. Zelikow, eds., *The Kennedy Tapes: Inside the White House during the Cuban Missile Crisis* (Cambridge, Mass.: Harvard University Press, 1997), pp. 492–629. The question of how close the two superpowers actually came to nuclear war is addressed with competing conclusions by two articles in *Cold War International History Project Bulletin*, no. 3 (fall 1993): James G. Blight, Bruce J. Allyn, and David A. Welch, "Kramer vs. Kramer: Or, How Can You Have Revisionism in the Absence of Orthodoxy?" and Mark Kramer, "Tactical Nuclear Weapons, Soviet Command Authority, and the Cuban Missile Crisis."

53. Anna Kasten Nelson ("Operation Northwoods and the Covert War against Cuba, 1961–1963," *Cuba Studies*, no. 32 [Pittsburgh: University of Pittsburgh Press, 2001]) demonstrates convincingly that the invasion plans were quite serious. She observes (p. 146) that "the plans for Cuba were not merely the product of underemployed colonels," but "were an integral part of Operation Mongoose and the attempts to overthrow the Castro government." Also see James G. Hershberg, "Before 'The Missiles of October': Did Kennedy Plan a Military Strike against Cuba," in *The Cuban Missile Crisis Revisited*, ed. James A. Nathan (New York: St. Martin's, 1992); Fursenko and Naftali, *One Hell of a Gamble*, pp. 149–51. The plans are included in *CINCLANT Historical Account of Cuban Crisis—1963*, Serial: 000119/J09H, April 29, 1963, in *CMC Document Set*, Document No. 003087.

54. "Memorandum from President Kennedy to Secretary of Defense McNamara," April 29, 1963, in *FRUS, 1961–1963*, vol. XI, Document No. 327, p. 791.

55. "Joint Resolution Expressing the Determination of the United States with Respect to the Situation in Cuba" (Public Law 87-733, October 3, 1962), in *American Foreign Policy, Current Documents, 1962*, Document III-44, pp. 389-90.

56. Jonathan Swift, *Gulliver's Travels*, ed., Robert A. Greenberg (New York: W. W. Norton, 1961), p. 8.

57. "Prepared Statement of Philip W. Bonsal," in U.S. Congress, Senate Committee on Foreign Relations, "U.S. Policy toward Cuba," Hearings before the Subcommittee on Western Hemisphere Affairs, 93rd Cong., 1st Sess., April 18, 1973, pp. 36-37. Bonsal was the last U.S. ambassador to Cuba and had been chosen for the post because of his reputation for working effectively with reformers in Latin America. In this statement he was advocating the normalization of relations between the United States and Cuba.

58. See, for example, "Memorandum of a Conference, Department of State: Questions Concerning the Program of Economic Pressures against Castro," June 27, 1960, in *FRUS, 1958-1960*, vol. VI, Document No. 536, p. 963; "Memorandum Prepared in the Department of State: The Problem of Cuba in the OAS," June 30, 1960, *FRUS, 1958-1960*, vol. VI, Document No. 540, p. 973.

59. Kissinger even revised the agreement to reduce the stipulations by which Cuba had to abide: "We defined [the understandings of 1962] as prohibiting the emplacement of any offensive weapon of any kind or any offensive delivery system on Cuban territory. We reaffirmed that in return we not use military force to bring about a change in the governmental structure of Cuba" (Henry Kissinger, *White House Years* [Boston: Little, Brown, 1979], p. 634). Kissinger was national security adviser at the time. In 1973 he became Secretary of State.

60. Ronnie Dugger, *On Reagan: The Man and His Presidency* (New York: McGraw-Hill, 1983), p. 229. On Reagan's belief that coercion was the only way to deal with the Soviet Union (and by extension its client states), see Russell J. Leng, "Reagan and the Russians: Crisis Bargaining Beliefs and the Historical Record," *American Political Science Review*, vol. 78, no. 2. (June 1984), pp. 338-39.

61. Haig was determined, William M. LeoGrande recounts (*Our Own Backyard: The United States in Central America, 1977-1992* [Chapel Hill: University of North Carolina Press, 1998], pp. 81-82) to "put an end to the Castro regime." At a March 1981 meeting of the National Security Council he reportedly told Reagan that if given the chance "I'll turn that fucking island into a parking lot" (quoted in *Our Own Backyard*, p. 82).

62. Kenneth N. Skoug, "Cuba as a Model and a Challenge," July 25, 1984, Current Policy No. 600, U.S. State Department, Bureau of Public Affairs, p. 5.

63. Michael Ranneberger, "Statement before the Subcommittee on Trade," May 7, 1998, in U.S. Congress, House Ways and Means Committee, "U.S. Economic and Trade Policy Toward Cuba," Hearing of the Trade Subcommittee on H.R. 1951, Cuban Humanitarian Trade Act of 1997, May 7, 1998, 105th Cong., 2nd Sess.; available at: www.state.gov/www/policy_remarks/1998/980507_ranneberger_cuba.html. Ranneberger was the State Department's coordinator for Cuban affairs.

64. Bureau of Democracy, Human Rights, and Labor, U.S. State Department, "Country Reports on Human Rights Practices—2001: Cuba," released March 4, 2002; available at: www.state.gov/g/drl/rls/hrrpt/2001/wha/8333.htm. Similarly, the State Department's Fact Sheet on "Medical Sales to Cuba" asserts, "The United States is the largest donor of medicine and medical equipment to Cuba. The Cuban government can also purchase medicines and medical equipment from U.S. companies. However, Cuban policy promotes medical tourism for foreigners over the welfare of average Cubans. For most Cubans, empty pharmacies are the norm."

65. Reich, "U.S. Foreign Policy in the Western Hemisphere."

66. Ranneberger, "Statement before the Subcommittee on Trade."

67. The phrase had been attributed to Eban before 1983, but without citation. In his 1983 version, he said: "In the final resort the Arab cause in the West Bank and Gaza will stand or fall by the decision of the Palestinian Arabs. Their diplomatic history refutes the idea that nations usually act in their own best interest. They have never missed a chance of losing an opportunity" (Abba Eban, *The New Diplomacy: International Affairs in the Modern Age* [New York: Random House, 1983], p. 229).

68. Peter Kornbluh and James G. Blight, "Dialogue with Castro: A Hidden History," *New York Review of Books*, October 6, 1994. The new regulations were listed in the Federal Register on October 8, 1975 (U.S. Congress, 1976. "U.S. Trade Embargo of Cuba," Hearings before the Subcommittees on International Trade and Commerce and International Organizations, Committee on International Relations, House of Representatives, on H.R. 6382, 94th Cong., 1st Sess., May 8 to September 23, 1975, pp. 562-64).

69. Henry Kissinger, *Years of Renewal* (New York: Simon and Schuster, 1999), p. 782; *New York Times*, August 21, 1975.

70. Kissinger, *Years of Renewal*, p. 782. *Tu quoque* is a Latin expression meaning "You're another." It is a form of argumentation in which a person responds to criticism by alleging that the critic engages in the very same behavior. Sánchez-Parodi maintains that the Cubans believed Puerto Rico and Angola were excuses: "the main reason, we have always believed, was the fear that if the secret talks were revealed during the election campaign, Ford would have been severely damaged" (quoted in Kornbluh and Blight, "Dialogue with Castro: A Hidden History").

71. Piero Gleijeses, *Conflicting Missions: Havana, Washington, and Africa, 1959-1976* (Chapel Hill: University of North Carolina Press, 2002), pp. 255-72; 285-93 329-38; Kissinger, *Years of Renewal*, pp. 290-93, 329-38; 797-98, 809-11; *New York Times*, December 21, 1975, p. 3.

72. "Statement on United States Policy toward Cuba," January 5, 1999, in *Public Papers of the Presidents of the United States, William J. Clinton, 1999*, Book I (Washington, D.C.: Government Printing Office, 2000), p. 7.

73. See, for example, Jorge I. Domínguez, "U.S.-Cuban Relations: From the Cold War to the Colder War," *Journal of Interamerican Studies and World Affairs*, vol. 39, no. 3 (1997); William LeoGrande, "Enemies Evermore," *Journal of Latin American Studies*, vol. 29, no. 1 (1997); Stephen A. Lisio, "Helms-Burton and the Point of Diminishing Returns," *International Affairs*, vol. 72, no. 1 (1996).

74. James Dobbins, special assistant to the president and senior director for inter-American affairs, NSC, "On-the-Record Briefing on Cuba," released by the Office of the Spokesman, U.S. Department of State, January 5, 1999.

75. Ellen Gamerman, "The Man behind O's Cuba Games," *Baltimore Sun*, March 26, 1999; Pettavino and Brenner, "More than Just a Game," p. 529; Philip Brenner, Patrick J. Haney, and Walter Vanderbush, "The Confluence of Domestic and International Interests: U.S. Policy toward Cuba, 1998-2001," *International Studies Perspectives*, vol. 3 (2002), p. 195.

76. "Statement on United States Policy toward Cuba," January 5, 1999, p. 7.

77. *Granma*, Daily Edition, January 9, 1999 (trans. from Spanish).

78. Quoted in Serge F. Kovaleski, "Warming Up a Cold War: Castro Cracks Down on Cubans Sympathetic to U.S. Policies," *Washington Post*, February 23, 1999, p. A13.

79. For analyses that have focused on key junctures in the relationship when there might have been a rapprochement see Philip Brenner, *From Confrontation to Negotiation: U.S. Relations*

with Cuba (Boulder, Colo.: Westview, 1988); Smith and Morales, *Subject to Solution*; Gillian Gunn, *Cuba in Transition: Options for U.S. Policy* (New York: Twentieth Century Fund Press, 1993); Jorge I. Domínguez and Rafael Hernández, eds., *U.S.–Cuban Relations in the 1990s* (Boulder, Colo.: Westview, 1989), especially Jorge I. Domínguez, "The Obstacles and Prospects for Improved U.S.–Cuban Relations: A U.S. Perspective."

80. Smith, *Closest of Enemies*, chapters 4–7; Brenner, *From Confrontation to Negotiation*, pp. 19–23; Robbins, *The Cuban Threat*, pp. 224–65; Raymond L. Garthoff, *Détente and Confrontation: American–Soviet Relations from Nixon to Reagan*, rev. ed. (Washington, D.C.: Brookings Institution, 1994), pp. 681–82.

81. William M. LeoGrande ("From Havana to Miami: U.S. Cuba Policy as a Two-Level Game," *Journal of Interamerican Studies and World Affairs* (spring 1998) provides a thoughtful analysis of the way U.S. foreign policy interests toward Cuba have been compromised by the difficulty presidents have had in simultaneously pursuing those interests while satisfying the interests of domestic constituencies.

82. Kissinger, *Years of Renewal*, p. 786. Bonsal offered a similar assessment in 1973 ("Prepared Statement of Philip W. Bonsal," p. 37) when he said, "In marked contrast to the evolution of American attitudes toward him, Castro's attitude toward the United States has remained rigid. . . . Castro, neglecting all contrary evidence, has maintained in his public utterances the concept that the 'unrepentant imperialists' are still plotting the overthrow of his revolution." In a meeting with us in 1993, Kissinger actually seemed mystified as to how Cuba could calculate that it had a greater interest in Angola than in establishing normal relations with the United States (the session was held at Pocantico Hills, New York, on August 23).

83. William Ratliff and Roger Fontaine, *A Strategic Flip-flop in the Caribbean: Lift the Embargo on Cuba*, Hoover Institution on War, Revolution and Peace, Stanford University, 2000, p. iii; available at: www-hoover.stanford.edu/publications/epp/100/100.pdf. This assumption leads them to argue that Castro's need to maintain the United States as an enemy means that trying to improve relations with Cuba now would only be an exercise in frustration. Similar positions can be found in: Mark Falcoff, "The Cuba in Our Mind," *National Interest*, summer 1993; Susan Kaufman Purcell, "Why the Embargo Makes Sense in a Post–Cold War World," in *Cuba: The Contours of Change*, eds. Susan Kaufman Purcell and David Rothkopf (Boulder, Colo.: Lynne Rienner, 2000).

84. Jorge I. Domínguez ("Castro's Staying Power," *Foreign Affairs*, March/April 1993), for example, contends that "The Castro regime endures in part because its enemies unwittingly help it to survive. . . . Continuing U.S. military maneuvers and overflights constantly remind Cubans of the possibility of a U.S. threat, making it easier for Castro to call for sacrifices to defend the homeland." Similarly, Alejandro Portes ("Strategic Neglect," *American Prospect*, September 25, 2000) argues that "Lifting the economic embargo and other hostile measures against Cuba would deprive aging revolutionaries of the single persuasive reason for their holding onto power."

85. This brief and stark summary of such an argument is intended to highlight the assumption that the embargo serves the narrow purposes of the Cuban leadership in holding onto power. It does not convey the nuances and complexity found in several thoughtful proposals of this sort by leading foreign policy groups. See, for example, Bernard W. Aronson and William D. Rogers, "U.S.–Cuban Relations in the 21st Century," Independent Task Force Report, November 26, 2000 (New York: Council on Foreign Relations, 2000); Inter-American Dialogue, *A Time for Decisions: U.S. Policy in the Western Hemisphere*, A Report of the Sol M. Linowitz Forum (Washington, D.C.: Inter-American Dialogue, 2000), pp. 17–18. Ratliffe and Fontaine (*A Strategic Flip-flop in the Caribbean*) are among the most prominent conservative critics of the embargo who have used this line of reasoning. Also see Daniel W. Fisk, "Cuba: The End of an Era," *Washington*

Quarterly, winter 2001; Richard N. Haass, "Sanctioning Madness," *Foreign Affairs*, November/ December 1997; David R. Henderson, "Why Our Cuba Policy Is Wrong,"*Fortune*, October 13, 1997; Editorial, "Coming to Our Senses on Cuba," *Chicago Tribune*, August 4, 2000.

86. Blight et al., *Cuba on the Brink*, pp. 298–300.

87. *Cuban Liberty and Democratic Solidarity (Libertad) Act of 1996*, Public Law 104-114 [H.R. 927], March 12, 1996, Sec. 2 (28); U.S. International Trade Commission, *The Economic Impact of U.S. Sanctions with Respect to Cuba*, Investigation No. 332-413, USITC Publication 3398, February 2001 (Washington, D.C.: U.S. International Trade Commission, 2001), p. 2-1; Donna Rich Kaplowitz, *Anatomy of a Failed Embargo: U.S. Sanctions against Cuba* (Boulder, Colo.: Lynne Rienner, 1998); Michael Krinsky and David Golove, *United States Economic Measures against Cuba* (Northampton, Mass.: Aletheia Press, 1993), pp. 85–117; Morris H. Morley, *Imperial State and Revolution: The United States and Cuba, 1952–1986* (New York: Cambridge University Press, 1987), pp. 187–93.

88. Ironically, one rationale underlying Kennedy's 1963 authorization supporting the terrorists was that active CIA engagement would enable the United States to limit "freelance exile raids." Secretary of State Rusk noted that some of their assaults could inadvertently force the United States into a confrontation with the Soviets, because "the hit-and-run raids against Cuba . . . will be blamed on us no matter what we say" ("Summary Record of the 42d Meeting of the Executive Committee of the National Security Council," March 29, 1963, *FRUS, 1961–1963*, vol. XI, Document No. 303, p. 740). Rusk observed in a letter to the president on the previous day that "hit and run raids by Cuban exiles may create incidents which work to the disadvantage of our national interest. Increased frequency of these forays could raise a host of problems over which we would not have control. Actions such as yesterday's exile attack which caused substantial damage to a Soviet vessel may complicate our relations with the USSR without net advantage to us" ("Letter from Secretary of State Rusk to President Kennedy," March 28, 1963, *FRUS, 1961–1963*, vol. XI, Document No. 302, p. 738). The phrase "freelance exile raids" is used in a September 12, 1963, memo ("Memorandum from Gordon Chase of the National Security Council Staff to the President's Special Assistant for National Security Affairs (Bundy)," *FRUS, 1961–1963*, vol. XI, Document No. 365, p. 864). Also see remarks by Samuel Halpern in Blight and Kornbluh, *Politics of Illusion*, p. 128. For Kennedy's authorization, see "Alleged Assassination Plots Involving Foreign Leaders," p. 173; Desmond Fitzgerald, "Memorandum for the Record," *FRUS, 1961–1963*, vol. XI, Document No. 348, June 19, 1963, pp. 837–38.

89. José Pérez Fernández, "Report on 40 Years of U.S. Aggression against Cuba," in *U.S. War on Cuba*, eds. José Ramón Fernández and José Pérez Fernández (Melbourne, Australia: Ocean Press, 2001), pp. 18–34.

90. Angus Deming, Anthony Marro, and Andrew Jaffe, "Terrorism: The Cuban Connection," *Newsweek*, November 1, 1976; "The World: Caribbean; Crash and Fall-out," *Economist*, October 23, 1976, p. 64; "Venezuela Frees Cuban Emigre," *New York Times*, August 8, 1987, Sec. 1, p. 5. Former Assistant U.S. Attorney Eugene Propper has suggested that the Venezuelan secret police arrested Bosch in part to prevent U.S. investigators from questioning him about his knowledge of and connection to the 1976 assassination of former Chilean Foreign Minister Orlando Letelier (Taylor Branch and Eugene M. Propper, *Labyrinth* [New York: Penguin, 1983], pp. 118–22).

91. Fidel Castro, "Funeral Oration for Cuban Victims of Cubana," October 15, 1976, *Foreign Broadcast Information Service*, Report Date October 15, 1975; available at: http://lanic.utexas.edu/la/cb/cuba/castro/1976/19761015.

92. The accord, "Memorandum of Understanding on Hijacking of Aircraft and Vessels and Other Offenses," is reprinted in U.S. Congress, House Committee on Foreign Affairs, "Hijacking

Accord between the United States and Cuba," Hearing before the Subcommittee on Inter-American Affairs, February 20, 1973; 93rd Cong., 1st Sess., p. 3-4. It came after a five-year spate of 147 airline hijackings in the United States, 92 of which had ended in Cuba. These incidents are what led to the installation of metal detectors at U.S. airports.

93. Senate Committee on Foreign Relations, "U.S. Policy toward Cuba," pp. 1–3, 5.

94. Laurence Doty, "Cuba's Abrogation of Pact Forces Tightened Security," *Aviation Week & Space Technology*, October 25, 1976, p. 30; *Economist*, October 23, 1976.

95. John Dinges and Saul Landau, *Assassination on Embassy Row* (New York: Pantheon, 1980), pp. 245–46; Ann Louise Bardach and Larry Rohter, "Life in the Shadows, Trying to Bring Down Castro," *New York Times*, July 13, 1998; "Cuban Extremists in U.S., A Growing Terror Threat," *U.S. News & World Report*, December 6, 1976.

96. Quoted in Andres Oppenheimer, *Castro's Final Hour: The Secret Story behind the Coming Downfall of Communist Cuba* (New York: Simon and Schuster, 1992), pp. 325–26. Also see *New York Times*, August 8, 1987; U.S. Department of Justice, Office of the Associate Attorney General, "Exclusion Proceeding for Orlando Bosch Avila," File: A28 851 622, A11 861 810, January 23, 1989; Dinges and Landau, *Assassination on Embassy Row*, pp. 250–51.

97. Bardach and Rohter, "Life in the Shadows."

98. Felix I. Rodriguez and John Weisman, *Shadow Warrior* (New York: Simon and Schuster, 1989), pp. 240–41. Though Rodriguez claims he was a minor figure, he acknowledges (p. 241) reporting to Vice President George Bush's national security adviser, Donald Gregg (a former CIA station chief), and dedicates the book to Gregg. This would not be typical of a low-level operative. Rodriguez had acquired some fame because he was present in 1967 when the Bolivians executed Che Guevara (pp. 160–65). Also see Robert Parry, "Lost History: The CIA's Fugitive Terrorist," *The Consortium*, January 6, 1997 (Arlington, Va.: Consortium for Independent Journalism, 1996); available at: www.consortiumnews.com/archive/lost.html.

99. Bardach and Rohter, "Life in the Shadows"; Parry, "Lost History: The CIA's Fugitive Terrorist."

100. Juan Tamayo, "Exiles Directed Blasts That Rocked Island's Tourism, Investigation Reveals," *Miami Herald*, November 17, 1997.

101. Glenn Garvin, "Panama: Exile Says Aim Was Castro Hit," *Miami Herald*, January 13, 2001. Though FBI agents interrogated him in 1992, Posada Carriles was not detained and U.S. officials have rejected Cuban government requests to bring him to justice.

102. *Alleged Assassination Plots Involving Foreign Leaders*, pp. 71–190. A 1994 study, based on Cuban files, alleges several hundred attempts: Claudia Furiati, trans. Maxine Shaw, *ZR Rifle: The Plot to Kill Kennedy & Castro* (Melbourne, Australia: Ocean Press, 1994). Also see Fabian Escalante, *CIA Targets Fidel: Secret 1967 CIA Inspector General's Report on Plots to Assassinate Fidel Castro* (Melbourne, Australia: Ocean Press, 1996).

103. George Crile III, "The Riddle of AM LASH," *Washington Post*, May 2, 1976; David Corn, "Our Man on Havana: From Poison Pens to Policy Planning—Nestor Sanchez's Brilliant Career," *Washington Post*, March 26, 1995, p. C2.

104. *Alleged Assassination Plots Involving Foreign Leaders*, p. 89; Corn, "Our Man on Havana."

105. *Alleged Assassination Plots Involving Foreign Leaders*, pp. 90, 176; Crile, "The Riddle of AM LASH."

106. Claiming there have been 637 "conspiracies," Col. José Pérez Fernández contends that "the main terrorists who continue planning to assassinate Fidel go free in [the United States], supported and protected by the U.S. authorities" ("Report on the U.S. Government's Plans for

Using the CIA and the Terrorist Organizations to Assassinate Leaders of the Cuban Revolution, Especially Commander in Chief Fidel Castro," in Fernández and Fernández, *U.S. War on Cuba*, pp. 72-73).

107. Ann Louise Bardach and Larry Rohter, "Investigation Leads to Plot to Kill Castro by Powerful Cuban Lobby," *New York Times*, May 5, 1998; Juan O. Tamayo, "Castro Death-Plot Defendant Charged in Drug Case," *Miami Herald*, January 25, 1999. The boat owner, Jose Antonio Llama, was a member of the CANF board of directors. He was one of those subsequently indicted for attempted murder by a federal grand jury in Puerto Rico. After the trial venue was moved to Miami from San Juan, a jury found all of the indicted were not guilty (Juan O. Tamayo, "Five Acquitted of Exile Plot to Kill Castro," *Miami Herald*, December 9, 1999, p. 1A).

108. Fidel Castro Ruz, "Address Commemorating the 25th anniversary of the Terrorist Act against a Cubana Jetliner off the Coast of Barbados," October 6, 2001; *Granma* (official translation); available at: www.granma.cubaweb.cu/temas12/articulo03.html.

109. Patrick J. Haney and Walt Vanderbush, "The Role of Ethnic Interest Groups in U.S. Foreign Policy: The Case of the Cuban American National Foundation," *International Studies Quarterly*, June 1999; Jonathan C. Smith, "Foreign Policy for Sale? Interest Group Influence on President Clinton's Cuba Policy, August 1994," *Presidential Studies Quarterly*, vol. 28, no. 1 (winter 1998).

110. Human Rights/Americas issued two reports in the 1990s which found a pervasive atmosphere of repression in Miami against any expression of moderation toward Cuba. It cited numerous instances of "violence and intimidation" and criticized both national and local government agencies both for tolerating the repression and for seeming to endorse it by funding groups engaged in terror tactics. See *Dangerous Dialogue Revisited: Threats to Freedom of Expression Continue in Miami's Cuban Exile*, November 1994 (New York: Human Rights Watch, 1994).

111. "Memorandum of Meeting With President Johnson," Washington, December 19, 1963, in *FRUS 1961-63*, vol. XI, Document No. 388, p. 907.

112. See, for example, Jean-Guy Allard, "Yielding to the Terrorist Mafia's Blackmail: Bush Imposes Reich on Latin America," *Granma International* (English), January 18, 2002.

113. Bradley Graham, "U.S. Tried to Restrain Group's Flights," *Washington Post*, February 27, 1996, p. A5; Mireya Navarro, "Nonviolence of Castro's Foes Still Wears a Very Tough Face," *New York Times*, February 28, 1996, p. A1; Rodriguez and Weisman, *Shadow Warrior*, pp. 109-11.

114. Jefferson Morley, "Shootdown," *Washington Post Magazine*, May 25, 1997; Jerry Meldon, "Behind the Elian Case," *The Consortium*, March 30, 2000 (Arlington, Va.: Consortium for Independent Journalism, 2000); available at: www.consortiumnews.com/2000/032600a.html.

115. Navarro, "Nonviolence of Castro's Foes Still Wears a Very Tough Face." Basulto allegedly also worked with Argentine military officers in 1981, training the *contras* in techniques of torture (Kerry Luft, "Dashing Symbol of Argentina's 'Dirty War' Quits," *Chicago Tribune*, March 3, 1996).

116. Robert Suro, "U.S., Cuba Agree on Stemming Raft Tide," *Washington Post*, September 10, 1994, p. A1; Philip Brenner and Peter Kornbluh, "Clinton's Cuba Calculus," *NACLA Report on the Americas*, September/October, 1995. The new agreement replaced a 1984 accord under which *up to* 20,000 Cubans could emigrate each year. In practice, less than 2,000 annually were granted permission.

117. Mireya Navarro, "U.S. Policy a 'Betrayal,' Cuban Exiles Protest," *New York Times*, May 8, 1995, p. A13; Walt Vanderbush and Patrick J Haney, "Policy toward Cuba in the Clinton Administration," *Political Science Quarterly*, fall 1999, p. 402.

118. Brenner and Kornbluh, "Clinton's Cuba Calculus"; Morley, "Shootdown."

119. Carl Nagin, "Backfire," *The New Yorker*, January 26, 1998, p. 32; Morley, "Shootdown." Film of the flight aired on Miami television that evening. Cuba's Ministry of Foreign Relations has its offices among the tourist hotels, apartment houses, and office buildings that line the Malecon.

120. Cuba claims he made more than twenty-five such flights (John M. Goshko, "Cuban Aide Defends Air Attack; Supporting Evidence Not Presented to UN," *Washington Post*, February 29, 1996, p. A16), and the State Department did acknowledge "numerous" instances in which planes from exile groups, including Brothers to the Rescue, violated Cuban airspace (Graham, "U.S. Tried to Restrain Group's Flights"). Basulto told journalist Carl Nagin ("Backfire," p. 32) that he dropped "half a million leaflets" over Havana on two flights in January 1996. He bragged on Radio Martí about the January flights, promising to make future overflights once a month (Thomas W. Lippman and Guy Gugliotta, "U.S. Data Forced Cuba to Retreat on Shooting; Basulto Bragged of Buzzing Havana Previously," *Washington Post*, March 16, 1996, p. A19).

121. Nagin, "Backfire," pp. 32–33. The trip of military officers was led by Rear Admiral Eugene Carroll, U.S. Navy (Ret.), who was then deputy director of the Center for Defense Information, and Robert White, director of the Center for International Policy, and a former U.S. ambassador to El Salvador and Paraguay.

122. Wayne S. Smith, "The U.S.–Cuba Imbroglio: Anatomy of a Crisis," *International Policy Report*, May 1996 (Washington, D.C.: Center for International Policy, 1996).

123. Barbara Crossette, "U.S. Says Cubans Knew They Fired on Civilian Planes," *New York Times*, February 28, 1996, p. A1.

124. International legal scholar Alfred P. Rubin ("U.S. Fixation on Castro May Do Us No Good: An Illegal Action?" *New York Times*, March 1, 1996, Letter to the Editor) argues that because "the Brothers to the Rescue flight was one in a series of political actions, and its flight plan was deliberately false," the Cuban action could be construed as falling under the UN Charter's guidelines that states have an "inherent right" to self-defense.

125. Daniel W. Fisk, "Cuba in U.S. Policy: An American Congressional Perspective," in *Canada, the US and Cuba: Helms-Burton and Its Aftermath*, ed. Heather Nicol (Kingston, Ontario: Centre for International Relations, Queen's University, 1999), p. 34.

126. "CBS Evening News (6:30 P.M. ET)," April 30, 1996, CBS News Transcripts, Burrelle's Information Services. Similarly, Cuban Foreign Minister Roberto Robaina commented at a UN press conference, "We ran out of alternatives" (Goshko, "Cuban Aide Defends Air Attack"). When asked by a radio interviewer what pressure the U.S. government had placed on him, Basulto joked that the authorities had been "on vacation" (Lippman and Gugliotta, "U.S. Data Forced Cuba to Retreat on Shooting").

127. *Cuban Liberty and Democratic Solidarity (Libertad) Act of 1996*, Public Law 104-114 [H.R. 927], March 12, 1996, Sec. 116 (a) (1) (2) (b) (3) <22 USC 6046>.

128. Cuban anger over the honor accorded the Brothers to the Rescue pilots who were killed in the incident erupted in December 2000 when Cuba threatened to cut off telephone service with the United States. The U.S. Congress had passed a law authorizing the president to use frozen Cuban assets in the United States to pay compensation to the families of the pilots. Cuba, in turn, added a 10 percent tax to phone calls to recoup the money. But the Clinton administration forbid U.S. firms from paying the tax, which led to the Cuban threat to curtail the telephone link. Calling the pilots provocateurs, Luis Fernandez, a Cuban-government spokesman, was quoted as saying that the administration and congressional actions are "going to encourage people to do more of that kind of thing, because they know they will be supported by the U.S. government" (Christopher Marquis, "Cuba Threatens to Cut Off Phone Service to the States," *New York Times*, December 9, 2000, p. A21).

129. This assessment is stated plainly in a June 1963 National Intelligence Estimate, which said:

> We believe that the current situation within Cuba favors this consolidation [of the Castro regime]. The mere passage of time tends to favor Castro as Cubans and others become accustomed to the idea that he is here to stay and as his regime gains in experience. It is unlikely that internal political opposition or economic difficulties will cause the regime to collapse. . . . The capabilities of the Cuban Armed Forces have been augmented by increased training, new equipment, and some reorganization. The Cuban ground forces are probably well able to control internal resistance and to repel small-scale external attacks. In the event of U.S. invasion, however, they would have to revert fairly quickly to static defense or guerrilla operations ("Situation and Prospects in Cuba," NIE 85-63, June 14, 1963, in *FRUS, 1961-1963*, vol. XI, Document No. 347, pp. 834-35).

130. Phyllis Greene Walker, "National Security," in *Cuba: A Country Study*, 3rd ed., ed. James D. Rudolph (Washington, D.C.: U.S. Department of the Army, 1985), pp. 250-52; Jorge I. Domínguez, *Cuba: Order and Revolution* (Cambridge, Mass.: Harvard University Press, 1978), pp. 346-48.

131. Carlos Alzugaray Treto, "Problems of National Security in the Cuban-U.S. Historic Breach," in Domínguez and Hernández, *U.S.-Cuban Relations in the 1990s*, pp. 93-95; Phyllis Greene Walker, "Challenges Facing the Cuban Military," *Cuba Briefing Paper Series*, no. 12, October 1996 (Washington, D.C.: Georgetown University's Center for Latin American Studies, 1996). At the 1989 Moscow conference on the missile crisis, Jorge Risquet (a member of Cuba's Communist Party Political Bureau) and Sergio del Valle (the Cuban Army chief of staff in 1962) pointedly argued that Cuba would have inflicted "terrible" casualties on an invading U.S. force in 1962. There were 270,000 people armed and mobilized in preparation for a U.S. invasion, del Valle Jiménez reported (Allyn et al., *Back to the Brink*, pp. 42, 106). A 1996 report by the Center for Defense Information, based on information gained during a trip to Cuba by former U.S. military officers, highlights the nature of Cuba's defense strategy ("Assessment on Cuba," February 13, 1996, Center for Defense Information, Washington, D.C.):

> Great emphasis is placed on the defense of Cuba through preparations for guerrilla war, relying on a massive network of tunnels which honeycomb the countryside to protect people and equipment. Following an assault by U.S. forces, the "war of all the people" would be waged by units emerging from the tunnels to conduct raids and ambushes of American troops. The impression Cuban leaders are striving to create is that while U.S. forces can certainly overwhelm Cuba militarily, the "war of all the people" would make it a bitter, costly victory.

132. Don Oberdorfer and John M. Goshko, "U.S. Gives Warning on Cuba-Salvador Arms Flow; Haig Warns U.S. Will 'Go to the Source' to Block Arms to Salvador," *Washington Post*, February 22, 1981; Juan de Onis, "Cuba Warned Direct U.S. Action against It on Salvador Is Possible," *New York Times*, February 23, 1981.

133. LeoGrande, *Our Own Backyard*, p. 84. The U.S. Defense Department estimated early in 1982 that Cuba's armed forces had 225,000 soldiers (including reserve divisions) and that "there are hundreds of thousands of reserves, militia, and other paramilitary forces" (Fred C. Ikle, "Testimony," in Senate Committee on the Judiciary, "The Role of Cuba in International Terrorism and Subversion," p. 87).

134. Walker, "National Security," pp. 252, 266-68; Don Oberdorfer, "Soviet Arms Shipments to Cuba Are Rising, Haig Tells Senator," *Washington Post*, July 31, 1981; Brenner, *From*

Confrontation to Negotiation, pp. 64–65. Planning for the new civilian forces actually began in 1980, as tension between Cuba and the United States increased. The first units of the *Milicia de Tropas Territoriales* (MTT) were formally commissioned on January 20, 1981. The MTT reached its full force of 1.2 million members in 1984.

135. U.S. Department of Defense, "The Cuban Threat to U.S. National Security," November 18, 1997; available at: www.defenselink.mil/pubs/cubarpt.htm. Anti-Castro groups attempted to discredit the report's findings in 2001 after one of its authors was arrested on charges of spying for Cuba (Christopher Marquis, "Spy Betrayed Agents to Cuba, Officials Say," *New York Times*, September 23, 2001, p. A32; Tim Johnson, "Cuba Spy Suspect Was Rising into Senior Intelligence Ranks," *Miami Herald*, September 29, 2001, p. A1). But the report was produced by several intelligence agencies, and the facts on which the conclusions were based have not been refuted. Also see Walker, "Challenges Facing the Cuban Military"; John Ward Anderson, "Cuban Military Still Looms Large; MiGs in Attack Recall Soviet Era, But Some Soldiers Now Farming," *Washington Post*, March 3, 1996, p. A26.

136. Domínguez, "Pipsqueak Power," p. 62.

137. However, a comparable fear did deter the United States from widening the war against North Vietnam (Robert S. McNamara, James G. Blight, and Robert K. Brigham, *Argument without End: In Search of Answers to the Vietnam Tragedy* [New York: Public Affairs Press, 1999], pp. 336–37).

138. Edward B. Atkeson, "Why Cuba Fired, *Washington Post*, March 13, 1996, p. A21."

139. Cubans' sense of vulnerability and fear of a U.S. attack is analyzed cogently in Margaret E. Crahan, "Cuba: Politics and Society," in *U.S. Policy toward Cuba*, ed. Dick Clark, Aspen Institute Congressional Program, First Conference (Washington, D.C.: Aspen Institute, 2000), p. 26.

140. Joseph Montville, "The Arrow and the Olive Branch: A Case for Track Two Diplomacy," in *Conflict Resolution: Track Two Diplomacy*, eds. John McDonald and Diane Bendahmane (Washington, D.C.: Foreign Service Institute/U.S. Department of State, 1987). Also see John Davies and Edward (Edy) Kaufman, eds., *Second Track Diplomacy for Ethnic and Nationalist Conflicts: Applied Techniques for Conflict Transformation* (Lanham, Md.: Rowman & Littlefield, 2002); John W. McDonald, "Further Exploration of Track Two Diplomacy," in *Timing the De-Escalation of International Conflicts*, eds. Louis Kriesberg and Stuart J. Thorson (Syracuse, N.Y.: Syracuse University Press, 1991); Ronald J. Fisher, *Interactive Conflict Resolution* (Syracuse, N.Y.: Syracuse University Press, 1997).

141. Harold Saunders, "Prenegotiation and Circum-negotiation: Arenas of the Peace Process," in *Managing Global Chaos*, eds. Chester Crocker, Fen Hampson, and Pamela Aall, (Washington, D.C.: United States Institute of Peace Press, 1996); Christopher C. Mitchell, "Track Two Triumphant? Reflections on the Oslo Process and Conflict Resolution in the Middle East," *ICAR Newsletter* (Institute for Conflict Analysis and Resolution, George Mason University, Fairfax, Va.), fall 1993, vol. 5, no. 6; Geir Dale, "Facilitating Oslo," *Track Two*, vol. 6, no. 2 (August 1997), Center for Conflict Resolution, Rondebosch, South Africa.

142. Mubarak Awad and Edy Kaufman, "Back from South Africa: Lessons for the Israeli–Palestinian Peace Process," *Tikkun*, September–October 1995. Unlike Israeli–Palestinian antagonism, U.S.–Cuban hostility is not rooted in deeply felt animosities between Americans and Cubans. Both Cuban and U.S. officials often emphasized over the last forty years that they harbor no ill will toward the citizens of the opposing country, and people on both sides of the Florida Straits genuinely respect and enjoy aspects of the other's cultures.

143. The *Cuban Democracy Act of 1992* is actually Title XVII of the National Defense Authorization Act for Fiscal Year 1993 (Public Law 102-484 [H.R. 5006], October 23, 1992).

Track II programs are designated as "Support for the Cuban People" (Section 1705 <22 USC 6004>). The Cuban Liberty and Democratic Solidarity Act of 1996 (the Helms-Burton Act) reaffirms support for Track II type programs in the CDA by asserting that "The policy of the United States is as follows: (1) To support the self-determination of the Cuban people. . . ; (3) To encourage the Cuban people to empower themselves with a government which reflects the self-determination of the Cuban people (Sec. 201 <22 USC 6061>).

144. James Gerstenzang, "U.S. Gets Tough on Its Cuba Restrictions," *Los Angeles Times,* July 14, 2001, p. A6. Earlier in the year Bush asserted that "The policy of our government is not merely to isolate Castro, but to actively support those working to bring about democratic change in Cuba. . . . We must explore ways to expand access to the Internet for the average Cuban citizen ("Remarks by the President in Recognition of Cuba Independence Day," May 18, 2001, Press Release, White House Office of the Press Secretary).

145. The first statement of policy in the act makes clear its approach: "It should be the policy of the United States—(1) to seek a peaceful transition to democracy and a resumption of economic growth in Cuba through the careful application of sanctions directed at the Castro government and support for the Cuban people" (Sec. 1703. <22 USC 6002> "Statement of Policy").

146. Edwin M. Martin, "Memorandum to Mr. [U. Alexis] Johnson; Subject: Track Two," October 12, 1962; in *CMC Document Set*, Document No. 00589. Martin was recommending to the under secretary of state for political affairs a plan outlined by Walt Whitman Rostow.

147. The CIA report was filed in response to an amendment in the 2000 Intelligence Authorization Act sponsored by Rep. Maurice Hinchey (D-NY). It is available on the CIA's web site under the title "CIA Activities in Chile, Report to Congress, September 18, 2000," at: www.cia.gov/cia/publications/chile/index.html. Also see Peter Kornbluh, *The Pinochet File: A Declassified Dossier on Atrocity and Accountability* (New York: New Press, forthcoming); Peter Kornbluh, "Chile; The CIA's Other Untold Scandal," *Los Angeles Times*, October 29, 2000, p. M2. The CIA report confirmed what a U.S. Senate committee had concluded in 1976, that "U.S. efforts to prevent Allende's assumption of office operated on two tracks between September 4 and October 24. Track II was initiated by President Nixon on September 15 when he instructed the CIA to play a direct role in organizing a military coup d'état in Chile" (U.S. Congress, Senate Select Committee to Study Governmental Operations with Respect to Intelligence Activities, Staff Report, "Covert Action in Chile 1963-1973," 94th Cong., 1st Sess., Committee Print, December 18, 1975, p. 25). CIA Director Richard Helms recorded Nixon instructing U.S. officials at the September 15 meeting to "make the [Chilean] economy scream." A copy of Helms's notes from the meeting with Nixon is housed at the National Security Archive, in its Chile Documentation Project, at: www.gwu.edu/~nsarchiv/NSAEBB/NSAEBB8/ch26-01.htm.

148. "Covert Action in Chile 1963-1973," pp. 30-31. "The most prominent of the right-wing paramilitary groups," the Senate report states (p. 31), "was Patria y Libertad (Fatherland and Liberty), which formed following Allende's September 4 election, during so-called Track II." One of its members, Michael Townley, was convicted in a U.S. court for planning the logistics in the Letelier Assassination (Dinges and Landau, *Assassination on Embassy Row*, pp. 100-115).

149. "Covert Action in Chile 1963-1973," pp. 29-30.

150. "Covert Action in Chile 1963-1973," pp. 32-35.

151. Karen DeYoung, "More U.S. Aid Sought for Cuban Dissidents; Anti-Castro Activists Hope Bush Will Boost Grants, Which Critics Call Ineffective," *Washington Post*, March 8, 2001, p. A16.

152. Even those who might want to create an opposition group, Domínguez ("The Secrets of Castro's Staying Power") notes, do not want it "to become 'the party of the United States.'" Portes ("Strategic Neglect") observes that the situation in Cuba is unlike those in Eastern Europe in the 1980s, where "anticommunism and nationalism worked together to undermine the entrenched communist regimes because the Soviet Union was the common target of both ideologies. In Cuba nationalism and anticommunism work at cross-purposes."

153. "Statement of Policy," *Cuban Democracy Act of 1992*, Sec. 1703 <22 USC 6002>. Cong. Robert Torricelli (D-NJ), the bill's sponsor, remarked one year after its passage that "On the one hand, we have tightened the economic noose. . . . On the other hand, the administration has now issued policy guidelines for implementing the telecommunications provisions of the Cuban Democracy Act. This is one of the ways envisioned by the Act for opening up Cuba to a flood of ideas, which is the other aspect of our strategy for bringing about Castro's downfall" (Robert G. Torricelli, "Testimony," in U.S. Congress, House Committee on Foreign Affairs, "Recent Developments in Cuba Policy: Telecommunications and 'Dollarization,'" Hearing before the Subcommittee on Western Hemisphere Affairs, August 4, 1993).

154. *Cuban Liberty and Democratic Solidarity Act*, Sec. 2 (28), Sec. 3 (2) and (5), Sec. 205 (a) (7).

155. Carlos Alzugaray Treto, *De la Fruta Madura a La Ley Helms-Burton* (Panama: Editorial Universitaria, 1997), p. 11. Historian Louis A. Pérez, Jr. (*Cuba and the United States: Ties of Singular Intimacy* [Athens: University of Georgia Press, 1990], p. 38) notes: "To many, the destinies of the two countries seemed not merely intertwined but indissoluble. . . . So powerful a hold did this proposition have over U.S. calculations that it soon became an axiomatic imperative." Ironically, Adams' argument was intended to dampen enthusiasm in the Congress for the immediate annexation of Cuba, because he did not want to provoke Spain or England (pp. 39–40).

156. Alzugaray, *De la Fruta Madura a La Ley Helms-Burton*, p. 18 (translation from the Spanish by the authors). The Platt Amendment stipulated that the United States had "the right to intervene for the preservation of Cuban independence," that is, whenever it deemed necessary. Louis A. Pérez, Jr. (*Cuba: Between Reform and Revolution* [New York: Oxford University Press, 1988], p. 186) observes that the amendment "served to transform the substance of Cuban sovereignty into an extension of the United States national system."

157. Lars Schoultz, *Beneath the United States: A History of U.S. Policy toward Latin America* (Cambridge, Mass.: Harvard University Press, 1998), pp. 147–48.

158. Quoted in Pérez, *Cuba and the United States*, pp. 108–9.

159. Pérez, *Cuba and the United States*, pp. 106–7; 113–19; Schoultz, *Beneath the United States*, pp. 150–51.

160. Soraya Castro Mariño, "Cuba–U.S. Relations: Détente in the Third Millennium?" Paper presented at the 43rd Annual Meeting of International Studies Association, New Orleans, La., 23–27 March 2002, p. 18. Similarly, Domínguez ("U.S.–Cuban Relations: From the Cold War to the Colder War," p. 58) observes: "The Helms-Burton Act is quite faithful to the theme of the Monroe Doctrine and the Roosevelt Corollary. It claims for the United States the unilateral right to decide a wide array of domestic policies and arrangements in a nominally sovereign post Castro Cuba."

161. David Rieff, "Cuba Refrozen," *Foreign Affairs*, July/August, 1996.

162. Even before the CDA became law, Miami was giddy with rife predictions of the Cuban Revolution's demise. See, for example, Oppenheimer, *Castro's Final Hour*, chap. 15.

163. Andrew Zimbalist, "Whither the Cuban Economy?" in Purcell and Rothkopf, *Cuba: The Contours of Change*, pp. 14–17.

164. Castro, "Cuba–U.S. Relations," p. 17; Zimbalist, "Whither the Cuban Economy?" pp. 17–18.

165. USITC, *The Economic Impact of U.S. Sanctions with Respect to Cuba*, table 3-2, p. 3-35. However, in a report submitted to the United Nations in 2001, the Cuban government cites a cumulative impact of $121 billion: "Cuba's Report to the Secretary General of the United Nations Organization on Resolution 55/20 of UN's General Assembly, 'Necessity of Ending the Economic, Commercial and Financial Blockade Imposed by the United States of America Against Cuba';" available through the Cuban Ministry of Foreign Relations at: www.cubaminrex.cu/versioningles/infingCubaONU.htm.

166. USITC, *The Economic Impact of U.S. Sanctions with Respect to Cuba*, p. 3-30.

167. USITC, *The Economic Impact of U.S. Sanctions with Respect to Cuba*, pp. 3-32 and 3-33.

168. American Association for World Health, *Denial of Food and Medicine: The Impact of the U.S. Embargo on Health and Nutrition in Cuba* (Washington, D.C.: American Association for World Health, 1997).

169. *Denial of Food and Medicine*, Summary of Findings.

170. Office of the Spokesperson, U.S. Department of State, "The U.S. Embargo and Healthcare in Cuba: Myth versus Reality," Fact Sheet, May 14, 1997; Anthony F. Kirkpatrick, "The U.S. Attack on Cuba's Health," *Canadian Medical Association Journal*, vol. 157, no. 3 (August 1, 1997), pp. 282–83.

171. The Trade Sanctions Reform and Export Enhancement Act of 2000 (Public Law 106-387) does relax some of the onerous requirements on the sale of food and medicine to Cuba. But Cuba refused to make any purchases under the terms of the new law, in part because it prohibits U.S. entities from extending credit to Cuba for the sale of food and medicine, which makes regular trade untenable. However, after Hurricane Michelle devastated Cuba in November 2001, the Bush administration did respond to pressure from humanitarian groups (as well as UN General Assembly vote of 167–3 against the U.S. embargo), to permit Cuba to purchase U.S. food using expedited procedures that circumvented restrictions in the 2000 Trade Act (Karen DeYoung, "U.S. Food Sale Is Hailed by Cuban Minister; 'Positive Gesture Could Aid Relations,' He Says," *Washington Post*, November 29, 2001, p. A29).

172. "Cuba's Report to the Secretary General of the United Nations."

173. Brenner et al., "The Confluence of Domestic and International Interests: U.S. Policy toward Cuba, 1998–2001," pp. 203–4; James M. Lindsay and Randall B. Ripley, "How Congress Influences Foreign and Defense Policy," in *Congress Resurgent: Foreign and Defense Policy on Capitol Hill*, eds. Randall B. Ripley and James M. Lindsay (Ann Arbor: University of Michigan Press, 1993), pp. 18–22.

174. LeoGrande, "From Havana to Miami: U.S. Cuba Policy as a Two-Level Game," pp. 74–75.

175. Richard A. Nuccio, "Cuba: A U.S. Perspective," in *Transatlantic Tension: The United States, Europe, and Problem Countries*, ed. Richard N. Haass (Washington, D.C.: Brookings Institution, 1999), pp. 17, 17n9, 27.

176. Brenner et al., "The Confluence of Domestic and International Interests: U.S. Policy toward Cuba, 1998–2001," pp. 196–97; Peter Slevin, "Pursuing an Opening to Cuba; Lawmakers Form Working Group," *Washington Post*, March 9, 2002, p. A5.

177. *Economic Eye on Cuba*, April 22–28, 2002, p. 5 (newsletter published by U.S.–Cuba Trade and Economic Council, Inc., New York); Anthony DePalma, "Cuban Cash Reopens U.S. Food Trade," *New York Times*, February 14, 2002, p. 1W.

178. In February 2001 Sen. Helms asserted, "I don't care how Castro leaves office, vertically or horizontally, but Fidel Castro has got to go" (Jesse Helms, "Towards a Compassionate Conservative Foreign Policy," Address before the Conservative Political Action Conference Arlington, Virginia, February 15, 2001; available at: www.senate.gov/~helms/Speeches/CPAC/cpac.html). Also see Wayne S. Smith, "The Cuba Stalemate," *Cigar Aficionado*, spring 1996.

179. Philip Peters, *U.S.–Cuba Bilateral Relations: Cooperation at Arm's Length* (Arlington, Va.: Lexington Institute, 2001).

180. For example, see Bernard W. Aronson and William D. Rogers, "U.S.–Cuban Relations in the 21st Century," Independent Task Force Report, November 26, 2000 (New York: Council on Foreign Relations, 2000).

181. Saul Landau, "After Castro," *Mother Jones*, July/August, 1989; Carollee Bengelsdorf, *The Problem of Democracy in Cuba: Between Vision and Reality* (New York: Oxford University Press, 1994).

182. Reich, "U.S. Foreign Policy in the Western Hemisphere."

183. Philip Peters, "The U.S. Embargo on Cuba: Voices from the Island," Lexington Institute *Issue Brief*, May 27, 1999 (Arlington, Va.: Lexington Institute, 1999); Human Rights Watch (*Cuba's Repressive Machinery: Human Rights Forty Years after the Revolution* [New York: Human Rights Watch, 1999], chap. 12) asserted that the organization "opposes the embargo against Cuba . . . [which] remains a sledgehammer approach aimed at overthrowing the Castro government."

184. "Pope John Paul II, Castro Texts," Associated Press, January 25, 1998.

185. The State Department's *International Narcotics Control Strategy Report 2001* states that "Coordination between the Government of Cuba (GOC) and the United States on international drug trafficking issues has increased since September 2000." Despite the fact that "Cuba's location and geography present an inviting environment to both air and maritime smugglers," it notes, "Cuba has not been designated as a major illicit drug producing or major drug-transit country" (U.S. State Department, Bureau for International Narcotics and Law Enforcement Affairs, *International Narcotics Control Strategy Report 2001*, March 2002, p. VI-9). Also see Peter Kornbluh, "Cuba, Counternarcotics, and Collaboration: A Security Issue in U.S.–Cuban Relations," *Cuba Briefing Paper Series*, No. 24, December 2000 (Washington, D.C.: Georgetown University's Center for Latin American Studies, 2000); Peters, *U.S.–Cuba Bilateral Relations*, pp. 8–9.

186. Ralph K. White, *Fearful Warriors: A Psychological Profile of U.S.–Soviet Relations* (New York: Free Press, 1984), p. 160. For an elaboration of how *realistic empathy* might have prevented international conflicts in the past and could help to prevent them in the future, see Robert S. McNamara and James G. Blight, *Wilson's Ghost: Reducing the Risk of Conflict, Killing, and Catastrophe in the 21st Century* (New York: Public Affairs, 2001), chaps. 2 and 5.

187. Atkeson, "Why Cuba Fired."

188. The 1997 Defense Department study concluded that "Cuba's weak military poses a negligible conventional threat to the U.S. or surrounding countries" ("The Cuban Threat to U.S. National Security").

189. Domínguez, *To Make the World Safe for Revolution*, pp. 6–7, 116–20, 152–62; 219–24; Erisman, *Cuba's Foreign Relations in a Post-Soviet World*, pp. 28–30, 33–47; Gleijeses, *Conflicting Missions*, chaps. 3–5 and pp. 374–79; Nelson P. Valdés, "Revolutionary Solidarity in Angola," in *Cuba in the World*, eds. Cole Blasier and Carmelo Mesa-Lago (Pittsburgh: University of Pittsburgh Press, 1979), pp. 87–117; Donna Rich, "Cuban Internationalism: A Humanitarian Foreign Policy," in Brenner et al., *The Cuba Reader*, pp. 405–13.

190. In November 1975 Cuban troops helped to defend the refineries and oil fields owned by U.S.-based Gulf Oil in Angola from attacks by U.S.-backed mercenaries operating against the new government there. See Gleijeses, *Conflicting Missions*, pp. 311–12.

191. In 1981 Cuban Vice President Carlos Rafael Rodríguez told Haig that "We had long maintained our ties with the MPLA [Popular Movement for the Liberation of Angola] in its struggle against Portuguese colonialism. . . . I can assure you unequivocally, inasmuch as I played a direct role in this matter, that when the decision to dispatch Cuban forces into Angola was made, we communicated nothing about it to the Soviet Union. We were not even aware of its point of view on that account. . . . When we became involved in the events in Angola, we had absolutely no concept of the geopolitical conceptions about the importance of Angola in light of the interests of the Soviet Union. We saw in Angola a friendly country, a group of revolutionaries struggling against colonialism, against South Africa, and embarked on all of this ("Transcript of Meeting between U.S. Secretary of State Alexander M. Haig, Jr., and Cuban Vice Premier Carlos Rafael Rodríguez, Mexico City, 23 November 1981," *Cold War International History Project Bulletin*, nos. 8–9 (winter 1996/1997), p. 210. Also see Gleijeses, *Conflicting Missions*, pp. 260, 305–7; William M. LeoGrande, *Cuba's Policy in Africa, 1959–1980*, Policy Papers in International Affairs, No. 13 (Berkeley: Institute of International Studies, 1980), pp. 21–22; Anatoly Dobrynin, *In Confidence* (New York: Times Books, 1995), p. 367. In contrast, the 1977 Cuban deployment to Ethiopia appears to have been coordinated with the Soviets. But Cuba seems to have acted for its own interests and not at the Soviet's behest. This deployment came after Castro independently failed in an attempt to mediate the Ethiopian–Somalian border dispute over the Ogaden region. See LeoGrande, *Cuba's Policy in Africa*, pp. 35–45; Domínguez, *To Make the World Safe for Revolution*, pp. 157–62; Donna Rich, "Cuba's Role as Mediator in International Conflicts: Formal and Informal Initiatives," in *Cuban Foreign Policy Confronts a New International Order*, eds. H. Michael Erisman and John M. Kirk (Boulder, Colo.: Lynne Rienner, 1991), pp. 127–28.

192. For example see Thomas O. Enders, "Testimony," in "The Role of Cuba in International Terrorism and Subversion," Hearings Before the Subcommittee on Security and Terrorism, Senate Committee on the Judiciary, U.S. Congress, 97th Cong., 2nd Sess., March 12, 1982, Serial No. J-97-97, pp. 147–59; U.S. Department of State and Department of Defense, *The Challenge to Democracy in Central America*, Washington, D.C., October 1986; Lars Schoultz, *National Security and United States Policy toward Latin America* (Princeton, N.J.: Princeton University Press, 1987), chap. 6; LeoGrande, *Our Own Backyard*, especially chaps. 3–5, 9, and 13.

193. Larry Rohter, "Sandinista Government Viewed as Leftist Hybrid," *New York Times*, March 23, 1985, p. 3; William M. LeoGrande, "Cuba," in *Confronting Revolution: Security through Diplomacy in Central America*, eds. Morris J. Blachman, William M. LeoGrande, and Kenneth Sharpe (New York: Pantheon, 1986), pp. 252–53; Dusko Doder, "Castro Faults Soviets on Managua Aid: Dispute Said to Account for Cuban's Absence from Funeral," *Washington Post*, March 24, 1985, p. A1; Cole Blasier, "The Soviet Union," in Blachman et al., *Confronting Revolution*, pp. 266–68.

194. The directive, PD-52 (October 29, 1979), came in the wake of Carter's ill-informed reaction to news that the Soviets had upgraded their 3,000-soldier contingent in Cuba to a "combat brigade." The unit had been in place since the missile crisis, but Carter insisted it had to be removed because it could be used for military intervention in the Western Hemisphere. However implausible such a scenario seemed, the administration refused to concede that it had misconstrued the nature of the brigade, which had not changed much over the years. For full accounts of the incident and how it affected U.S.–Soviet relations, see Garthoff, *Détente and Confronta-*

tion, chap. 24; David D. Newsom, *The Soviet Brigade in Cuba* (Bloomington: Indiana University Press, 1987); Gloria Duffy, "Crisis Mangling and the Cuban Brigade," *International Security*, vol. 8, no. 1 (summer 1983). Carter's disposition to improve relations with Cuba was signaled by Secretary of State Cyrus Vance eleven days after the January 20, 1977, inauguration, when he said that he hoped the United States and Cuba could quickly move toward normalization (Murray Marder, "Vance Warns Rhodesia," *Washington Post*, February 1, 1977; Graham Hovey, "Possibility Is Raise of U.S.–Cuba Meeting," *New York Times*, February 4, 1977). Five weeks later Carter relaxed the embargo by permitting U.S. citizens to travel to Cuba.

195. Smith, *Closest of Enemies*, pp. 128–40. Brzezinksi (*Power and Principle*, pp. 178–90) explains how he influenced Carter to see that the Soviet Union was using Cuba as a "military proxy" in Africa to serve its own expansionist aims in his memoirs.

196. Smith, *The Closest of Enemies*, pp. 141–42.

197. Barry Sklar, "Cuban Exodus 1980: The Context," in Brenner et al., *The Cuba Reader*, pp. 339–42.

198. Raymond L. Garthoff, "American–Soviet Relations in Perspective," *Political Science Quarterly*, vol. 100, no. 4 (winter 1985–86), pp. 544–54.

199. Garthoff, "American–Soviet Relations in Perspective," p. 553 (emphasis in original).

200. Castro, "Cuba–U.S. Relations: Détente in the Third Millennium?" p. 1.

201. Alzugaray, "Problems of National Security in the Cuban–U.S. Historic Breach," p. 86.

202. "Memorandum from the President's Assistant Special Counsel (Goodwin) to President Kennedy," August 22, 1961 in *FRUS, 1961–1963*, vol. X, Document No. 256; "Memorandum From the President's Assistant Special Counsel (Goodwin) to President Kennedy," August 22, 1961, in *FRUS, 1961–1963*, vol. X, Document No. 257. Reflecting on his response thirty-five years later, Goodwin remarked: "It wasn't a bad deal, if he meant it, and given what was to come later, a detached analyst might urge that it be pursued. But the mood in America was not one of detachment. The emotion that had always surrounded the 'problem' of Cuba had, if anything, been heightened by our defeat at the Bay of Pigs. To make a deal with Castro, any kind of deal, would have been politically difficult, perhaps impossible" (Richard Goodwin, "Cigars & Che & JFK," *Cigar Aficionado*, Autumn 1996).

203. "Transcript of Meeting between U.S. Secretary of State Alexander M. Haig, Jr., and Cuban Vice Premier Carlos Rafael Rodríguez, Mexico City, 23 November 1981," pp. 212–13.

204. Peter Kornbluh, "A 'Moment of Rapprochement': The Haig-Rodríguez Secret Talks," *Cold War International History Project Bulletin*, nos. 8–9 (winter 1996/1997), p. 219.

205. Purcell, "Why the Cuban Embargo Makes Sense in a Post–Cold War World," p. 93.

206. Steven Mufson, "Leahy, Hatch Seek Ashcroft Testimony on Civil Liberties," *Washington Post*, November 26, 2001, p. A4.

207. Garthoff ("American–Soviet Relations in Perspective," p. 549) notes that both the United States and the Soviet tended to apply double standards toward each other, which contributed to the lack of empathy.

208. U.S. State Department, Bureau of Democracy, Human Rights, and Labor, *Country Reports on Human Rights Practices–2001: Cuba*, March 4, 2002, Section 1c; available at: www.state.gov/g/drl/rls/hrrpt/2001/wha/8333.htm.

209. On police brutality, see Human Rights Watch, *Shielded from Justice: Police Brutality and Accountability in the United States* (New York: Human Rights Watch, 1998). On prisons, see the quarterly *Journal of the National Prison Project*, sponsored by the American Civil Liberties Union (733 15th Street, NW, Washington, D.C. 20005).

210. *Country Reports on Human Rights Practices–2001: Cuba*, Section 6a.

211. Human Rights Watch, *Unfair Advantage: Workers' Freedom of Association in the United States under International Human Rights Standards* (New York: Human Rights Watch, 2000).

212. Isaiah Berlin, "Giambattista Vico and Cultural History," in Isaiah Berlin, *The Crooked Timber of Humanity: Chapters in the History of Ideas* (New York: Knopf, 1991), p. 59.

213. Isaiah Berlin, "The Bent Twig: On the Rise of Nationalism," in Berlin, *The Crooked Timber of Humanity*, p. 259.

214. Faure Chomón, interview with the authors, Havana, Cuba, April 29, 1995.

215. Gen. Nguyen Dinh Uoc, interview with the authors, Hanoi, Vietnam, November 9, 1995.

216. See Robert S. McNamara, James G. Blight, and Robert K. Brigham, with Thomas Biersteker and Col. Herbert Y. Schandler, *Argument without End: In Search of Answers to the Vietnam Tragedy* (New York: PublicAffairs, 1999), especially chap. 5, "Escalation, 1961–1965."

217. Michael Ignatieff, *The Warrior's Honor: Ethnic War and the Modern Conscience* (New York: Metropolitan Books, 1997), pp. 189–90.

218. José Antonio Arbesu, at a conference on the missile crisis in 1991, thoughtfully highlighted the idea that empathy must start with the powerful country. "I think it is useful to put ourselves in each other's shoes," he said. But in order to avoid another confrontation like the missile crisis, "it is important to take these lessons into account, in view of the relations between big and small countries" (Blight et al., "Cuba between the Superpowers," p. 53).

INDEX

ABOUT THE AUTHORS

James G. Blight is a professor of international relations at Brown University's Watson Institute for International Studies, where he has resided since 1990. He is a pioneer of the research method known as critical oral history, in which declassified documents, former decisionmakers, and scholars are combined in conference settings to yield new insights about recent history. Projects under his direction using the method have been carried out on the Cuban missile crisis, the Bay of Pigs invasion, the Vietnam War, and the breakdown of U.S.–Soviet detente. Dr. Blight is the author or coauthor of more than a dozen books on U.S. foreign policy, including five on the Cuban missile crisis. His most recent books are *Cuba on the Brink: Castro, the Missile Crisis, and the Soviet Collapse*, with Bruce J. Allyn and David A. Welch (2nd, expanded edition, Rowman & Littlefield, 2002), and *Wilson's Ghost: Reducing the Risk of Conflict, Killing and Catastrophe in the 21st Century*, with Robert S. McNamara (2001). He lives in Milton, Massachusetts, with his wife, Janet Lang, a psychologist and epidemiologist who has collaborated with him on these pathbreaking projects.

Philip Brenner is a professor of international relations at American University in Washington, D.C., and chair of American University's Inter-Disciplinary Council on the Americas. A specialist in U.S. foreign policy toward Latin America, he has been engaged in research about U.S.–Cuban relations since 1974. He is the author or coeditor of several books and articles about Cuba and U.S.–Cuban relations, including *From Confrontation to Negotiation: U.S. Relations with Cuba* (1988) and

The Cuba Reader (1989). Since 1986, Dr. Brenner has been involved with efforts of the National Security Archive to secure and disseminate documents about the Cuban missile crisis, and he has served on the Advisory Board of the Archive since its founding in 1985. He is completing a textbook on contemporary U.S. foreign policy. Dr. Brenner lives in Washington, D.C., with his wife, Betsy Vieth, and two children, Lily and Isaac.